Teaching in the Middle School

M. Lee Manning

Katherine T. Bucher

Old Dominion University

Upper Saddle River, New Jersey
Columbus, Ohio

Library of Congress Cataloging-in-Publication Data

Manning, M. Lee.
Teaching in the middle school / M. Lee Manning, Katherine T. Bucher.—1st ed.
p. cm.
Includes bibliographical references and index.
ISBN 0-13-950420-6
1. Middle school teaching—United States. I. Bucher, Katherine Toth. II. Title.

LB1623 .M286 2001
373.1102—dc21

99-086514

Vice President and Publisher: Jeffery W. Johnston
Editor: Debra A. Stollenwerk
Editorial Assistant: Penny S. Burleson
Production Editor: Mary Harlan
Design Coordinator: Diane C. Lorenzo
Cover Design: Jeff Vanik
Cover Art: Stephen Schildbach
Text Design and Illustrations: Carlisle Publishers Services
Production Coordinator: Amy Gehl, Carlisle Publishers Services
Production Manager: Pamela D. Bennett
Director of Marketing: Kevin Flanagan
Marketing Manager: Amy June
Marketing Services Manager: Krista Groshong

This book was set in Times Roman by Carlisle Communications, Ltd. It was printed and bound by R. R. Donnelley & Sons Company. The cover was printed by Phoenix Color Corp.

Photo Credits: All photos by Richard Overbaugh.

10 9 8 7 6 5 4 3 2 1
ISBN 0-13-950420-6

Dedication

To my wife, Marianne, for her support and encouragement, and to middle school educators everywhere who diligently teach and nurture young adolescents.

MLM

To my husband, Glenn, for his patience and understanding, and to all of the adults who make a difference in the lives of young adolescents.

KTB

Preface

> There is more support for change in education now than at any other time in my memory. . . . A number of trends . . . will indeed bring about the kind of fundamental change that has long been needed. If we do not assume the initiative, however, the gains we have made and the supportive climate are likely to fade, and several more decades would pass before another time as ripe for reform would come along (John H. Lounsbury).

This statement was made, during an interview, by John H. Lounsbury (Manning, 1997), one of the founding fathers of the middle school movement. As Lounsbury indicated, the events of the past 10 to 15 years have placed major emphasis on understanding young adolescents and implementing effective middle school practices. Several state departments of education, the Children's Defense Fund, the Carnegie Council on Adolescent Development, the National Middle School Association, the National Association of Secondary School Principals, and the Association for Childhood Education International have led the way. The result has been the increasing acceptance of middle schools, the increasing knowledge about young adolescents and their developmental period, and the increasing recognition that middle school teaching methods need to be developmentally responsive. This does not mean that the battle for acceptance of the middle school concept is over. Rather, it means that middle school educators need to take advantage of the momentum and to continue to implement genuine reforms in middle school education.

Our challenge in writing this book was to find a way to take all of the information about young adolescents and middle schools and translate it into a 12-chapter book. We also wanted to balance the practical and the theoretical, for it is our belief that a mixture of the two is necessary. Thus, in this book, we wanted to provide both preservice and in-service teachers with basic information about young adolescents, ages 10 to 14. We also wanted to provide a solid core of essential knowledge about middle schools, including information about young adolescent development, middle school organization, core and exploratory curricula, middle school instructional strategies, and essential middle school concepts. Our aim was to emphasize young adolescents' diversity (developmental, cultural, and gender) and the importance of these differences reflected in educational experiences and guidance efforts. In determining "what effective middle schools and teachers do," we used respected documents such as *This We Believe* (the official position paper of the National Middle School Association, 1995), *Great Transitions: Preparing Adolescents for a New Century* (Carnegie Council on Adolescent Development, 1996), and *Turning Points: Preparing American Youth for the 21st Century* (Carnegie Council on Adolescent Development, 1989). Last, we wanted a strong research base, and a focus on teaching methods, strategies, materials, resources, and technology.

This book is the result of our work. It is our hope that through our scenarios, case studies, and anecdotes, we have captured the practical essence of young adolescents and middle schools. We also hope that our narrative, explanations of research, references, and recommended readings present both the philosophical and the pedagogical foundations of middle school education.

Rationale for *Teaching in the Middle School*

As we wrote *Teaching in the Middle School,* our overarching goal (albeit lofty, we admit) was to improve the lives and educational experiences of young adolescents. Reflecting this, our specific objectives were to (1) tell readers about middle schools today—what they are and what they can become; (2) describe young adolescents and their developmental period; (3) identify essential middle school concepts that have potential for this age group; and (4) identify educational experiences that are developmentally responsive for young adolescents.

We are realistic enough to know that even if we are able to achieve our objectives, this book alone will not be sufficient to change middle schools. We believe that classroom teachers will be the key reformers of middle school education and that the ultimate success of middle school reforms will depend upon these teachers—people whom we highly respect and who work daily to improve the lives and educational experiences of young adolescents. Thus, we wrote this book with middle school classroom teachers in mind.

Organization of this Book

This book is divided into the following four parts:

Part I: Understanding Middle Schools and Young Adolescents
 Chapters 1, 2
Part II: Developing the Curriculum and Organizing the School
 Chapters 3, 4, 5, 6
Part III: Planning, Implementing, and Assessing Instruction
 Chapters 7, 8, 9, 10
Part IV: Guiding Students and Working with External Communities
 Chapters 11, 12, Epilogue

Chapter 1 looks at middle schools today and provides an overview of middle school concepts and teaching, while chapter 2 examines young adolescents, their development, and related issues. Chapters 3 and 4, respectively, examine the core curriculum and the integrated and exploratory curriculum. Organization of middle schools and young adolescents in classes is the topic of chapter 5. In chapter 6, we explore positive middle school environments and effective classroom management procedures. Planning and implementing instruction are the topics of chapters 7 and 8. Looking at research on effective teaching from a middle school perspectives, chapter 9 explains teaching behaviors that we think will be most effective with young adolescents. Assessment, a timely and somewhat controversial topic, is the focus of chapter 10. Chapter 11 explores ways both teachers and professionally trained guidance counselors can provide all young adolescents with developmentally responsive guidance experiences. The final chapter, chapter 12, examines the relationships between schools and communities and suggests ways to involve parents in middle schools. Last, the Epilogue presents some challenges and possibilities for middle schools and suggests what they might become when teachers are committed to young adolescents and effective middle school practices.

Special Features and Pedagogical Aids

As you read this book, we want you to be able to visualize what happens in real middle schools. While we wanted to be practical, we also wanted to include pertinent research and we wanted a book that will be up-to-date. To do all of that, we have included several special features that we think will help you understand the realities of teaching in a middle school.

Diversity Perspectives In this feature we use examples to reflect our nation's cultural diversity and our increasing recognition of gender differences. Thus, each Diversity Perspective looks at a particular topic that is actually discussed in the chapter and considers how middle school educators can be cultural- and gender-responsive.

Theory into Practice (TIP) Our students always want to know about the "real world." While researchers often offer perceptive findings, we find that they do not always explain how to implement them. TIP takes concepts found in each chapter and provides practical classroom or school examples, indicates how to use research findings in a school setting, or offers a checklist for evaluating the existence of a concept in a middle school. Each TIP has at least one reference that we used to develop it.

Anecdotal Accounts In our many years of teaching and working with middle schools, we have had a variety of experiences and accumulated a number of stories. While we have changed the names of the participants, we have tried to integrate these stories throughout the text. We wanted you to feel that you were looking over our shoulders and listening to actual middle school teachers, middle school students, college students, and parents.

Chapter Objectives To provide an overview and to help focus your reading, we have provided objectives at the beginning of each chapter. You can also use this advance organizer or outline as a study or review guide.

Scenarios Each chapter starts with a scenario that prepares you for the topics that will be discussed. In the scenario, we try to describe "real-life" conversations and events that middle school educators might encounter and to pose problems that often arise. Try reacting to the scenario before you read the chapter and then revisiting it when you finish the chapter.

Case Studies In each chapter, a case study examines the topics being discussed and shows how middle school teachers responded. Sometimes these case studies are a continuation of the situation found in the opening scenario. Other times, they present a new problem. As you read them, consider how you might react to the situation and whether you agree with the responses found in the case study.

Keeping Current with Technology We are constantly adding to our knowledge of middle schools, and it is impossible to put everything into one book. With our technology feature, you can use the resources of the Internet to access additional information related specifically to the topics discussed in each chapter. Additional resources can be found at the Companion Website at www.prenhall.com/manning.

Glossary Specialized terms related to young adolescent development, middle school concepts, and the education profession in general can be somewhat confusing. Therefore, a glossary is included at the end of this book.

ACKNOWLEDGMENTS

Any project of this magnitude calls for our sincere appreciation being offered to a number of people. First, we want to thank Richard Overbaugh of Old Dominion University for taking the photographs used in the text. We appreciate his donating his time and providing his photographic expertise. Also, for their helpfulness and advance planning for the photograph sessions, we want to thank Dr. Edith Eidson, principal at Corporate Landing Middle School in Virginia Beach, Virginia, and her staff: Dr. Ward, sixth-grade principal; Mr. Thomas, seventh-grade principal; Mr. Disharoon, eighth-grade principal; Mr. Anglin, student activities coordinator; and Ms. Mitchell, library media specialist.

Second, we want to offer our appreciation to Debbie Stollenwerk at Prentice Hall for her patience and encouragement, as well as to Penny Burleson for her help, for her prompt handling of the reviews, and for keeping us "on track." Last, we are particularly grateful to the following individuals who reviewed the book and offered numerous constructive suggestions:

Elaine Chakonas, Dominican University
Tom Erb, University of Kansas
Linda Carol Gabbard, Eastern Kentucky University
Fred H. Groves, Northeast Louisiana University
Michael A. James, Wichita State University
Karen Kusiak, Colby College
Ann Lockledge, University of North Carolina, Wilmington
Sara Delano Moore, University of Kentucky
Connie H. Nobles, Southeastern Louisiana University
Michael Perl, Kansas State University
Linda Schlosser, SUNY, Brockport
James E. Watson, Trinity International University

MLM
KTB
Old Dominion University

Discover the Companion Website Accompanying This Book

The Prentice Hall Companion Website: A Virtual Learning Environment

Technology is a constantly growing and changing aspect of our field that is creating a need for content and resources. To address this emerging need, Prentice Hall has developed an online learning environment for students and professors alike—Companion Websites—to support our textbooks.

In creating a Companion Website, our goal is to build on and enhance what the textbook already offers. For this reason, the content for each user-friendly website is organized by topic and provides the professor and student with a variety of meaningful resources. Common features of a Companion Website include:

For the Professor–

Every Companion Website integrates **Syllabus Manager**™, an online syllabus creation and management utility.

- **Syllabus Manager**™ provides you, the instructor, with an easy, step-by-step process to create and revise syllabi, with direct links into Companion Website and other online content without having to learn HTML.
- Students may log on to your syllabus during any study session. All they need to know is the web address for the Companion Website and the password you've assigned to your syllabus.
- After you have created a syllabus using **Syllabus Manager**™, students may enter the syllabus for their course section from any point in the Companion Website.
- Clicking on a date, the student is shown the list of activities for the assignment. The activities for each assignment are linked directly to actual content, saving time for students.
- Adding assignments consists of clicking on the desired due date, then filling in the details of the assignment—name of the assignment, instructions, and whether it is a one-time or repeating assignment.
- In addition, links to other activities can be created easily. If the activity is online, a URL can be entered in the space provided, and it will be linked automatically in the final syllabus.
- Your completed syllabus is hosted on our servers, allowing convenient updates from any computer on the Internet. Changes you make to your syllabus are immediately available to your students at their next logon.

For the Student–

- **Topic Overviews:** outline key concepts in topic areas
- **Electronic Blue Book:** send homework or essays directly to your instructor's email with this paperless form
- **Message Board:** serves as a virtual bulletin board to post—or respond to—questions or comments to/from a national audience
- **Chat:** real-time chat with anyone who is using the text anywhere in the country—ideal for discussion and study groups, class projects, etc.
- **Web Destinations:** links to www sites that relate to each topic area
- **Professional Organizations:** links to organizations that relate to topic areas
- **Additional Resources:** access to topic-specific content that enhances material found in the text

To take advantage of these and other resources, please visit the *Teaching in the Middle School* Companion Website at

www.prenhall.com/manning

Brief Contents

Part IV *Guiding Students and Working with External Communities 239*

Contents

Part II Developing the Curriculum and Organizing the School 47

Part I

Understanding Middle Schools and Young Adolescents

In chapter 1, you will be able to look at middle schools today and see how they have evolved during the past 50 years. In addition to reading about what all middle schools need to be like, you will review reports of selected states and professional associations. We pose several questions that you can consider to determine whether middle school teaching is really for you.

In chapter 2, you can read about the early adolescence developmental period as well as young adolescents themselves as we discuss young adolescents' physical, psychosocial, and cognitive development and suggest implications for middle school educators who want to provide developmentally responsive educational experiences. Be sure to read our cautions about making generalizations about this very diverse group of learners.

After you read these two chapters, we hope you will have an understanding of the purposes of middle schools as well as an understanding of young adolescents, their development, and the challenges they face.

Chapter 1

Middle Schools Today—Concepts and Teaching

Scenario—The First Day of Student Teaching

Ami Chen took one last look at herself in the car's rearview mirror. Then she opened the door and slid out. Taking a deep breath, she squared her shoulders and walked resolutely toward Harrison Lakes Middle School. A 21-year-old teacher education student, Ami was both excited and apprehensive as she walked into her first student-teaching assignment.

She had been thinking about this day for 4 years. Now those days of sitting in college classes were over and she would face the ultimate test. Could she really teach middle school students? In her mind, Ami knew her professors had prepared her for middle school teaching; she knew about young adolescents, understood the essential middle school concepts, and knew the recommendations of the various reports on reforming middle school education. She felt prepared; still, this was the real thing, and she had heard "stories" of the pranks young adolescents pulled on green student teachers. To say young adolescents were "challenging" to teach seemed like an understatement.

Ami had been assigned to Eva Maria Gillespie, a seventh-grade teacher with 19 years of middle school experience. In addition to being well-liked by her colleagues and by the students, Mrs. Gillespie had been named Teacher of the Year and had several other awards for good teaching. Ami had also found out that Mrs. Gillespie was known for her high expectations, both in student behavior and academic achievement.

As arranged, Ami met Mrs. Gillespie in the main office before the students were scheduled to arrive. As the two were walking back toward the seventh-grade rooms, Mrs. Gillespie turned to Ami and asked, "Butterflies in your stomach?"

Ami grinned. "How did you know?"

"I think we all feel that way at times," replied Mrs. Gillespie. "Want to talk about it?"

"Well," said Ami, "I'm concerned about student teaching. I always thought I wanted to teach in the middle school, but now I don't know. When I visited last week, I kept watching the students. They're so . . . diverse! I mean, physically, they're all different sizes. And, I bet they're on all different learning and ability levels, too. I spent the weekend worrying about today."

As Mrs. Gillespie took the "long way" back to her room, she talked to Ami. "It's true that these students are diverse. In fact you'll find almost every one of the developmental, learning, cultural, gender, and social class differences that you read about in college here at Harrison Lakes."

As they walked, Mrs. Gillespie explained some of the ways the staff at Harrison Lakes addressed the differences. She talked about the school climate, developmentally responsive instruction, and guidance efforts.

As she listened to Mrs. Gillespie, Ami began to smile. She thought to herself that Mrs. Gillespie sounded just like she was teaching a college class and listing all those essential concepts found in good middle schools. Ami also reminded herself that the reason she had majored in middle school education was that she liked the idea of working in a school that was "student-centered" and that she was looking forward to working collaboratively with other teachers.

As they neared the seventh-grade cluster, Mrs. Gillespie slowed and said, "Come on into the teacher area and let me introduce you to our interdisciplinary team."

Ami followed her into the bright, cheerful room. "Maybe, just maybe, this will work out," she thought.

Overview

Many prospective teachers have shared Ami Chen's feelings as they entered the middle school classroom for the first time. The middle school is a unique place that differs distinctly from elementary and secondary schools. In this chapter, you will find an overview of many of the essential middle school concepts. In addition you will have a chance to examine what it means to be a middle school teacher and to look at the challenges in this exciting profession.

Objectives

After reading and thinking about this chapter on middle schools today, you should be able to:

1. explain a brief history of the junior high school and the middle school;
2. define "student-centered" and "developmentally responsive middle schools";
3. provide a rationale for middle schools being distinctly unique from elementary and secondary schools;
4. name and explain selected middle school concepts such as those prescribed by the National Middle School Association;
5. suggest directions for effective middle schools as proposed by selected states such as California, Florida, Maryland, and Virginia;
6. explain the recommendations for middle school education as espoused by the Carnegie Council on Adolescence; and
7. describe what middle school teaching is like and what young adolescents are really like.

A Brief History of the Junior High School and the Middle School

Before we look at middle schools, let's briefly examine what existed before middle schools and how middle schools developed.

Junior High Schools

Harvey Allen (1992) explained that during much of the nineteenth century, the traditional school organization plan was the 8-year elementary and 4-year high school pattern. This 8-4 arrangement provided opportunities for large numbers of students to obtain a common schooling in the elementary school and for a select number of students to receive specialized academic preparation for college in the 4-year high school. By the 1890s, dissatisfactions regarding this arrangement grew. Educators and others have spent the 100 years since trying to develop a successful school in the middle that would meet the developmental needs and interests of young adolescents and that would serve as a transition between the elementary school and the high school.

With higher education pressing the issue, numerous national committees met between 1890 and 1920 to discuss ideas related to altering the curriculum of the 8-4 plan. These committees considered shortening the elementary school program in years and enriching the curriculum in grades 7 and 8 by the introduction of more rigorous academic subjects such as natural history, physics, foreign languages, algebra, and geometry (Allen, 1992; Bossing & Cramer, 1964).

Gradually, the concept of 6-3-3 emerged, with an elementary school of 6 years and a secondary school of 6 years with the first three of those years spent in a junior high school. The first 3-year junior high schools, incorporating grades 7 to 9, were established in Columbus, Ohio, in 1909. Then, in 1918, the National Education Association Commission on the Reorganization of Secondary Education approved the junior high school concept.

Early junior high school programs focused on enriched academic programs for college-bound students and vocational programs for students bound for work settings. However, as the junior high school stabilized its curriculum, instruction, and organization, it became apparent that the school also needed to meet the unique social, personal, and academic needs of young adolescents. This developmental purpose soon became the guiding principle of the junior high school and the yardstick by which its proponents measured its success or failure (Allen, 1992; Perlstein & Tobin, 1988).

A uniquely American institution, the junior high school experienced steady growth over the next several decades and became the dominant school organizational pattern for young adolescents. However, despite its growth, the junior high school experienced philosophical problems. Organizationally, the junior high school was a bridge between elementary and secondary schools, but philosophically, the junior high school was caught between competing elementary and secondary viewpoints. Instead of becoming what young adolescents needed, the junior high school was dominated by the high school. By failing to identify and develop a rationale of its own, the junior high school grew into its name and became a "junior" high school (Allen, 1992, p. 2).

Middle Schools

Growing disenchantment with the junior high school accelerated the emergence of the middle school. Beginning in the 1960s and developing rapidly in the 1970s and 1980s, middle schools soon outnumbered junior high schools, and the middle school concept dominated.

In developing the middle school, educators wanted to avoid the mistakes of the junior high school. They wanted the middle school to be a learner-centered school that would meet young adolescents' developmental needs. The middle school, itself, was to consist of grades 6 to 8 and possibly grade 5. The ninth grade, with its Carnegie units and its subject-centered emphasis, distorted the image of a learner-centered middle school and was generally excluded from the middle school organizational pattern.

Two of the more prominent theorists of the early development of middle schools were Donald Eichhorn and William Alexander. They emphasized the student focus of the middle school. Eichhorn coined the term *transescence,* which was defined as the developmental period beginning in late childhood prior to puberty and extending through the early years of adolescence. Research into the school performance of transescents or young adolescents suggested that, because of their earlier maturation and sophistication, sixth graders were more appropriately placed with seventh and eighth graders than with fourth and fifth graders.

Alexander and Williams (1968) published *The Emergent Middle School,* which became an influential book in the middle school movement. In their book, they described the middle school as a new and emergent school rather than a reorganized junior high school. Ideally, the middle school should build its programs on some of the positive contributions of the junior high school (i.e., core curriculum, guidance programs, exploratory education, and vocational and home arts). Simultaneously, the middle school would eliminate high school practices such as academic honor societies, competitive sports, and subject matter orientation. Additionally, the middle school would include team teaching and interdisciplinary teaming (Allen, 1992).

Middle Schools

Definition

For the purposes of *Teaching in the Middle School,* we define the *middle school* as:

> a school organization containing grades 6 to 8 (and sometimes grade 5) that, first, provides developmentally appropriate and responsive curricular, instructional, organizational, guidance, and overall educational experiences and, second, places major emphasis on 10- to 14-year-olds' developmental and instructional needs.

Other definitions may differ slightly from ours. For example, the National Middle School Association (1995) contends that the age range extends from 10 to 15 years old. Richard Kellough and Noreen Kellough (1999) suggest that the middle school often includes the fifth grade and, conversely, might span only the seventh and eighth grades. Another definition suggests the middle school includes any school that takes its design specifically from the analysis of 10- to 14-year-olds, their characteristics, and their developmental needs (George, Lawrence, & Bushnell, 1998).

Rationale

Why, you might wonder, was it necessary to place special emphasis on middle schools? Unfortunately, for many years, the school in the middle, regardless of whether it was called an intermediate school, junior high school, or middle school, did not fully understand its purpose. While the K–5 school perceived its mission as teaching basic skills, the secondary school perceived its mission as providing general, academic, or vocational education. However, the school in the middle lacked a "mission"—it was a school without a clear sense of purpose and accompanying direction. Fortunately, this has changed.

Serving a far greater role than just being a "transition school" between the elementary school and the high school, modern middle schools:

- provide unique educational experiences that reflect the developmental and instructional needs of 10- to 14-year-olds;
- meet young adolescents' educational needs by implementing proven middle school concepts such as advisor-advisee programs, exploratory programs, interdisciplinary teaming and organization, and positive school climates;
- continue to refine young adolescents' basic skills originally learned in the elementary school; and

- offer opportunities for young adolescents to explore curricular areas as well as to discover unique abilities and talents.

Its Students—Young Adolescents

The terms used to describe students in this developmental period include *early adolescents, preadolescents, transescents,* or *middle schoolers.* We prefer *young adolescents,* who we define as:

> students between the ages of 10 to 14 who experience the physical, psychosocial, and cognitive changes associated with the early adolescence developmental period, yet who also exhibit tremendous cultural, gender, developmental, and individual diversity that deserves to be considered by middle school educators who plan educational experiences.

Middle Schools: Today and Tomorrow—Selected Concepts

"So, what's so different about a middle school? Isn't it just a junior high school with a new name?"

We can not remember how many times we have heard comments such as these. To help point out the differences between junior high schools and middle schools, let's look at a few of the middle school concepts in more detail. Throughout this book, we will refer to and build upon these basics in our discussions of what makes middle schools unique.

Developmentally Responsive

Middle schools provide 10- to 14-year-olds with developmentally appropriate educational experiences that emphasize the education and overall well-being of the learners. Working collaboratively, teachers, counselors, administrators, and parents address young adolescents' developmental needs and ensure some degree of success for all learners. They recognize and address young adolescents' developmental diversity as well as cultural and gender differences. In turn, young adolescents know educators value academic achievement.

Our students who are preparing to teach in the middle school sometimes ask us, "How can teachers tell whether a middle school is developmentally responsive?" We tell them the list of questions to ask is almost endless, but in essence, they can ask themselves whether all middle school experiences reflect young adolescent development. Theory into Practice 1–1 provides a list (certainly a beginning rather than a definitive list) that you can use to determine developmental responsiveness.

In addition to the list presented in Theory into Practice 1–1, there are some other principles of developmentally responsive middle schools that you can look for. See if the middle school (1) uses a wide range of instructional strategies in response to the variety of learning needs in the classroom (e.g., simulations, experiments, community-based learning, and cooperative learning); (2) has implemented an exploratory program so that students may expand and develop individual interests; (3) encourages continuous progress for each

Theory into Practice 1–1

Determining a Middle School's Developmental Responsiveness

The Developmentally Responsive Middle School

Yes _____ No _____ 1. The school's written philosophy states that curricular, instructional, and environmental practices are based upon young adolescents' physical, psychosocial, and cognitive developmental characteristics.

Yes _____ No _____ 2. The school's curricular and instructional practices reflect the unique nature and needs of young adolescents, rather than perceiving 10- to 14-year-olds as children or adolescents.

Yes _____ No _____ 3. The school's administration, faculty, and staff have professional preparation in understanding young adolescent development and are experts in teaching 10- to 14-year-olds.

Yes _____ No _____ 4. The school provides "communities of learning" where close, trusting relationships with adults and peers create a climate for personal growth and cognitive development.

Yes _____ No _____ 5. The school's policies and practices recognize and address young adolescents' cultural and gender differences, as well as their tremendous diversity in physical, psychosocial, and cognitive development.

Yes _____ No _____ 6. The school ensures some degree of success for all young adolescents in more than one developmental area.

Yes _____ No _____ 7. The school has functional strategies (i.e., appropriate for this particular developmental period) for re-engaging families in the education of young adolescents.

Yes _____ No _____ 8. The school provides an organization that includes cross-age grouping, alternatives to ability grouping and tracking, school-within-a-school, and other organizational strategies that address young adolescents' physical, psychosocial, and cognitive development.

Yes _____ No _____ 9. The school actively seeks to connect schools with communities and tries to provide young adolescents with opportunities for community service.

Yes _____ No _____ 10. The school actively empowers administrators and teachers to make decisions based on young adolescent development and effective middle-level practices.

Developed from: Manning, M. L. (1993b). *Developmentally appropriate middle level schools.* Olney, MD: Association for Childhood Education International.

individual so that each learner may progress at a preferred pace and in a preferred learning style; and (4) charts student progress in ways that stress individual growth rather than comparison to peers (Tomlinson, Moon, & Callihan, 1998). It is also important for middle school educators to recognize and address young adolescents' cultural and gender differences and place emphasis on helping students develop positive and healthy cultural and gender identities.

High Expectations and Success for All Students

You might question why we grouped "high expectations for all students" *and* "success for all students" together as qualities of a good middle school. We believe the two are not contradictory, and in fact, effective middle school educators can ensure both to some degree.

Too often, we have seen middle schools that have low expectations for their students, both in terms of behavior and academic achievement. Perhaps unknowingly, the educators in these schools either do not realize the capabilities of their students or fail to insist that their students perform at the highest level. *This We Believe* (National Middle School Association, 1995) suggested that middle school educators should hold high expectations for all learners; in fact, students themselves should have high expectations for success. These high expectations promote positive attitudes and behaviors and motivate students to achieve; low expectations lead to alienation, discouragement, and a lack of effort. As a teacher, your expectations are quickly conveyed to young adolescents through your gestures, comments, and overall attitudes.

When setting high standards, you must keep in mind that young adolescents differ significantly—not all will achieve the same degree of success, become school leaders, or win "end-of-the-year awards" for outstanding scholarship. However, as suggested in *Turning Points* (Carnegie Council on Adolescent Development, 1989), you must provide all young adolescents with the opportunity to succeed at least to some degree in all aspects of the middle school program. As one seventh-grade teacher told us, "I try to help all of my students feel successful at something. None of my students should go home in the afternoon thinking he or she failed all day."

In setting high expectations and ensuring some degree of success, you must remember the developmental needs of 10- to 14-year-olds. Young adolescents have fragile self-esteem and are developing expectations for both behavior and academic achievement that might last a lifetime. As a middle school educator, you should constantly consider the effects of high expectations on self-esteem and make necessary adjustments.

School Climate and Communities of Learning

A positive middle school climate is safe, inviting, and caring; it promotes a sense of community and encourages learning (National Middle School Association, 1995, p. 18). As you might recall, this is one of the aspects that Mrs. Gillespie described to Ami Chen in the chapter's opening scenario.

What actually constitutes a positive school climate? You might look at how students treat each other, how staff members interact with each other, and how student behavior and rules reflect democracy and fairness. You might also look at the emphasis placed on human relationships, dignity, and respect; how students and teachers recognize and accept one another; and the evidence of respect for cultural and gender differences (National Middle School Association, 1995). As you will read in chapter 6, a healthy school climate should be a "place where close, trusting relationships with adults and peers create a climate for students' personal growth and intellectual development" (Carnegie Council on Adolescent Development, 1989, p. 10).

One solution to unacceptably large schools and to students feeling anonymous in overly large groups is the creation of smaller learning environments. These communities might be called "school-within-a-school" or "houses" and might contain 125–150 students (Carnegie Council on Adolescent Development, 1989). A positive middle school climate, both in the whole school and in the smaller learning communities, provides opportunities for students to interact, to find meaning in schoolwork and relationships, and to feel a sense of recognition.

Even small things contribute to the climate of a middle school. Thus, in speaking with young adolescents, focus not only on the content but also on the affective impact of your words. Use appropriate words to show caring and affection, speak courteously and listen attentively, plan spontaneous opportunities to talk with each learner, and avoid making judgmental comments about learners (Kostelnik, Stein, Whiren, & Soderman, 1988).

Adult Advocate for Every Student

In addition to providing a positive school climate and small communities of learning, effective middle schools also provide an adult advocate for each young adolescent. According to *This We Believe* (National Middle School Association, 1995), all adults in developmentally responsive middle schools serve as advocates for young adolescents. However, each student should have at least one adult who knows her or him well, genuinely cares for her or him, and supports her or his academic and personal development. This advocate should be of good character and should be knowledgeable about young adolescent development and middle school education. While these advocates are not counselors, they can identify behavioral changes in students that need to be considered by counselors, administrators, other teachers, and parents. This advocate can also act as the primary person with whom the family makes contact when communicating about the child.

To assist with advocacy efforts, many schools provide advisory programs, home-based groups, and team-based mentorships, as well as comprehensive guidance and counseling efforts. The ultimate result should be that no student feels unknown or neglected. This is especially important with students in this developmental period and in larger middle schools (National Middle School Association, 1995).

Curriculum

John Lounsbury (1996) maintained that, while the advancements in middle school education have been remarkable, these changes have been largely organizational and have not reached middle school curriculum. This was in spite of the fact that the 1991 publication of *A Middle School Curriculum: From Rhetoric to Reality* (Beane, 1990) by the National Middle School Association had pointed out that the middle school curriculum had not received the attention that it deserved.

What should be in the curriculum of an effective middle school? Your answer will depend on whether you approach this question on a global basis or whether you look at it in a more traditional, discipline-specific manner.

Ideally, curriculum in an effective middle school reflects the interests, concerns, and thinking levels of young adolescents. More than a time to review elementary content or preview secondary content, a responsive middle school should base its program content upon young adolescents' physical, psychosocial, and cognitive levels (Manning, 1993a, 1994/1995) as well as upon their need to achieve, to experience success, and to have continuous learning experiences. While you will need to consider the content that students learned in the elementary school and the content that they will learn in the secondary school, you must also keep in mind the uniqueness of young adolescents.

Middle-level students are unlike any other age group, and, in fact, are more unlike each other than their elementary and secondary school counterparts. Thus, middle school educators must provide young adolescents with a curriculum that meets varying rates of development as well as motivational levels (National Association of Secondary School Principals, 1993).

Specifically, the middle school curriculum should:

- equip students with skills for continued learning—i.e., skills associated with the collection of information, the organization and expression of ideas (mathematics, writing, speaking), and the evaluation of information and ideas.
- teach students how to organize for action, both as individuals and as a group, including planning, group processes, management, evaluation, and self-evaluation.
- teach students the universality of the human condition, giving special attention to the ways that people satisfy needs and seek personal fulfillment in various times, places, and conditions.
- teach students about the differences that exist among people and their cultures and the ways in which these differences affect individuals' views of the world, their values, and their interpretations of the events of their lives.
- provide students with opportunities to develop skills in and respect for artistic expression and aesthetic sensitivity.
- provide students with the study of foreign languages to gain a better understanding of the ways that language and culture affect how people think and act.
- engage students in productive thinking, systematic reasoning, and the evaluation of information (National Association of Secondary School Principals, 1985).

Other selected curricular essentials include efforts to improve young adolescents' self-concept; provide appropriate responses to cultural and gender diversity; demonstrate an understanding of physical, psychosocial, and cognitive development; and provide a balance between skills, academic content, and experiences.

As you will read in chapter 4, *This We Believe* (National Middle School Association, 1995) calls for a challenging, integrative, and exploratory middle school curriculum. By *challenging,* we mean curricular experiences that engage young adolescents, emphasize important ideas and skills, provide relevant experiences, and emphasize developmental responsiveness. The *integrative* dimensions help young adolescents make sense of life experiences and include courses and units that are taught by individuals and teams, and that integrate issues that are relevant to the students. The *exploratory* components should allow students to discover their interests and skills, and acquaint them with healthy leisure pursuits.

Turning Points (Carnegie Council on Adolescent Development, 1989) recommends a common core of knowledge that teaches middle school students to think critically, lead a healthy life, behave ethically and lawfully, and assume the responsibilities of citizenship in a pluralistic society. As an educator, you should allow students to participate actively in discovering and creating solutions to problems. You should also use integrating themes across curricular areas to help students see relationships rather than disconnected facts. Students should learn to use coping skills such as collaboration, problem solving, and conflict resolution. By emphasizing ethical and lawful behavior, you can expose young adolescents to the value of citizenship, compassion, regard for human worth and dignity, and appreciation of diversity.

It would be wonderful if everyone accepted these recommendations as the core curriculum for any middle school. Realistically, however, most educators continue to consider the core curriculum as language arts, social studies, science, and mathematics. This will be true as long as test-makers continue to design tests that place priority on these four curricular areas, and as long as teachers feel pressure (from administrators, parents, and the overall community) for young adolescents to excel in these four areas.

Instruction

If curriculum is the "what is taught," then instruction is the "how things are taught." Your perspectives and instructional strategies will be very important to young adolescents. When you are planning instruction in a middle school, you must:

- recognize and accept differences in young adolescents' physical, psychosocial, and cognitive patterns and rates of development by setting developmentally appropriate curriculum goals;
- place emphasis on thinking and learning how to learn rather than focusing only on isolated skills and content;
- view guidance, both counselors and teacher-advisors, as an essential component of middle school education;
- place value on gender and cultural differences and provide classroom organization and instructional approaches that recognize these differences;
- provide curricular materials that enhance young adolescents' acceptance of self and others and that enable them to accept differences and similarities among people;
- promote integrated curricular approaches, so young adolescents will perceive relationships among and between curricular areas;
- allow young adolescents to make significant choices and decisions about grouping, organization, curricular, and management practices;
- ensure some degree of success for all young adolescents in all aspects of the school program;
- recognize the importance of self-esteem and its influence on academic achievement, socialization, and overall personal development; and

- promote heterogeneous grouping and seek other alternatives to homogeneous ability grouping and tracking.

Too often, when we think of diversity, we think only of cultural and gender diversity. While you will be reading about these throughout this book, we also want you to keep in mind other forms of diversity. In Diversity Perspectives 1–1, Tomlinson, Moon, and Callahan (1998) look at academic diversity and how well middle school educators address this lesser-mentioned diversity.

Assessment

In chapter 10, you will read about assessment in middle schools in considerable detail; however, because of the importance of this often controversial topic, it deserves to be mentioned here. Although some educators (as well as students and parents) might wish the current emphasis on testing will go away, the call for student assessment may even become more intense.

Middle school educators will be expected to provide assessment and evaluation that reflect young adolescents' development. *This We Believe* (National Middle School Association, 1995) aptly stated the challenge: "In developmentally responsive middle level schools, assessment and evaluation procedures reflect the characteristics and uniqueness of young adolescents" (p. 27). For example, young adolescents' concern for peer approval calls for individualized evaluation, so students will not be compared. Cooperative learning, with assessment based on both group and individual performance, capitalizes on this need and promotes both academic learning and the development of social skills. You can emphasize what students have accomplished rather than labeling them as failures to reach some arbitrary standard. Furthermore, you should also help students and parents understand how a student's performance corresponds with national or state norms and how such information can be useful when planning careers and further education. Still, assessment should not be a dominating concern during the middle school years (National Middle School Association, 1995).

Organization

One essential component of developmentally responsive schools for young adolescents is "interdisciplinary team organization" (McEwin, 1997) or "interdisciplinary team teaching," an organization pattern in which two or more teachers representing different subject areas share the same students, schedule, and adjoining areas of the school.

This team organization is a more fundamental structural change than the team teaching that was popular in the 1960s and early 1970s (Erb, 1997). Teachers on an interdisciplinary team plan together and work to draw connections between their subjects. While these teachers might sometimes teach together, it is not required. The real distinction between team teaching and interdisciplinary team teaching is a curricular one; that is, a team of teachers becomes an interdisciplinary team when its members engage in purposeful efforts to integrate learning from normally disparate disciplines (Wraga, 1997).

Diversity Perspectives 1–1

Academic Diversity

Tomlinson, Moon, and Callahan (1998) maintained that despite the range of academic, affective, social, cultural, and gender differences that typify the middle grades, relatively little research has been undertaken to determine how teachers deal with diversity in the middle school. In this study of 1,988 middle schools, the authors examined four themes. The themes and findings include:

1. The nature of middle school learners

Findings: Most respondents considered middle school learners more social than academic, more concrete thinkers than abstract, able to work effectively with an established routine, easily discouraged, and extrinsically motivated. Interestingly, most principals thought middle school learners were not weak in basic skills, while most teachers thought the opposite.

2. Barriers to modifying curriculum and instruction for academic diversity

Findings: Barriers included fear of loss of control, lack of knowledge of how to modify, lack of appropriate materials, lack of planning time, grading concerns, inadequate time block in schedules, and seeing no need to modify or differentiate instruction.

3. Tools used for differentiating instruction

Findings: An interesting finding was that principals are far more optimistic about the frequency of teacher use of varying instructional strategies than are teachers themselves. Popular instructional strategies included preassessing student knowledge, peer tutors, advanced organizers, breaking work into small parts, offering varied modes of expressing learning, independent study, interest groups, learning centers, computers for remediation, advanced computer programs, flexible pacing, and mentorships for remedial or students at-risk.

4. Nature of instructional modifications made for academically diverse learners

Findings: Responses included few efforts to provide complex, integrated, or high-level materials or tasks; some adaptation for student readiness, yet far fewer for student interest and cultural differences; more adaptations for slower learners than for advanced learners; reliance on school specialists (e.g., resource teachers, after-school tutoring programs, and pull-out programs) to make adaptations; and most readiness-based adaptations being made for struggling learners with peer tutoring being the most common effort.

The researchers concluded that since middle schools strongly endorse heterogeneous teaming, efforts must be made to address the needs of academically diverse learners who vary greatly in readiness, interest, learning profile, culture, and gender. Middle school educators must not only champion responsive education, but must work to ensure that this rich intent is translated into an equally rich classroom reality.

Source: Tomlinson, C. A., Moon, T. R., & Callahan, C. M. (1998). How well are we addressing academic diversity in the middle school? *Middle School Journal, 29*(3), 3–11.

Effective interdisciplinary organization and teams require several essentials. Erb (1987) maintained that teachers sharing common planning times and sharing students were two absolute necessities for teams to function. He also listed a common block-time schedule and the spatial proximity of team members' classes as two other features.

Other characteristics of effective interdisciplinary teams include: a balance in the teachers' expertise, age, sex and race; team leaders with specific responsibilities; an established team decision-making process (e.g., goals, grouping, scheduling, homework, and discipline); agreed-upon procedures to assess students' strengths and weaknesses; the development of a team identity; flexibility in student and master schedules; the support of school and district administration for the teaming concept and team efforts; sufficient time for team planning; adequate staff development; and team members who are proficient in human relations skills (Dickinson & Erb, 1997; Erb, 1997; Merenbloom, 1991).

Guidance and Counseling

Effective middle schools provide guidance programs that are specifically planned and implemented to address the ever-changing needs of 10- to 14-year-olds. Rather than guidance being only one hour a week or occurring only when a student requests an appointment with the counselor, classroom teachers provide guidance and advice throughout the school day (Cole, 1992; MacLaury, 1995) in both planned advisory programs as well as in their daily interaction with young adolescents.

In the planned advisor-advisee program (also called advisories, teacher advisories, or home-based guidance), each student has the opportunity to participate in a small interactive group with peers and staff to discuss school, personal, and societal concerns. The advisory program helps each student develop a meaningful relationship with at least one significant adult in the middle school (Allen, Splittgerber, & Manning, 1993). In this way, all faculty members serve as advisors, plan and implement advisory programs, assist advisees in monitoring their academic progress, provide times for students to share their concerns, refer advisees to appropriate resources, maintain appropriate records, and encourage the advisee's cognitive and psychosocial growth (James, 1986). They also meet with individual students about problems; offer career information and guidance; discuss academic, personal, and family problems; address moral or ethical issues; discuss multicultural and intergroup relations; and help students develop self-confidence and leadership skills (Epstein & MacIver, 1990).

As one middle school teacher said; "Everything I do relates to guidance in some way—I have my advisor-advisee program; I counsel individual students nearly everyday; I even try to work affective aspects into my exploratories." That is quite a big job. But it is a very important part of being a middle school teacher.

Family and Community Partnerships

Another important part of being a middle school teacher is establishing good relationships with adults outside the school. According to *Turning Points* (Carnegie Council on Adolescent Development, 1989), parental involvement declines progressively during the elementary school years. In fact, by the middle school years, the home-school connection is virtually abandoned. Yet, while young adolescents need greater autonomy, they neither need nor desire a complete break from their parents and families (Carnegie Council on Adolescent Development, 1989).

Developmentally responsive middle schools must emphasize the importance of parents and community members becoming active partners in young adolescents' education. Thus, schools should take the initiative to provide a wide array of opportunities for parent and community involvement. In chapter 12, you will be able to read about these partnerships in more detail and explore ways to reengage parents and other adults in the education of young adolescents.

DIRECTIONS FOR EFFECTIVE MIDDLE SCHOOLS

Harvey Allen (1992) maintained that in recent years, there has been a flurry of activity in middle-grades education on both the state and national level. The result has been a number of important publications. While we can only briefly mention these works here, we encourage you to read them and become familiar with their recommendations.

Significant state initiatives include California's *Caught in the Middle* (1987), Maryland's *What Matters in the Middle Grades* (1989), and Virginia's *Framework for Education in the Middle School Grades in Virginia* (1990). In Florida, a group of leading school educators studied the status of middle-grade education and published the findings in *The Forgotten Years* (1984). Based upon the recommendations in this report, Florida enacted *Progress in Middle Grades Education (PRIME),* a comprehensive middle grades improvement program. Table 1–1 summarizes these state initiatives.

The Carnegie Council on Adolescent Development issued two impressive reports on improving the education of young adolescents. The first report, *Turning Points: Preparing American Youth for the 21st Century* (1989), provided a comprehensive examination of the condition of young adolescents and the extent to which schools address their needs. The more current report, *Great Transitions: Preparing Adolescents for a New Century* (1996), examined a similar topic. Table 1–2 provides a look at the themes of these two reports.

Several other documents stand out as essential reading on middle school education. *This We Believe: Developmentally Responsive Middle Level Schools* (1995), the National Middle School Association's official position paper on effective middle-level schools, is probably one of the most influential documents on improving middle school education. It is a resource that we will continually refer to in this book. Other reports on improving middle-grades education include *An Agenda for Excellence at the Middle Level* (1985) and *Achieving Excellence through the Middle Level Curriculum* (1993), both published by the National Association of Secondary School Principals, and *Developmentally Appropriate Middle Level Schools* (1993), published by the Association for Childhood Education International.

TABLE 1–1 *Selected State Initiatives in Middle School Education*

State	Year	Report	Recommendations
Florida	1984	*The Forgotten Years, PRIME*	Provided philosophy and goals for middle-level education in curriculum, organization, and student support services
California	1987	*Caught in the Middle*	Addressed 22 principles such as curriculum and instruction, students' potential, organization, teaching, and leadership
Maryland	1989	*What Matters in the Middle Grades*	Looked at development in young adolescents and provided recommendations around seven key questions such as self-esteem, curriculum and instruction, and student support
Virginia	1990	*Framework for Education in the Middle School Grades in Virginia*	Looked at 23 areas such as connections between schools and society, curriculum, instruction, and special needs

Developed in part from: Allen, H. A., Splittgerber, F. L., & Manning, M. L. (1993). *Teaching and learning in the middle level school.* Columbus, OH: Merrill, page 34.

TABLE 1–2 *Themes of Selected Reports by the Carnegie Council on Adolescent Development*

Turning Points: Preparing American Youth for the 21st Century (1989)
1. Creating a community of learning
2. Teaching a core of common knowledge
3. Ensuring success for all students
4. Empowering teachers and administrators
5. Preparing teachers for the middle grades
6. Improving academic performance through better health and fitness
7. Reengaging families in the education of young adolescents
8. Connecting schools with communities
***Great Transitions: Preparing Adolescents for a New Century* (1996)**
1. Reengaging families with their adolescent children
2. Educating young adolescents for a changing world
3. Promoting the health of adolescents
4. Strengthening communities with adolescents
5. Redirecting the pervasive power of the media
6. Leading toward a shared responsibility for young adolescents

Keeping Current with Technology 1–1

For more current information about the topics discussed in this chapter, visit the following Internet sites:

Visit a few online middle schools:

Jordan Middle School, Palo Alto, CA
http://www.jordan.palo-alto.ca.us

Meads Mill Middle School, Northville, MI
http://mmwww.northville.k12.mi.us/mmill.htm

Raymond B. Stewart Middle School, Zephyrhills, FL
http://199.164.105.18/RBSMS_index.html

Winona Middle School, Winona, MN
http://wms.luminet.net/

For some general information about middle schools, try:

California League of Middle Schools
http://clms.net/

MiddleWeb, a World Wide Web site "exploring the challenges of middle school reform"
http://www.middleweb.com/Links.html

National Middle School Association
http://www.nmsa.org/

Implementing all of the recommendations found in these resources is not easy. Certainly all of the changes proposed in these documents can not happen overnight. Keeping Current with Technology 1–1 lists some Internet sites that you can visit to learn more about these recommendations and how some schools have attempted to implement them. Case Study 1–1 shows how a site-based management team developed a plan to implement middle school concepts.

TEACHING IN THE MIDDLE SCHOOL: QUESTIONS TO CONSIDER

If you are reading this book, you probably fit into one of two categories. You may be a "preservice" teacher education student like Ami Chen in the chapter's opening scenario, wondering if middle school teaching is really for you. Or you may be an experienced "inservice" teacher like Ami's teacher, Mrs. Gillespie, looking to find new ways to work with young adolescents. No matter which category you are in, as you read the following sections, ask yourself if you have the personal and professional commitment to teach or to continue teaching in the middle school and to provide quality educational experiences to young adolescents.

Case Study 1–1

Implementing Middle School Concepts

The members of the site-based management team at Oakwood Middle School decided that, while the school had some effective student-centered programs, much more needed to be done before Oakwood could accurately be called a "middle school." The team agreed to study publications such as *Great Transitions* (Carnegie Council on Adolescent Development, 1996), *Turning Points* (Carnegie Council on Adolescent Development, 1989), and *This We Believe* (National Middle School Association, 1995) to find some recommendations for changes. But when they made a list of all of the recommendations in those documents, some skepticism arose. Clarence Bates, a sixth-grade teacher, shook his head and declared, "There's too much in these documents. Why even bother when we know we'll never be able to do everything they recommend?" But Maurice Kinessi, a guidance counselor, countered: "Can't we still be a good middle school without doing it all?"

After a lively, and sometimes quite heated, discussion, the members of the site-based management team agreed that giving teachers too many implementation plans at one time might result in only half-hearted efforts that would not lead to substantial and long-lasting changes. Instead, they decided to hold school meetings to involve as many teachers as possible, to discuss changes and issues of concern, and to attempt to set an agenda for change. The team, with the help of the teachers, would try to address concerns and problems, set some goals and develop a long-range plan. The idea would be to avoid change just for the sake of change and to avoid too many changes at one time.

While the planning took almost a year, the administrators and teachers at Oakwood finally decided upon a course of action in the form of a 3-year plan. The first year would focus on interdisciplinary teaming because they realized that much progress could be accomplished during team meetings. In the second year, they would continue the work on the teams but add an emphasis on building effective advisor-advisee programs. If all worked well, by the third year, the school's focus would shift to developing exploratory programs. During all 3 years, an emphasis on "making the overall school climate more positive" would be paramount. They also agreed to "revisit" the 3-year plan periodically to assess their progress and redirect their efforts if necessary.

What Are Young Adolescents Really Like?

Ami Chen, our fictitious student teacher in the chapter's opening scenario, mentioned the tremendous diversity of young adolescents. You could say that young adolescents are so diverse that they are difficult to describe. But, remember, they are caught between childhood and adolescence. As one of our students stated, "They are old enough to find their bus home, yet young enough that we [teachers] can still influence them."

One group of authors (Tomlinson, Moon, & Callahan, 1998) described young adolescents by saying:

> Diversity is the hallmark of middle level learners. Middle schoolers range from childlike to adult-like, from socially awkward to socially adept, from emotionally insecure to brimming with confidence, and from concrete to abstract in thinking—sometimes seemingly all in the same student on the same day. (p. 3)

What Does Middle School Teaching Require?

We have observed hundreds of middle school preservice and inservice teachers. To us, middle school teaching requires:

- a genuine commitment to teach young adolescents and to teach in the middle school;
- knowledge of the curricular area(s);
- knowledge of young adolescents, their development, and their diversity; and
- knowledge and expertise in essential middle school concepts such as advisor-advisee programs, exploratory programs, interdisciplinary teaming, and positive school climates.

Please notice that we put "a genuine commitment to teach young adolescents" as our first priority. That was intentional. If you want to be an effective middle school teacher, you should be committed to young adolescents. As *This We Believe* (National Middle School Association, 1995) points out, this commitment will be significant in determining the effectiveness of the middle school and its ultimate success at addressing the needs of young adolescents.

What exactly does this mean? First, you have to make a conscious choice to teach young adolescents. Just as you know the subject that you teach, you have to understand the developmental uniqueness of young adolescents. But more than that, you should enjoy being with 10- to 14-year-olds and should understand the culture of this ever-changing age group. You should be sensitive to individual differences and make sound educational decisions based on young adolescents' needs, interests, and special abilities. Be prepared to serve as a role model; your behavior can be as influential as the curriculum you teach. In your curriculum, provide your students with a rigorous and relevant education based on their developmental needs (National Middle School Association, 1995).

Don't take a job in a middle school to just hold you over until you can find a teaching position in a high school. It takes commitment and dedication to teach young adolescents. "I'm just teaching in this middle school until I can get a science job at the high school," one teacher told us. While she had a firm grasp of science content, she had little understanding of young adolescents and middle school education. As a result, she was unhappy and her students were frustrated.

As a middle school educator, you need to have professional preparation in middle school education, including field experiences in exemplary middle schools. Having said that, we are realistic enough to know that not all teachers can be trained specifically for middle schools. Some teachers will be either elementary or secondary trained and, then, will work toward a middle school certification. We know of many teachers like this who presently teach in the middle school and who are excellent teachers. However, *they chose to teach at the middle school and are not waiting for another teaching job to become available.* We applaud the efforts of these dedicated teachers.

When one bright and enthusiastic young woman in our middle school teacher education program received her practicum placement in a seventh grade, we could tell that she was excited as well as a bit skeptical of teaching young adolescents, just as the fictitious Ami Chen. Although she was open to the experience, we did not think she was totally convinced that middle school teaching was for her. After the practicum, she sheepishly admitted that she had decided to pursue early childhood education. Although our middle school teacher preparation program had lost an excellent teacher candidate, we congratulated her on her decision, and we were glad that she had found where she wanted to be. We were also glad that middle school education would not have a teacher who actually preferred to be elsewhere.

We think teachers who are most successful with young adolescents:

- want to teach and work with the age group;
- are genuinely caring and concerned about their welfare;
- have high expectations for behavior and achievement;
- understand the "culture" of 10- to 14-year-olds;
- serve as advocates—not excusing bad behavior or poor choices—but willing to help students learn from their behaviors and choices, both good and bad;
- know the subject that they are teaching; and
- believe in and support basic middle school concepts.

Undoubtedly, many other characteristics exist, but if you have these qualities, you should make a good middle school teacher. Care to join our team?

Closing Remarks

Middle schools are maturing and developing into schools whose curricular, organizational, teaching, environmental, and guidance practices reflect the developmental and instructional needs of young adolescents. Educators have begun to understand the early adolescence developmental period and have implemented effective middle school practices. However, while the goals set forth in documents prepared by state departments of education, foundations, and professional associations are in sight in many schools, other schools are facing a long, and perhaps difficult, journey. Fortunately, most middle school educators are working toward the same major goal: to improve the lives and educational experiences of young adolescents.

Suggested Readings

Beane, J. A. (1999). Middle schools under siege: Points of attack. *Middle School Journal, 30*(4), 3–9. Examines the attacks on the middle school concept and the toll these attacks are taking.

Beane, J. A. (1999). Middle schools under siege: Responding to the attack. *Middle School Journal, 30*(5), 3–9. Suggests ways middle school advocates might respond to various criticisms.

Carroll, P. S., & Taylor, A. (1998). Understanding the culture of the classroom. *Middle School Journal, 30*(1), 9–17. A look at a collaborative project, and at a class as culture, setting, and social group.

Childhood Education Association for Childhood Education International 1997 (Theme Issue on Young Adolescents), Annual Theme Issue 1997, 73(5). This theme issue provides articles on interdisciplinary teaming, middle school reform, holistic language learning, literacy, technology, and teacher education—all related specifically to young adolescents and middle school education.

Love, C. (1998). On middle schools and middle level education. A conversation with John H. Lounsbury. *Current Issues in Middle Level Education, 7*(1), 5–12. In this conversation, John Lounsbury, one of the founding fathers of the middle school movement, talks about challenges and opportunities of middle school education, ways Schools of Education can work with public schools, and schools that call themselves middle schools, but in reality, are not.

Stevenson, C., & Erb, T. (1998). How implementing *Turning Points* improves student outcomes. *Middle School Journal, 30*(1), 49–52. Explains how implementing the recommendations requires putting multiple elements in place that support and reinforce each other.

Tomlinson, C. A., Moon, T. R., & Callahan, C. M. (1998). How well are we addressing academic diversity in the middle school? *Middle School Journal, 29*(3), 3–11. Middle schools must address student differences because they endorse heterogeneous grouping and serve a diverse group of students.

Chapter 2

Young Adolescents—Development and Issues

Scenario—Ms. Ortega Reflects

When Ms. Christina Ortega, a language arts teacher on an interdisciplinary seventh-grade team, shared her thoughts about teaching, she explained what an eye-opening experience her first year had been:

"We talked about diversity in my college classes, but I didn't grasp what that meant until now. Within our team, we have early maturers and late maturers, fast maturing girls and slower developing boys, socially outgoing students and some too shy to speak, independent students and some needing constant attention, and both abstract and concrete thinkers.

Then, there are gender and cultural differences. It seemed so easy back in college. I was sure that I would not stereotype my students, but now I see that girls and boys do appear to learn differently. While some of the boys like competition; some of the girls like collaboration. Of course, crossover between the genders exists, but there still are predominant differences in how girls and boys learn. There are also the cultural differences.

And I can't forget about all the developmental problems. After a great beginning, academic achievement took a dip in November, and peer pressure continued to take its toll on attitudes and behavior. Three of my students were caught smoking. A rumor spread about a pregnant student in another cluster. Is Heather anorexic or just a little too slim for her age? Is there some reason Lamont can't stay in his seat in class? My list of concerns could go on and on. I know middle school is supposed to be different. But how can I deal with the diversity among the students that I teach and meet all of their needs? I know my subject matter, but I realize now that content is only part of teaching. If I am going to be a successful middle school teacher, I really need to focus on the students I'm working with. And that means I need more information about them."

Overview

Christina Ortega is facing a problem shared by many middle school educators. Today's 10- to 14-year-olds, commonly called young adolescents, differ significantly from the individuals found in this age group 30 or 40 years ago. Contemporary young adolescents develop faster—physically, they mature earlier; cognitively, they know more (although their cognitive experiences might not be the type that contribute to school achievement); and socially, many have a preoccupation with friends and peers. They also face issues such as dieting and eating disorders; alcohol, drugs, and tobacco; AIDS and STDS (sexually transmitted diseases); peer pressure; and physical and psychological safety concerns that previous generations might not have confronted at this age.

Whether you are a beginning teacher like Ms. Ortega, an experienced educator, or a student in a teacher education program, there is a wealth of detailed information on 10- to 14-year-olds' developmental characteristics to help you work with middle school students. A number of publications focus extensively on young adolescent development (Manning, 1993a, 1993b: Milgram, 1992; Tanner, 1971; Thornburg, 1983a; Van Hoose & Strahan, 1988).

In this chapter, rather than reading lists of young adolescent's developmental characteristics, you will be able to look briefly at the physical, cognitive, and psychosocial development of 10- to 14-year-olds and focus on the issues facing young adolescents as they develop. Then, you can examine some ways that middle school educators can provide educational experiences that reflect young adolescent development.

Objectives

After reading and thinking about this chapter on young adolescents, you should able to:

1. explain the need to consider the tremendous diversity (developmental, cultural, and gender) among young adolescents;

2. explain issues such as general health, diet, and eating disorders; alcohol, drugs, and tobacco; AIDS and teenage pregnancy; peer pressure; and how these issues affect young adolescents' physical, psychosocial, and cognitive development;
3. list and describe young adolescents' physical, psychosocial, and cognitive developmental characteristics;
4. name several contributors who have conducted research and written about young adolescent development and list their primary contributions;
5. explain why middle school educational experiences should reflect young adolescent development; and
6. name several sources of additional information that will assist you in understanding 10- to 14-years-olds' development.

Generalizations about Development—The Need for Caution

Teaching a subject would be easy if there were no need to worry about learners' individuality. However, it is impossible to overlook the uniqueness of the students and still be a good teacher. Only by matching instruction to the needs and capabilities of individual learners can we provide developmentally appropriate and responsive education. In middle-level grades, more than in any other, the emphasis needs to be on whom we teach, rather than on what we teach. This is not to say that curriculum is unimportant. Rather, this statement is a realization of the complexity of middle-level boys and girls. The middle-level years are a time of growth and development, with changes occurring in individual students on a daily basis. What makes working with 10- to 14-year-olds challenging is realizing and accepting that change.

While developmental characteristics can be listed with considerable certainty, any objective discussion of young adolescents must emphasize that change is a constant and that diversity is the hallmark characteristic of young adolescents (Thornburg, 1983a). The wide range of physical developmental characteristics can readily be seen—some 12-year-olds look like 16-year-olds while others resemble 8-year-olds. Other characteristics are more subtle. Psychosocially, some young adolescents place priority on friendships and socialize at every opportunity; others might continue to be somewhat shy and even avoid social opportunities. Cognitive development is even less evident, with some young adolescents performing formal and higher level thinking, while others continue to think in concrete terms (Manning, 1994/1995). Every young adolescent is growing up, but each is taking a different road and going at a different speed on his or her journey from childhood to adulthood.

Young Adolescent Development

Many writers have looked at the physical, psychosocial, and cognitive developmental characteristics of young adolescents. (Manning, 1993a, 1993b; Milgram, 1992; Tanner, 1971; Thornburg, 1983a; Van Hoose & Strahan, 1988). While it is important for you to know and understand these characteristics, we think it is also important to look at these characteristics in light of the issues that today's young adolescents face. Just as middle-level educa-

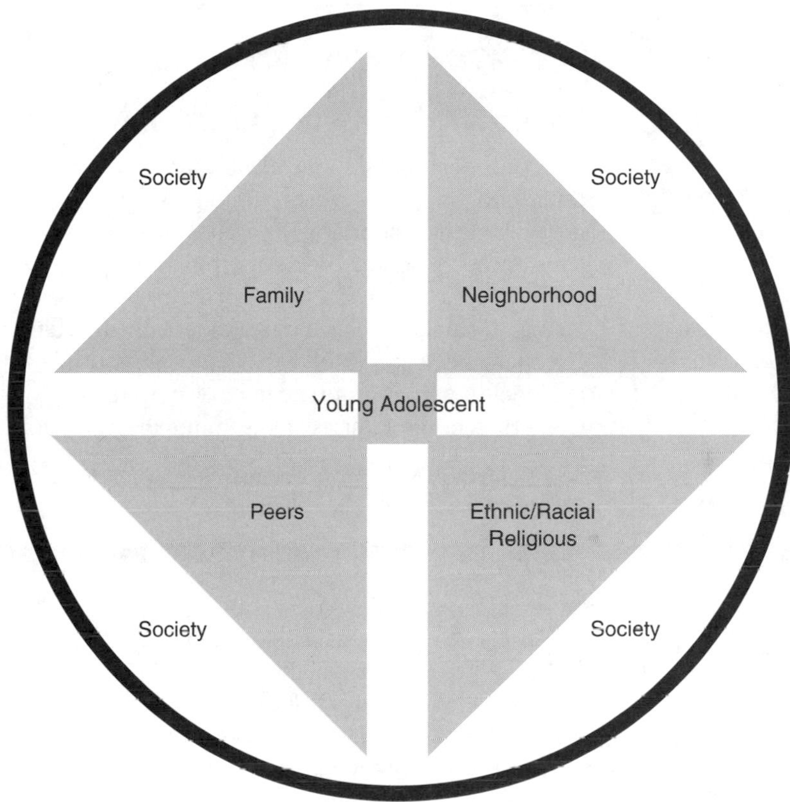

FIGURE 2–1 Communities Affecting the Young Adolescent

tors must be concerned with the total environment of the school and the community, not just what happens in their own classrooms, we believe that, in order to understand middle school students, educators have to look at young adolescents and the ways they develop in light of what we call their communities.

As each young adolescent develops, he or she undergoes many changes—both internal and external. One middle school librarian mused, "I just stand back and watch the hormones at work." That thought was echoed by a teacher who said, "My job is to help my students maintain some order in their lives and perhaps learn a few things while the hormones take over the control of their bodies." Certainly, physical changes are a major part of the development of young adolescents. However, the final effect that these changes have is tempered by the environment or "communities" in which a young adolescent lives. To us, these communities include the family and its socioeconomic group, the neighborhood (including the school), the ethnic/racial/religious community, and young adolescent peers (Figure 2–1). Each of these groups and their approach to the issues of contemporary society will impact the development of a young adolescent.

Often these communities exert conflicting influences on the young adolescent. Expectations from an ethnic community may be different from those of peers or the neighborhood, while family expectations may conflict with the neighborhood or peer norms. Girls might,

Diversity Perspectives 2–1

Ethnicity, Identity, and Risk Behaviors

Marcell looked at ethnicity, identity, and risk behaviors in Mexican American adolescents and offered recommendations for helping these students. One of the fastest growing ethnic minorities, Mexican American adolescents face a number of problems: substance abuse, unsafe sexual practices, poor academic achievement, and delinquency. While disturbing in and of themselves, these problems also affect adolescents' identity formation, rates of cultural retention/acculturation, and ethnic identities. Marcell offers a detailed list of recommendations, divided into three groups: promoting ethnic identity and appropriate level of prevention; promoting interaction among social workers, schools, families, and communities; and adapting program activities.

Source: Marcell, A. V. (1994). Understanding ethnicity, identity formation, and risk behavior among adolescents of Mexican descent. *Journal of School Health, 64,* 323–327.

for a variety of reasons, actually seek to avoid success (George, 1986; Grossman & Grossman, 1994) because they might feel that success, which results from competition, conflicts with their sense of connectedness with others; excelling in a male-oriented school system might result in unpopularity or outright ridicule; and success will portray them as less feminine and less popular with boys (Grossman & Grossman, 1994). African, Asian, and Hispanic Americans often differ in their learning styles as well as their perceptions of school success and motivation (Manning & Baruth, 1996). This can lead to some unique pressures on middle school adolescents. As Diversity Perspectives 2–1 shows, ethnic groups often face special problems, as evidenced in Marcell's study of Mexican American adolescents.

Realizing that the four communities exert tremendous pressures on the young adolescent, we want to look briefly at the characteristics of young adolescent development and then explore the relationships that exist between adolescent development and the realities of contemporary society. Although we look at physical, psychosocial, and cognitive development separately in this chapter, we want to stress the interconnectedness of these developmental characteristics (Figure 2–2). For example, adultlike behavior brought on by physical development can be strengthened or tempered by family and peer relationships.

While we realize that we may be glossing over some very complex topics that are often explored in detail in adolescent development or psychology texts, we provide references and resources for further exploration. Remember, just as a team approach is basic to the middle school concept, so is the need to rely on a variety of resources to build your knowledge as a middle-level educator.

Throughout all areas of young adolescent development, change is a constant, as are individual differences among students. Some students are more likely to develop unacceptable behavior or participate in unacceptable acts than others. Development, changes in family structures, pressures and pitfalls of school, and societal pressures are community forces

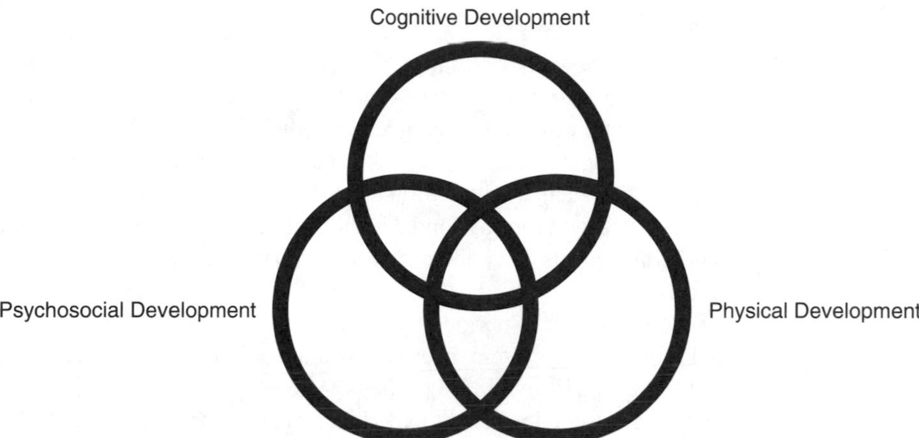

FIGURE 2–2 Interconnectedness of Young Adolescent Development

that make all middle school students at-risk at one time or another. Walker (1991) aptly summarized the situation: "Every student is at risk for some reason. We cannot wait until a student is labeled as such to intervene; rather, we must plan for the success of all students" (p. 112).

Although all young adolescents experience at-risk conditions and behaviors at some time, at-risk conditions affect youngsters in different ways or not at all. While two students may be experiencing similar situations, one may develop unacceptable behavior while the other might function capably. Thus, middle school educators must use great caution when trying to determine who is and who is not at-risk for a certain condition or as a result of a specific situation.

Physical Development

Early adolescence, the developmental stage between childhood and adolescence, was recognized as a separate developmental period in the 1970s (Thornburg, 1983b) and has received less research examination than other developmental stages. Still, some researchers have provided important information on physical development.

Tanner offered significant contributions to the research in his *Growth at Adolescence* (1962), his research findings and conclusions published in the *Scientific American* (1968), and his studies of 12- to 16-year-olds published in *Twelve to Sixteen: Early Adolescence* (Kagan & Coles, 1972). He focused on several areas of physical development such as sequence and tempo of growth, diversity and variations, the onset of puberty, the trend toward larger body sizes, early and late maturers, and how physical growth affects mental growth, emotion, and physiological development. Terming the young adolescent developmental period as "forgotten," Lipsitz (1977) in *Growing Up Forgotten* examined myths and misconceptions about young adolescent development.

Selected Physical Developmental Characteristics

As a result of the work of Tanner, Lipsitz, and others, we now realize that physical development during early adolescence includes a number of changes, each with the potential for having powerful effects on young adolescents and their daily lives.

First, young adolescents experience a growth spurt with a rapid increase in body size and obvious skeletal and structural changes. During an approximate 2-year time span, 9 to 10 inches of growth for boys and 7 inches for girls may occur. Girls sometimes weigh more than boys since girls reach their growth spurt peak around age 12 and boys reach their peak around 14.

Second, puberty, a period of physiological changes that include the development of the sexual reproductive system, begins in young adolescence. While considerable diversity exists, 88% of the girls and 83% of the boys reach puberty by age 14.

Third, young adolescents experience gender-specific physical development. For example, girls' hips widen and breasts develop while boys' voices deepen, shoulders grow, and facial hair appears (Milgram, 1992).

Implications and Issues

These three selected physical developmental characteristics can have profound effects on young adolescents and the issues affecting their lives.

1. **Restlessness and fatigue.** Young adolescents often experience restlessness and fatigue due to growing bones, joints, and muscles. Sitting for long periods of time becomes difficult and perhaps even painful if the desks and chairs are too small. Lamont had problems sitting still in Christina Ortega's class because of an ill-fitting and uncomfortable chair rather than any serious emotional problem. Even exercise is not always the answer. While youngsters should participate in developmentally appropriate exercise, physical competitions between early and late maturers should be avoided since these often become very one-sided and can add to self-esteem problems.
2. **Physical diversity.** Look around a middle school and notice the wide range of physical diversity among young adolescents (e.g., a physically small 14-year-old and large 11- or 12-year old). On a recent visit to a middle school library, we saw a young woman working at the circulation desk who, by her dress, attitude, and overall appearance, seemed to be a parent volunteer or paraprofessional. Later when we saw her again in a classroom, we learned that this young lady was a very mature eighth grader. This physical diversity can affect self-esteem and can result in youngsters worrying about when growth will begin or end. Also, early developers sometimes feel more "grown up" and engage in adultlike behaviors, often participating in activities that have potentially dangerous consequences.

   Among these adultlike behaviors is the use of *alcohol, drugs, and tobacco.* Whether students use these substances to act grown up or to conform to neighborhood and peer expectations, this action can lead to major health problems and to other problems such as teenage pregnancy and alienation from family, friends, and school. Equally disturbing is the increasingly younger ages at which children begin to experiment with dangerous substances. While exact figures are not available for 10- to 14-year-olds, a study of 12- to 17-year-olds by the Census Bureau reported the following drug use: marijuana and hashish (16.8%), alcohol (38.8%), and tobacco (36.3%) (U.S. Bureau of the Census, 1998). Physical growth can be stunted; psychosocially, young adolescents might withdraw or grow dependent on alcohol; and cognitively, their thought processes might be slowed or delayed. Of course, there is always a chance of brain damage or even death.

3. **Nutritional problems.** Boys and girls develop differently, with girls maturing at a faster rate and often feeling self-conscious due to their faster growth. Middle school educators need to keep these gender differences in mind and recognize how these differences might affect girls' psychosocial development or lead to nutritional problems (especially anorexia nervosa and bulimia).

   Some young adolescents experience an obsession with thinness. Anorexia nervosa, an extreme quest for thinness, is a psychological and physical disturbance in which the teenager starves herself (females make up 95% of anorexics), exercises compulsively, and develops an unrealistic view of her body. Bulimia is another closely related eating disorder. However, while the anorexic aims to lose weight by not eating, the bulimic tries to eat without gaining weight. For example, the young person experiences eating sprees or binges, fears not being able to stop eating, and experiences a depressed mood and self-disparaging thoughts after eating binges. Then, the bulimic self-induces vomiting to avoid gaining weight. Complex causes and treatment underlay these disorders, and between 10% and 20% of youngsters who do not receive professional help die of starvation and its consequences (Seifert & Hoffnung, 1991). Christina Ortega was right to be concerned about Heather. She fits the profile of an adolescent, usually a girl in a middle or upper socioeconomic group, who appears unhappy, shows an inordinate concern about his/her weight and appearance, and evidences frequent weight fluctuations (Atwater, 1988).

4. **Sexual awareness.** The onset of puberty sometimes results in a sense of sexual awareness, which can have dangerous consequences if sexual experimentation occurs. If that happens, young adolescents can become pregnant or can contract diseases.

   Recent increases in figures reporting *sexual activity, pregnancies, and abortions* indicate that adolescents and often children participate in at-risk behaviors (Carnegie Council on Adolescent Development, 1996). In fact, U.S. teenagers under the age of 15 are 15 times more likely to give birth than their peers in other Western nations (Buie, 1987). According to Barth, Middleton, and Wagman (1989), teenage pregnancy remains the major reason for students leaving school; by the age of 15, 6.6% of females and 17.5% of male teenagers have had intercourse; sexually active adolescents do not use contraception consistently or effectively, and almost 20% of all teens have an unintended pregnancy.

   Teenage pregnancy was becoming a major concern for the teachers in Christina Ortega's middle school, especially when one 14-year-old girl became pregnant for the second time! Realizing that the middle school concept tries to tackle the whole problem with a variety of resources, Ms. Ortega's school decided to try a school wide effort to combat teenage pregnancy—through science and health classes, sex-ed and exploratory programs, and, perhaps more importantly, teacher advisories. The school nurse, guidance counselor, and library media specialist were also involved in the effort to help the young adolescents.

Unlike many of the other risks that young people face, *AIDS* is a life-or-death matter. Unfortunately, inexperience, a feeling of invincibility, and a lack of knowledge make young adolescents particularly vulnerable. One in four new HIV infections in the United States occurs in people younger than 22 (Rosenberg, Biggar, & Goedert, 1994). Through June 1994, more than 15,000 persons aged 20–24 and more than 60,000 persons aged 25–29 had been diagnosed with AIDS (Unks, 1996). Since the 20–29 age group accounts for one in five AIDS cases, and the incubation period between HIV infection and AIDS diagnosis is many years, it is clear that large numbers of people diagnosed with AIDS in their twenties became infected with HIV as teenagers.

Sexually active young adolescents are also at risk of contracting *sexually transmitted diseases (STDS).* Curious about sexual activity and sometimes prone to sexual experimentation, youngsters can contract a STD, which can impede their development and overall health.

5. **Sexual identity.** With the onset of puberty, young adolescents begin to develop and examine their sexual identity. While all young people confront biological and social developmental changes, gay and lesbian young adolescents often struggle with an identity formation that differs from the majority of their peers. Estimates suggest there are 2.9 million gay or lesbian young adolescents in the United States. Representing all cultural, religious, social, and racial groups and from both rural and urban schools, gay and lesbian young adolescents often are isolated by their fears as well as by the taboos of society and the ridicule of others (Bailey & Phariss, 1996).

   Some educators believe that being both gay or lesbian and a young adolescent results in double jeopardy. Not only are some of these young people fearful, withdrawn, depressed, and full of despair, they often also experience harassment and violence, and exhibit suicidal tendencies (Vare & Norton, 1998). In addition to attempting to clarify their sexual orientation, some gay and lesbian young adolescents may resort to substance abuse, exhibit low self-esteem, develop conflicts with their family, and become emotionally isolated. These "invisible" students are becoming more visible each day through increased numbers of referrals to counselors, social workers, and substance abuse personnel (Bailey & Phariss, 1996, p. 39).

6. **Depression and acute health conditions.** Compared to adults, young adolescents suffer fewer illnesses and general health problems. However, their physical development can be affected by their general health, depression, and days missed from school due to acute health conditions.

   Depression, a contemporary and common problem, often affects young adolescents. Symptoms may include a change in appetite or weight, sleep disturbances, psychomotor problems, loss of interest in usual activities, loss of energy, feelings of worthlessness or excessive guilt, complaints about difficulty to concentrate, and thoughts of death or suicide. Depression, however, may not always be termed as such and may be cited as learning disabilities, hyperactivity, school phobia, somatic complaints, and conduct disorders.

When taken to the extreme, depression can lead to *suicide.* Over the past 30 years, the teenage suicide rate has tripled and currently accounts for more than 5,000 deaths each year, or nearly 20% of all the deaths among young people. Children and young adolescents who attempt suicide tend to be female, by a ratio of four to one, but completed suicides are higher among males. Boys typically use "active" methods such as shooting or hanging, and girls commonly use "passive" methods such as taking poisons or drugs (Strother, 1986). Reported suicides are greatly outnumbered by unreported suicides, attempted suicides, and other types of self-destructive behavior.

Some young adolescents also experience acute health conditions. While the Census Bureau does not report heath data specifically for 10- to 14-year-olds, typical acute health conditions for children age 5 to 17 years include infective and parasitic conditions, common colds, influenza, digestive system problems, and injuries (U.S. Bureau of the Census, 1998).

Nutrition to build growing bodies is not a topic of great interest to young adolescents. As one girl told us: "I looked at my cereal this morning, but that's all I did." When a sixth-grade boy got off the bus eating a bag of potato chips and drinking a soda, a teacher kidded him that it was too soon after breakfast for a snack. The boy replied, "This is my breakfast."

Health concerns, however, can lead to serious consequences for young adolescents. First, not taking reasonable care of the body or taking unnecessary risks can result in injuries or death. Second, inadequate nutrition can interfere with a teenager's ability to concentrate at school and to engage in peer-related activities. Third, an obsession with thinness can result in serious health problems and even death.

What Can Middle-Level Teachers Do?

Being aware of the changes is a major step in helping young adolescents deal with the developmental problems that they face. Just as Christina Ortega noted the changes in her students, you need to become aware of the physical development of your own students. You can discuss developmentally appropriate topics in health and family life classes as well as in advisor-advisee programs and exploratory programs. With the help of others such as the school nurse and the guidance counselor, you can provide factual information about young adolescent sexuality that also addresses the concerns of gay and lesbians. Information on young adolescent physical development can be added to the school library collection and featured in displays or booktalks. This includes providing age-appropriate literature that explains all sexual orientations and that also includes factual accounts of gay and lesbian young adolescents and their experiences. The Web sites in Keeping Current with Technology 2–1 provide additional sources of information about the development of young adolescents. Finally, you can help young adolescents understand the need to protect the human and civil rights of all people, no matter what their physical appearance, developmental characteristics, or sexual orientation.

Keeping Current with Technology 2–1

Adolescence Directory On-Line
http://education.indiana.edu/cas/adol/adol.html
Links for teachers, counselors and teens provided by the Center for Adolescent Studies at Indiana University.

Adolescent Health On-Line
http://www.ama-assn.org/adolhlth/adolhlth.htm
Resources from the American Medical Association

American Academy of Child and Adolescent Psychiatry
http://www.aacap.org
Information on teen suicide, alcohol use, and eating disorders.

Antigang and Youth Violence Initiative
http://www.usdoj.gov/ag/anti-gang.htm

Carnegie Corporation
http://www.carnegie.org

Office of Population Affairs
http://www.dhhs.gov/progorg/opa/
Describes adolescent pregnancy programs.

U.S. Bureau of the Census
http://www.census.gov/

U.S. Department of Health & Human Services
http://www.hhs.gov/
Search under the term "adolescent" for health information.

Psychosocial Development

While middle-level youngsters are developing physically, their social behaviors are changing too—friendships and social networks are expanding; allegiances and affiliations are shifting from adults to peers; their self-esteem is growing; and their lives are often plagued by mood swings. Youngsters become preoccupied with themselves, and they desire freedom and independence. Several theorists have attempted to explain these changes in young adolescents.

Erik Erikson (1963) proposed that people develop through eight psychosocial stages, each having a distinct age range and distinct characteristics. Within each respective stage is a crisis period for social and emotional development. The resolution of each stage depends on a person's ability to achieve a positive or negative outcome that influences ego development. An unresolved crisis may interfere with progress during the next psychosocial stage. Unfortunately, Erikson did his work prior to early adolescence being accepted as a legitimate developmental period, so he did not designate a distinct psychosocial stage for the 10- to 14-year-old range. That means the early adolescence developmental period falls within two of Erikson's psychosocial stages: Industry vs. Inferiority (6 to 11 years) and Identity vs. Role Confusion (12 to 18 years) (Manning, 1988).

In the Industry vs. Inferiority stage, children form an opinion of themselves as either "industrious" or "inferior." During this stage, youngsters need to accomplish specific and worthwhile social, physical, and academic tasks, complete all assignments, and feel a sense of pride. Inability to complete relevant tasks successfully may lower the young adolescents' self-esteem and lessen the chances of future success.

In the Identity vs. Role Confusion stage, young adolescents seek an identity by striving for increased independence from adults and for peer acceptance by concerning themselves with the kind of person they are becoming. As students seek a sense of self, there is a danger of role confusion where they have doubts about their identity. Youngsters also look for role models and heroes and try to integrate these ideals into their own value system (George & Alexander, 1993).

Robert Havighurst (1972) proposed a social stage theory that divides a person's life into six developmental stages, each with its own respective developmental tasks. In discussing developmental tasks, Havighurst explained that living is actually a "long series of tasks to learn, where learning well brings satisfaction and reward, while learning poorly brings unhappiness and social disapproval" (Havighurst, 1972, p. 2). Middle school students fall within the later part (i.e., 10- to 12-year-olds) of the childhood period and the beginning years (or the 12- to 14-year-olds) of the adolescent period. They need to be successful with social and emotional tasks and must learn to place the common goals over personal interests. Specific developmental tasks for this age group include achieving new and more mature relations with age-mates of both sexes, continuing to learn an appropriate masculine or feminine role, beginning to achieve emotional independence from parents and other adults, and working toward socially responsible behavior.

Selected Psychosocial Developmental Characteristics

Psychosocial development is a function of the interaction of physical and intellectual development with the communities in which the young adolescent lives. Being a friend, having friends, and spending time with friends become all-important. In their study of young adolescent friendships, Crockett, Losoff, and Peterson (1984) reported that friendships boost self-esteem and reduce anxiety as trust and respect develop; help young adolescents develop a sense of identity; contribute to interpersonal skills important for future social relationships; and assist in the adjustment to the physical and psychological changes associated with puberty.

Young adolescents shift their allegiance and affiliation from teachers and parents to peers who become the prime source for standards and behavior. As youngsters reach outside the family community for social experiences, companionship, and approval, contact with parents begins to decrease and the nature of social interactions gradually changes (Thornburg, 1983a). This shifting of allegiance results in peers having tremendous influence on the behavior, speech, and attire of young adolescents. Examining long-held beliefs and allegiances, young adolescents expend considerable energy moving toward greater control over their lives and increased autonomy (George & Alexander, 1993).

During this developmental period, young adolescents become preoccupied with themselves. They compare themselves physically and socially with peers and question their "developmental progress" if differences exist. Those with noticeable weight and height differences or early- or late-maturers might be the only ones to notice; however, these differences can play an enormous role in influencing perceptions of themselves and others. The smallest differences can make young people feel self-conscious and can also make them reluctant to participate in physical or social activities.

Finally, young adolescents also experience changing self-esteems that might vary from situation to situation. A student might have a positive self-esteem in science class yet feel totally inadequate in physical education. The transition from the elementary school to the usually larger middle school may also affect their self-esteem. Rather than being the oldest and perhaps biggest, they must reassess their standing with peers and teachers (Thornburg & Glider, 1984). Diversity Perspectives 2–2 looks at how girls experience a greater decline in self-esteem.

Implications and Issues

Psychosocial development can affect young adolescents in a number of ways.

1. **Rapid physical development.** Problems can arise when physical development is not matched by emotional or social development. For example, Lamont, Christina Ortega's student, was a good example of an early maturing young adolescent. In 6 to 8 months, he grew nearly 6 inches, gained weight, developed a deep voice, and experienced the growth of considerable hair on his legs and arms. As a result, peers and older acquaintances expected more mature behavior from Lamont. However, Lamont's rapid physical growth had not been matched with psychosocial maturity, and the expectations of his peers and friends left him feeling uncomfortable.
2. **Peer pressure.** Without a doubt, peers represent a powerful and often underestimated source of influence in the social, academic, and overall development, behavior, and attitudes of young adolescents. We saw an excellent example of peer pressure applied to clothing in a sixth-grade classroom. Out of 24 students, 22 wore the same blue-and-white cloth shoes. When we asked several students why they chose those shoes, each indicated a desire to conform to what they saw as class standards, with the usual response being: "Everybody wears them."

   Unfortunately, at times, peer pressure can lead youngsters to participate in risky behaviors, something that affects substantial numbers of young people (Carnegie Council on Adolescent Development, 1990). These at-risk behaviors can result in underachievement; pregnancy and sexually transmitted diseases; tobacco, drugs, and alcohol abuse; health problems; physical and psychological violence; and eating disorders. All of these can be affected by peer pressure.

   However, in spite of the problems often associated with peer pressure, middle school educators need to remember that attempts by adults to compete with peers for a place of importance in a young adolescent's life are usually doomed to fail. A healthy self-concept still serves as one of the best antidotes to negative peer pressure (Manning & Allen, 1987). Confident and successful students who feel good about

Diversity Perspectives 2–2

Females and Self-Esteem

The research indicates that self-esteem declines as girls grow older and includes aspects such as stereotyping, self-ratings, efforts to boost self-esteem, effects of and on body image, and effects on academic achievement, especially during the middle school years (Brown & Gilligan, 1990; "Education and gender," 1994; Jackson, Hodge, & Ingram, 1994; Loeb & Horst, 1978; Lundeberg, Fox, & Puncochar, 1994; Schmuck & Schmuck, 1994). Lundeberg et al. (1994) reported declining self-esteem in girls as early as the sixth grade, with these differences increasing with age, and with girls showing a far greater loss than boys. For example, girls in elementary, middle, and secondary schools experience continuous decreases in self-esteem of 60%, 37%, and 29%, respectively ("Education and gender," 1994). This lack of confidence, however, does not often result from lack of ability. Instead, even when girls achieve as well or better than their male counterparts, they tend to underestimate their ability and to overestimate others' abilities (Lundeberg et al., 1994). Around adolescence, girls tend to accept stereotyped notions of how they should be, and they repress their true feelings to accept more traditional feelings (Brown & Gilligan, 1990). The effects of self-esteem on young adolescent girls' academic achievement, overall motivation, and general outlook on life should prompt middle school educators to provide gender-appropriate school experiences designed to increase girls' self-esteems.

A survey (Daley, 1991) sponsored by the American Association of University Women (AAUW) found culture is also a factor in self-esteem. Many more African American girls were still confident in high school compared to European and Hispanic girls, and European girls lost their self-assurance earliest of all three groups. African American girls may feel more self-confident because they often see strong women around them. They seem less dependent on school achievement for their self-esteem, drawing their sense of themselves more from family and community.

themselves and their relationships to their communities are usually less likely to "go along with the crowd." Conversely, students who already exhibit risky behavior and who may already feel unsuccessful and lack confidence may be even more likely to give in to peers in an attempt to feel accepted or part of the group.

Not all peer pressure is negative; some can be a positive influence. For example, peer pressure can be used to encourage academic achievement and to promote socially acceptable behaviors (Manning & Allen, 1987). Peers can exert pressure to eat the right foods, avoid abusive substances, and behave appropriately. The difficult task is to decide how most effectively to lessen the influence of negative peer pressure and how to use peer pressure to encourage desirable behaviors such as working toward a group goal. As one 12-year-old girl told us, "Everyone is tempted to give in to peer pressure at times; and sometimes that's OK. What's important is knowing when to say yes and when to say no."

3. **Shifting allegiances.** Young adolescents need educators' and parents' support even as their allegiances shift and they move away from associating with adults. Youngsters who used to look forward to a trip with their family would now rather "hang out" with their friends. Realistically speaking, adults often feel rejected or even hurt when this occurs. Still, both educators and parents need to show support and caring attitudes toward young adolescents. Young people who feel rejected might try even harder to move toward peers and away from adults. Understanding young adolescents' motives and perspectives during this shifting process can actually contribute to positive relationships between younger and older generations.
4. **Preoccupation with appearances.** Young adolescents need to understand that it is normal to be preoccupied with their appearances and behavior. Mirrors, combs, brushes, and even cans of hair spray emerge from backpacks for a fast touch-up (for both girls and boys) during classes.
5. **Adult behaviors.** Divorce, the apparent decline of parental and institutional authority, and the media seem to force adult behaviors on youngsters. While the quest for independence and freedom can seem exciting and quite grown-up, young adolescents need to learn that they must assume responsibility for their actions and that they should not participate in risky adventures and behaviors.

How does the idea of a youngster adopting adult attitudes and behaviors relate to development? From a psychosocial perspective, young adolescents often feel rushed to socialize too early, to engage in cross-sex relationships, to participate in adult activities, and to see events from perspectives beyond their years. Rather than feeling hurried to move through the 10- to 14-year-old period to more adultlike behaviors, young adolescents should experience age- and developmental-appropriate tasks and challenges.

The increasing standardization of many schools adds to the problem. For example, Elkind (1981) cites textbooks that are standardized on a national level, machine-scored tests, rigid-age grouping, and tightly sequenced curriculum and teaching as evidence of this. Ten years later, Elkind (1993) reiterated his concern that the disappearance of the childhood years contributed to children engaging in risky behaviors.

Educators need to teach decision-making skills so that young adolescents will be equipped with the ability to make informed decisions. Having the knowledge, however, does not often suffice—young adolescents tend to feel immortal and often make poor decisions. Taquisha, a shy seventh grader who had recently moved into the neighborhood, thought having her tongue pierced would make her seem more grown-up and would help her be accepted by her peers. Unfortunately, her tongue became infected. Unable to hide the tongue ring from her family, Taquisha went through some physically and psychologically unpleasant days before she "swallowed" the tongue ring and ended the controversy.

While it would be easy to write off Taquisha's problems because of her immaturity, young adolescents need the help that a middle school can provide. Rather than being condemned, young adolescents need educators who will work with them and prepare them to make informed and mature decisions in their quest for independence and freedom.

6. **Changing self-esteems.** With young adolescents' changing self-esteems, middle school educators need to recognize how self-esteem dips and must take appropriate action. Changing from the elementary school to the middle school, developing bodies, making new friendships, and tackling more difficult subject matter can have negative effects on self-esteems. Middle school educators' face a twofold challenge. First, they need to teach young adolescents to make accurate assessments of their self-esteems and, second, educators need to provide educational experiences that contribute to positive self-esteems.
7. **Aggressive behaviors and violence.** Educators need to provide young adolescents with the skills necessary to cope with physical and psychological violence. Incidents of aggression and violence are increasing annually at alarming rates in our schools. The U.S. Department of Justice reports 3 million crimes—or about 11% of all crimes—occur each year in public schools (Sautter, 1995). According to *Turning Points:* "Where petty theft from lockers and occasional fights were once problems, today assaults, carrying of weapons, drug transactions, and robberies are constant worries in schools" (Carnegie Council on Adolescent Development, 1989, p. 65).

   While violent assaults on students and teachers grab media attention, most aggression consists of less extreme acts such as bullying, verbal/physical threats, shoving, and fist fights. Boys are three times more likely than girls to be involved in aggression (Carnegie Council on Adolescent Development, 1989). There is no isolated cause for this aggression. Rather, research suggests that substance abuse, victimization, marital discord/spouse abuse, depression, exposure to violence in the mass media, and extreme poverty all play a role (Gable, 1994).

   While aggressive acts take a toll at all grade levels, there are several reasons why middle school students are frequently affected. First, young adolescents have left the supposedly safe elementary school to enter a usually larger and more impersonal middle level school setting. Second, during their development, young adolescents form long-lasting attitudinal assumptions and perceptions of others (e.g., how others treat them, how others should be treated, what makes others aggressive or violent, and how to respond to aggressive behavior or violence). Third, during these formative years, young adolescents might conclude that aggressive behavior calls for aggressive responses, a reaction that often leads to additional problems.

   Youngsters who fall victim to aggressive behavior may develop feelings of inferiority or a lower self-esteem as they struggle to answer questions such as: "Why do others want to hurt me?" Fear and stress stemming from aggressive behavior can exact a heavy toll on young adolescents, often impinging upon their social development, self-esteem, and even academic achievement.

What Can Middle-Level Teachers Do?

In advisor-advisee sessions, exploratory programs, and health classes, middle school educators need to convey the idea that developmental differences are normal and that development in one area does not imply comparable development in other areas. Middle school educators can also use small groups (e.g., cooperative learning sessions) that allow friends to study and work together and that allow new friendships to form. While educators should probably refrain from trying to make friends for social isolates, educational experiences can be planned that involve all students in social endeavors. Advisory and exploratory sessions can include topics such as ways to make friends, select "good" friends, and develop cross-gender and cross-cultural friendships.

Cognitive Development

While several researchers and writers have proposed theories about cognitive development and how children and adolescents learn, most have not focused their attention solely on the early adolescence developmental period. That means that it is necessary to pull information on 10- to 14-year-olds out of a larger body of work.

The learner's cognitive development includes the ability to organize information around categories or concepts, which allows for generalizations and contributes to increasingly higher levels of cognitive functioning. Jean Piaget divided this development into four stages. Most young adolescents function in a transitory stage between Piaget's concrete (7 to 12 years) and formal operations (12 and beyond) stage. Some young adolescents in the early formal operations stage can comprehend concepts, reason about the future, and test hypotheses (Ginsburg & Opper, 1988). While Piaget's developmental ages suggest young adolescents should be able to deal with abstract tasks, most young adolescents continue to think in concrete terms. Milgram (1992) warns that considerable evidence contradicts the belief that formal operational thinking begins around age 11 or 12.

Lev Vygotsky (1978) agreed with most of Piaget's conclusions, but he argued that other people (such as parents, peers, teachers, counselors, and others) play influential roles on an individual's cognitive development. Language, an essential component of social interaction, provides opportunities for young adolescents to interact and socialize with other people.

Howard Gardner (1983, 1993b) based his multiple-intelligences theory on brain research, developmental research, experiments with animals, psychological testing, cross-cultural studies, and the works of Dewey, Bruner, Piaget, and Eisner. Gardner (1983) considers intelligence to be biologically based and represented in multiple ways. He believes learners have at least seven intelligences: (1) logical mathematical—enjoy solving problems, finding patterns, outlining, and calculating; (2) linguistic—relate to the meaning of words, their rhythms, and sounds; (3) spatial—like to design, invent, imagine, and create; (4) bodily kinesthetic—learn through physical movement, mimicking, and touching; (5) musical/rhythmic—enjoy the human voice and environmental and instructional sounds; (6) interpersonal—can understand the feelings of others; and (7) intrapersonal—can understand own emotion, motivations, and moods.

Theory into Practice 2–1 shows how the assignments in one unit can reflect Gardner's theory of multiple intelligences.

Considerable research (Cornett, 1983; Dunn & Dunn, 1979; Keefe, 1987, 1990; Titus, Bergandi, & Shryock, 1990) suggests that matching learning styles and teaching-learning activities contributes to meeting cognitive needs. Cornett (1983) considered learning styles to be consistent patterns of behavior. To some degree, learning styles indicate how individuals

Theory into Practice 2–1

Multiple Intelligences

Bucher and Fravel (1993) showed how a seventh-grade social studies and an English/Language arts teacher can team with a library media specialist, music teacher, art teacher, and physical education teacher to teach a 4-week unit on the 1920s. The following are examples of activities within the unit that reflect multiple intelligences.

Linguistic: (1) Interview people who lived in the town during the 1920s. If possible, locate pictures and/or postcards to show how the town looked and then prepare a written description. (2) Use a desktop publishing program to create a newspaper featuring information about the 1920s such as the death of Floyd Collins and the Scopes trial in Tennessee.

Spatial: (1) Identify the major events of the 1920s and create a timeline. (2) Research people such as Jessie Redmond Faussett, Walter White, Zora Neal Hurston, Langston Hughes, and Countee Cullen who made literary and artistic contributions during the Harlem Renaissance. Using a map of New York City, pinpoint key places where literary and artistic accomplishments occurred.

Interpersonal: (1) Work in cooperative learning groups to discuss several government scandals such as the Teapot Dome Scandal and the Continental Trading Company, Ltd. that began during President Harding's administration. (2) Select four or five famous people from the 1920s and have them "appear" on a panel to discuss their contributions. Make a list of guidelines for students maintaining positive rapport with other panel members.

Intrapersonal: (1) Share your feelings and impressions about the Roaring Twenties with another student. Were these positive or negative times in which to live? Why? (2) Select a person from the "Roaring Twenties" and research her or his life. Step into that person's shoes and compare her or his life with your life today.

Kinesthetic: (1) Learn dances popular in the 1920s and try to show how the movements reflect the perspectives of the time period. (2) Produce a short video using the format of a "you were there" look at history.

Musical: (1) Identify and describe some of the music of the decade and explore the lives of 1920s African American musicians. (2) Write a song that reflects the 1920s and tells about various events and people.

Logical-Mathematical: (1) Compare and contrast the lifestyles of wealthy people, farmers, and industrial workers who faced hard times during the 1920s. Draw bar graphs that compare the income levels of the two groups and the various levels of unemployment among industrial workers. (2) Research how some people became wealthy in Florida as the state grew rapidly in the real estate boom of the 1920s. Suggest causes of the growth and the problems and display them in some descriptive form.

Adapted from: Bucher, K., & Fravel, M. (1993). Social studies: The roaring twenties. *School Library Media Activities Monthly 10*(3), 27–29.

Case Study 2–1

Jason—A Troubled 13-Year-Old

The first time we saw Jason, he seemed remarkably well-behaved for a 13-year-old. Well-liked by his teachers, he cut grass for several elderly neighbors, and even volunteered at the public library. He was a teenager who seemed to be on the right track.

When we saw him a few months later, his growth spurt had begun, and, in addition to growing an amazing 8 to 9 inches, his voice had deepened. He had developed a few skin problems, but what surprised us most were the psychosocial changes. Teachers reported that Jason had made new friends and was very concerned about dressing and acting like them. Although he had been one of the top students in his class, he did not want others to know that he was intelligent. Talking to his parents, we found that they had noticed Jason's mood swings—one day, he was a happy-go-lucky 13-year-old; the next day he appeared angry, frustrated, and resentful.

From a cognitive perspective, while Jason continued to make good grades, his once intense interest had waned. Although he continued to excel in science and social studies, math was becoming difficult. He could not seem to grasp the abstract thinking required to excel in algebra.

His parents and teachers (and perhaps Jason, too) wondered about his future. Would he grow out of the moodiness and angry feelings? How far would the allegiance to peers extend? Would his academic excellence continue, or would he decline like some other middle school students? Was he concerned about his sudden growth, and was he wondering how tall he would grow? Were illegal substances involved in the personality changes?

After much discussion, Jason's parents and teachers developed the following plan of action to help him.

1. The teaching team decided to determine Jason's cognitive readiness level. Perhaps his decline in mathematics resulted from his cognitive development rather than any other specific reason.
2. The guidance counselor agreed to meet with Jason to discuss new friends and his being overly concerned about dress and peer expectations.
3. The teaching team decided to include topics such as peer pressure, substance use, and growth spurts in their advisory programs—not just because of Jason but because most of the students probably had similar concerns.
4. The teachers and Jason's parents decided to monitor his mood swings. They realized many young adolescents had mood swings, but they wanted to rule out any substance abuse problems.
5. The teachers agreed to review Jason's behavior at their weekly team sessions and to invite his parents to return in 4 weeks to talk some more. Of course, if problems developed, the parents were urged to contact the team or guidance counselor at once.

process information and respond to the instructional process. In the Titus et al. (1990) study of adolescent learning styles, researchers found girls to be more concretely oriented than boys, girls as a group showed more similarity in their learning styles, and slow-track students demonstrated tendencies toward being active and less abstract than fast-track students.

Selected Cognitive Developmental Characteristics

Researchers (California State Department of Education, 1987; Dorman & Lipsitz, 1984; Ginsburg & Opper, 1988; Manning, 1993c; Milgram, 1992) have identified and described young adolescents' cognitive developmental characteristics. However, remember that the onset of these cognitive developmental areas differs dramatically among individuals.

First, youngsters in the concrete operations stage (7 to 11 years) learn most effectively with concrete objects and have difficulty dealing consistently and effectively with abstractions and generalizations. Learners in the formal operations stage (11 or 12 years and above) can conceptualize abstract relationships, employ inductive thinking, and expand the logical thinking processes. During this stage, learners can consider more than one aspect of a problem and can experiment, hypothesize, and analyze to arrive at conclusions (Pikulski, 1991). In addition, they can analyze and synthesize data, pose and explore questions, apply different strategies and solutions to problems, and develop higher levels of intellectual thought (California State Department of Education, 1987). Likewise, young adolescents begin to think about the future, make commitments to abstract ideals, and experience excitement about learning new concepts (Dorman & Lipsitz, 1984).

Second, young adolescents develop the ability to make reasoned moral and ethical choices and to internalize the rightness and wrongness of events. Thus, they can make reasoned ethical choices concerning personal moral behavior and can test and determine the moral and ethical validity of ideas (Thornburg, 1982). They also develop the ability to take another's point of view and to develop self-discipline.

Third, young adolescents develop personal attitudes and perspectives toward other people and institutions. They engage in self-examination, and form opinions toward concepts such as justice, equality, and acceptance. Looking at how and why people treat others as they do, young adolescents often voice concerns about injustices received by individuals or a group of people.

Finally, young adolescents develop cognitive skills that allow them to solve real-life problems. These problems vary with individuals, cultures, genders, and socioeconomic groups. However, youngsters learn to work through the basic processes of gathering evidence about the problems, considering their consequences, considering possible options and the effects of options on others, and selecting the most feasible solution. Case Study 2–1 looks at one young adolescent and the developmental changes in his life.

Implications and Suggestions for Educators

1. Educators can determine cognitive readiness levels by judging students' thought processes and complexity of thought (Brooks, Fusco, & Glennon, 1983) and by using the Arlin Test of Formal Reasoning to determine performance levels (Toepfer, 1985). One middle school, known for its academic rigor, began algebra in the seventh grade.

After one exhausting year (for both students and teachers), the district decided that some young adolescents did not have the formal reasoning skills to deal with algebra and discontinued the practice. Educators admitted that students deserve careful assessment to determine whether they have the cognitive ability to handle such mathematics.

2. Middle school educators should plan organizational strategies such as continuous progress educational experiences, which allow students to progress according to their own levels and rates, learning styles, and cognitive developmental characteristics (National Middle School Association, 1995). While we do not advocate "watering-down" education, we do believe that educators should beware of piling on so many educational experiences that young adolescents feel overwhelmed or frustrated. These feelings can hurt motivation or cause feelings of resentment. The key is knowing how much pressure to apply rather than avoiding the pressure altogether.
3. Art, music, health, and physical education can be powerful sources of academic growth and can contribute to enhanced conceptualizations and understandings of other academic areas (National Association of Secondary School Principals, 1989). Too often, however, these are regarded as educational frills. Yet, in a middle school, they should be part of a total learning experience that appeals to the learning styles of all students.
4. Young adolescents need educational experiences that challenge them to think and excel academically without frustrating them and lowering their self-esteems. Underachievement or failing to achieve at one's potential is a common problem facing many students. It can have serious repercussions on cognitive development, motivation, attitudes toward learning, and self-esteem.

   Often one failure leads to additional failures or to the expectation of failing. This is especially serious with young adolescents because of their need to develop a positive belief in their own ability to meet personal and school expectations. Once teachers label young adolescents (or young adolescents label themselves) as lower achievers, the task of catching up and achieving at expected levels becomes difficult. In fact, once students begin functioning below grade level, the tendency to fall further behind increases with each additional grade.

   When Robbie entered seventh grade, he told each teacher: "Don't expect me to make good grades; I've made bad grades for the last 5 years and I can't change now." After discussing Robbie at a team meeting, all of the team teachers started giving him special attention. By the end of the fall semester, Robbie was making B's. He would probably never be a straight A student, but his academic achievement had increased, and he began to believe that he could learn and achieve.
5. Middle-level teachers can use integrated curricular designs and interdisciplinary approaches to teach broad concepts and relationships between subject area lines. They can also provide educational experiences that challenge yet do not frustrate young adolescents, provide opportunities (e.g., small heterogeneous groups or cooperative learning) so learning can result from social interaction (Muth & Alvermann, 1992), and offer appropriate left brain/right brain educational experiences (Sperry, 1974).
6. Exploratory programs can address intellectual curiosity, rapidly changing interests, and diverse cognitive levels. Using the theory of multiple intelligences (Gardner,

1987), teachers can (1) involve students in learning experiences, (2) help students develop particular intelligences that they may lack, and (3) design culturally responsive approaches to reach learners who have trouble learning. The goal is to allow students to achieve at their own pace, provide positive reinforcement, and help students reach their fullest potential (Teele, 1990).

Closing Remarks

No longer considered children or adolescents, young adolescents have their own legitimate developmental period, with their own unique physical, psychosocial, and cognitive developmental characteristics. The needs of young adolescents will be met only when middle school educators *change* educational practices to reflect middle schoolers' growth and development and when they *understand* how communities and their contemporary issues affect development. Perceptive middle school educators must also provide educational experiences that reflect cultural, gender, individual differences, and sexual orientation. Only when this is done can middle schools reach their potential and meet the developmental needs of young adolescents.

Suggested Readings

Alaniz, M. L., Cartmill, R. S., & Parker, R. M. (1998). *Hispanic Journal of Behavioral Sciences, 20*(2), 155–174. Suggests that youth violence is related to alcohol availability and the percentage of divorced adults rather than to the percentage of immigrants in the neighborhood.

Butler, D. A., & Manning, M. L. (1999). Helping middle schools address gender differences. *Focus on Middle School, 11*(3), 1–6. Looks at the early adolescent developmental period and tells what teachers, counselors, and administrators can do.

Gable, R. A., & Manning, M. L. (1996). Facing the challenge of aggressive behaviors in young adolescents. *Middle School Journal, 27*(3), 19–25. Examines student aggression at the middle level and suggests organizational, curricular, programmatic, and philosophical modifications to combat aggression.

Hamburg, D. A. (1997). Toward a strategy of healthy adolescent development. *American Journal of Psychiatry, 154*(6), 7–12. Looks at how technological and social changes of recent decades have provided many young people with both material benefits as well as risks and stresses.

Manning, M. L. (1994/1995). Addressing young adolescents' cognitive development. *The High School Journal, 78,* 98–104. Examines young adolescents' cognitive developmental characteristics and suggests appropriate educational experiences.

Marinoble, R. M. (1998). Counseling and supporting our gay students. *The Education Digest, 64*(3), 54–59. Covers identity conflict, feelings of isolation and stigmatization, peer relationship problems, family disruptions, and staff development for counselors and educators.

McCadden, J., & Swendseid, R. (1997). Providing a secure environment for students with emotional problems. *Middle School Journal, 28*(4), 10–17. Focuses predominantly on students with emotional problems; however, the suggestions apply to all young adolescents.

Reiff, J. (1997). Multiple intelligences, culture, and equitable learning. *Childhood Education, 73*(5), 301–304. Examines multiple intelligences, equitable learning environments, and provides readers with practical teaching-learning experiences.

Taylor-Dunlop, T., & Norton, M. M. (1997). Out of the mouths of babes: Voices of at-risk adolescents. *The Clearing House, 70*(5), 274–278. Presents 11 young women who discuss their desire to have adults communicate with them in a caring way and to be talked "with" instead of "at."

Part II

Developing the Curriculum and Organizing the School

In chapter 3, you can examine the middle school curriculum and the goals of the various core subject areas as well as the related domains. Then, in chapter 4, you can extend your focus on curriculum to include integration and exploration. Both curriculum chapters call for educators to provide young adolescents with developmentally responsive learning experiences.

In chapter 5, you will read about middle school organization, the need for flexibility, several scheduling options, and heterogeneous learning communities. In addition to reading about teacher collaboration and how it can result in improved professional relationships, you will also look at interdisciplinary teams, a hallmark of effective middle schools.

In chapter 6, you can explore another crucial aspect of effective middle school education—strategies and techniques of managing young adolescents and the learning environment. Note that emphasis is placed on the need for positive learning environments and effective classroom management.

These four chapters examine three very important aspects of the middle school—curriculum, organization, and management—and in some ways, make up the heart of the book as well as middle school education.

Chapter 3

Middle School Curriculum—Core and Related Domains

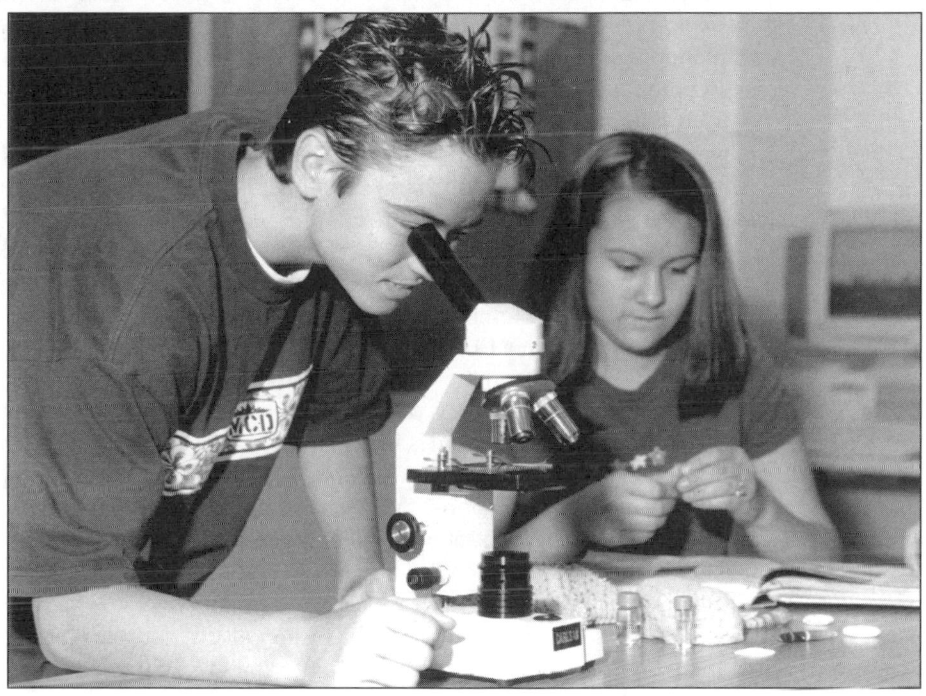

Scenario—The Williams Middle School Curriculum Committee

Early one morning on a teacher work day, Karen Whitmore, library media specialist at Williams Middle School, was using one of the library's Internet-access computers. She stopped when she heard the sound of someone entering the library and turned to see her friend Midge Ashami, a seventh-grade language arts teacher, walking toward her. "What brings you to school so early, Midge?" Karen asked.

"Well, I'm trying to get some things together for today's meeting of the new curriculum committee," Midge responded. "I think Mr. Bateman has big plans for the group. And, since he's such a great principal, I don't want to let him down. I thought you might be able to help me find a few things and maybe do an ERIC search for me. With all the information on middle schools and language arts that's coming out today, I can't keep track of it. There's a lot of junk published but there's also a lot of great information that we can use here at Williams Middle. I guess someone else beat me to the punch," she noted, glancing at the information displayed on Karen's computer screen.

"What do you mean?" Karen asked.

"Well, it looks like you've been searching for curriculum information on the Internet, so I guess someone else asked you to look things up for them first."

"No, Midge, you're the first teacher to ask me. What I'm doing is locating information to take to the curriculum meeting myself. You know, I have a curriculum of information literacy skills that I'm responsible for teaching and I want to go to the meeting prepared to present it."

"Gee, that might explain why Mr. Bateman put you on the committee. I just thought you were there to find information for the rest of us on science, math, social studies, and, of course, language arts. I didn't know, Karen, that there was a library curriculum in middle school."

Just then a male voice came from behind Karen and Midge. "Why did you think Bateman put me on the committee? Was it just so I could provide illustrations in the guide the curriculum committee will come up with?"

Turning, the two saw Don Crow, one of the school's art teachers.

"That's right, you're on the curriculum committee too," Midge said. Shaking her head, she added, "It seems that I focus on my own area of language arts. What I need to remember is that the curriculum is more than the four core subjects."

"Maybe," said Don, "that's why Bateman put us all on the curriculum committee. We have ideas from the professional meetings we attend and even curriculum guidelines from our professional associations. But, we need to do a better job of sharing this information. Just like we teach the students to respect each other, work together, and make strengths out of differences, we faculty members need to do the same things. Now, Karen, could you find the Web site of the National Art Education Association for me? I hear there's some good middle school art information on it."

"Even better," smiled Karen. "I'll teach you to find it yourself."

"Don't tell me," joked Midge. "Helping teachers locate information must be one of your information literacy curriculum skills."

Overview

Until about 10 years ago, educators often neglected the middle school curriculum and focused on other aspects such as school organization, teacher advisories, and positive school climates. Undoubtedly, these were worthwhile pursuits, but the curriculum suffered from neglect. Since the early 1990s, however, this has begun to change. Like the faculty at Williams Middle School, educators are giving more attention to the middle school curriculum. *The Middle School* journal has devoted several issues to curriculum, and the National Middle School Association has published *This We Believe* (National Middle School Association, 1995), and a second edition of James Beane's (1993a) *A Middle School Curriculum: From Rhetoric to Reality.*

Too often educators, like Midge Ashami in the scenario, focus only on their special core curriculum area, whether it is language arts/English/communication skills, mathematics, science, or social studies. We disagree with this for two reasons. First, when working on teams and engaging in interdisciplinary teaching, all educators need a basic understanding of the core subjects. Also, we believe that the related subjects of art, music, vocational/career education, physical education, and informational literacy (sometimes called library skills) are important too. Thus, in this chapter you will find information about the core curriculum and what we call the related domains. While you will only find an overview of each of these eight areas, you will find references to places where you can obtain additional information. We believe that, when all of the eight curriculum areas work together, the middle school curriculum has the best chance of meeting the needs of young adolescents.

Objectives

After reading and thinking about this chapter on middle school curriculum, you should be able to:

1. define learner-centered and subject-centered curriculum frameworks and explain why these two frameworks should not result in "either/or" situations;
2. propose a rationale for informational literacy, art, music, and physical education being considered an integral part of the middle school curriculum;
3. explain selected considerations for developing responsive middle school curriculum;
4. identify and discuss the four core areas commonly taught in middle schools; and
5. identify and discuss the related domains commonly taught in middle schools.

Curriculum Definitions

There are many definitions of curriculum. For some educators, it is the total of everything that happens in a school (Figure 3–1). For others it is the "what is to be taught" that focuses the instruction on "how to teach." In this chapter, we will be using a fairly narrow view of curriculum that will allow you to focus briefly on each of the core curriculum elements and then on the related domains. Discussing these separately may seem like a contradiction to our belief in an integrated, interdisciplinary approach to middle school education. However, in many middle schools, the core subjects are still taught separately, and the state and national standards, curriculum guides, and textbooks still dictate what many teachers teach. However, we believe as Beane (1993a) does that, if we are to help 10- to 14-year-olds maximize their potential as learners, we must have an integrated curriculum. If you understand the basics of the core and related domains, you will be better prepared to integrate your subject specialities with the other disciplines. You will find more about this in chapter 4.

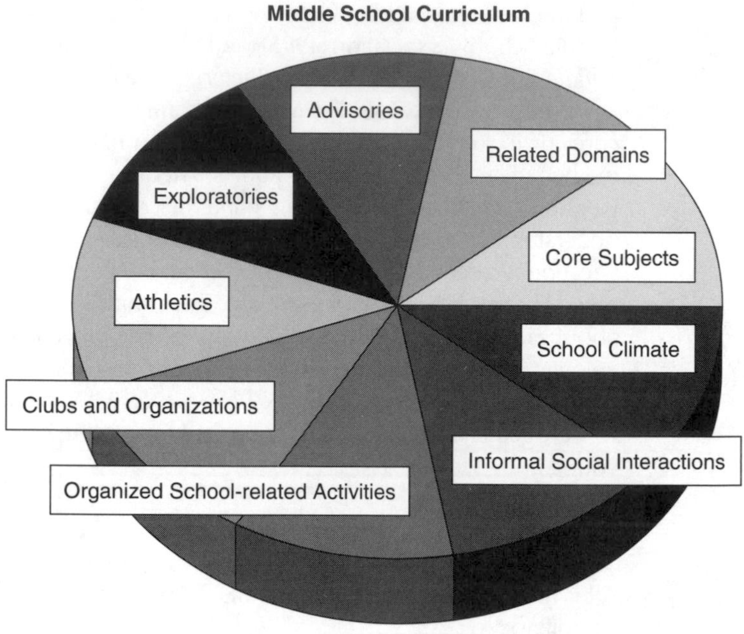

FIGURE 3–1 Components of the Middle School Curriculum

Throughout the chapter, you will find different terms used to refer to the curriculum of a school. We want to remind you to refer to the glossary at the end of this book for complete definitions.

CURRICULUM FRAMEWORKS

Many educators define a curriculum framework as either learner-centered or subject-centered. Table 3–1 shows the differences between the two.

Probably, you will not be surprised to find that we think middle school educators should use elements of both. One middle school teacher aptly summarized the necessity of avoiding an "either/or" perspective when she told us, "I was trained in mathematics—in fact, I see myself as a mathematician. However, my math abilities will not do my students any good if I don't consider each of them when I teach—their development, motivation, and personal concerns. I love math, but I also believe I cannot just 'teach' mathematics; I 'teach' children."

CURRICULUM STANDARDS

Most of the professional associations for subjects in the core curriculum and related domains have issued guidelines or standards for what should be taught in middle school. While we will summarize some of this information for you in order to help you understand

TABLE 3–1 ***Learner-Centered and Subject-Centered Curricular Frameworks***

Learner-Centered Curriculum	Subject-Centered Curriculum
Places major emphasis on learner rather than subject	Places major emphasis on subject rather than learner
Places priority on learners' individual needs, overall well-being, self-esteem, and attitudes	Focuses on cognitive development and acquisition of knowledge
Stimulates and facilitates student activity	Places emphasis on textbooks and other sources of knowledge
Focuses on student individuality	Focuses on the group and group welfare
Stresses individualization or small groups	Stresses large groups, lectures, and questioning
Focuses on personal and social problems young adolescents might face	Focuses on main ideas and methods of inquiry
Seeks students' input on content to be studied and instructional methods	Uses textbooks and curriculum guides as sole source of knowledge
Emphasizes independence and self determination	Emphasizes group welfare and obedience

the curriculum content of each discipline, we encourage you to examine the complete curriculum by reading some of the materials cited in the resources sections and by locating information found on the Web sites listed in the Keeping Current with Technology 3–1. These will provide you with up-to-date information from many professional associations and other organizations.

In addition to national guidelines, many states and even some local school districts have their own curriculum content standards. If you examine these standards, you will see that, rather than prescribing instructional approaches, they provide a framework upon which individual teachers can build developmentally appropriate instructional activities for their students.

There are many national and state pressures to reform the curricular content of schools, in part to provide higher standardized test scores, a topic that we will discuss in more detail in chapter 10. While curriculum reform might be a means of improving test results, other areas of education such as teacher preparation, assessment and evaluation, and school organization also need to be considered (Pinar, 1992). In addition, for meaningful curriculum reform, Michael Fullan (1995) maintains that teachers need to accept change as being loaded with uncertainty; to become committed to, skilled at, and involved in collaborative cultures; and to become continuous learners who assume direct responsibility for reforming both the school and the profession (Fullan, 1995, 1998; Fullan & Miles, 1992).

Developmentally Responsive Middle School Curriculum

As the math teacher's comments pointed out, successful teachers blend a knowledge of their subjects with a knowledge of their students. While there are some characteristics of 10- to 14-year-olds that have special significance for certain subjects in the curriculum,

Keeping Current with Technology 3-1

Examine the curriculum standards and related information at these Internet sites:

National Standards and Associations:

American Alliance for Health, Physical Education, Recreation and Dance
http://www.aahperd.org/

American Association of School Librarians
http://www.ala.org/aasl/

Arts/Music Education National Standards
http://artsnet.hein2.cmu.edu:70/0/AMC/NSAE

Association for Career and Technical Education
http://www.acteonline.org

Mathematics Standards–Eisenhower Clearinghouse
http://www.enc.org/reform/fworks/national.htm

National Art Education Association
http://www.naea-reston.org/

National Association for Music Education
http://www.menc.org/

National Business Education Association
http://www.nbea.org/

National Council for the Social Studies
http://www.ncss.org/

National Council of Teachers of English
http://www.ncte.org/

National Council of Teachers of Mathematics
http://www.nctm.org/

National Science Teachers Association
http://www.nsta.org/

State standards and guidelines–Here are representative sites:

Utah–Curriculum Database
http://www.uen.org/cgi-bin/websql/lessons/curriculum.hts

Virginia–Standards of Learning
http://www.pen.k12.va.us/VDOE/Instruction/sol.html

A few other sites with curriculum information:

ArtsEdge–Linking the arts and education
http://artsedge.kennedy-center.org/artsedge.html

Keeping Current with Technology 3-1 (cont.)

A few other sites with curriculum information: (*cont.*)

Eisenhower National Clearinghouse–Science and Mathematics Curriculum Information
http://www.enc.org/

Federal Resources for Educational Excellence (FREE)
http://www.ed.gov/free

Kentucky School Media Association–Resources for curriculum/literacy skills
http://www.uky.edu/CommInfoStudies/SLIS/ksma/cur.htm

PE Central–A clearinghouse for physical education
http://pe.central.vt.edu

there are some general things to keep in mind when you are examining a developmentally responsive middle school curriculum. Reflect back to chapter 2 and the discussion of young adolescent development. For any curriculum to be successful, it must take into consideration these developmental needs. The physical needs of 10- to 14-year-olds affect their self-esteem and sense of identity, their psychosocial needs address their search for independence, and their cognitive needs include their wide range of thinking abilities, attention spans, and interests.

The middle school curriculum must reflect a genuine concern for young adolescents by addressing self-esteem, self-identity, peers, and friendships. Subjects should be taught through genuine, interesting, and relevant activities that are assessed authentically and that reflect both the diversity of learners and the usefulness and importance of the subject to contemporary society. Especially valuable in science and mathematics are curricular experiences such as predicting, inferring, and experimenting.

Core Curriculum

The core curriculum traditionally has consisted of the language arts/English/communication skills, social studies, science, and mathematics (Figure 3–2). As you read about these areas, remember, however, that other curricular areas, such as art and music, and curricular experiences, such as advisories and exploratories, are all vital to the education and overall welfare of young adolescents. In a contemporary middle school, most educators strive to create a sense of a "community of learners" where 10- to 14-year-olds work collaboratively in meaningful, functional, and genuine activities that are relevant to their world. However, you must also remember that there are forces, external to the school, that have a direct impact on the curriculum.

FIGURE 3–2 Core Curriculum, Related Domains, and External Forces

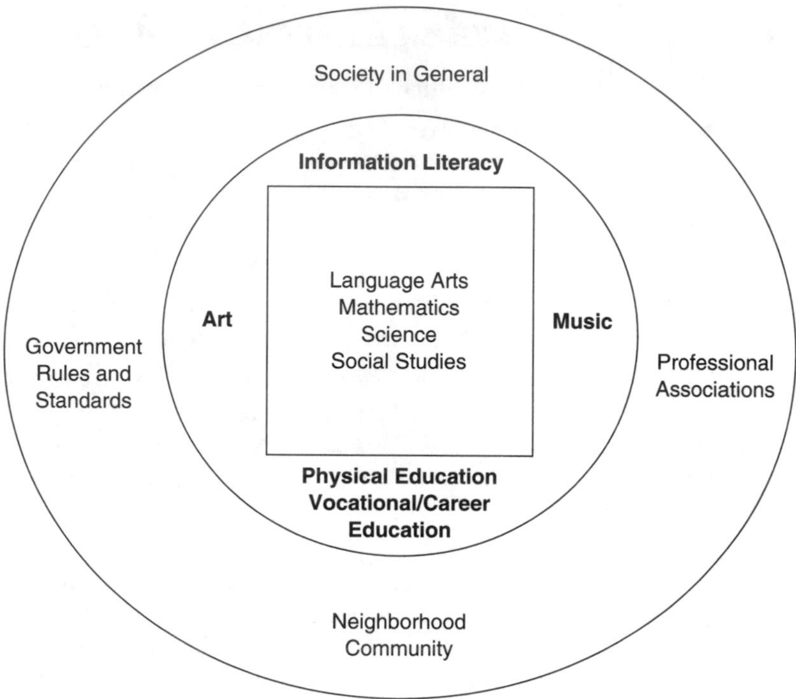

English/Language Arts/Communication Skills

Overview. Included in the language arts are important "skills" that young adolescents use daily. The National Council of Teachers of English (NCTE, 1996) considers language to be a means of communication, an instrument of thought, a defining feature of culture, and a mark of personal identity. These language arts skills give young adolescents the ability to communicate in their widening social worlds by developing their receptive and expressive abilities as shown in Table 3–2. When these skills are integrated with each other as well as with other subject areas, students can see the relevance of becoming competent readers and writers.

Goals of Language Arts. *The Standards for the English Language Arts* (NCTE, 1996) identified several goals for all students. We think a few of them have particular importance for young adolescents. The middle school language arts program should address the students' increasing need to:

1. read, comprehend, and appreciate written material,
2. listen effectively,
3. speak in formal and informal situations to both large and small groups,
4. communicate in written form using a wide range of writing strategies,
5. plan argumentative communication in a logical and convincing manner, and
6. communicate effectively during activities such as advisor-advisee sessions and other nonacademic school programs.

TABLE 3–2 ***Language Arts Skills***

Receptive Language Arts Skills	Expressive Language Arts Skills
Reading	Writing
Listening	Speaking
Viewing	Visually representing

TABLE 3–3 ***Emphases in Contemporary Language Arts***

Creating literature-focus units (Tompkins, 1998)
Reading in the content areas (e.g., science) not just in reading texts
Using a whole language approach (Schurr, Thomason, & Thompson, 1995)
Providing real communication situations (Lapp & Flood, 1992)
Using authentic activities and real literature focused on student needs and interests (Myers & Hilliard, 1997)
Reading to students every day (Watson & Crowley, 1988)
Providing opportunities for the integrated practice of reading, writing, speaking, and listening skills

Curriculum Recommendations. Literacy learning, a major focus of language arts education, is a complex process. In the middle school, it is influenced not only by cognition and motivation, but also by the social context of the school itself. Middle schools teem with language. Students eagerly relate stories of last night's events or triumphs on succeeding levels of a video game. Mounds of notes are passed, read, answered, and sometimes collected throughout a normal day. Young adolescents read, write, speak, listen, and think enthusiastically and for reasons that are very important to them (Irvin, 1997). These social aspects of reading and writing are also important for language arts teachers. For, as students gain experience socially, they learn acceptable responses while reading or listening. That is, they learn the norms of the "interpretive community." When teachers encourage students to read and write about things from their own environment, they may read and write more naturally and with more sophistication (Irvin, 1997).

Unfortunately, in some middle school classes, the teacher is the only audience for writing, and the purpose for reading is solely to answer questions on a worksheet. There are, however, many alternatives. Students can participate in supervised Internet "chats," post their writing on the Internet, or make a radio play for younger students. These and similar activities provide students with meaningful tasks for literacy development and, at the same time, give them natural ways to interact with others (Irvin, 1997).

A few of the current emphases of language arts instruction are shown in Table 3–3. The contemporary focus on literacy and approaches such as whole language and literature-focus units suggests young adolescents will have more genuine and meaningful language arts experiences (and we hope fewer worksheets). If educators make language arts experiences meaningful to the social worlds of students and reflective of their communication situations, young adolescents will view language arts as meaningful and enjoyable.

Case Study 3–1

Developmentally Responsive Language Arts

During the afternoon of a teacher work day at Williams Middle School, the language arts teachers met to work on their goals for the next year. As they discussed their students and the school environments, they realized that 10- to 14-year-olds spend a lot of time listening to others.

"With all the listening our students do," remarked Kim Leszner, "they need good listening skills. But do you really think they can handle that on all of our grade levels?"

"I'm not sure," replied Sal Lebo, "but I think I remember that the cognitive development of most 10- to 14-year-olds creates enhanced listening capabilities. And, as our students get older, their increasing attention spans allow more focused listening."

"Well, that sounds impressive," interjected Chip Leary. "Anyway, a goal to improve listening would tie in well with the school's increasing emphasis on abstract learning throughout the curriculum."

"This morning at the school curriculum meeting, Mr. Bateman mentioned focusing our efforts on helping students make reasoned moral and ethical choices. Listening skills would fit right in with that," added Midge Ashami. "Our students need to be able to handle increasingly complex social tasks and situations without adult supervision. Also, with their increasing tendencies to engage in what I politely call "argumentative behaviors," we better give them the skills they need to debate with others or to clarify their own thinking."

After much discussion, the language arts teachers came up with five general suggestions that could be implemented at all grade levels to help teachers improve student listening skills at Williams Middle School:

1. provide in-class opportunities for guided communication,
2. give students significant opportunities to make genuine choices after listening to both sides of an argument,
3. organize classes to provide opportunities for small group work with assignments requiring both speaking and listening,
4. focus on providing clear directions and explanations related to daily assignments, and
5. read aloud to students on a regular basis.

"This looks like a pretty good list, and it's doable," remarked Sal when the list was finished. "I especially like the emphasis on reading aloud. I know we once considered this appropriate only for younger children, but I think it provides an excellent means to teach listening, especially when we select high-interest books and other materials written for young adolescents.

"Speaking of books," added Midge, "don't you think we ought to involve Karen Whitmore in the library with this? I'm sure she would like some advance notice of what we're planning and could make some good book recommendations."

Case Study 3–1 (cont.)

"That's a great idea, Midge. You know, the more I look at this list, the more I realize that these listening skills are something the students need in all their subjects, not just in language arts," added Kim. "Say, didn't you say you're on the school curriculum committee?"

"Yes, I am," replied Midge.

Kim continued, "If we made listening skills a goal for language arts, do you think you could present it to the whole school curriculum committee? I mean, maybe some of the other teachers have listening skills as part of their curriculum."

"I'd be glad to! That's just the sort of thing Mr. Bateman was talking about this morning when he told us that he put people from every part of this school on the committee so that we could learn what everybody does and look for links." Midge paused a moment before adding: "You won't believe what Becky Rice said. She mumbled something about only looking for the missing link in science, but I don't think Bateman heard her."

"Well, that's Becky," said Chip. "Now weren't we going to divide up the new classroom book sets today? I'd like to use *Dealing with Dragons* on the sixth-grade level, but didn't you want to use it with seventh grade, Kim?"

Case Study 3–1 revisits Williams Middle School to show how the language arts teachers planned developmentally responsive listening experiences. Keep this case study in mind, and look for ways these same skills might be incorporated in other core subjects.

Social Studies

Overview. Social studies has been described in a number of ways, but the definition we like best is that of Michael Allen and Robert Stevens (1994). They see social studies as an integration of experience and knowledge concerning human relations for the purpose of citizenship education. Achieving this requires knowledge, the skills necessary to process information, a set of values and beliefs, and social participation.

In the middle school, most students are introduced to their first serious and systematic exploration of social studies in a curriculum that usually emphasizes history, government, and geography. However, instead of teaching these topics in isolation, middle school educators are encouraged to work toward the integration of these and other social science disciplines with the humanities and should teach in an interdisciplinary manner (Allen & Stevens, 1994).

The middle school social studies program should reflect young adolescents' development by addressing their increasing ability to see others' perspectives and by building on their own expanding social worlds. In addition, it should give them an opportunity to become informed participants in their own community and to see how that could be extended to participation in their state, nation, and world. Ideally, it should be integrated into the various curricular areas, so 10- to 14-year-olds will see social studies as something they can use rather than a collection of facts to which they cannot relate. Some of the trends in social studies are seen in Table 3–4.

TABLE 3–4 ***Emphases in Social Studies Education***

Social Studies Educators Should:
Increase the emphasis on history
Make geography a primary foundation
Use literature to teach social studies
Focus on the multicultural nature of American society
Renew attention to Western civilization
Study the role of religion
Increase attention given to contemporary and controversial issues
Cover issues in more depth
Increase the use of writing as a means to learn and understand social studies

Source: Risinger, C. F. (1992, October). *Trends in K–12 social studies.* (ERIC Document Reproduction Service No. ECO-SO-92-8).

Goals of Social Studies. In the report *Charting A Course: Social Studies for the 21st Century,* the Curriculum Task Force of the National Commission on Social Studies in the School offered several goals for social studies education including the development of the following:

1. civic responsibility and citizen participation;
2. a global perspective through an understanding of students' life experiences as part of the total human experience;
3. critical understandings of situations in America;
4. a multicultural perspective on the world's peoples through an understanding of their differences and commonalities throughout time and place; and
5. students' capacities for critical thinking about the human condition (Mullins, 1990).

In addition, the National Council for the Social Studies (1994) recommended a scope and sequence model that includes 10 broad themes (including cultural heritage, global perspective, political and economic systems, tradition and change, social history, spatial and environmental relationships, social contracts, technology, peace and interdependence, and citizenship) that should be addressed at each grade level. Depending on the maturity and ability of the students, topics derived from these themes are emphasized at specific grade levels. For middle schools, the overall topic to be emphasized is "Viewing the World from Different Perspectives." Within this topic, young adolescents can begin to develop a respect for others by examining regions of the earth and differing perspectives on values, life views, and modes of living.

Curriculum Recommendations. The Curriculum Task Force divided its specific curricular recommendations for social studies in two major sections—grades K–6 and grades 7–12. However, even with these divisions, we can determine the social studies content for grades 5–8.

According to these guidelines, teachers in grades 5 through 6 will focus on one or more of the following content areas: U.S. history, world history, and geography (both physical and cultural). In seventh grade, emphasis is placed on state and local history and geography. The teacher is to help students understand the human interactions that take place within a social system, and the relationship of the local community to the state, nation, and world. Finally, in eighth grade, the focus is on U.S. history and stresses the political and economic development of the United States and its relationship with the rest of the world. Teachers are expected to use case studies and comparative studies as curriculum resources (National Council for the Social Studies, 1994).

Science

Overview. Science should appeal to young adolescents since their increasing psychosocial development allows for more collaboration on projects and experiments, and their cognitive development allows for higher-order thinking and the testing of hypotheses. Thus, rather than relying solely on textbook approaches, middle school science educators should use a process approach to encourage students' active participation. Frequently used processes include predicting, inferring, controlling variables, defining operationally, and experimenting. In addition, teachers should provide students with science topics and applications that are relevant to young adolescents' worlds.

Specifically, young adolescents should be able to plan, design, and conduct a scientific investigation and communicate their findings. Implicit in this is the use of critical thinking to connect evidence and explanations. When linking science and technology, students should be able to identify appropriate problems for technological design and follow through with a solution of product. You should remember, however, that the diverse nature of young adolescents means that some students will not attain all of these abilities until seventh or eighth grade (Howe & Jones, 1998).

Other current emphasis areas of science education are shown in Table 3–5.

Goals of Science. In the National Science Education Standards, goals for science are defined in terms of students' ability to (Peters, 1998):

1. experience the richness and excitement in knowing about and understanding the natural world;
2. use appropriate scientific processes and principles in making personal decisions;
3. engage intellectually in public discourse and debate about matters of scientific and technological concern; and
4. increase their economic productivity through the use of knowledge, understanding, and skills of the scientifically literate person in her or his career.

Curriculum Recommendations. The National Science Education Content Standards identify what students should understand in the areas of physical, life, earth, and space science. They also identify the concepts and processes that students should understand. Differing from traditional science textbooks or district curriculum guides, these Content Standards

TABLE 3–5 ***Current Science Emphases***

Science Educators Should:
Promote independent thinking
Encourage learners' creativity and curiosity
Build on learners' ideas
Reduce the amount of material covered so that more time can be devoted to developing thinking skills
Make connections between science and other areas of the curriculum
Begin instruction with questions rather than answers
Focus on the needs of all learners, including those from all ethnic groups and those with special psychological or physical needs

Source: Howe, A. C. & Jones, L. (1998). *Helping children learn science.* Columbus, OH: Merrill.

provide depth of coverage on the most important topics instead of breadth of content with learners studying numerous topics in minimal detail (Peters, 1998).

In a similar manner, *Science for All Americans* (American Association for the Advancement of Science, AAAS, 1990) identifies broad areas of knowledge that can be taught at many levels and in many ways. Details and facts are not important in themselves and are only useful to the extent that they lead to understanding the principles involved. The focus is on depth of understanding and on having students use scientific knowledge to make choices in their daily lives (Howe & Jones, 1998). Table 3–6 shows both the Content Standards for grades 5 to 8 and the AAAS knowledge areas.

An important issue in science education is equity. Most educators believe that science should be comprehensible, accessible, and exciting for all students throughout their school years and that all students should have scientific literacy. In reality, few educators achieve such lofty goals. A document from the National Science Foundation (1996) showed that males score higher than females, and White students score higher than African and Hispanic Americans on national science assessments.

Part of the problem may be that students often view a scientist as "a white male, with a lab coat, pocket protector full of pencils, and long unkempt hair, a nerd with glasses" (Gega & Peters, 1998, p. 18). As long as this occurs, it is difficult for girls and minority students to value and appreciate science. Changing these stereotypical images of scientists may bring more women and minorities into science endeavors (Gega & Peters, 1998).

Another problem may be that middle school educators, perhaps unconsciously, sometimes discourage females and minorities from taking active roles in science. Too often we've heard comments such as: "Jessica, you take the notes while Jamal and Charles do the experiment." Or, "Now I know all of you girls are going to be squeamish about what we're going to do next. . . ." What should educators do? For one thing, middle school educators can encourage girls and minority students to take math, science, and technology classes. They also need to use additional sources of information to supplement the textbook and to show women and minorities in roles as successful scientists.

TABLE 3–6 *Science Curriculum Standards*

National Science Education Content Standards	*Science for All Americans*
Physical Science	**Physical Science**
Properties and changes of properties of matter Motions and forces Transfer of energy	The universe The earth Forces that shape the earth The structure of matter Energy transformations Motion and forces
Life Science	**Life Science**
Structure and function in living systems Reproduction and heredity Regulation and behavior Populations and ecosystems Diversity and adaptations of organisms	Diversity of life Heredity Cells **The Human Organism** Human identity Life cycle Basic functions
Earth and Space Science Structure of the earth system Earth's history Earth in the solar system	Included with **Physical Science**
Science and Technology Abilities of technological design Understandings about science and technology	
Science in Personal and Social Perspectives Personal health Populations, resources, and environments Natural hazards Risks and benefits Science and technology in society	Interdependence of life Flow of matter and energy Evolution of life
History and Nature of Science Science as human endeavor Nature as science History as science	

Source: Peters, J. (1998). *A sampler of National Science Educational Standards.* Columbus, OH: Prentice Hall.
Source: American Association for the Advancement of Science. (1990) *Science for all Americans.* Washington, DC: Author.

Mathematics

Overview. Mathematics helps students explore, develop their problem-solving abilities, and reason logically. Unfortunately, according to the National Council of Teachers of Mathematics

(NCTM), the traditional mathematics curriculum was dull and irrelevant. Thus, the NCTM has proposed changes in the content and teaching of mathematics. In their publications such as *Professional Standards for Teaching Mathematics* (1991) and *Assessment Standards for School Mathematics: Working Draft* (1993), they have pushed for a curriculum that is useful, exciting, and creative and that can be enjoyed by students in grades 5 to 8.

The NCTM reform efforts call for mathematics teachers to engage students both intellectually and physically. That means teachers should use hands-on activities in tactile, auditory, and visual instructional modes. While we know that young adolescents are beginning to develop their abilities to think and reason more abstractly, we also know that concrete experiences still provide the means by which most students construct knowledge. From these experiences, they can then draw more complex meanings and ideas. The use of language, both written and oral, helps students clarify their thinking and report their observations as they form and verify their mathematical ideas. For all of this to happen, educators must create an educational environment in which students can evaluate their own mathematics achievement and accept responsibility for their learning. As students become more responsible, they can learn to initiate their own questions and problems in order to become powerful mathematics problem solvers (Steele & Arth, 1998).

Goals of Mathematics. While educators such as Diana Steele and Alfred Arth (1998) have written about the general mathematics curriculum, Rhoda Powers Collins (1994) specifically addressed middle school mathematics. She maintained that mathematics reform should include:

1. enhancing students' critical, creative, and logical problem-solving abilities,
2. increasing students' chances for succeeding in higher-level mathematics—students from all levels and backgrounds should have relevant mathematics experience rather than working only on lower-level skills,
3. preparing young adolescents for life experiences with mathematics,
4. increasing the linkages within mathematics, with other disciplines, and with the real world to strengthen students' understandings, insights, and competence, and
5. allowing students to work collaboratively and engage in participatory and interactive learning—they communicate mathematically through discussions; listening, reading, and writing about mathematics with a partner or in small groups (Collins, 1994).

Curriculum Recommendations. The NCTM maintains that the middle school curriculum should include the following features. First, problem situations should establish the need for new ideas and should motivate students. Teachers should emphasize the application of mathematics to real-world problems, especially those to which middle school students can relate. Also, students should be encouraged to communicate with and about mathematics with "mathematical reasoning" permeating the middle school curriculum. A broad range of mathematics should be taught, such as number concepts, computations, estimation, functions, algebra, statistics, probability, geometry, and measurement. Plus, they should be taught as an integrated whole that shows curricular connections. Finally, technology, including calculators, computers, and videos, should be used when appropriate. Paper-and-pencil computation should become less important.

Diversity Perspectives 3–1

Young Adolescents, Multiculturalism, and the Middle School Curriculum

Young adolescents have several psychosocial and cognitive developmental characteristics that suggest the need for experiences emphasizing diversity. Here are a few of those characteristics and things that you can do to provide appropriate curricular experiences.

Characteristic 1—*Young adolescents form cultural identities.* Your curricular materials should provide factual and objective information and perspectives. Stay away from materials with sexism, racism, or stereotypes. Look for materials that are written by a variety of authors who incorporate a wide range of perspectives on historical events, and who use poetry, artwork, journals, music, and illustrations of men and women as well as varied cultural groups (Saravia-Shore & Garcia, 1995). Also, suggest books about the positive accomplishments of people in specific cultural groups.

Characteristic 2—*Young adolescents form close friends, social networks, and opinions of others' similarities and differences.* Provide various organizational options to encourage students to work with students they have not previously worked with. If you are working with a diverse population, use cooperative learning to increase the likelihood of interethnic friendships and to improve attitudes and behaviors toward students of different backgrounds (Manning & Lucking, 1993).

Characteristic 3—*Young adolescents develop a sense of justice, a perception of fairness, and an overall sense of how people should be treated.* Use activities such as role playing, reading appropriate young adolescent literature, and integrated curricular activities (i.e., exploring a common theme of injustice or celebrating a culture's achievements).

Source: Manning, M. L. (1999/2000). Developmentally responsive multicultural education for young adolescents. *Childhood Education 76,* 82–87.

A major change in these recommendations, and one that is difficult for some teachers to embrace, is the acceptance of calculators and the belief that mastery of computational skills is not a prerequisite for all higher level math. Students' ability to reason and solve problems does not depend on their ability to calculate. Thus, students who have not learned basic computational skills by the middle grades should not be held back from more advanced mathematics when the calculator can help them move forward (Cauley & Seyfarth, 1995).

As in science, equity is another issue in mathematics. One report looking at gender differences in mathematics achievement, *Everybody Counts: A Report to the Nation on the Future of Mathematics Education* (National Research Council, 1989), maintained that, as girls and boys progress through the mathematics curriculum, they show little difference in ability, effort, or interest until the adolescent years. Then, as social pressures increase, girls reduce their effort in the study of mathematics and thereby limit their future education and career choices. The report continued that gender differences in mathematics performance result from the accumulated effects of sex-role stereotypes in family, school, and society (National Research Council, 1989, p. 23).

Also, looking at mathematics achievement, Terwilliger and Titus (1995) studied participants in the University of Minnesota Talented Youth Mathematics Program (UMTYMP). Boys showed significantly higher levels of motivation, confidence, and interest in mathematics than females. Despite efforts of the UMTYMP program staff to provide an atmosphere that supported and encouraged the girls, gender differences increased over the 2 years of the study.

These studies point to the need for middle school educators to provide gender-responsive learning environments. This is especially important since young adolescents form their gender identities and self-esteems during these developmental years. While knowledge of the problem is a first step, there must be a genuine commitment to respond to the needs of female learners. Diversity Perspectives 3–1 looks at how young adolescents' developmental characteristics suggest a need for a middle school curriculum that teaches acceptance and respect for diversity.

Related Domains

Although educators attach a great deal of importance to the four disciplines of the core curriculum, they often view the related domains as poor relatives. As Rikard &Woods, (1993) point out, one reason may be because activities using motor abilities are often given less value than activities using cognitive abilities (except when those motor abilities are used in professional sports). Other educators contend that, since the standardized tests given by most school districts do not evaluate art, music, or physical education, these are less important. In the case of information or library skills, since students do not receive a grade in "library," whatever is in the information skills curriculum cannot be too important.

Whatever the reasons, however, the related domains are often relegated to a secondary place in the curriculum. Typically, these subjects are scheduled throughout the school day more for the convenience of core classroom teachers than for the purposes of teaching and learning (Rikard &Woods, 1993). Why then, you may ask, are we including them in our discussion of the middle school curriculum? It is our belief that the related domains are important. In fact, for many students they provide the most successful experiences that these students will have in middle school.

Developmental Responsiveness of the Related Domains

Each of the related domains plays an important role in the development of young adolescents. Mary Stokrocki (1997) contends that young adolescents need art experiences that allow them to express feelings associated with their developmental changes or "rites of passage." For example, when students learn about clay and mask making, they begin to understand other cultures, think about the past, explore changes in identities, and develop a vision of their own. In the same vein, Robert Woody (1998) and June Hinckley (1992) write about the importance of an active, cooperative, and accessible music program in helping 10- to 14-year-olds make the transition from childhood to adolescence.

Few educators doubt that middle school students are at a unique point of physical development. They have special psychomotor needs and interests as they experience body changes due to rapid growth spurts. Their sense of body awareness increases as these physical changes occur, and they compare themselves to their peers. In addition to the physical changes, middle school students experience intense emotional and psychological challenges. As Linda Rikard &Woods, (1993) point out, young adolescents often seek risk-taking and confidence-building activities. They want chances to push themselves to test newly acquired physical abilities along with opportunities to refine, practice, and use skills already acquired.

Information literacy skills build on the cognitive development of young adolescents as they engage in more sophisticated research and problem solving. By using information skills and technology, teachers are moving away from rote learning and "are striving to bring more of the creative process into the classroom" (Smith, 1996, p. 47).

As you read about each of the subjects in the related domains, keep these developmental characteristics in mind.

Art Education

Overview. The Consortium of National Arts Educators Association (American Alliance for Theater & Education; Music Educators National Conference; National Art Education Association; and National Dance Association) developed the Arts Standards and prepared a document on "What Every Young American Should Know and Be Able to Do in the Arts." According to the Consortium, the arts disciplines provide their own ways of thinking. Also, they are a gift to humanity—linking hope to memory, inspiring courage, enriching celebrations, and soothing tragedies (Music Educators National Conference, 1994).

In the middle school, art should not be limited to one area; instead, it should include dance, music, theater, and visual arts. During this impressible developmental period, middle school students should have experiences with a number of art forms that allow them to express their originality, freedom, concerns, and happiness. While art is worthwhile in and of itself, it should be taught in an integrated fashion—integrated with the core curriculum as well as other related curricular domains. All young adolescents should have access to art experiences, both as a source of enjoyment and as a source of the knowledge that can be acquired from learning about art forms that represent our human intellectual and cultural heritage.

The middle school art program helps young adolescents develop self-confidence in their abilities to create artwork and acquire knowledge about the content of art production, art history, art criticism, and aesthetics. Through art, they should also begin to assume more academic responsibility and become creative problem solvers (Harrison, 1996).

Goals of Art. The Consortium of National Arts Educators Association lists several benefits of an education in art. Students educated in the arts disciplines should gain powerful tools for:

1. understanding human experiences, both past and present;
2. learning to adapt to and respect others' ways of thinking, working, and expressing themselves;

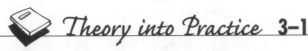

Theory into Practice 3–1

Encouraging Artistic Reflection

To encourage artistic reflection in your students, provide them with opportunities to do the following:

- *record* in journals the evolution of their work–brainstorming ideas, sketches, cartoons, stages, notations, and final results,
- *share* and draw in each others' journals,
- *evaluate* individual performances to which the teacher might add reactions,
- *grade* themselves with teacher input,
- *critique* popular art forms (e.g., advertisements and films),
- *videotape* celebrations for successful work accomplished, and
- *organize* artwork, photographs, and written performance of their ritual performance.

Source: Developed from Stokrocki, M. (1997). Rites of passage for middle school students. *Art Education, 50*(23), 48–55.

3. learning artistic modes of problem solving;
4. understanding the influence of the arts—their power to create and reflect cultures and the impact of their design on our daily lives;
5. making decisions in situations where there are no standard answers;
6. analyzing nonverbal communication and making informed judgments about cultural products and issues; and
7. communicating their thoughts and feelings in a variety of modes (Music Educators National Conference, 1994).

Curriculum Recommendations. In grades 5 to 8, young adolescents should learn the characteristics of the visual arts by using a wide range of subject matter, symbols, meaningful images, and visual expressions. Students need to reflect on their feelings and emotions and to evaluate the merits of their efforts. As a result, they will gain in their ability to apply the knowledge and skills in the visual arts to their widening personal worlds. The curriculum to meet such goals could include: drawing and painting, sculpture, architecture, film, and folk arts. In addition, the visual arts can involve varied tools, techniques, and processes and can include vocabularies and concepts associated with the various types of work in the visual arts (Music Educators National Conference, 1994). Theory into Practice 3–1 shows some ways to encourage art in the classroom.

While researchers such as Gilbert Clark and Enid Zimmerman (1998) write of the importance of nurturing the arts for gifted and talented students, the discipline-based art education (DBAE) programs provide systematic, sequential teaching experiences that involve *all* students rather than just a talented few. In DBAE programs, students engage in the activities people do with the arts—they make works of art, they appreciate art, they learn to understand art, and they make judgments about art (Brandt, 1987/1988).

Information Literacy

Overview. Lenore was a middle school education student who was returning to college after an absence of several years. After one of her observations in a seventh-grade science class, she reported what she saw. "I didn't realize school libraries had changed so much. My teacher and the librarians had planned a series of activities related to the student's projects on endangered species. The students were using all kinds of resources to find information, not just the encyclopedia. But what really impressed me was how the students seemed to be selecting the information that they needed, not just copying pages from a book."

Lenore was right. School libraries have changed into media centers, and the emphasis today is on information literacy with the middle school playing an important role in preparing young adolescents to locate information and use that information to solve problems. The information literacy curriculum helps 10- to 14-year-olds begin to develop complex analytical skills at a developmentally appropriate time in their lives.

What is information literacy? According to Hancock (1993), it is a "resource-based" approach to learning. Students are encouraged to participate in learning activities in the classroom, the library media center, the school, and the community. Teachers and school librarians work together to make a wide array of resources available to students.

Goals of Information Literacy. *Information Power* (American Association of School Librarians, 1998) is the set of national guidelines developed by the American Association of School Librarians (AASL) and the Association for Educational Communications and Technology (AECT). Contained in these guidelines are nine information literacy standards. For a student to be information literate, he or she must:

1. access information efficiently and effectively,
2. evaluate information critically and competently,
3. use information accurately and creatively,
4. pursue information related to personal interests,
5. appreciate literature and other creative expressions of information,
6. strive for excellence in information seeking and knowledge generation,
7. recognize the importance of information to a democratic society,
8. practice ethical behavior in regard to information and information technology, and
9. participate effectively in groups to pursue and generate information.

Curriculum Recommendations. Middle school students can benefit from an information literacy curriculum. In addition to developing their cognitive skills, students improve their lifelong learning skills, learn democratic values, and demonstrate ethical behavior. As Eleanor Howe (1998) pointed out, the idea behind information literacy is not to bring the fish (resource/information) to the students. Rather it is to help the students learn how to fish for themselves. Her feelings were echoed by researchers such as Kulthau, Paul, and Nosich, who have pointed out the benefits of information literacy and have concluded that every student should develop an internalized information literacy model (Loertscher & Woolls, 1998).

In most middle schools, the information literacy curriculum is usually considered the domain of the school library media specialist. However, one of the AASL and AECT's key learning and teaching principles for school library media programs is that the teaching of information literacy and its use by students must be integrated throughout the school's curriculum (American Association of School Librarians, 1998). This is usually done by using a model such as I-Search (Tallman, 1995) or the Big Six (Eisenberg & Berkowitz, 1992).

One problem facing the information literacy curriculum is that it is a process, not a product. Unfortunately, standardized tests usually measure only products. Yet, as young adolescents mature, their jobs and careers will ask them to solve increasingly complex problems. From how to increase the milk production of a herd of cows to how to convince the city not to put a waste treatment plant in their neighborhood, as adults, today's middle school students will need to locate, analyze, and use the skills of information literacy.

Parents often become concerned with any curriculum reform, especially when the results are not directly reflected on standardized achievement tests. Theory into Practice 3–2 provides some practical steps to follow to involve parents in the revision of any curriculum.

Music

Overview. While writers such as Timothy Gerber (1992) maintain that music should be part of the core curriculum, most middle schools consider it one of the related domains or disciplines. According to Robert Woody (1998), the ultimate goal of the middle school music program is not great student performances; instead, it is musical learning that will allow young adolescents to participate actively in musical experiences for their entire lives. Whether performance-oriented (such as band and chorus) or general music, music classes should familiarize students with the nature of music.

As David Reul (1992) pointed out, there are many benefits to an effective music program. Not only has music been proven to develop the areas of reading, mathematics, and language, it is also one of the few curricular areas that speaks to the intuitive, right side of the brain. Reul also emphasized that music activities can be a direct answer to state curriculum guides that mandate a differentiated curriculum for students identified as gifted and talented. However, he also contended that music allows for the study and appreciation of an art form that is vital to each student's education (Reul, 1992).

A quality music program impacts the total school environment and builds character traits such as discipline, cooperation, and self-control (Woody, 1998). Similarly, when students are encouraged to perform solos, improvise, and compose their own original works, they develop their creative energy. The school music program often contributes to academic achievement and may be an area of accomplishment for some students who are less successful in the core disciplines. The most successful music educators participate actively in the total life of the school and work closely with other faculty members (Gerber, 1992).

Goals of Music. To better meet students' needs, the music curriculum called for in *The School Music Program: A New Vision* (Music Educators National Conference, 1994) differs from traditional music curricula in several ways. Many of these differences fall into seven categories:

1. Skills and knowledge as objectives—including a well-planned sequence of learning experiences.

Theory into Practice 3–2

A Middle School Curriculum

Sixth-Grade Level	Seventh-Grade Level	Eighth-Grade Level
Required Courses	**Required Courses**	**Required Courses**
Language arts	English	English
Social studies	Social Studies	Social studies
Science	Mathematics	Mathematics
Mathematics	Science	Science
Physical education	Physical education	Physical education
Electives	Instructional enrichment	Instructional enrichment
	Electives	Electives
Exploratory Courses	**Semester**	**Semester**
Art	Art	Art
Introduction to technology	Computer applications	Computer applications
Keyboarding	Technology education	Technology education
Teen living–boys and girls	Teen living	Teen living
Year-Long Electives	**Year-Long**	**Year-Long**
Chorus 6	Band	Band
Sixth-grade band	Chorus	Chorus
Sixth-grade orchestra (strings)	Orchestra	French 1
		German 1
		Latin 1
		Orchestra
		Spanish 1

Developed from: Great Bridge Middle School, Chesapeake, VA.
http://pen1.pen.k12.va.us:80/Anthology/Chesapeake/Schools/GBMSS/curric.html

2. Diverse genres and styles of music—reflecting the musical diversity of America's pluralistic culture.
3. Creative skills—including improvisation and composition.
4. Problem-solving and higher-order thinking skills—moving beyond the acquisition of facts toward the synthesis of knowledge.
5. Interdisciplinary relationships—extending across curricular areas rather than being confined to artificial boundaries.
6. Technology—utilizing current technology to individualize and expand music learning.
7. Assessment—reflecting reliable, valid, and appropriate techniques for assessing student learning.

Curriculum Recommendations. Rather than just a collection of musical experiences, music classes should encourage students to employ and develop their problem-solving and higher-order thinking skills, in the form of musical decision making, self- and peer evaluation, and other activities (Woody, 1998). Music educators need to dispel the five myths that influence the attitudes and actions of many educators (Reimer, 1997). These myths include the following: listening is passive; listening is uncreative; listening is boring, and the teaching of it is boring; listening cannot be assessed; and teaching listening only includes teaching performing. Once these myths are overcome, more educators should realize the important role that music plays in the development of young adolescents.

Physical Education and Health

Overview. Included in the domain of physical education are both physical fitness and health education. A well-organized, expertly taught physical education program, one that includes a variety of physical fitness activities, can keep students excited and interested.

In the middle school, educators need to modify or adjust the fitness program to meet developmental differences and to ensure that students will be successful and interested in a lifetime of regular physical activity. One way to do this is to help students find activities that appeal to them personally. Activities should emphasize health-related components of physical fitness: cardiovascular endurance, flexibility, abdominal strength and endurance, and body composition (Darst, Pangrazi, & Stillwell, 1995).

In middle school, students should have access to school health services to aid in disease prevention, screening, and detection. In health classes, they should use factual information to begin to develop attitudes and behaviors that will lead to healthy lifestyles. However, health programs must go beyond the wellness approach, which focuses primarily on physical fitness, nutrition, and stress management. Students need help making decisions about crucial health issues such as: substance use and abuse, accident prevention and safety, mental and emotional health, personal health, disease prevention and control, environmental, community and consumer health, and family life (Messick & Reynolds, 1992).

Steven Grineski (1995) wrote that when students shared memories of physical education classes, "hundreds of [them] reported negative experiences associated with competitive games" (p. 8). One reason may be that their physical education programs did not take into consideration their diverse abilities. A single middle school physical education class will likely contain students of many different sizes from the late-maturer to the early-maturer. While all young adolescents should be expected to engage in some physical activity (some accommodations might have to be made), they should not be subjected to competitive activities that lead to loss of self-confidence and self-esteem, or that lead them to seek ways to avoid physical education altogether.

Goals of Physical Education. Debra Vogel (1995) stated that the primary purpose of physical education programs should be to encourage and inspire students to develop healthy habits to ensure future wellness. To make this a reality, the physical education program should:

1. have students participate in various fitness and sports activities that not only enhance their level of fitness but also encourage fitness as a way of life (Rikard & Mays, 1993);

TABLE 3–7 ***Sample Activities in Three Curricular Categories***

Skill Development Units (4–5 weeks)	Fitness (2 weeks)	Special Activities (1–2 weeks)
Field & court	Jogging	Team handball
Basketball	Speed walking	Floor hockey
Soccer	Rope jumping	Self-defense
Volleyball	Track	Adventure/risk activities
Speedball	Bicycling	Frisbee golf
Racket sports	Weight training	"Jump Rope for Heart"
Badminton	Aerobic dance	
Tennis		
Wall ball		
Dance		
Square		
Folk		
Gymnastics		
Educational		
Olympic		

Source: Rikard, L. G., & Woods, A. M. (1993). Curriculum and pedagogy in middle school physical education. *Middle School Journal, 24*(4), 51–55.

2. advance the understanding of the relationship between lifestyle choices and health;
3. use and encourage personal fitness assessment as the first step in making lifelong changes and/or adaptations;
4. have students learn and practice effective strategies for changing behaviors in various health-related areas, such as diet, exercise, safety habits, and stress management; and
5. have students understand that daily physical activity will help ensure a longer life and a higher quality life (Vogel, 1995).

Curriculum Recommendations. Table 3–7 shows sample physical education activities in three curricular categories.

Vocational/Career Education

Overview. Sometimes referred to as business education, technical education, or industrial education, vocational/career education is another related domain. Found most frequently in the eighth grade, its focus is often on providing aptitude tests and interest inventories designed to assist students in their selection of career interests. Some middle schools also provide specific vocational/career classes or experiences in technology education, building trades, cosmetology, or automobile mechanics.

Goals of Vocational/Career Education. The Association for Career and Technical Education (ACTE) stresses the importance of preparing students for the challenges and demands of the workplace by giving young adolescents a chance to study career possibilities and to understand how interest and aptitude affect their vocational choices. Thus, a vocational/career education program should include:

1. systematic career development programs that include preferred life roles as well as personal abilities and interests,
2. a focus on work, family, education, and leisure/recreations activities with academic content and basic skills,
3. the exploration of future employment opportunities as well as financial rewards, and
4. the development of occupational skills, attitudes, and work habits.

Curriculum Recommendations. To be successful, the middle school vocational/career education experiences need to be developmentally appropriate for young adolescents and have a clear scope and sequence that prevent gaps and duplication. In addition to presenting knowledge and skills, the experiences should include opportunities for 10- to 14-year-olds to begin to learn the socialization skills necessary to get along with others in the workplace. Finally, all students should be required to become involved in some type of vocational or career education experience in the middle school with expanded opportunities provided for some students.

Closing Remarks

The middle school curriculum should be distinctly unique—neither elementary nor secondary. Likewise, it should be far more than just a holding pattern between the other two levels of schooling. In essence, while it is articulated with both the elementary and secondary school, the middle school curriculum should stand on its own and reflect the unique developmental characteristics and needs of young adolescents. Efforts toward middle school curriculum development and integration should include both the core curriculum *and* the related curricular domains. Art, music, informational literacy, and physical education should be viewed as integral to the overall curricular mission of the school. Only then will young adolescents have access to a curriculum that meets their academic and developmental needs. Theory into Practice 3–2 shows how one middle school designed its curriculum.

Suggested Readings

American Association for Health Education. (n.d.). *Responsibilities and competencies for teachers of young adolescents in coordinated school health programs for middle level classroom teachers.* Reston, VA: Author. Provides valuable information on coordinated health programs, especially teacher competencies.

Blasewitz, M. R., & Taylor, R. T. (1999). Attacking literacy with technology in an urban setting. *Middle School Journal, 30*(3), 33–39. Shows how technology can address the literacy needs of the lowest readers in a middle school.

Colvin, C., & Schlosser, L. K. (1998). Developing academic confidence to build literacy: What teachers can do. *Journal of Adolescent & Adult Literacy, 41*(4), 272–281. Outlines characteristics of academically marginal and successful middle school students and offers suggestions for helping teachers create classrooms where literacy is emphasized and promoted.

Cooke, L. B., & Adams, V. M. (1998). Encouraging "math talk" in the classroom. *Middle School Journal, 29*(5), 35–40. Discusses how having students talk about mathematics can help them prove conceptual understandings and realize that problems can be solved in more than one way.

Irvin, J. L. (1998). *Reading and the middle-school student: Strategies to enhance literacy* (2nd ed.). Boston: Allyn and Bacon. Looks at a wide array of literacy topics such as literacy and the curriculum, learning environments, and exemplary literacy programs.

Middle Ground: The Magazine of Middle Level Education (1998, February). 1(3). Spotlights social studies: civic responsibility, geography projects, performance assessments, and history research.

Middle Ground: The Magazine of Middle Level Education (1998, October) 2(2). Spotlights science: inquiry learning, experiments, and science fairs.

Middle School Journal (1998, January). Includes articles on creating literature environments, middle school cultures of literacy, motivating young adolescents, and improving literacy through collaboration.

Woody, R. H. (1998). Music in the education of young adolescents. *Middle School Journal, 29*(5), 41–47. Focuses on music and the middle school concept, integrated curricula, and students at-risk.

Chapter 4

Middle School Curriculum—Integrated and Exploratory

Scenario—Mr. Costa Considers the Curriculum

The following exchange took place before a meeting of the seventh-grade Tiger team at Great Meadows Middle School between Mr. Fred Costa and Ms. Bette Hampson, two experienced teachers.

"Bette, you know that I don't think our curriculum meets the academic needs of our students. And, I'm not sure we're preparing them for the real world. When they're faced with going to college, tracking down a job, or dealing with other people in a working environment, some of our students are going to have real problems."

"Fred, we've talked about this before. I know you favor giving our students real-world experiences. But what can we realistically do? Better yet, why should we do it? These students have a few years to go before they have to make career decisions. In the meantime, I'm happy just to get a few facts into their heads and get them ready for the state's mandated seventh-grade achievement tests."

"Did you forget what Dr. Wilson said at the last faculty meeting?"

"If you're talking about that task force on revamping our curriculum, Fred, sure I heard it. But, how can I teach basic skills to some, advanced content to others, and still have time to worry about . . . oh what did she say?"

"She said we need to look at what we're doing now and explore how much more we really could do for our students. Just think, in addition to the cooperative planning that we do, there are things like integrated curriculum planning, interdisciplinary teaching, student-centered activities, experiential education, simulations, and even service learning that we could try. And, while our current exploratories are a good beginning, we could be doing a lot more with them too. Didn't you hear Wilson mention an integrated and exploratory curriculum that promotes the concept of human dignity? Haven't you read those books and articles that she keeps putting in our mailboxes?"

"Fred, you sound like you're giving me a lecture. You know that I don't have time to read everything that winds up in my mailbox."

Fred cut her off with a quick comment. "Bette, I know you're a great teacher and you really care about our students. But can't you see that some of those books like *This We Believe* and *Turning Points* are our future? More important, they're a blueprint for helping our students. If we work together, we really can make a difference for our students. Isn't that what teaching is all about?"

Overview

In the last chapter, we looked at the middle school core curriculum of language arts, mathematics, science and social studies and the related domains of informational literacy, art, music, vocational/career education, and physical education. But, as Fred Costa was trying to explain in this opening scenario, the middle school curriculum is more than a collection of separate subjects. While each core curricular area is essential "in and of itself," we believe that the best curricular experiences for young adolescents should also be integrated and exploratory. That means that educators should plan curricular experiences around themes that are of personal and social significance to 10- to 14-year-olds in the real world. It also means that educators should provide mini-courses or other learning experiences designed to help young adolescents investigate curricular areas based on their personal needs, interests, and aptitudes. In this chapter, you will have the opportunity to examine the integrated and exploratory curricula in more detail and to read about the issues surrounding both of them.

Objectives

After reading and thinking about this chapter on middle school integrated and exploratory curriculum, you should be able to:

1. explain why middle school educators should use integrated curricular approaches;
2. identify several dimensions of curriculum integration such as organizing around problems and issues that are relevant to the young adolescents' world;
3. discuss James Beane's (1993a) proposal that the integrated curriculum should reflect democracy, human dignity, and the prizing of cultural diversity;
4. explain the role of teachers, learners, and school library media specialists in planning and implementing integrated curricular experiences;
5. define and describe exploratory programs, their purposes, and how they should reflect young adolescents' interests and aptitudes;
6. identify several essentials for successful exploratory programs such as considering young adolescents' shorter attention spans, varying interest levels, and abilities to think; and
7. suggest several selected considerations for developing middle school curriculum.

Contemporary Curriculum Perspectives

We believe that the middle school curriculum should be distinctly unique for young adolescents. But what, you might ask, makes it unique? First, the middle school curriculum should be neither elementary nor secondary in content or approach to learning, nor should it be a holding pattern between the other two levels of schooling. As William Glasser (1997) suggested, the middle school curriculum should nurture the warm, supportive human relationships that young adolescents need to succeed in school. According to *This We Believe* (National Middle School Association, 1995), the curriculum should be challenging, integrative, and exploratory. To most educators, that means the curriculum should challenge all ability levels of young adolescents; no group should be slighted at the expense of another. In addition, as proposed by Beane (1993a) and *This We Believe* (National Middle School Association, 1995), the middle school curriculum should be integrated, so young adolescents can see relationships and connections among the disciplines and domains and so that they can explore issues and problems that are important to them. With an exploratory curriculum, young adolescents can discover their unique abilities and interests.

In one school we visited, only a courtyard separated the middle school and the high school; in fact, the schools shared the same principal and several teachers taught in both the middle and the high school. We heard these teachers debate what the middle school curriculum should be. While some thought it should be more like the elementary school, others thought making the middle school curriculum more like the secondary curriculum would better "prepare" students for high school. Unfortunately, these educators had fallen into the "either-or" perspective—neither felt the curriculum should be distinctively "middle school."

We hope, however, that you will not fall into this trap and that you will see the need for a uniquely "middle school" curriculum that, while it is articulated with both the elementary and secondary school, reflects the particular developmental characteristics and needs of young adolescents.

INTEGRATED CURRICULUM

Definitions

In chapter 3, we defined curriculum in several ways. In this chapter, we want you to think about the middle school curriculum as a pyramid resting on a broad discipline-centered base and rising to a defined learner-centered apex (Figure 4–1). As the curricular focus

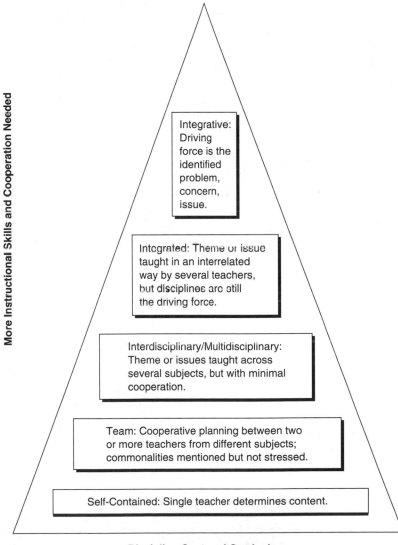

Self-Contained: Single teacher determines content.

FIGURE 4–1 Curriculum Integration Continuum

moves away from subject dominance to student focus, there are five levels, each of which, to us at least, requires more instructional skill and cooperation. Moving from the discipline centered, self-contained classroom, you next find the team/cooperative planning level. Here interconnections among the subjects are noted but not stressed. The multi- or interdisciplinary level finds themes or threads uniting the content in the various disciplines. However, the "multidisciplinary [approach] still begins and ends with the subject-based content and skills" (Beane, 1996, p. 7). At the integrated level, subjects are finally taught in an interrelated manner. This level is related to the constructivist approach to teaching. Finally, at the integrative level, a student/teacher-identified issue becomes the driving force behind the curriculum. In this book, we will frequently use the term *curriculum integration* to refer to the two top levels of the pyramid.

While we believe that the integrated and integrative levels are the most exciting and hold the greatest promise for teaching middle school students, we do not believe that the curriculum must remain at one level at all times. Teachers who do not always teach at the integrated or integrative levels should not consider themselves failures. External community forces, internal school pressures, as well as the needs of 10- to 14-year-olds demand a flexibility in approaches. What would concern us, however, is a curriculum that never moves beyond the team or interdisciplinary level. Unfortunately, as Figure 4–2 shows, some middle schools rarely reach even the interdisciplinary levels of curriculum.

Rationale

Why is the topic of curriculum integration enjoying such interest and support among middle school educators? The answers may be found in the writing of James A. Beane, one of the most vocal proponents of the integrated curriculum. According to Beane (1996), there are several reasons for the attention. First, more educators are supporting curriculum arrange-

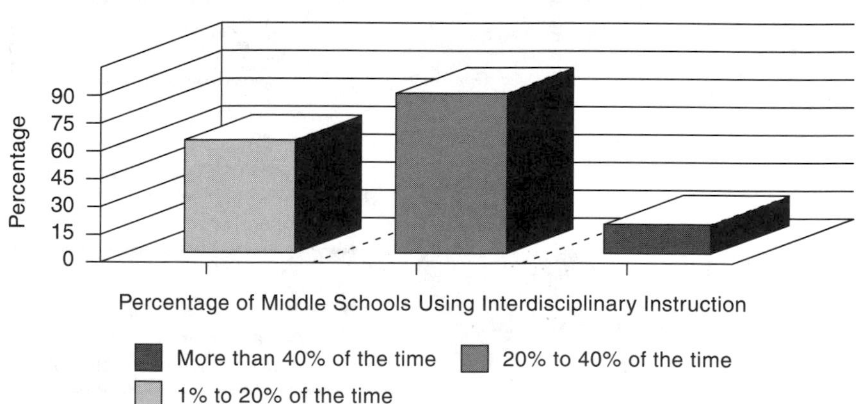

FIGURE 4–2 Use of Interdisciplinary Instruction in Middle Schools.
Based on data from: McEwin, C. K, Dickinson, T. S., & Jenkins, D. M. (1996). *America's middle schools: Practices and progress–A 25 year perspective.* Columbus, OH: National Middle School Association.

ments that involve application of knowledge rather than rote memorization. Then, too, research on brain functions has shown that, when processing information, the brain looks for patterns and connections and emphasizes coherence over fragmentation. By extension, the more learning and knowledge is unified, the more accessible and "brain-compatible" it is. Third, there is a shift in education from knowing the "right answer" to knowing how to find the best solution. Knowledge is neither fixed nor universal. Today's students are being asked to answer questions and face situations that did not exist when their parents went to school. When solving today's complex problems dealing with the environment, medical ethics, or human relations, students need to apply information from an assortment of disciplines and to use a collection of information-gathering strategies. Finally, the movement toward an integrated middle school curriculum is being driven by professional educators who are seriously interested in progressive educational ideas such as whole language, unit teaching, thematic curriculum, and problem- and project-centered methods (Beane, 1996).

Components of an Integrated Curriculum

As we stated before, as a curriculum moves up the pyramid from subject-centered to learner-centered, there is an increasing emphasis on interrelated planning and teaching. While it is beyond the scope of this book to describe, in detail, each of the levels in the pyramid, we do want to spend just a little time looking more closely at the top levels. Table 4–1 shows some of the characteristics of integrated teaching as identified by Beane (1996).

According to Beane, the integrated curriculum should reflect democracy, human dignity, and the prizing of cultural diversity. Consider three of Beane's (1993a) statements:

- "The idea of democracy ought to permeate the middle school, including its curriculum." (p. 65)

TABLE 4–1 *Integrated Middle School Curriculum*

Characteristics of an Integrated Middle School Curriculum
• Central problem or issue is identified by teachers and students collaboratively.
• Issue is of personal and social significance to 10- to 14-year-olds.
• Problem or issue becomes central focus of the curriculum.
• Learning experiences are planned that are related to the issue.
• Learning experiences integrate knowledge from all disciplines and domains.
• Subject lines dissolve as the emphasis is placed on the exploration of the issue.
• Students acquire knowledge and skills to solve the problem or issue being studied rather than merely to accumulate isolated facts or skills, or to prepare for a standardized test.
• Projects and activities involve the real application of knowledge.
• Young adolescents see how this experience can be used in other circumstances.
• Students see the benefits of democratic problem solving.

Based on: Beane, J. (1996) On the shoulders of giants! The case for curriculum integration. *Middle School Journal, 28* (1), 6–11.

- "A second enduring concept that ought to permeate the curriculum is that of human dignity and the related ideas of freedom, equality, caring, justice, and peace." (p. 66)
- "A third enduring concept, related to the first two, is the ostensible prizing of cultural diversity. While the history of schooling presents a somewhat bleak picture in this area, we are now at a historical moment when this concept may have brighter prospects." (p. 67)

When an integrated curriculum reflects these contexts, young adolescents can recognize and thoughtfully consider all views, content, and cultures. They can also learn about human dignity and the related ideas of freedom, equality, caring, justice, and peace and can have active opportunities to practice these ideals. Likewise, they can learn to value cultural and other forms of diversity.

Within the framework of the integrated curriculum, teachers should use examples and information from a wide range of cultures and groups to illustrate the key concepts, principles, generalizations, and theories in their subject areas. Similarly, they should include activities and experiences that reduce prejudice and that promote gender equity.

The Intersection of Personal Concerns and Social Issues

James Beane (1993a) also contends that considerable overlap exists between young adolescents' personal concerns and the larger issues affecting our world. Table 4–2 shows several curriculum themes with the corresponding young adolescent and social concerns. Beane (1993a) feels that in these intersections, there might be a promising way of conceptualizing a general education that serves the dual purpose of addressing young adolescents' personal issues and needs, and the problems and the concerns of the larger world. He feels these needs, issues, and problems might be the themes that should drive the middle school curriculum as a general education program.

Integrated Curriculum: Themes, Questions, and Concerns

You might wonder how the integrated curriculum is developed. Ideally, it begins with an issue of concern to 10- to 14-year-olds. Themes suggested by students in one class included: "Living in the Future," "Careers, Jobs, and Money," "Conflict," "Environmental Problems," and "Sex, Health, and Genetics" (Beane, 1993b). Other organizing themes might include contemporary concerns such as homelessness, hunger, drug abuse, and pollution (McEwin & Thomason, 1991). Any of these topics can be examined using more than one cultural perspective and with consideration of the effects of culture and gender on learning and achievement.

Realistically speaking, many middle school teachers have mixed feelings about using integrated, cross-curricular themes. Often these educators perceive a conflict between the disciplines and the integrated curriculum. Beane's contention is that the integrated curriculum "does not ask whether there should be subject matter or skills but rather how those are brought into the lives of young people and used by them" (Beane, 1993b, p. 19). Most teachers are willing at least to entertain the idea because they agree that young adolescents need to see relationships between curricular areas. Still, others remain reluctant. As one middle school teacher recently told us, "I have two concerns. Can I make the theme fit my curriculum guide and how will curricular integration affect my students' scores? In this school, these are the primary concerns."

TABLE 4–2 ***(Sample) Intersections of Personal and Social Concerns***

Early Adolescent Concerns	Curriculum Themes	Social Concerns
Understanding personal changes	TRANSITIONS	Living in a changing world
Developing a personal identity	IDENTITIES	Cultural diversity
Finding a place in the group	INTERDEPENDENCE	Global interdependence
Personal fitness	WELLNESS	Environmental protection
Social status (e.g., among peers)	SOCIAL STRUCTURES	Class systems (by age, economics, etc.)
Dealing with adults	INDEPENDENCE	Human rights
Peer conflict and gangs	CONFLICT RESOLUTION	Global conflict
Commercial pressures	COMMERCIALISM	Effects of media
Questioning authority	JUSTICE	Laws and social customs
Personal friendships	CARING	Social welfare
Living in the school	INSTITUTIONS	Social institutions

From: Beane, J. A. (1993). *A middle school curriculum: From rhetoric to reality.* 2e. Westerville, OH: National Middle School Association.

Role of Teacher

The basic difference between the subject-centered and the learner-centered curriculum is what we, as educators, want students to do. If we want students to "know" (usually regurgitate) a set number of facts for each discipline, we favor a curriculum near the base of our pyramid (see Figure 4–1). If, however, we want students to solve problems by identifying those problems and then by learning and applying the skills and information needed to solve those problems, we tend to favor a curriculum closer to the apex of the pyramid.

An integrated curriculum that focuses on personal and social concerns is near the apex. With such a curriculum, the role of the teacher has to change (Beane, 1993b). No longer can middle school teachers view themselves only as teachers of subject matter, only concerned with meeting content objectives, and only as conveyers of knowledge. In addition to demonstrating an understanding of young adolescents' social and personal concerns, they need to commit to implementing a middle school curriculum that addresses those concerns and issues.

This does not mean that the integrated curriculum is unstructured or that it allows students to do whatever they want (Beane, 1993b). Middle school teachers are still responsible for setting the stage and changing the environment within which young adolescents engage in learning activities that reflect their interests, needs, capabilities, personalities, and motivations. While structuring and guiding the explorations of 10- to 14-year-olds, teachers must have the skills and the resources to build upon students' interests, while simultaneously providing appropriate and workable learning activities (Kellough & Kellough, 1996).

Our university students who are completing their practicum experiences in middle schools have remarked that the integrated curriculum requires teachers to perceive roles differently. As one said, "Teachers don't plan alone anymore. They plan in teams that go

Theory into Practice 4–1

Action Research and the Integrated Curriculum

The following tips for implementing an integrated curriculum project are based on an article by Douglas Arnold (1998).

1. Make a firm commitment to curricular integration–be sure teachers realize the work and advantages involved.
2. Provide students, their parents, and other teachers with explanations of curricular integration.
3. Address the potential barriers of lack of planning times and teachers not sharing the same students and consider other barriers that the school might have.
4. Begin slowly but eventually involve as many teachers as possible.
5. Make sure exploratory programs and teacher advisories (if possible) reflect the topics being studied.
6. Ask students for their suggestions on how to make future action projects more productive and enjoyable.

Source: Arnold, D. E. (1998). Action research in action: Curricular articulation and integrated instruction. *NASSP Bulletin, 82*(596), 74–78.

beyond their own subjects. While I can see that they're working toward higher, more lofty goals, I also see that the way they view their own role in the classroom is changing. They seem to be functioning more as guides than as suppliers of knowledge."

Implementing an integrated curriculum requires skill and planning. Theory into Practice 4–1 provides some practical guidelines to follow based on one school's attempt to develop an action research project across the curriculum.

Role of Learner

"It's been really great to take a problem and try to solve it. In most classes, we just learn facts from the textbook. But when Mr. Hanzelik gives us a topic, we get to choose what we want to do with it." An eighth-grade student.

"If I like the theme we're studying, it's great to study it all day long. Working on the whale thing was fun. It was almost like we weren't even in school." A seventh-grade student.

"We've studied some great themes this year, but I don't like studying the same theme for more than two or three weeks. I get tired of the same thing, especially if the themes are boring. Then, studying them all day is really bad." A seventh-grade student.

As these students suggest, the exploration of themes (such as those shown in Table 4–2) in an integrated curriculum can be interesting. Young adolescents have the opportunity to apply a variety of skills (i.e., the skills [such as communicating, computing, and researching] usually taught and promoted in most middle schools). They can also use other skills including reflective thinking, critical ethics, problem solving, valuing, self-esteem and self-concept, social action skills, and searching for completeness and meaning (Beane, 1993a).

In an integrated curriculum, the student needs to be involved; learners are no longer passive and waiting for knowledge to be conveyed. They are expected to assume at least some responsibility for their learning. Whether involved in the planning of the integrated curriculum, offering input on learning methods to use, selecting materials and resources that complement the curricular content, or choosing the most effective means of evaluating outcomes, young adolescents begin to take an integral role in the learning process. This intense involvement allows young adolescents to perceive how curricular content relates to their personal and social concerns and interests. In other words, they become active participants and stakeholders in both the process and the products.

Several authors have provided examples of integrated teaching units (Smith & Johnson, 1993; Stevenson & Carr, 1993) in which student interests were combined with discipline-related goals. You will read more about them in chapter 7 of this book. Theory into Practice 4–2 provides an overview of an integrated unit that includes the book *A Family Apart* by Jean Lowery Nixon (1987) and incorporates the themes of "family, overcoming difficulties, familial love, orphan experiences, separation, death, poverty, self-reliance, rejection, adaptive behavior, and final acceptance of reality," all revolving around the central theme of relationships (Smith & Johnson, 1993, p. 7).

Social Action
Medical Technology (1800s–Today)
Social Workers and Guest Speakers
Orphans Today and Results

Completeness
Stress and Its Effects
Study Arts of 1800s

Valuing
Child Labor and Production
Mother's Last Letter
Unwanted Children and Abortion
Story Scene Dramatization

Critical Ethics
Orphan Trains and Their Purposes
Poetry Writing

Relationships
Finding a Place in the Group
Living in a Changing World

Reflective Thinking
Inventions and Their Impacts
Book Review

Problem Solving
Pollution (History of)
Transportation Problems
Travel Logs, Simulation of Book Travel

Self-Conceptualizing Self-Esteem
Nutrition and Wellness
Role of the Family: Separation and Divorce

Social/Cultural Diversity
Career Fair
Underground Railroad and Slavery
Assimilation of U.S. Cultures
Race Relations
Urban Versus Rural

Source: Smith, J. L., & Johnson, J. (1993). Bringing it together: Literature in an integrative curriculum. *Middle School Journal 25,*(1), 3–7. Used with permission.

Theory into Practice 4–2

Teaching the Theme of Relationships

This integrated curriculum unit revolves around the theme of responsibility and the young adolescent book *A Family Apart.*

Source: Smith, J. L., & Johnson, J. (1993). Bringing it together: Literature in an integrative curriculum. *Middle School Journal 25,*(1), 3–7. Used with permission.

Role of School Library Media Specialist

"You'd think teachers would welcome the chance to cut their student/teacher ratio in half! That's what would happen if teachers would let me teach my information curriculum skills integrated with their subject skills. It's not like I'm trying to take over their job—they know the subjects and I know research skills and resources. Instead of just assigning a topic and then sending the students to the library, we could be planning and teaching together and the students would benefit. With some teachers, the first time I find out about an assignment is when the fourth or fifth student asks for the same information. By then, the first students have checked out all the books and I have to scramble to find sources. If the teachers would just include me in their team planning, it would be a win-win situation. Teachers would have another professional to assist them, students would find what they need, and I could be sure we have the materials to help them. Hey, it's not like I don't know what goes on in a classroom. I was a classroom teacher for 8 years before I became a school librarian. Sure, I know there are some librarians who aren't sold on integrated teaching. But that's not me. I want a chance to be part of the middle school teams! Why don't they include me?" Flo Naugle, middle school library media specialist.

Like many of the other so-called special teachers in the related domains, the school library media specialist has a role to play in the integrated curriculum. As Judy Pitts (1994) found, when subject matter and information-seeking skills are combined and teachers and school library media specialists plan cooperatively, students have the greatest opportunity for learning. School library media specialists often know appropriate materials and technologies that complement the teacher's curricular efforts and that address the learning styles of young adolescents.

Instead of participating only when called upon, library media specialists and other teachers of the related domains should work collaboratively with core discipline teachers. In addition to providing materials (books, magazines, electronic databases, etc.) that are appropriate for 10- to 14-year-olds and the topics they study, library media specialists can suggest specific technological resources that advance the goals and objectives established by the interdisciplinary team.

Use of Resources

With an integrated curriculum, teachers need to use a wide variety of learning materials and resources to meet the interests, learning styles, and cognitive levels of young adolescents

(Kellough & Kellough, 1996). Teachers also need to select materials that address students' multiple intelligences (Gardner, 1993a, 1995, 1997). These materials or resources should provide young adolescents with opportunities to handle, construct, manipulate, experiment with, and explore their curricular themes (Kellough & Kellough, 1996). While materials, such as books, magazines, videos, videodiscs, CD-ROM databases, pictures, and maps, should be readily available in the school library, other resources should include motors, science equipment, computers and software, historical artifacts, construction kits, art supplies, and musical instruments. These resources should be both specific and general. That is, they should be specific so as to relate to particular themes or integrated units and should be sufficiently general to allow students to "make their own meanings" to themes and units under consideration.

One of the greatest class of resources available in most schools today falls under the broad heading of "technology." Computers, related hardware, and software assist students with problem solving and help teachers integrate instruction. By using computers, students can collect, analyze, evaluate, and manipulate information. Electronic databases assist students in their search for information, while writing software allows them to write, revise, edit, and publish their written work with ease. Multimedia software and the World Wide Web appeal to a multitude of senses and provide an opportunity for students to take vicarious field trips. From collaborating with other students via e-mail and Web sites to developing graphic organizers such as webs, outlines, and concept maps, young adolescents relish the opportunity to use technology when examining issues in an integrated theme. This same technology then allows students to present their findings in a variety of ways ranging from traditional reports to multimedia "slide shows" and hypermedia presentations. Throughout the process, technology should be an integral part of integrated instruction (Hinton & Orlich, 1996).

In Diversity Perspectives 4–1, Powell, Fussell, Troutman, Smith, and Skoog (1998) discuss how a wide variety of resources are used to teach themes in a single unit.

Methods of Assessment

As you will read in more detail in chapter 10, educators' perspectives of assessment are changing. William Glasser (1992) maintained that test questions should never call for mere regurgitation of bare facts. Instead of asking students to recall only what they have memorized, teachers should allow students to use the information in real-world situations. Still, like educators on other levels, too many middle school educators rely on traditional assessment methods. Perhaps this is because these methods are objective and relatively easy to construct and administer. Whatever the reason, true-false, multiple-choice, and fill-in-the-blank test items continue to be popular.

If you are teaching in an integrated curriculum, you must be willing to try different techniques of assessing student progress. Teachers who are evaluating only factual knowledge and rote memorization might continue to use traditional objective assessments. However, teachers in an integrated curriculum need to provide opportunities for young adolescents to demonstrate their knowledge of relationships, and to produce projects and other learning products that cannot be measured on traditional paper-and-pencil tests. That is why teachers are using more authentic assessments such as rubrics, checklists, anecdotal records, and portfolios.

Diversity Perspectives 4–1

Integrative and Multicultural Curriculum

Powell, Fussell, Troutman, Smith, and Skoog reported on a thematic course of study (called stream) at Brown-Barge Middle School, a magnet school for technology in Pensacola, FL. In the American Tapestry unit, teachers sought ways to make the discipline-based content directly relevant to their multicultural content. During the 12-week thematic unit or stream, teachers designed activities in which students studied legislative actions and their effects on civil rights. For a field trip, students visited a civil rights memorial in Montgomery, AL. With the help of their teachers, students compared and contrasted the speeches and writings of Martin Luther King and Malcolm X, read multicultural literature selections, viewed documentaries of cultural and racial conflicts, and considered the contributions in the humanities made by minority groups. Also, they studied W. E. B. Dubois and Booker T. Washington, learned about key civil rights organizations of the 1970s and 1980s, researched the Japanese-American internment camps of the 1940s, and explored the discrimination against Chinese immigrants in the nineteenth and twentieth centuries. These lessons were not added onto other lessons. Instead, they provided the content to integrate and extend knowledge and skills acquired during the remainder of the American Tapestry instruction.

This study pointed out the need for educators to:

1. Commit to genuine multicultural education reform that is integrative rather than just superficial;
2. Make sure the thematic unit (stream) is a total school-day approach with exploratories and teacher advisories also reflecting the topic.
3. Become aware of and responsive toward the needs, interests, and backgrounds of students.
4. Work with all professionals in the school as well as parents about what is taught and how it is taught.

Source: Powell, R., Fussell, L., Troutman, P., Smith, M., & Skoog, G. (1998). Toward an integrative multicultural learning environment. *Middle School Journal, 29*(4), 3–13.

But this approach is not without problems. One eighth-grade teacher told us that she liked the idea of authentic assessments but she also wanted a undisputable basis for her students' grades. "I like using projects and rubrics. My students get to engage in solving real-world problems and they come up with some great results. But I also like the objectivity of a completion or multiple-choice test. Neither the parents nor the students are likely to question a grade when I can point to the number of questions missed on a test and show that the right answers are found in the textbook."

Keeping Current with Technology 4–1

There are a variety of sources of information about the integrated and exploratory curricula on the Internet. Visit a few of the following sites.

For bibliographies of information about the integrated curriculum:

Association for Supervision and Curriculum Development–Selected ERIC abstracts on Integrated Curriculum
http://www.ascd.org/services/eric/int.html

Middle School Bibliography from the Integrated Curriculum Research Circle of ACSA
http://www.acsa.edu.au/projects/middle/docs/biblioms.htm

Integrated curriculum strategies
http://cisl.ospi.wednet.edu/CISL/Strategies/INTEGCURR.html

Position statements and other information on the integrated curriculum:

The National Council for the Social Studies
http://207.69.210.46/standards/positions/middle.html

Seamless curriculum by Marion Brady
http://ddi.digital.net/~mbrady/page1.html

Interdisciplinary teamed instruction
http://www.ael.org/rel/iti/index.htm

Resources on information literacy and the integrated curriculum can be found at:

I-SEARCH
http://www.edc.org/FSC/MIH/

Big Six
http://www.kn.pacbell.com/wired/big6/

Information on schools with integrated and exploratory curricula

Brown-Barge Middle School, Pensacola, FL (Integrated Curriculum)
http://www.escambia.k12.fl.us/schscnts/brobm/Home.html

St. Gabriel's Middle School, Kansas City, MO (Exploratory Curriculum)
http://www.digitalhistory.com/schools/StGabriel/index.html

Central Middle School in San Carlos, CA (Exploratory)
http://central.sancarlos.k12.ca.us/curriculum.html#exp

Additional Information

As we have indicated before, it is impossible to cover a complex topic in depth within the confines of a single book. Use the resources in Keeping Current with Technology 4–1 to locate additional information and to see a variety of curriculum examples.

Other Perspectives on Integrated Curriculum

Is the integrated curriculum the ideal? Not all educators would answer affirmatively. While James Beane speaks out as a national authority for the integrated curriculum, other scholars have raised thought-provoking questions. Some educators such as Paul George (1996) and Tom Gatewood (1998), while not opposed to an integrated curriculum, suggest several possible obstacles and problems with its complete implementation. While we, too, support Beane's ideas for an integrated curriculum, we also believe that these other educators have raised questions that must be considered.

Among those who believe that not everything can be taught in full integration is Tom Gatewood (1998). He feels that students need to spend time being prepared in the individual subject matter disciplines. Sharing his views are other educators, personnel in state departments of education, textbook authors, and test publishers who continue to suggest lists of information that should be learned within the various curricular areas. Gatewood (1998) finds it ironic that, at a time when exciting changes are occurring in the various middle school subject-area disciplines, curriculum integration, as proposed by most of its advocates (despite their protestations to the contrary) still seems to diminish and devalue the traditional subject areas. While organizations (such as National Council of Teachers of English and National Council of Teachers of Mathematics) have called for curricular integration, none of these organizations has called for eliminating individual curricular areas (Gatewood, 1998). As a result, many teachers are caught between their positions as teachers of mathematics, language arts, social studies, science, or related domains and their positions as teachers of young adolescents. They are anxious that their allegiance to their respective disciplines might suggest that they are failing young people. They are criticized because of their belief in the importance of subject matter and their role as subject specialists. As one seventh-grade teacher told us, "I can't put all I teach in a number of themes, especially if I want my students to have subject-matter expertise. But I don't let the administration hear me say that. All they preach is theme, theme, theme. Then they get upset at the results of the standardized tests the students take each year. Can't they see there are benefits in both approaches?"

Other questions raised about the integrated curriculum focus on the use of themes as the principal source of curriculum content and on the way those themes are identified by students and teachers (Gatewood, 1998). If middle schools belong to the people of a community and state, who gives a small group of students and teachers the right to determine the themes to be taught? To whom are they accountable? And, who determines whether the themes are significant or trivial; mainstream or marginal; diverse or ethnocentric? Some educators believe that advocates of an integrated curriculum sometimes are trying to push their agenda too far.

While making it clear that he is not opposed to an integrated curriculum, Paul George (1996) could find no research to support the claims that an integrated curriculum would be better at 12 specific items including addressing the "living concerns" of students, providing more problem-solving situations, fostering more independent learning, providing more involvement with the environment, encouraging greater depth of learning, or improving the transfer or retention of learning. While he found that the integrated curriculum "has the potential to be a valuable addition to the educational experiences we offer young adolescents" (George, 1996, p. 15), he also found that the vast majority of educators, parents, and policy makers do not seem to understand the concept of integrated curriculum. In some cases, speakers and consultants inaccurately give the curriculum integration label to any and all thematic teaching without knowing the true essence of curriculum integration.

George (1996) also found that some teachers feel threatened with an unfamiliar curricular approach. Although many teachers have studied a single subject for years, the integrated curriculum does not allow them to take advantage of this expertise. While effective teachers improve yearly as they learn more about the subject area, accumulate resources, and refine lessons, constantly changing themes may negate these advances. With national testing focusing on specific subject areas, parents are often concerned with academic success as measured solely on those tests (George, 1996).

There are other obstacles to the successful implementation of an integrated curriculum. Basics such as a common planning time, a block schedule, and a common group of students are essential to an integrated curriculum. Regrettably, these fundamentals are still lacking in some middle schools. In addition, as the teacher's role changes from lecturer to facilitator, more demands are placed on often overworked educators. They must deal with large and small group instruction, monitor a number of student-choice projects, appeal to a variety of learning styles, and teach a mandated set of learning competencies via a theme.

Obviously, the integrated curriculum is an excellent instructional practice. While it will not solve all discipline and learning problems, it can turn some students into avid learners and can help young adolescents make necessary connections between their personal worlds and society as a whole. Unfortunately, the integrated curriculum takes time and is difficult to implement. In order to be successful, middle schools need to provide teachers with administrative support, staff development opportunities, and in-school preparation time and resources. They also need to include all educators on the integrated curriculum development teams. Educators need to enlighten the external communities and work with them in the development of meaningful learning experiences for young adolescents.

As we leave the discussion of the integrated curriculum, Case Study 4–1 tells how a middle school faculty decided to restructure its curriculum.

Exploratory Curriculum/Programs

Definition and Description

One definition of the exploratory program is that it consists of minicourses or other learning experiences that are designed to help young adolescents explore curricular areas based on their needs, interests, and aptitudes. Exploratories allow 10- to 14-year-olds to learn more about a specific subject. Rather than being expected to master a subject, students can learn a sufficient amount to determine whether they want to pursue the topic in greater detail.

Exploratories usually last a semester; however, some schools change them every 6 to 8 weeks. For example, a seventh grader might take computers during the first half of the fall semester and home arts the second half. Then, he or she might take theater and careers during the spring semester, each lasting about 6 to 8 weeks. Then, students who have an interest can either continue with the exploratory or take responsibility for learning on their own.

Case Study 4–1

A School Restructures the Curriculum

Like Fred Costa in the opening scenario of this chapter, some of the teachers and administrators at Great Meadows Middle School realized that they needed to develop a curriculum that was more integrated than what they presently had. While they had always taught curricular material from a single-subject approach, they realized that students did not see relationships between curricular areas, and, in fact, did not see the relevance of the curriculum to their lives. Although the educators had hesitations about a wholesale "switchover" at one time, they knew they wanted to make at least a slow move toward an integrated curriculum.

A Curriculum Integration Task Force of administrators and teachers from the core and related domains was established, and the members discussed their reasons for wanting to move from a single subject to an integrated curriculum approach. While they thought the transition was needed, they, understandably, had concerns: How would they find the time needed to develop integrated curricular units, how would the students (and parents) react to the change, what effects would the change have on academic achievement, and could the state-mandated learning objectives still be taught in each grade level?

Assessing their strengths, the task force agreed that Great Meadows Middle School had several advantages that would contribute to their effort. First, there were effective interdisciplinary teams. That meant the team meetings could be used to plan integrated units. Second, the school had successfully implemented block scheduling that would provide the flexibility to have longer or shorter teaching periods to accommodate the needs of an integrated curriculum. Finally, while some teachers like Bette Hampson were skeptical, the fact that most of the teachers were motivated and excited about a curriculum change would be a big help.

Starting slowly, but deliberately and with commitment, the task force debated the use of student-generated versus teacher-generated themes. The decision was to begin with teacher-generated themes, but to try to base those themes on observed students interests. They wanted to select, carefully, the themes that would allow curricular integration (to the maximum extent possible) through traditional curricular areas. Second, since the teachers were concerned about time, they decided to encourage each team to prepare one integrated unit in the fall and one in the spring; then, in the future years, each team would refine the previously prepared units, and prepare others. Third, they wanted to prepare both students and parents for the move toward an integrated curriculum. It would be important to convince both groups that the move toward curricular integration was the most prudent course of action. Last, they made a commitment to have each team include all the school professionals in the effort. As one teacher stated, "Everybody in the school—the library media specialist, the counselors, and the special resource teachers—can play instrumental roles in this effort."

There are several reasons for middle school exploratories. First, they provide young adolescents with opportunities to investigate areas of interest and personal concern (usually without receiving a grade based on mastery). In addition, exploratories take into consideration the shorter attention spans and diverse interests of young adolescents. Learners are allowed to change topics often before their interest wanes. Finally, exploratories give young adolescents an opportunity to decide who they are, what they might want to become, and what is personally important for them to believe.

Teachers' Roles

"Developing our exploratories was fun. We began by listing our areas of expertise. Then, the Exploratory Committee used our lists to develop a master list, which they let the students react to. From there, the committee made up a schedule for the exploratories to be taught. It took a lot of time and effort to match up the student interests with teacher expertise. I'm glad the committee allowed some duplication so that nobody had to work with too large a group or too many sessions of exploratories. You know, some of the topics looked so interesting, I wish I could have taken them!" Comments of a sixth-grade teacher.

In the exploratory program, teachers try to pique students' interests and to motivate them to want to learn more about the topic. Some students will like the topic; others will not. A lot depends upon the topic, the student's interest, and the teacher's enthusiasm. This does not mean that the teacher acts as a fountain of knowledge and expects all students to have similar enthusiasm for the topic. Instead, the teacher works as a guide or as a resource person rather than as one who is trying to make experts of all students. The teacher also helps students select learning activities and materials, and then monitors their progress in the exploratory. Ideally, students will engage in a process of self-assessment as they move toward their individual goals.

Topics

It is important to conduct an informal survey to determine the exploratories that might interest boys and girls. Possible topics range from pottery making, computer technology, a 9-week survey of a foreign language (again just to determine or pique interest), a personal improvement program, or even dance. A potential problem is that students' exploratory interests must match teachers' areas of expertise. The exploratory should be a topic in which a teacher has a genuine interest and is able to conduct group sessions without a great deal of additional study and preparation. Figure 4–3 shows a course outline for a seventh-grade exploratory focusing on careers.

Functions

The exploratory program in the middle school has several functions—all with the ultimate purpose of meeting young adolescents' developmental, personal, social, and academic needs. First, they give young adolescents opportunities to explore their interests, talents, and skills within personal and educational constructs. In addition, they help 10- to 14-year-olds decide who and what they are and let them consider who and what they want to

7th Grade Exploratory–Careers

Teacher's Name: ________________________________ **Room Number:** ______________

Materials: A spiral notebook and a pencil

Course Description: This exploratory focuses on personal, educational, and career development of the student with major emphasis on the interrelationships of careers and academic preparation, aptitudes, interest, and abilities.

Objectives: During the 9-week course, the students will:

1. explain how educational achievement can impact on career options.
2. offer several reasons for beginning career planning during the middle school years.
3. show how peer pressure can influence decisions in school work.
4. explain how interest, aptitudes, and abilities relate to career goals.
5. explain the importance of having a good work ethic and name several characteristics or behaviors of individuals with good work ethics.
6. identify occupations in various career clusters.
7. identify skills in finding and using sources of career information.
8. identify career opportunities in the state and region.

Instructional Grouping: Students will be organized in large groups for general instruction and will work independently in classroom activities and projects. Teacher assistance will be available during class as appropriate and after class upon request of the student.

Grading Procedures: The 9-week grade will result from the tests, daily grades, and participation.

Rules for Student Behavior: Students are expected to abide by the rules in the student handbook when at school and by the following specifically in the Career Exploratory.

1. Be on time and have all necessary materials.
2. Be responsible for your own behavior.
3. Show respect for yourself and others.
4. Listen considerately while others are speaking.
5. Follow directions.

FIGURE 4–3 Exploratory Course Outline

become. By assisting young adolescents in defining and pursuing their current living and learning needs, exploratories also help students gain a better understanding of their emerging capacities and interests during this time of developmental changes (National Association of Secondary School Principals, 1993).

What topics do students like best? At the schools we visited, the most popular exploratories dealt with topics such as physical development, sex education, relationships, high-interest aspects of specific curricular areas, and other topics related to "growing up."

Essentials of Exploratories

Several essentials usually serve as the foundation of exploratories. Effective exploratories provide developmentally responsive experiences. That means they should take into consideration young adolescents' shorter attention spans, varying interest levels, and abilities to think abstractly. They should also enhance motivation and build interest in topics that young adolescents might want to pursue, and reflect core curriculum and other related domains. When exploratories relate to the middle school curriculum in some way, they provide young adolescents with opportunities to learn more about particular topics and to see other perspectives of a topic being studied.

Selected Considerations for Developing Middle School Curriculum

You have read about both the exploratory and the integrated curriculum. Before we leave this discussion, we would like to leave you with a few selected considerations that, we believe, can help you increase the effectiveness of both integrated and exploratory curricular experiences. Based on your own experiences, you might be able to add your own comments to this list.

In essence, the middle school integrative and exploratory experiences should:

1. *Be unique but exhibit a sense of continuity between the elementary and high school levels.* Some middle school educators still seem uncertain about whether the curriculum should be an extension of the elementary curriculum or a forerunner of the secondary curriculum. We believe that effective middle school curricular experiences, both integrative and exploratory, should be unique, should reflect the diversity of young adolescents, and should help them make the transition from elementary to high school.
2. *Reflect developmental responsive perspectives (that is, reflect young adolescents' physical, psychosocial, and cognitive developmental characteristics).* Educators need to recognize development as a basis for curricular integration and exploration.
3. *Be the basis of and be relevant to learners' experiences as well as their personal, social, and academic aspirations.* Young adolescents must see how the learning experiences relate to life (Diem, 1992) and must view schooling as a useful activity.

   Providing curriculum relevance does not mean either "dumbing down" the curriculum or having lower expectations and less demands for excellence. However, learners need to see how curricular experiences can improve their lives. The key is to consider each individual learner and his or her characteristics, and, then, to plan a curriculum to which students can relate and build upon for future educational success.

4. *Adopt student-centered perspectives.* With a student-centered integrative and exploratory curriculum that focuses on students' needs, interests, and developmental levels, many middle school students are motivated to behave, learn, and achieve. Making a student-centered curriculum a reality takes thought and commitment to understand individual students as well as the teaching-learning process.
5. *Achieve a balance between cognitive and affective.* Without doubt, middle school educators need to focus on the cognitive learning that young adolescents need to succeed in school and in life. However, teachers also need to focus curricular integration and exploration toward the affective domains—those areas where young adolescents form attitudes toward topics, people, and institutions. For example, while students need to learn facts about other cultures, they also need to explore racist feelings and prejudices.
6. *Reflect a clear belief in the relationship between learners' self-concept and their success with the middle school curriculum.* More than two decades ago, William Purkey clarified the relationship between self-concept and social and academic achievement in *Self-Concept and School Achievement* (1970). He also showed educators how to invite students to have a better self-concept in *Inviting School Success* (1984). An individual's self-concept continually accumulates experiences that "tells" the individual his or her degree of self-worth. Obviously, learners feel better about themselves when they do better in school, and vice versa. Unfortunately, many learners do not receive the positive reinforcement and positive nurturing attention that they need to succeed in school and to feel good about themselves (Canfield, 1990). Integrative and exploratory curricular efforts should address self-concept and its powerful effects on personal development and academic achievement.
7. *Provide for cultural and gender diversity.* The integrated and exploratory curriculum should help all students understand their cultural and gender diversity and should provide experiences that use diversity as strengths on which to build learning and socialization.

Closing Remarks

The emphasis on integrated curricular experiences and exploratories has grown during the past 10 years, especially since James Beane began his work on curriculum. Until this time, the middle school curriculum was basically ignored, while educators placed priority on other aspects of the middle school such as organization, teacher advisories, and interdisciplinary teaming. While these aspects should continue to be examined and refined, the middle school curriculum is now receiving much deserved consideration. Rather than being either an elementary or secondary curriculum, the middle school integrative and exploratory curriculum should be based specifically on the young adolescents' needs, interests, and concerns and should provide developmentally responsive curricular experiences. As suggested in *This We Believe* (National Middle School Association, 1995), these experiences should be challenging, integrative, and exploratory. To a great extent, however, the success to which young adolescents have developmentally responsive integrative and exploratory curricular experiences will depend significantly upon the commitment and actions of teachers, such as those at Great Meadows Middle School in this chapter's opening scenario.

Suggested Readings

Arnold, J. (1993). A curriculum to empower young adolescents. *Midpoints Occasional Papers, 4*(10), 1–11. Looks at stereotypes of young adolescents, societal forces and development, principles of empowerment, and examples of empowering curricula.

Beane, J. (1996). On the shoulders of giants! The case for curriculum integration. *Middle School Journal, 28*(1), 6–11. Defines the term, and looks at its past and contemporary progress.

Doda, N. M., & George, P. A. (1999). Building whole middle school communities: Closing the gap between exploratory and core. *Middle School Journal, 30*(5), 32–39. Looks at curriculum integration, home-base/advisiory alliances, extended team, and core-exploratory liaisons as a means of combining exploratory and core efforts.

Gatewood, T. (1998). How valid is the integrated curriculum in today's middle school? *Middle School Journal, 29*(4), 38–41. Discusses practical, intellectual, and accountability problems.

George, P. (1996). The integrated curriculum: A reality check. *Middle School Journal, 28*(1), 12–19. Suggests 21 possible problems with integrated curriculum.

McCullen, C. (1998). The electronic thread: Blending standards & technology. *Middle Ground, 2*(1), 7–8. Includes suggestions for integrating technology into the disciplines.

Simmons, S. L., & El-Hindi, A. E. (1998). Six transformations for thinking about integrative curriculum. *Middle School Journal, 30*(2), 32–36. Redefines learning and teaching in middle-level schools as requiring six transformations in teachers' thinking.

Tomlinson, C. A. (1998). For integration and differentiation choose concepts over topics. *Middle School Journal, 30*(2), 3–8. Compares topics-based integrated study and concept-based integrated study.

Windschitl, M., & Irby, J. (1999). Tapping the resources of the World Wide Web for inquiry in middle schools. *Middle School Journal, 30*(3), 40–46. Calls for cautiously expanding the use of the Web in the middle school curriculum.

Chapter 5

Middle School Organization—Educators and Learners

Scenario—Cheryl Walker Chairs the Organization Committee

With a few last-minute jitters, Cheryl Walker, a sixth-grade teacher, opened the first meeting of the Brookside Junior High School (B.J.H.S.) Organization Committee. B.J.H.S. would become Brookside Middle School next year, but, if Cheryl had her way, the change would include more than a new name. Three weeks ago, Ervin Renso, the principal of B.J.H.S., had asked her to chair this subcommittee of the larger School Restructuring Committee. As Mr. Renso had explained, the subcommittee's responsibilities would be to (1) review the school's current organization and schedules, (2) consider whether a change was needed in the switch to a middle school, and, if so, (3) propose possible organization restructuring plans.

Although Cheryl Walker welcomed the challenge, she thought about the crucial questions the committee needed to address: How receptive would her committee members be to changing the status quo? Would they ever have the "nerve" to suggest block scheduling or an interdisciplinary team organization? She thought to herself, "Those are big steps, and the overall School Restructuring Committee as well as the school's faculty might not want such broad and sweeping changes. While this is a great faculty to work with, I know how much apprehension there is about the switch from junior high to middle school. If I try to push too much, I may do more harm than good!"

One thing Cheryl did like about the way the switch was being handled was that her principal had asked her committee to "review, consider, and propose" rather than just mandate changes, so perhaps this was the opportunity she had been looking for. Ever since she had begun attending the National Middle School Association meetings, Cheryl had been lobbying the administration to develop a flexible school organization that would meet the different developmental, social, and academic needs of the young adolescents at Brookside. Now Ervin Renso was giving her an opportunity to make some changes. But could she get others to see what a difference these changes would make for them as teachers and for their students?

Overview

The challenges facing Cheryl Walker and her committee are nothing new. Since American education outgrew the one-room school, finding the ideal organization pattern for schools to meet the needs of students has always been a challenge. Today, a new option in that search is the organization found in the modern middle school. In this chapter, we will look at the ways that contemporary middle schools have tried to provide developmentally appropriate educational experiences for 10- to 14-year-olds. This includes the use of flexible organizational patterns such as block scheduling, heterogeneous learning communities, and interdisciplinary team organization (ITO). While we support these concepts, we also realize that there is not a "one-size-fits-all" approach to education. To be successful, middle-level educators need to consider their individual school situations to determine the school and class organizations that most effectively meet their young adolescents' academic, social, and developmental needs and interests.

Objectives

After reading and thinking about this chapter on middle school organization, you should be able to:

1. describe the need for middle school organization to be adaptable and to meet young adolescents' developmental, social, and academic needs;
2. define traditional departmentalized schedules and explain how they work;

3. define flexible scheduling and two types–alternating-day block schedule and flexible interdisciplinary block schedule.
4. describe block scheduling and explain how teachers can use smaller or larger blocks of time to provide developmentally responsive educational activities for young adolescents;
5. define heterogeneous learning communities, explain reasons for heterogeneous instructional groups, and suggest teaching methods that address young adolescents' individual needs;
6. define interdisciplinary teams and explain their contributions to both young adolescents and teachers in middle schools; and
7. describe how interdisciplinary team organizations work, explain team member and leaders' roles, and suggest ways to evaluate the effectiveness of teams.

ORGANIZATION—THE NEED FOR FLEXIBILITY

"Too often we do anything to eliminate a problem. Later we even think up reasons for what we did. This 'anything' then becomes hallowed tradition." Overheard during a meeting.

The Beginning of Schools

When formal American school systems began, students of all ages often attended the same school and, frequently, were in the same classroom. As school attendance grew, educators developed a compartmental system in which they assigned students to grade levels based on age, similar to school organizational patterns today. The result was a rigid classification and organization of students. Above the elementary level, educators taught only certain subjects, usually in a particular grade. In these schools, education was based on set time blocks that were controlled by a system of bells. The resulting educational organization pattern left little opportunity for curricular integration, innovation, and interdisciplinary activities.

The hallowed tradition of rigid schedules began to change with the development of middle-level education. For the first time, educators looked at the learning characteristics of 10- to 14-year-olds as an aid to developing a schedule that was both flexible and responsive to student and teacher needs. According to *This We Believe* (National Middle School Association, 1995), "developmentally appropriate middle level schools are flexible in grouping, scheduling, and staffing" (p. 28). Examples of this flexibility can be found in school-within-a-school arrangements or "houses," block scheduling, heterogeneous learning communities, and interdisciplinary teaming. Differing greatly from their junior high school predecessors (Table 5–1), middle schools are designed to be flexible enough to address the developmental, social, and academic needs of young adolescents.

Cheryl Walker's Brookside Junior High School had the epitome of an inflexible schedule with 55-minute periods all day—even lunch was 55 minutes. Bells ruled the instructional day; periods could not be changed. There was no time for interdisciplinary meetings, except before or after school. When the school decided to adopt essential middle school

TABLE 5–1 *Differences between Middle Schools and Junior High Schools*

Middle School	Characteristics	Junior High School
Interdisciplinary teams	**Organization of Teachers**	Subject departments
Instructional grouping within heterogeneous learning communities	**Organization of Students**	Homogeneous groups
Cooperation	**Instructional Planning**	Isolation
Flexible blocks	**Scheduling**	Rigid periods
Team-based learning	**Student/teacher interaction**	Different teacher every 40 to 55 minutes
Nurturing/caring	**Student/teacher environment**	Impersonal
Team cohort group	**Student/student environment**	Constantly shifting groups in separate classes
One adult advisor/mentor for 25 or less students	**Guidance**	Guidance counselor for 300–600 students
Advisories on daily or biweekly basis	**Frequency of guidance**	Guidance once or twice a year

concepts, one of Cheryl's committee's first recommendations was to remove the bells and adopt a schedule that would allow flexibility as well as time for teacher advisories and student exploratories. Some teachers lobbied against the change because they had always planned their lessons to fit 55-minute periods and did not want to have to redo the lesson plans they had been using for years! Others were sure that flexibility was a synonym for chaos. After all, how could you teach the required curriculum if you did not have 55 minutes every day to cover the material?

In considering the scheduling alternatives found in middle-level schools, we find that there are three primary types: traditional departmentalized schedule, alternating-day block schedule, and the flexible interdisciplinary block schedule.

Traditional Departmentalized Schedule

The traditional departmentalized schedule typically associated with junior high schools and high schools has a fixed number of daily periods of uniform length, with instruction delivered according to departmental classifications (Hackman & Valentine, 1998). Table 5–2 shows a traditional schedule with a 30-minute lunch occurring within the fourth period.

Although 76% of middle-level schools used this traditional schedule in 1969 (Alexander et al., 1969), today the percentage is much lower. McEwin, Dickinson, and Jenkins (1996) found traditional departmentalized schedules are used in less than 50% of seventh grades and in a little over 50% of eighth grades. The number of instructional periods per day in the traditional schedule varies between five and ten with 94% of the middle schools

TABLE 5–2 ***Traditional Departmentalized Schedule***

Time	Monday	Tuesday	Wednesday	Thursday	Friday
8:00–8:25	Advisory	Advisory	Advisory	Advisory	Advisory
8:30–9:25	1	1	1	1	1
9:30–10:25	2	2	2	2	2
10:30–11:25	3	3	3	3	3
11:30–12:55	Lunch/4	Lunch/4	Lunch/4	Lunch/4	Lunch/4
1:00–1:55	5	5	5	5	5
2:00–2:55	6	6	6	6	6
3:00–3:10	Homeroom	Homeroom	Homeroom	Homeroom	Homeroom

in a national survey reporting the use of a six-, seven-, or eight-period day (Valentine, Clark, Irvin, & Melton, 1993). Educators are urged to use this scheduling pattern cautiously because it can perpetuate practices such as ability grouping (Canady & Rettig, 1995).

Flexible Scheduling

In an attempt to avoid the rigid scheduling found in junior high schools, middle-level educators have looked at various types of flexible schedules. These schedules organize classes and educational experiences to allow for daily variations, thus reflecting a sound middle school concept and ensuring more equal access to all instructional programs and student support services (California State Department of Education, 1987). For example, flexible schedules permit the allocation of time and effort according to the needs of students and the nature of the course content.

When combined with other middle school concepts such as interdisciplinary teaming and mixed-ability grouping, flexible schedules also provide opportunities for the use of a variety of instructional strategies, including both whole-group and small-group instruction, and integrated interdisciplinary instruction (Hopkins & Canady, 1997; Rettig & Canady, 1996). In a middle school, flexible schedules should provide for the diversity of students' cognitive and affective abilities, as well as their need for exercise and rest. This means allowing time for exploratory programs (discussed in chapter 3), advisor-advisee programs, extended blocks of uninterrupted instructional time in which a variety of activities can occur, teacher planning time, integration of subjects, varied lengths of instructional time, and innovation and experimentation with varied time schedules (Arnold, 1991).

Block Schedules. One type of flexible schedule is the block schedule, which is frequently found in high schools. Within this schedule, large blocks of time, typically 90 minutes or more, are allocated for each class, with fewer classes each day and fewer class changes. Almost any class in the core disciplines such as language arts and science, the related domains of art or music, as well as exploratories, can be held within the large blocks of time. Since teachers do not feel rushed to complete instructional activities within short time periods, some schools report a dramatic improvement in overall school climate (Hackmann, 1995b).

Block scheduling can take several forms. During "Horace's Friday," students at a Massachusetts middle school spend four blocks with one teacher (Murdock, Hansen, & Kraemer, 1995), while, in the Intensive Core Program at a Colorado middle school, students spend 4 1/2 weeks on one core subject (Alam & Seick, 1994). With four-by-four daily schedules, students can enroll in four classes each semester for a total of eight classes each academic year (Edwards, 1995). A Copernican schedule includes seminars on topics of student interest and classes on a trimester basis (Carroll, 1989). Both the four-by-four and Copernican modifications allow students to enroll in more courses than would be possible under traditional six- or seven-period schedules.

While block schedules such as the Copernican and four-by-four schedules may provide numerous advantages for high schools, they often present problems for middle schools. Frequently, these schedules do not always allow schools to offer year-long classes in selected subjects. Also, since courses are offered on a semester or trimester basis, students would not be enrolled in all required core classes during the same semester. This makes it difficult, if not impossible, to develop interdisciplinary units that integrate even the core disciplines of language arts, social studies, science, and mathematics (Hackmann & Valentine, 1998).

Alternating-Day Block Schedules. To cut down on the number of classes that students and teachers have each day, some middle schools use an alternating-day block schedule (Hackmann & Valentine, 1998). Most common is an eight-block arrangement in which even-numbered and odd-numbered classes meet on alternating days (Hackmann, 1995b). In a variation of this block schedule (Table 5–3), some schools hold all classes on either Monday or Fridays to ensure that all teachers see their students either at the beginning or the end of the week. Other variations include maintaining one constant period of 45–50 minutes each day for classes such as foreign language, which may need daily academic instruction (Hackmann & Valentine, 1998).

Middle schools can benefit from alternating-day block schedules (Canady & Rettig, 1995). By having subjects every other day, young adolescents have more time to concentrate on individual studies without having to juggle a large number of assignments, tests, and other school responsibilities on a single day. A disadvantage is that the day is still divided into uniform time blocks. While some teachers may be able to implement interdisciplinary instruction within this structure, others may still find that the block format is too rigid for them to develop a thematic, integrated curriculum (Hackmann & Valentine, 1998).

Flexible Interdisciplinary Block Schedule. The flexible interdisciplinary block schedule, sometimes called the flexible block schedule or the interdisciplinary block, provides blocks of teaching times. Within these blocks, interdisciplinary teams can decide how to allocate the time for students on their team (Hackmann & Valentine, 1998).

TABLE 5–3 ***Alternating-Day Block Schedule***

Time	Monday	Tuesday	Wednesday	Thursday	Friday
8:00–8:20	Advisory	Advisory	Advisory	Advisory	Advisory
8:25–9:10	1	1	2	1	2
9:15–10:00	2				
10:05–10:50	3	3	4	3	4
10:55–12:10	Lunch/4	Lunch	Lunch	Lunch	Lunch
12:15–1:00	5	5	6	5	6
1:05–1:50	6				
1:55–2:40	7	7	8	7	8
2:45–3:30	8				

Thus, this scheduling pattern relies on interdisciplinary team organization, the basic organization of exemplary middle schools (George & Alexander, 1993). Table 5–4 shows a flexible interdisciplinary block schedule with a team core in the mornings and directly after lunch and then three afternoon class periods that can be used for the related domains (art, music, health/physical education), specialized studies (reading, foreign language), and exploratories.

Within the flexible interdisciplinary block schedule, teachers can individualize and personalize learning, and students can concentrate on areas of interest (Drake & Roe, 1994). When teachers take advantage of the flexibility of this schedule, the length of individual lessons can vary daily, depending on the needs of the teachers on the team (Merenbloom, 1991). The core block time might be divided into equal parts for subject-specific instruction or may be opened up for team-taught interdisciplinary units. On some days, a greater amount of time may be allocated to one teacher for activities such as laboratory experiments that require extended class time (Hackmann & Valentine, 1998).

Benefits of Block Schedules. We have mentioned some advantages of block schedules, but there are others. When teachers use block scheduling with a team approach, they can remedy the compartmentalized routine of separate subject classes by allowing several teachers to work with a group of students within a single block. This allows students to see the interconnectedness of the subjects that they study. Also, block scheduling helps young adolescents to adapt to varying academic and behavior requirements by giving them more time in an individual classroom setting. At the same time, block scheduling allows more time for reteaching or retesting. Finally, block scheduling can help 10- to 14-year-olds and

TABLE 5–4 ***Flexible Interdisciplinary Block Schedule***

<table>
<tr><th>Time</th><th>Monday</th><th>Tuesday</th><th>Wednesday</th><th>Thursday</th><th>Friday</th></tr>
<tr><td>8:00–8:20</td><td>Advisory</td><td>Advisory</td><td>Advisory</td><td>Advisory</td><td>Advisory</td></tr>
<tr><td>8:25–9:10</td><td rowspan="4">Core block</td><td rowspan="4">Core block</td><td rowspan="4">Core block</td><td rowspan="4">Core block</td><td rowspan="4">Core block</td></tr>
<tr><td>9:15–10:00</td></tr>
<tr><td>10:05–10:50</td></tr>
<tr><td>10:55–11:40</td></tr>
<tr><td>11:40–12:10</td><td>Lunch</td><td>Lunch</td><td>Lunch</td><td>Lunch</td><td>Lunch</td></tr>
<tr><td>12:15–1:00</td><td>Core</td><td>Core</td><td>Core</td><td>Core</td><td>Core</td></tr>
<tr><td>1:05–1:50</td><td>1</td><td>1</td><td>1</td><td>1</td><td>1</td></tr>
<tr><td>1:55–2:40</td><td>2</td><td>2</td><td>2</td><td>2</td><td>2</td></tr>
<tr><td>2:45–3:30</td><td>3</td><td>3</td><td>3</td><td>3</td><td>3</td></tr>
</table>

their teachers eliminate the stress found in a traditional schedule. Educators who serve more than 100 students per day face serious emotional demands. Similarly, young adolescents can find that dealing with five or more different teachers a day can be stressful and confusing (Francka & Lindsey, 1995).

While these reasons provide a sound rationale for block scheduling, the basic reason for using a block schedule should be that the shorter and/or longer blocks of time better meet the needs of young adolescents. Longer class periods allow students more time for extended hands-on projects, lab assignments, more in-depth discussions, and varied approaches to learning. While results vary with individual schools, projected benefits of block scheduling include improved academic success and achievement, increased opportunity for individualized attention, fewer classes for teachers to plan for and teach in a 24-hour period, more opportunities for students to make up work during resource periods, and improved school climate through reduced stress and a calmer school day (Gerking, 1995).

Guidelines for Implementing Block Scheduling. Hackmann (1995a) suggests 10 guidelines and contends that a collaborative approach to school reform emerges when teachers, students, administrators, and parents design and implement a block schedule. Hackmann's guidelines can be found in Table 5–5.

Case Study 5–1 continues the saga of Brookside Junior High School and shows how a group of professional teachers and administrators adopted block scheduling in the switch from junior high to middle school.

TABLE 5–5 ***Guidelines for Implementing Block Scheduling***

1. *Employ a systems thinking approach*—Implement a block schedule because the approach empowers teachers to rethink and restructure their system rather than because it is the latest fad.
2. *Secure the support of superiors*—Restructuring may affect areas beyond the faculty's jurisdiction such as reducing staff, altering bus schedules, and deviating from negotiated contract agreements.
3. *Understand the change process*—The change process can be difficult for both students and teachers. Give the change serious consideration, move when the momentum peaks, and address all faculty concerns.
4. *Involve all stakeholders*—All changes should be teacher-driven, and teachers should be actively involved in developing the schedule. Obtain the support of administrators, and involve parents and students whenever possible.
5. *Consult sources outside the school*—Use sources such as books, journal articles, the World Wide Web; attend state and national conferences; and invite educators who have first-hand experiences planning and implementing block schedules.
6. *Brainstorm creative alternatives*—Focus attention on the reasons for the change and for implementing a new schedule, and pilot one or two schedules before full implementation occurs.
7. *Examine the budgetary implications*—Consider costs and how block scheduling will result in teachers teaching more or less subjects and how special-area teachers and special activities will be affected.
8. *Plan faculty inservices*—Address teachers' anxieties by planning for an "implementation dip" (p. 26), and encourage teachers to rely on their collaborative and collective expertise.
9. *Include an evaluative component*—Employ a variety of evaluative measures to determine the effectiveness of block scheduling and its effects on all stakeholders.
10. *Share and celebrate our successes*—Provide a celebrative occasion to share positive classroom experiences, to brainstorm creative approaches for the longer or shorter teaching periods, and to consider ongoing evaluations of student progress.

Adapted from: Hackmann, D. G. (1995). Ten guidelines for implementing block scheduling. *Educational Leadership, 53*(3), 24–27.

ORGANIZATION—HETEROGENEOUS LEARNING COMMUNITIES

For a long time, American educators have tracked or grouped students on the basis of achievement level and academic ability (e.g., standardized achievement tests, teacher-made tests, and previous teachers' recommendations) (Vaughn, Bos, & Schumm, 1997). They have assumed that most students share essentially the same personal attributes and learner characteristics and therefore can be placed in a single homogeneous group. Unfortunately, those students who deviate from the norm because of things such as special needs; racial, cultural, religious, or gender differences; or conflicting perceptions toward school have sometimes received an inferior education because many educators have not been trained to teach mixed-ability groups of students (Gable & Hendrickson, 1997).

In a report entitled *Turning Points: Preparing American Youth for the 21st Century,* the Carnegie Council on Adolescent Development (1989) characterized tracking as "one of the

Case Study 5–1

A School Adopts a Block Schedule

When Brookside Junior High School was switching to the middle school concept, the Organization Committee, chaired by Cheryl Walker, realized the problems and pitfalls (i.e., the lack of flexibility) associated with their six-period day. After careful deliberations, the committee recommended a switch to flexible interdisciplinary block scheduling. However, since the magnitude of such a change would require careful planning, the committee also recommended hiring a consultant. Inviting their colleagues to join them, the committee members also planned visits to middle schools to talk with teachers who had first-hand experiences with block scheduling.

After the switch was approved by the Brookside faculty and the administrators, Cheryl and her committee worked with the consultant to develop a model for planning the flexible block schedule and a detailed implementation plan. Approximately 12 of the 48 Brookside teachers, including four of the members of Cheryl's committee, received training in flexible scheduling and its implementation. Then, these 12 (in many cases, former grade level or subject leaders) worked with and trained the remaining 36 teachers. Part of both faculty meetings and the new interdisciplinary team meetings was devoted to discussions of flexible block scheduling, its advantages, and the potential problems to consider and address. Two PTA meetings were devoted to the possible implementation of block scheduling, and the input of both parents and young adolescents was actively sought. Building a schedule to meet the needs of as many students as possible was not easy, but Cheryl and two other teachers of the initial twelve worked with the assistant principal.

The next year, flexible interdisciplinary block scheduling was implemented in a format similar to Table 5–4 with times for exploratories and advisory programs. It reflected *This We Believe* (National Middle School Association, 1995) in that it provided flexibility to use enrichment groups, cooperative learning, and independent study groups; and to allow teachers to design and operate educational experiences, collaborate across teaching specialties, and share responsibility for literacy development, guidance and advocacy, and student life.

Two years later, most teachers in Brookside agreed that the implementing of flexible interdisciplinary block scheduling was successful, but even with the careful planning, problems did exist that had to be addressed. For example, teachers had to plan differently, and some teachers felt uncomfortable teaching without formal structured class periods. They were overshadowed, however, by the teachers who liked the longer periods of time and the accompanying flexibility. In addition, the flexibility and the heterogeneous groupings that accompanied the new schedule had a positive impact on student attitudes and performance.

most destructive of current practices" (p. 14). The National Middle School Association (1995), in its publication *This We Believe,* advocated more flexible organization structures in "lieu of academic tracking" (p. 28). Finally, Hastings (1992) has even proposed that ending ability grouping of students is a moral imperative for educators. Thus, it is clear that current thinking reflects a realization that homogeneous grouping has a deleterious effect on students' self-esteem and their feelings about their ability to achieve academically (Gamoran, 1992; Oakes, 1985; Slavin, 1996).

To find out what often happens to young adolescents when they are grouped homogeneously, we need only to look at Kirk, a seventh grader we met. Three teachers decided to group their classes homogeneously after the midsemester break by using reading scores, overall academic scores, and teachers' opinions. After the students received their assignments, Kirk came up to one of the teachers and said, "Well, Mr. Soto, you put me in the dumb group." Although the teacher tried to explain that the groups would allow more instruction and assessments on the "right level," and that the overall school day would improve, it was clear that Kirk was not accepting the response. When the teacher was done, Kirk looked at him again and stated matter-of-factly, "Like I said, Mr. Soto, you put me in the dumb group." That day, Kirk's self-esteem took a nose dive.

What is the alternative? Middle school educators have two basic options to lessen the negative effects of homogeneous ability grouping: heterogeneous learning communities and heterogeneous instructional grouping.

When middle school educators use heterogeneous learning communities, they organize young adolescents into teams, "houses," or learning communities without regard for common characteristics. For example, a sixth-grade team may consist of 100 students who have a wide range of personal attributes and learning characteristics. Like the neighborhoods from which they come, the students will be diverse in learning styles, abilities, levels of motivation, and previous academic achievement.

With heterogeneous instructional groups, teachers place students in groups for instruction, without regard to their academic ability and expertise, intelligence, or previous learning experiences. With these groups, teachers can use a variety of instructional techniques such as mastery learning, individualized instruction, peer tutors, and cooperative learning to meet the needs of the students.

At times, within the heterogeneous communities and the heterogeneous instructional groups, teachers can group together students with similar learning needs. In fact, putting students together because they have similar learning needs is a way to avoid the "one-size-fits-all" educational experiences often associated with large heterogeneous groups. For example, seventh-grade teacher Rodi Segear had a science class of 28 heterogeneously grouped students. After learning each student, he grouped them into four homogeneous groups, based on learning abilities and interests. To keep these homogeneous groups from becoming permanent, Rodi constantly reevaluated the students and moved students from group to group accordingly. He knew that students can be grouped homogeneously within heterogeneous teams or classes as long as the groups are not permanent. In the Suggested Readings at the end of this chapter, Fred Nolan describes how math classes can be grouped by level and still maintain the spirit of a learning community.

ORGANIZATION—INTERDISCIPLINARY TEAMS

For many years, teachers have planned for classes, collected teaching materials, decided on teaching methods, and taught in isolation. Working alone, they did not know other teachers' goals, methods, and successes; nor did other teachers know theirs. Each teacher had "her or his own little world" in the classroom and taught a group of students without benefit of other teachers' praise or constructive criticism. A degree of respect existed whereby teachers assumed that other teachers taught in about the same manner and used the same materials. Naturally, since teachers never planned together, such a system did not allow for curricular integration. Students went from class to class without seeing any connections between the subject they were studying. Students were even taken to the school library for isolated "library lessons" that had no connection to the topics studied in any classes.

In an attempt to address the problems that resulted from teaching in isolation, middle schools have adopted interdisciplinary team organization (ITO). When carefully planned, implemented, and maintained, ITO is a key component of highly successful middle schools programs (McEwin, 1997). This integrated approach has expanded so that teachers look beyond their own classrooms and view the middle school as a resource-based learning environment where library media specialists and other teachers in the related domains join with core team members to provide active learning experiences for young adolescents who now see relationships among the subjects that they study. We'll look at interdisciplinary instructional strategies in chapters 6 and 7; however, in this chapter, we want to examine the organizational qualities of interdisciplinary teaming.

Definitions

It is important to define what we mean by "team teaching," "interdisciplinary team organization," and "interdisciplinary team teaching." Team teaching, a teaming approach developed several decades ago, can be defined as two or more teachers working together to provide instruction to a group of students. The term is often used to describe a situation in which two or more teachers on the same grade level share students and common planning time (Wraga, 1997). Interdisciplinary team organization (ITO) is defined as an organization pattern of two or more teachers representing different subject areas and sharing the same students, schedule, and adjoining areas of the school. Team organization is a more fundamental structural change than the team teaching that was popular in the 1960s and early 1970s (Erb, 1997). In fact, ITO is now widely recognized as an essential component of developmentally responsive schools for young adolescents (McEwin, 1997). The terms *interdisciplinary team organization* and *interdisciplinary team teaching* (*ITT*) have been used interchangeably in the literature.

Sometimes, ITO and ITT are confused with team teaching. Interdisciplinary team teaching involves a team of two or more subject teachers who share students and planning time and who work to draw connections between their subjects. While these teachers might sometimes teach together, it is not a requirement for interdisciplinary team teaching. According to Wraga (1997), the real distinction between team teaching and interdisciplinary team teaching is a curricular one; that is, a team of teachers become an interdisciplinary team when its members set out to integrate learning from normally disparate disciplines (Wraga, 1997). But there is also an organizational difference. With true interdisciplinary teams, the professional work life of teachers and the basic organizational structure of the school are changed. Teachers collaborate and have an opportunity to learn from one another about teaching and young adolescents, in ways that never existed within the departmentalized organization.

We also need to make a distinction between interdisciplinary teaming and interdisciplinary curriculum. The former refers to the way teachers organize to relate to each other and to work with students. The latter refers to the ways of organizing the learning content and experiences for students. Some teachers confuse these two terms because, although they refer to separate concepts, they are interdependent at their most sophisticated levels of implementation. An interdisciplinary team that has achieved its highest levels of functioning engages in delivering interdisciplinary curriculum (discussed in more detail in chapter 4). In the past two decades, the most successful middle schools are those that have discovered how to combine interdisciplinary teaming and interdisciplinary curriculum into a mutually supportive process (Erb, 1997).

Brief Look at Origins

The history of teaming dates back at least to the Platoon School, the Winnetka Plan, and the Pueblo Plan of the early twentieth century (Wraga, 1997). During the 1950s, many educators promoted team teaching or "teaming" as a solution to a number of educational problems, especially the chronic teacher shortages the nation faced following World War II. By the mid-1960s, team teaching was touted as a solution to a variety of educational problems such as making instruction relevant to students, utilizing staff in a cost-effective manner, providing effective special-education services, rejuvenating "burnt out" (Wraga, 1997, p. 328) staff, and integrating a variety of school subjects. Educators looked to teaming as a way to make the curriculum more relevant to students' needs, and to spur American education in the wake of the Soviet launching of *Sputnik.*

Unfortunately, team teaching did not live up to expectations. One quick example will show you why. In the early 1970s, one of us went to visit a student teacher in a teamed classroom and found one teacher instructing 75 seventh graders. The student teacher was duplicating copies of worksheets, and the other team teacher was planning lessons. It seems that this was the usual arrangement for this team-teaching situation. One teacher "taught" 75 students while the other teacher "planned." Clearly, this was not what team teaching was meant to do. There was no way for one teacher to meet the needs of 75 young adolescents.

Fortunately, on the middle school level, teaming has outlived the fad period of the 1960s and has matured into the approved middle school practice of interdisciplinary team organization (ITO). ITO is now a hallmark of genuine middle school education (Wraga, 1997).

When Kenneth McEwin (1997) reviewed several major studies such as a comprehensive study of middle schools conducted by Alexander in 1968, a 20-year follow-up study by Alexander and McEwin (1989a, 1989b), and a 25-year partial replication study by McEwin, Dickinson, and Jenkins in 1993 (1996), he found that the use of ITOs has increased significantly during the past 25 years. For example, the percentage of sixth- to eighth-grade middle schools in which sixth-grade language arts is taught on interdisciplinary team has increased from 8% in 1968 (Alexander, 1968) to 33% in 1988 (Alexander & McEwin, 1989b) to 59% in 1993 (McEwin, Dickinson, & Jenkins, 1996). Overall, 70% of schools containing seventh grade reported having implemented ITO and providing at least some common planning time for team members.

McEwin (1997) also reported that the subjects most likely to be taught on core teams are English, mathematics, science, and reading; fewer than 20% of the schools with ITO teach subjects such as foreign language, home economics, and industrial arts on teams. In about 40% of middle schools, teachers can decide which team they want to join. In other cases, the assignment of teams is most often made by school administrators.

Rationale

Why do so many middle schools use interdisciplinary teaming? The basic rationale for ITO in middle schools is that it provides a more effective means of meeting developmentally responsive needs and individual interests of 10- to 14-year-olds. It minimizes the number of young adolescents who feel unknown, who think that teachers do not know their progress in other classes, or who believe that other students do not know them well enough to accept them as friends. Because of the closer, more coherent supervision and caring that occurs on a team, ITO helps students build team spirit and improves attitudes and work habits. On interdisciplinary teams where teachers share a common planning time, students have higher self-concepts, and both students and teachers have more positive feelings about school (Warren & Muth, 1995).

In addition to improving instruction and developing better interpersonal relationships, effective teams can become powerful forces in creating learning communities for both teachers and students (Martin, 1999). Other advantages include ITO's contributions to both the school environment and curriculum. Interdisciplinary team organization is necessary to create a positive school environment that emphasizes caring, respect, success, and interdependence (Felner et al., 1997). From a curricular perspective, interdisciplinary teaming establishes a curricular balance among content, instruction, and skills for general, career, and fine arts education and, also, provides students with a better understanding of the interconnectedness of the various content areas. Similarly, planning time, materials, and other resources can be shared by professionals.

Essentials

In an extensive report on a longitudinal study of a school network engaged in *Turning-Points*–based school transformation, Felner et al. (1997) offered some interesting findings on the structure of teams. First, they found that team sizes can range from 60 to 70 students with 2 to 3 teachers to more than 240 students with 9 to 12 teachers. Student-to-teacher ratios on a team vary from 20 students per teacher to more than 40 students per teacher. Also, the amount of common planning time varies from no common planning time to the shared use of individual planning times to daily common planning times that is provided in addition to individual planning time for every teacher.

Looking at the effects of ITO, Felner et al. (1997) reported that team size, student/teacher ratio, and amount of common planning time appear to have significant instructional effects. For example, teams that exceed approximately 120 students, that have fewer than four planning periods a week, and that have student/teacher ratios beyond the middle twenties tend to have little impact on instructional practices or students' well-being. While small numbers of students in a team may somewhat improve students' reports of their levels of support and feelings of connectedness to the school, unless teachers have common planning times, actual instruction does not seem to improve. Teams that are too large, both in terms of students *and* teachers on the team, can experience a number of problems. In addition to team members failing to engage in critical team planning such as curriculum integration, coordination, and collaboration around students' needs, both students and teachers on large teams report increased psychological and behavioral problems. Students also report a more negative climate and lags in student achievement (Felner et al., 1997).

Ten years before this study, Erb (1987) identified four necessary features of effective ITO: common planning or meeting time, shared students, common block of time schedule, and spatial proximity of team members' classes. He maintained that teachers sharing common planning times and students were two absolute necessities for teams to function. Not having a common time to plan prevents teachers from discussing issues related to teaming efforts; not having the same students fails to make maximum use of the teaming process. However, when these basic essentials are in place, teaming can provide a more effective environment for learning that includes the following:

1. *An atmosphere for effective collegiality.*

Effective ITO cannot develop in isolation since teaming is more than an organizational feature. Good ITO affects the school's social, cultural, and power dimensions. Although subject-matter expertise and grade-level preferences should be considered when forming teams, schools that organize teams using only information about content and grade level fail to recognize that teaming affects all facets of the school's culture.

According to Burkhardt (1997), a team functions most effectively when team members subscribe to a shared set of common expectations. He tells of a team that placed emphasis and priority on specific words, such as *appreciation, acknowledgment, communication, risk,* and *respect.* While these might not be priorities for all teams (for example, other words might be *compassion, individuality,* and *trust*), each team needs to establish an atmosphere that reflects its priorities. Burkhardt also believes that a significant whole-team experience early in the school year pays dividends later in the year. He recommends a field trip to build a sense of community and feelings of collegiality.

Throughout the year, successful teams need regular activities to keep the team spirit alive. These activities have a positive impact on young adolescents and also address the social and emotional needs of 10- to 14-year-olds who learn better when they are in a caring and supportive school environment.

2. *A better way to provide a supportive environment for students.*

Along with the ITO should come new ways of providing education to young adolescents. This might mean including the school library media specialist and exploratory teachers on teams, and providing common times for special area and exploratory teachers to meet with the regular team. It may also mean that educators model good peer relations and demonstrate the importance of diverse individuals learning to work together. According to Burkhardt (1997), teachers serve as exemplars for young adolescents when they model cooperation, caring, and common sense. Some of the most powerful teachings come when teachers demonstrate how to act civilly and how to handle adversity and unexpected situations (Burkhardt, 1997).

ITO addresses the basic need of 10- to 14-year-olds to belong. As team members, young adolescents feel less alienation, have less misbehavior, engage in less vandalism, and have fewer tendencies to act out for attention (Burkhardt, 1997). As Thomas (1997) stated, teaming requires a changing of the school's culture—the way teachers and young adolescents think, perform, and react. Looking for short-term gains such as rapid increases in academic achievement or improvement in student behavior might result in disappointment since team building takes time, effort, and determination.

3. *The provision of staff development.*

Effective teaming does not happen as an accident but occurs only with effective staff development. Teachers need initial staff development to learn how to form a team and how to function as a team. They also need on-going staff development to provide assistance as teams plan to utilize flexible scheduling, employ alternative student-grouping arrangements, develop integrated units, and implement other curricular innovations.

4. *A recognition of the realities of a middle school.*

Team organization can help overcome the fear and uncertainties of working in a middle school. In a textbook, it is easy to overlook the fact that ITO must function in a real world. Middle-level educators need to work around realities such as overcrowded schools and cramped work spaces, lack of uninterrupted blocks of time, and paperwork that often takes precedence over teaching and curriculum development. Teachers and administrators need to accept these realities and work around or with them, rather than use them as reasons not to implement ITO.

For teachers who have worked in isolation for many years, another reality is that collaboration can be difficult. We have known teachers who considered themselves subject-matter specialists and, yet, felt threatened by the idea of working on a team. Fears about getting along, working with "difficult" team members, and teaching in the same room as another teacher are very real to some teachers. Fears of change and of the unknown are very real in most schools. But, once teaming succeeds, few teachers would return to working in isolation.

5. *The collaborative relationships between schools and universities.*

Currently there is a great deal of interest in middle schools. University faculty research middle school curriculum, organization, and instruction; specialists in state departments of education create middle school endorsements and licensure requirements; and faculty in teacher education programs develop specialized preservice and inservice middle school programs. ITO provides a collaborative base within which professionals from outside agencies can work with school educators to improve instruction for young adolescents (Thomas, 1997).

Development of ITO

Teaching teams do not develop overnight. They mature through what George (1982) identified as four operationalization phases: the *organizational phase* is characterized by the emergence of common procedures; the *community phase* is marked by conscious promotion of team identity among teachers and students; the *team-teaching phase,* which George considered nonessential to the existence of team organization, involves team members planning and teaching together; and, the *governmental phase* is characterized by the involvement of team members in participatory decision making. Plodzik and George's (1989) study corroborated these phases, pointed to the importance of staff development in the implementation efforts, and reaffirmed the critical role of administrators in providing constructive leadership.

Benchmarks of Effective Teams

What do effective interdisciplinary teams look like? Here are a few characteristics identified by research and scholarly opinion (Erb, 1997; Clark & Clark, 1997; Dickinson & Erb, 1997; Jones, 1997; Martin, 1999; Merenbloom, 1991). Effective, mature teams:

- Consist of members who recognize that the acquisition of professional knowledge is a lifelong process. "Teaching and learning are lifelong pursuits—very sophisticated, often enigmatic, and generally beyond the trappings of college coursework" (Jones, 1997, p. 209).
- Have members who are confident, express job satisfaction, and are proud of their schools. They have positive adult attitudes that are reflected in students' attitudes as well. Because positive attitudes set the tone of the classroom, these teachers report high levels of student enthusiasm and few disruptions that require disciplinary action.
- Build for a long-term gain rather than scramble for a short-term gain (Burkhardt, 1997). Successful and effective teams take time to develop and result from cooperation, planning, and maintenance where team members look for and seize opportunities to strengthen team relationships and improve team effectiveness. Team members looking for a quick fix to the problems facing a school will likely be disappointed.
- Nurture the relationship among team members and develop a team identity. While team and individual activities vary (such as cookouts and ball games), team members move toward a connection that often extends beyond the professional into the personal realm. Yet, even when team members do not mesh personally, mature teams can still function effectively.
- Are curriculum risk takers who seek autonomy to accomplish their goals. They are thoughtful in their planning, interactive in their discussions, rigorous in their academic expectations, and clear in their communications. They monitor their instruction to be certain that it is integrated with literacy skills and relevant life experiences. They reference other team members' teaching and often join them for lessons. They endorse each others' content area in their teaching just as they do their own.
- Function in harmony with the school's administration. Mature teams generally agree that they teach for administrators who both allow and expect autonomy and flexibility. Administrators contribute to the autonomy of teams by selecting instructional leaders who offer total commitment to young adolescents. Also, "administrators have the same standards for their faculty that they expect faculty to have for their students—spontaneity with intent, creativity with abandon,

achievement with integrity" (Jones, 1997, p. 217). Above all, the school and district administration support the teaming concept and team efforts and provide sufficient time for team planning and for adequate staff development.

- Have a balance in teachers' expertise, age, sex, and race.
- Select team leaders with specific responsibilities and develop an established team decision-making process (e.g., goals, grouping, scheduling, homework, and discipline) with agreed-upon procedures to assess students' strengths and weaknesses.

By listing these characteristics, we do not mean that a team must possess all of them to be successful. While some characteristics (e.g., acquiring professional knowledge and developing a team identity) might be excellent for all teams, each individual team needs to reach a consensus on the characteristics that team members deem most important.

In one school that we visited, this was clearly demonstrated when the principal pointed with pride to the Tiger Team. She stressed how far they had come in only 3 years and listed the team's accomplishments for us. Yet, when we talked with team members, they felt frustrated about what they had done. One teacher remarked, "We are not doing all we could and should do." Other members agreed that they had not achieved the "benchmarks" of a successful team. As we continued the conversation with the teachers, they began to realize that the team did not have to be able to check off all the characteristics on some list in order to have an effective team. They needed to establish their own ideas of success.

Evaluation of Team Efforts

Maintaining effective interdisciplinary teams requires establishing goals in light of the unique situation and providing continuous evaluation and reflection. Theory into Practice 5–1 shows some questions to consider in determining the effectiveness of a team.

Obstacles to Change

It can be very difficult to implement interdisciplinary teams, especially in the middle school where teaching can be emotional, demanding, and intense. However, the issues and challenges facing contemporary young adolescents suggest teaming in the middle school is more important today than it was 30 years ago. Rather than teachers working in isolation to prepare young adolescents to deal with issues and challenges, interdisciplinary teams can better provide developmentally responsive educational experiences (Jones, 1997).

Unfortunately, in the majority of middle schools, especially on the seventh- and eighth-grade levels, departmentalization continues to dominate—isolating teachers, fragmenting curriculum, and allowing many young adolescents to "fall through the cracks" (McEwin, 1997, p. 322). Additionally, in some middle schools, ITO is only a "paper plan" (McEwin, 1997, p. 322) In such schools, some teams recognize the powerful potential of teaming, while other teams operate as if teaming and departmentalization were synonymous (McEwin, 1997).

In one school that we visited, we observed a very dysfunctional team. During a team meeting, one teacher refused to sit with the group and instead sat at her desk, another appeared afraid to speak, one looked out of the window for most of the time, and one nearly

Theory into Practice 5–1

Questions for Middle School Teams

Here are some questions to consider when evaluating the effectiveness of middle school teams:

1. How has interdisciplinary teaming affected student behavior, self-concept, and achievement in our school? How do students perceive interdisciplinary teaming?
2. How has interdisciplinary teaming affected young adolescents' transition from elementary to high school?
3. How has teaming reduced the feeling of isolation among teachers and students and contributed to a positive school climate? Has the school climate improved?
4. Does the school administration support risk taking and work to secure increased time and resources for teamwork?
5. To what extent are teachers and staff members involved in and supportive of interdisciplinary teaming? Have efforts been made to help teachers–including those not specifically involved in teaming organizations–understand teaming's rationale?
6. Is there common planning time for members of each interdisciplinary team? Is planning time organized and used effectively (e.g., planning agendas; weekly, quarterly, semester, and annual goals)?
7. Do interdisciplinary teams have leaders? How are they selected?
8. How are teams functioning? Are they using time flexibly? Are they using appropriate grouping practices? Have they developed commonly shared organizational procedures (e.g., classroom management, student expectations, student evaluation)? Is there a collegial process base for determining team goals?
9. To what extent is content being integrated? Are teachers working to make connections in their content areas? Are thematic units being developed and implemented?
10. After being involved in interdisciplinary teaming, what do teachers perceive as the advantages and disadvantages? What changes need to be made?
11. How do parents and community members perceive interdisciplinary teaming?
12. How are library media specialists and other teachers in the related disciplines contributing to the interdisciplinary teams?

Based in part on: Clark, S.N., & Clark, D.C. (1997). Exploring the possibilities of interdisciplinary teaming. *Childhood Education, 73*(5), 267–271; and on Martin, K. M. (1999). Building and nurturing strong teams. *Middle School Journal, 30*(3), 15–20.

cried as she was saying that no one ever listened to her and everyone refused to consider her comments. This team had more obstacles than any we observed. We later learned that the principal decided to break up the team the next year.

Complacency and isolation are two obstacles to the success of ITO. Often teams become too complacent after reaching a high level of success. While achieving a difficult goal deserves a quiet period, it should not be stretched into a time of complacency when team leaders and members lose their energy and focus. Other teams isolate themselves, sometimes to the point that relationships rarely extend beyond core teachers. Instead, a team needs to relate to all people who touch the lives of the students on the team (Jones, 1997). All educators—core, exploratory, library media specialists, administrators, special needs, and gifted—need to be involved on the team and offer their contribution to young adolescents on the team.

Mature teams recognize these and other obstacles and plan appropriate responses to deal with them. The challenge is for all middle school educators to see the potential that interdisciplinary teaming holds and, through commitment and staff development, work toward making the concept a reality, thus improving both the lives and educational experiences of young adolescents.

Teachers' Roles in ITO

The willingness of teachers to commit to teaming as well as their knowledge of how efficient teams work will determine, to a large extent, the team's productivity and overall effectiveness. While specific roles may vary with schools and individual teams, several behaviors that most teachers on ITOs will want to adopt include:

- collaborating on teaching and learning;
- participating in group decision making;
- creating an interdisciplinary mind set and perspective;
- designing and implementing interdisciplinary educational programs;
- sharing responsibility for learning, guidance, advocacy, and student life;
- making effective use of time, space, staff, grouping arrangements, and student schedules;
- planning and implementing heterogeneous communities of learning;
- using flexible scheduling to maximize the school's effectiveness;
- cooperating with the library media specialist and other special-area teachers;
- planning and implementing developmentally responsive exploratory and advisory programs;
- selecting materials that contribute to interdisciplinary methods and approaches; and
- designing a system for contacting parents to keep them informed of the team's goals and plans.

Team leaders also have specific roles that contribute to and often determine the overall effectiveness of team efforts. In addition to functioning as a liaison between the team and the administration, the team leader also coordinates interdisciplinary activities between the various teams. In fact, in addition to the regular team meetings, team leaders should conduct periodic meetings among themselves to discuss items of interest to all teams. Team leaders should also be responsible for (or at least involved in) scheduling and conducting testing programs, preparing the team budgets and purchasing educational materials, scheduling and conducting team meetings, assisting in the selection of new team members, assisting in organizing community-service projects, coordinating reporting procedures and parent-teacher conferences, and facilitating communication among team members. Middle schools should also provide team leaders with some form of compensation—either monetary, one less class to teach, or fewer students. Being an effective team leader requires time, energy, and commitment, and team leaders deserve compensation.

Keeping Current with Technology 5–1

For more information on topics mentioned in this chapter, check out the following resources found via the Internet.

Louisiana Middle School Journal On-Line
http://www.tec.nsula.edu/LMSA/frjourna.htm

On-line journal of the Louisiana Middle School Association.

Reforming Middle Schools and School Systems
http://www.middleweb.com/Reformingschools.html

Information on middle school reform efforts in Long Beach, CA, Louisville, KY, and other U.S. cities.

Visit some middle schools to find information on middle school organization, teams, and interdisciplinary curriculum:

General Site: Yahoo! Education
http://dir.yahoo.com/Education/K_12/Schools/Middle_Schools/By_Region/U_S__States/

Click on a state name to visit middle schools on the Web.
Specific Schools:

Deep Creek Middle School, Chesapeake, VA
http://eclipse.cps.k12.va.us/public/Schools/DCMS/dcms.html

Holden Middle School, Holden, Missouri
http://oseda.missouri.edu/holden.k12.mo.us/HMSpage.html

Rye Neck Middle School, Mamoroneck, NY
http://www.ryeneck.k12.ny.us/MS/ms.html

Slauson Middle School in Ann Arbor, MI
http://aaps.k12.mi.us/~slauson2/index.html

South Middle School in Arlington Heights, IL
http://www.ahsd25.n-cook.k12.il.us/south.html

Talley Middle School, Wilmington, DE
http://www.k12.de.us/talley/default.htm

Unit 4 Schools, Champaign, IL
http://squire.cmi.k12.il.us/Champaign/buildings/buildings.html#mid

ORGANIZATION—INTERDISCIPLINARY METHODS

Interdisciplinary instructional methods are discussed in chapters 6 and 7; however, you need to realize that middle school organization does not exist in a vacuum. It affects and is affected by both the curriculum and the instructional methods. Visit some Web sites of the schools listed in Keeping Current with Technology 5–1 to see how these factors impact a school.

Interdisciplinary methods address three major dimensions. The academic dimension represents the basic content areas of mathematics, language arts, social studies, science, foreign language, health, physical education, unified arts, career, technology, home arts, and information retrieval. The social dimension includes the necessary opportunities for socialization, extracurricular activities, and interaction with peers, teachers, and adults in the school, home, and community. The personal dimension includes health, physical education, unified arts, career, and exploratory activities (Allen, Splittgerber, & Manning, 1993).

Through the use of a true middle school organization and interdisciplinary methods, middle schools can eliminate or lessen curricular boundaries, provide opportunities for collaboration among young adolescents and their teachers, allow teachers and library media specialists to correlate skills and concepts across disciplines, improve school environments and climates, and improve interpersonal and intracultural relationships. This combination of organization and methodology addresses problems and shortcomings that result from educators being preoccupied with only one or two specific subjects. Also, this approach provides the flexibility needed to young adolescents' diversity.

Organization—Multiage Teams and Looping

Before we leave our discussion of middle school organization, there are two additional concepts you should become familiar with. First, multiage, developmental, or nongraded teams consist of several teachers who share the same planning time and the same students. The difference is that the students are not from one grade level. Thus, a multiage team of 90 students would have 30 students from sixth grade, 30 from seventh grade, and 30 from eighth grade. Students would stay on the same team for each of the 3 years they were in middle school. While it would appear that these multiage teams could be organized by developmental stages of the students, the complexity and the multiple developmental characteristics of young adolescents make it difficult to place students. The alternative is to assign student to multiage teams on a random basis (Kommer, 1999).

A second organizational concept is looping. When a middle school is organized for looping, the teams of students and teachers remain together for more than one year (i.e., seventh-grade teachers follow their students and teach them again in eighth grade). Advantages of looping are that it promotes stability, facilitates advisor and advisee relationships, gives teachers a better understanding of their students, results in more effective classroom discipline, and allows teachers a quick reconnect with parents. A problem is that teachers must be prepared to teach at two or more grade levels on a rotating basis and must have extensive inservice training (Lincoln, 1997).

Closing Remarks

Deciding how most effectively to organize schools and classes to best meet the needs of students has been a major concern for decades. Middle school educators today acknowledge the deleterious effects of homogeneous grouping on students, recognize the advantages of planning and teaching on interdisciplinary teams, and recognize that block scheduling can provide flexibility by allowing longer or shorter times to teach and learn. However, we cannot say that the definitive word on school and class organization has been written. Middle school educators continue to experiment with grouping students, to pilot organizational patterns such as looping and multiage teams, and to improve the effectiveness of interdisciplinary teams. Undoubtedly, worthwhile debates over school and class organizations will continue as middle school educators persevere in their efforts to determine how to most effectively organize to meet young adolescents' diverse needs, abilities, and interests.

Suggested Readings

Erb, T. (1999). Team organization reconsidered. *Middle School Journal, 30*(3), 2. Explains that barely half of the middle-level schools in the United States even claim to engage in interdisciplinary teaming.

Gable, R. A., & Manning, M. L. (1999). Interdisciplinary teaming: Solution to instructing heterogeneous groups of students. *The Clearing House, 72*(3), 182–185. Provides a 10-step interdisciplinary problem-solving method to improve the effectiveness of heterogeneous grouping.

Gallagher, H. (1999). Teaching in the block. *Middle Ground, 2*(3), 10–15. Examines the successes and failures of middle schools that have switched to block schedules.

Hackman, D. G., & Valentine, J. W. (1998). Designing an effective middle level schedule. *Middle School Journal, 29*(5), 3–13. Discusses traditional departmentalized schedules, alternating-day block schedules, and flexible interdisciplinary block schedule.

Kain, D. (1999). We all fall down: Boundary relations for teams. *Middle School Journal, 30*(3), 3–9. Maintains that educators need to consider the relations between teams and other forces in the school.

Martin, K. M. (1999). Building and nurturing strong teams. *Middle School Journal, 30*(3), 15–20. Provides answers to questions such as why some teams function more effectively than others; what factors contribute to creating and nurturing strong teams; and what administrators can do.

Nolan, F. (1998). Ability grouping plus heterogeneous grouping: Win-win schedules. *Middle School Journal, 29*(5), 14–19. Describes a scheduling solution within block scheduling that allows for heterogeneous grouping (i.e., how math classes can be grouped by level and still maintain the spirit of a learning community).

Rottier, J. (1997). *Implementing and improving teaming: A handbook for middle level leaders.* Columbus, OH: National Middle School Association. Offers specific suggestions to guide administrators and/or team leaders in various team designs, scheduling possibilities, and roles of leaders.

Chapter 6

Managing Young Adolescents and Environments—Strategies and Techniques

Scenario—Westview Middle School Educators Tackle the School Environment

As Pete Bronowski, an eighth-grade teacher, was leaving Westview Middle School on a blustery Thursday, he noticed Lew Carson walking slowly to his car. To Pete, Mr. Carson's slumped shoulders and slow shuffle sent a message that something was wrong with the normally enthusiastic assistant principal. "Weather got you down?" Pete asked as he caught up with Lew. "Oh, it's more than the weather, Pete."

Lew replied. "Nothing's wrong with the family, is there?" Pete's voice showed his concern. "Oh, no," Lew said, "Marianne and the girls are fine." As Lew started to get in his car, Pete put his hand on the door. "Come on Lew," Pete said. "We've been friends long before you became an administrator. You can level with me. Something's really bothering you!"

"I guess you could say it's an accumulation of things, Pete. Increased discipline referrals, a loss of motivation by the staff, increased conflicts between teachers and students, fights and even brawls among students, and more downright meanness." Lew paused a moment before continuing. "We impose stricter rules, punish, bribe, and suspend—nothing seems to work! And it's only November. I hate to think what it will be like by the end of the year. I usually enjoy my job; but I'm an educator, not a police officer or a prison warden."

"Lew, you're not alone with those feelings," Pete said reassuringly. "There are quite a number of teachers who have been expressing the same concerns. In fact, a few of us even started our own support group. We call ourselves the Dunk and Debate Bunch and meet every Friday morning before school at the Do-Nut Delight."

"What do you talk about?" Lew asked.

"Oh, we have the usual gripes and complaints. But we're really working to put a positive spin on things. You know, trying to identify practical things that we can do to improve the climate of our own classrooms. Karen Smithson from the Dolphin team is working on her master's so she summarizes the stuff she's learning in her classes. The rest of us chip in from our experience or things we've read. Kate Andrews, the media specialist, has been great in sticking articles in our mailboxes whenever she comes across them. Since Kate's a regular in the group, we sometimes tell her things we want her to look for and she does an Internet search of ERIC for us. Most of our discussions have focused on school environment and classroom management procedures."

Lew nodded. "You folks are hitting at the heart of the problem. Now, if only you could come up with some solutions. I've been doing a lot of reading and thinking and keep coming back to a basic question. How can we create a caring environment at Westview where the emphasis is on teaching rather than on punishing and where everyone has a respect for everyone else?"

Pete laughed. "Lew, even though you're an administrator, you'd fit right in with our group. Why don't you come join us tomorrow morning? It's a lot warmer than this cold parking lot."

A smile came to Lew Carson's face. "That sounds like a great suggestion. What time should I be there?"

Overview

Like Lew Carson and the members of the Dunk and Debate Bunch, effective middle school educators realize that both the school environment and the teachers' choice of classroom management strategies can have a powerful effect on relationships between educators and students. Educators are looking for ways to create a positive environment in which students learn and teachers teach. But this is not always easy. Many factors influence the school and classroom climate. Some, such as the external communities we discussed in chapter 2, play an important role. Students come to school with a set of expectations for behavior that has been formed by their family, neighborhood, religious and ethnic culture, and their prior educational experiences. In middle schools, educators must not only deal with these external factors, but they must also work with 10- to 14-year-olds who are going through some of the most chaotic developmental years of their lives. What most middle school educators try to do is create a school environment that teaches both rights and responsibilities while it allows some individual freedom and flexibility.

In this chapter you will have an opportunity to look at the components of a positive school environment and to examine several theories of classroom management by educators such as Lee Canter and Marlene Canter, Rudolph Dreikurs, Haim Ginott, and Frederic Jones. What appears here is not an in-depth discussion of each theory. Therefore, you will find references to these and other theorists such as Fritz Redl and William Wattenberg, William Glasser, Thomas Gordon, and Richard Curwin and Allen Mendler.

As you read about these theories, keep the following in mind. As much as we believe in the importance of learning about these theories, we believe that these theories are only a beginning. Each middle school teacher needs to build his or her own personal model of classroom management–one that works for the individual and the young adolescents that he or she teaches. This means you should examine each theory and learn its basic principles so that you have a repertoire of ideas from which you can select those that best meet the needs of your students and your teaching environment.

Objectives

After reading and thinking about this chapter on managing young adolescents and environments, you should be able to:

1. define *positive middle school environment,* recognize the need for such an environment, state the reasons for maintaining such an environment, and list practices that can help make such an environment a reality;
2. discuss the ways in which respected middle school publications (e.g., *This We Believe* [National Middle School Association, 1995] and *Turning Points: Preparing American Youth for the 21st Century* [Carnegie Council on Adolescent Development, 1989]) urge middle-level educators and students to develop a sense of a healthy community that is composed of persons of differing ages, roles, and responsibilities;
3. explain the need for developmental responsiveness–a belief that the school environment and classroom management practices should reflect young adolescents' developmental characteristics;
4. summarize essential beliefs about effective middle school classroom management systems such as young adolescents' accepting responsibility for misbehaviors; teachers knowing classroom management models; and teachers teaching (and students learning) self-discipline;
5. discuss the theories of several classroom management experts such as the Canters, Dreikurs, Ginott, and Jones; and
6. explain why teachers need to construct their own personal models of classroom management based on strategies that actually work for individual teachers.

Understanding Positive Middle School Learning Environments

In chapter 2, you read about the environments or communities that affect the young adolescent and the conflicting influences that they often have on a 10- to 14-year-old. Although the school is part of the neighborhood community, you should not assume that it is a single entity. Rather, within the school itself are another set of communities as shown in Figure 6–1. More and more attention is being focused on the development of a positive learning environment throughout the school communities in an effort to provide a place in which 10- to 14-year-olds can feel a sense of belonging.

This emphasis on school environment has come about for several reasons. In part, it is the result of additional research into school environments and how they influence young adolescents and teachers. Our increasing knowledge of the early adolescence developmental period suggests that 10- to 14-year-olds need a positive atmosphere in which to learn and socialize. Also, there is a growing movement in schools to instill closer interpersonal

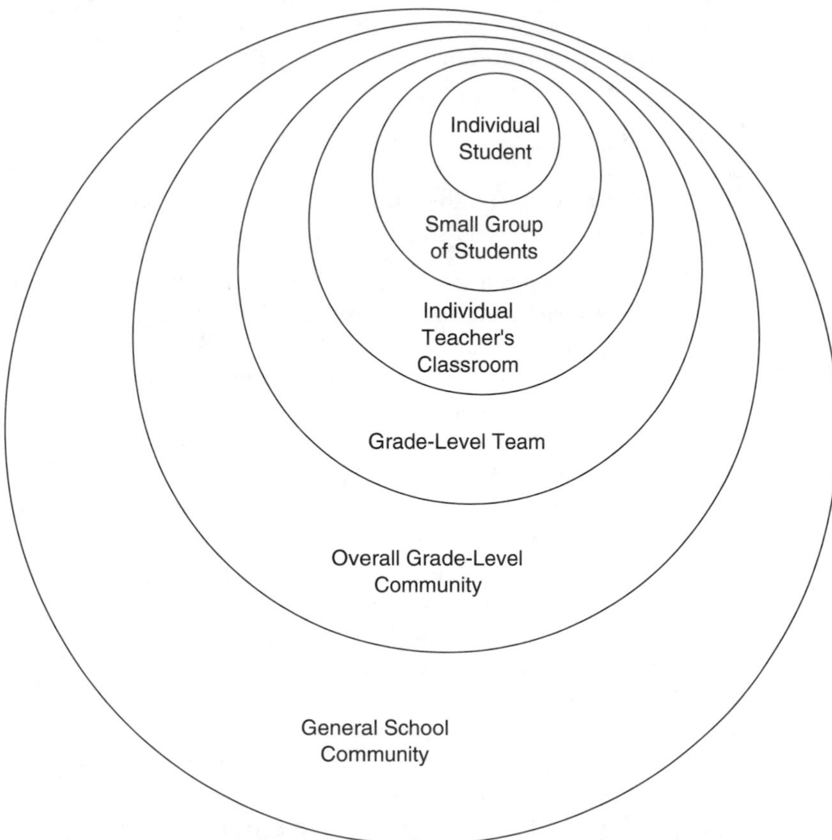

FIGURE 6–1 Communities within the Environment of a Middle School

relationships between learners and teachers as well as among learners themselves. It is important that this caring environment occur not only in the overall structure of the middle school, but also within each of the school communities. In particular, it should extend into the classroom environment where it can play a major role in the teacher's selection of classroom management strategies.

Several aspects of the middle school concept contribute to this caring culture. Advisor-advisee programs encourage young adolescents to become known and feel part of a small group, and they provide a place where educators and young adolescents work collaboratively to discuss problems and concerns. In exploratories, students examine areas of interest (such as community relationships), and educators and students can learn from each other. Interdisciplinary teams and teaming encourage small groups or clusters of teachers and young adolescents to work together toward agreed-upon and common goals. In learning teams and in individual classrooms, teachers use classroom management strategies that promote an atmosphere of trust and respect. While all of these factors together create the culture of an individual school, in this chapter we will first focus on the components of a positive school environment throughout its communities and then explore effective classroom management strategies.

The Call for Positive Middle School Environments

Pete Bronowski and Lew Carson in the opening scenario of this chapter are not the only educators who are concerned about the school environment. Several publications show the importance of positive school and classroom environments. The California State Department of Education (1987) called for every student to experience a positive school climate that reflects a strong student-centered educational philosophy. In each classroom, the teacher plays a major role in determining the extent to which the school demonstrates warmth, caring, and respect. Another publication (National Association of Secondary School Principals, 1985) suggested that the school environment should support excellence and achievement by providing "opportunities for students and teachers to socialize informally outside the classroom" (p. 3) and by creating "a caring, supportive atmosphere that tolerates and welcomes wide ranges of student diversity" (p. 3). Students' personalities and abilities unfold under the supervision of individuals who have the highest levels of caring and sensitivity (California State Department of Education, 1987).

Definition and Characteristics

Unfortunately, the somewhat elusive nature of the phrase "positive middle school environment" makes the term a little difficult to define. However, most people will be glad to describe what that environment is like. The following are a few phrases that we have heard teachers, staff, administrators, and students use.

A positive school environment:

- "encourages a sense of collaboration among students and educators."
- "emphasizes teamwork and trust."
- "has everyone committed to working toward common goals."

- "is centered around the learner." (student-centered)
- "is a safe place where you can feel free to say what you believe and know that other people will listen to you."
- "is a place where we all try to work together to make things better. Not just in our classroom but throughout the whole school."
- "encourages students to achieve."
- "is a place where other people respect what you say."
- "helps you teach more than academics. Students feel a commitment toward each other as well as toward the whole school."

The Need for Developmental Responsiveness

In a caring middle school, the environment and the management practices should be developmentally responsive. That means they reflect young adolescents' developmental characteristics. Table 6–1 identifies some common changes experienced by 10- to 14-year-olds and suggests some things that you can do to provide a positive school environment that can respond to those changes.

TABLE 6–1 *Young Adolescent Development and Positive School Environments*

Young Adolescents Experience:	Positive School/Classroom Environments Can Help Young Adolescents:
Changes in self-esteem	Feel better about themselves and their abilities to cope in middle schools. Have increased socialization.
Shifts in allegiances from parents and teacher to peers	Learn that allegiances do not have to be either/or situations. See that caring people want to care for, interact with, and support others. Develop personal attitudes toward other people and institutions.
Increased desire for friendships and social interaction	Examine the similarities between making friends and building a community. Make choices concerning their behavior toward individuals and groups. Determine characteristics and traits they want in friends.
Changes in reasoned moral and ethical choices about behavior	Realize the rightness and wrongness of events.
Engagement in social analysis and making judgments about people and institutions (Manning, 1994/1995; Manning, 1993b)	Analyze how and why people treat others in certain ways. Make choices concerning behavior toward individuals and groups.

Character education has become an important topic to middle school educators. According to Kohn (1997), character education can refer to anything, outside of academics, that schools can provide to help young adolescents grow into good people. In a more narrow sense, it can also indicate a style of moral training that reflects particular values as well as assumptions about the nature of children and how they learn (Kohn, 1997). Many educators think that a positive school environment has the potential for lessening conflicts between educators and students, reducing discipline referrals, and reducing confrontations between students. By eliminating the "students versus educator" mentality, students perceive the harmonious relationships in the school and are less inclined to engage in hostile and confrontational behaviors.

Diversity Perspectives 6–1 looks at how cultures should reflect caring in a world of differences.

A Sense of Community

For centuries, people have experienced the need for a "sense of community" and have realized the benefits of considering themselves a part of a genuine community. Figure 6–2 presents two definitions of community. Some educators believe that the development of a sense of community is an important part of creating a positive middle school environment. This involves the creation of a general community environment for the total school and the development of learning communities in the grades, teams, and individual classrooms. Recent scholarly writing (Graves, 1992; Sergiovanni, 1994a, 1994b; Westheimer & Kahne, 1993) has provided considerable insight into learning communities and their characteristics, purposes, and development.

Rationale for Communities

The call for the development of learning communities throughout the middle school has come from professional associations, foundations, and individual researchers. In *This We Believe,* the National Middle School Association (1995, p. 19) described a good middle

A community is:

"... a process marked by interaction and deliberation among individuals who share common interests and commitment to common goals" (Westheimer and Kahne 1993, p. 325).

"... an inherently cooperative, cohesive, and self-reflective group entity whose members work on a regular face-to-face basis toward common goals while respecting a variety of perspectives, values, and life styles" (Graves, 1992, p. 64).

FIGURE 6–2 Defining a Sense of Community

Diversity Perspectives 6–1

Caring Cultures in a World of Differences

Louise Derman-Sparks (1993/1994) called attention to the racism, sexism, classism, heterosexism, and ableism that continue to be deeply entrenched and pervasive in our society. Derman-Sparks gave numerous examples of how these "-isms" affect children's development of identity and attitudes. Undoubtedly, these ills of society will affect the school environment—it will be as difficult for young adolescents to develop a sense of community as it will be for middle school educators to build a positive school environment.

Louise Derman-Sparks suggested several goals for empowering children:

1. Nurture each child's construction of a knowledgeable, confident self-concept and group identity. Educators can create education conditions in which all children are able to like who they are without feeling superior to anyone.
2. Promote each child's comfortable, emphatic interaction with people from diverse backgrounds. Educators can guide children's development of the cognitive awareness, emotional disposition, and behavioral skills needed to respectfully and effectively learn about differences, and comfortably negotiate and adapt to differences.
3. Foster each child's critical thinking about bias. Educators can help children develop the cognitive skills to identify "unfair" and "untrue" images, comments, and behaviors directed at one's own and others' identities.
4. Cultivate each child's ability to stand up for her/himself and for others in the face of bias. Educators can help children learn and practice a variety of ways to act when another child acts in a biased manner toward her or him and/or when a child or adult acts in a biased manner.

Derman-Sparks also suggests that teachers need to know how to:

1. teach their own culture in relationship to society's history and current power realities
2. adapt their teaching style and curriculum content to their children's needs
3. engage in cultural conflict resolution with people from cultural backgrounds other than their own
4. be critical thinkers about bias in their practice
5. be activists—engaging people in dialogue about bias, intervening, working with others to create change.

How can Derman-Sparks' (1993/1994) theories affect middle school education? As they implement positive school environments, middle school educators can provide

- exploratory topics that focus on "-isms" such as racism and sexism
- advisory sessions that examine young adolescents' feelings about self and others such as self-esteems and cultural identities

Diversity Perspectives 6–1 (cont.)

- curricular experiences that integrate cognitive learnings as well as affective learnings such as studies of people and "feelings and attitudes" toward people
- concerted schoolwide efforts to examine feelings, positively and negatively, that affect the school environment
- experiential exercises in which middle school students gain a better understanding of self and others.

Source: Derman-Sparks, L. (1993/1994). Empowering children to create a caring culture in a world of differences. *Childhood Education 70,* 66–71.

school as "a healthy community composed of persons of differing ages, roles, and responsibilities." The Carnegie Council on Adolescent Development's (1989) *Turning Points: Preparing American Youth for the 21st Century* stated that:

> The student should, upon entering the middle grade school, join a small community in which people—students and adults alike—get to know each other well to create a climate for intellectual development. Students should feel that they are part of a community of shared educational purpose. (p. 37)

According to Canning (1993), members in a genuine community interact in a spirit of peace, feel comfortable expressing feelings, consider themselves accepted by other members, listen to others with empathy, support others unconditionally in a nonthreatening situation, and feel a sense of synergy that makes the community highly productive.

Unfortunately, this ideal of learning communities is often in direct contrast to the neighborhood, families, and general society in which many students live. With the increased divorce rates, single-parent homes, highly mobile society, and decline of the extended family support system, many students do not have a strong family, ethnic, or religious community within their lives. Within many large schools, students feel "lost" or anonymous, turning to the mass media to help them develop patterns of acceptable behavior. However, as Graves (1992) pointed out, television-viewing often promotes an individualistic perspective and features violent, nonrational solutions to problems. This carries over into some schools where, according to the U.S. Department of Justice, 3 million crimes (about 11% of all crimes) occur each year in public schools (Sautter, 1995). These are some reasons why everyone in a middle school needs to work together to create interdependent, cooperative communities where students and teachers can learn and work in a comfortable, safe, inspiring environment. As Sergiovanni (1994a) said, communities consist of individuals bonded together by natural will and a set of shared ideas and ideals.

Designing Positive Middle School Learning Environments

A goal of each middle school educator should be to create a positive caring environment consisting of a number of learning communities. In fact, many middle schools claim to be organized into learning communities and include the concept in their mission statements. One middle school may state that it is "a community organized around social relationships and interdependencies that nurture relationships and foster learning." Another might insist that it "promotes the empowerment of learners and educators by focusing on commitments, obligations, and duties that people feel toward each other and toward the school." But creating learning communities and a positive school environment takes time and effort.

Theory into Practice 6–1 contains a checklist that can be followed to plan an environment that is student-centered, collaborative, harmonious, and positive, or to evaluate the planning process. You can use this checklist to evaluate the efforts of one middle school in Case Study 6–1, which revisits Westview Middle School and looks at the efforts of one group of middle school educators to make sure a positive school environment became a reality.

Classroom Management in the Middle School

"Sit down, shut up, and get to work." We heard these commands as we walked by the door of an eighth-grade classroom. Brenda DeLuca, the eighth-grade teacher we were visiting, saw the look on our faces. "That's a lively class in there," she remarked. "But," we protested, "isn't that the same group of students we saw you teaching earlier this morning? You weren't yelling at them." Ms. DeLuca seemed to be struggling for words. Finally she said, "Ms. Meyers and I have different approaches to working with students. She disciplines; I try to manage a class."

The effort to develop a positive middle school environment filters down to the individual teacher and his or her classroom. The ideal is to create a climate where everyone works together and learns together. Easy as this may sound, classroom management is one of the most challenging parts of teaching. Family and community norms, the environment of the school, the physical room setting, the development of the individual adolescents in the class, group dynamics, the curriculum, and the instructional methods are a few of the factors that must be considered in implementing any discipline, or classroom management, system.

Particularly in the middle school, the classroom management or discipline system should be developmentally responsive. It should be based upon a solid understanding of the early adolescence developmental period and, more specifically, on how young adolescents think and behave (and reasons for their behavior), and on what works as well as what does not work. This is no small task, especially when you consider the tremendous diversity of the age group and the daily changes taking place in 10- to 14-year-olds. Young adolescents might demonstrate acceptable behavior one day and misbehave the next. They might be a behavior problem for one teacher and be perfectly well-behaved for another. While the assertive discipline model might work for some students and teachers, other teachers might be more successful with the democratic teaching model.

Theory into Practice 6–1

Checklist for Designing a Positive Middle School Environment

Yes	No	Characteristic
_____	_____	The school has a school environment committee consisting of educators who have a genuine commitment to improve the school environment and who will work collaboratively toward group goals.
_____	_____	This group communicates with other faculty members in the school. Other educators know the group's efforts, understand reasons for decisions, and feel they can offer opinions that will be thoughtfully considered.
_____	_____	At least one administrator, two or three parents, and perhaps one or two students are involved on the environment committee.
_____	_____	The environment committee has the assistance of other middle school educators who have firsthand experience with improving school environments, either from within the school system or from another school system.
_____	_____	There is a consensus among the committee members, other educators in the school, students, and parent representatives on the characteristics of an environment that meet students' and educators' needs in the particular school.
_____	_____	The group has identified specific efforts or programs that hold potential for achieving the characteristics of a positive environment.
_____	_____	The group has assessed present school practices and policies to determine changes that hold potential for making the school environment more positive.
_____	_____	The group realizes that a positive school environment is a continuing and evolving *process* that can be both frustrating and rewarding.
_____	_____	The group has lofty goals, but avoids too many major simultaneous organizational or instructional changes, so teachers will not be overwhelmed with too many changes at one time.
_____	_____	The group celebrates its accomplishments by taking time to reflect upon what has been achieved.

Developed from: Saddlemire, R., & Manning, M. L. (1999). Five solutions for a humane and respectful learning environment: A case study. *American Secondary Education, 27*(3), 47–52.

Case Study 6–1

Creating a Positive School Environment at Westview

Although they might not have realized it, when assistant principal Lew Carson joined the teachers in the Dunk and Debate Bunch, the educators at Westview Middle School were taking the first step toward developing a positive school environment with a commitment toward common interests and shared educational goals. As the informal group continued to meet, the phrases "caring" and "respecting others" kept appearing in their discussions. They also agreed that they wanted a classroom management system that "taught" rather than only "punished." But the problem was how to convey this attitude to the rest of the staff and the students.

Finally, the group asked Lew to present their ideas about the school environment to Bonita Banks, the school principal. It was a relief to everyone when Dr. Banks agreed to appoint a formal school committee that was quickly nicknamed "the environmental control board," or ECB for short. While this new committee included some members of the informal group, membership was expanded to include other teachers, administrators, staff, parents, and students from each grade level.

The ECB discussed scheduling, discipline procedures, teaching methods, school organization, guidance programs, and the overall culture of the school. Committee members reported to their constituents and asked for their advice and suggestions. Practicing teachers from other school systems, as well as administrators, and the superintendent were invited to meet with the group. The ECB members decided to assess the school's program to determine the existing practices that supported a positive school environment. In addition they asked for input from student organizations and individual students and held focus groups of parents.

As a result of their work, the committee made the following suggestions for improving the climate at Westview Middle School.

Discipline code. School rules should be simplified and made more positive. Fewer rules would be better than a longer, detailed list. Instead of being overly harsh and punitive, consequences should "teach."

Collaborative opportunities. "Positive school climate" should be a continuing topic for interdisciplinary teams to discuss. Goals of the interdisciplinary teams included knowing students as individuals, improving interpersonal relationships between educators and learners, and developing more positive teaching-learning environments.

Exploratories. Exploratory topics should emphasize collaboration, caring, and getting along with others.

Teacher advisory. Teacher advisories should be structured so that each student is known well by at least one significant adult. Advisory groups should promote students' social, emotional, and moral growth while providing

Case Study 6–1 (cont.)

personal and academic guidance. Teacher-advisory programs should provide times for students to share concerns and feelings and opportunities to meet in small groups where advisors know learners as individuals on a regular and face-to-face basis.

The ECB members understood that designing a positive school environment was more a process than a product–it would be an ongoing effort, one that would be continually refined. Therefore, they requested that the ECB become an ongoing committee at Westview with members chosen by each of the constituent groups: faculty, staff, parents, administration, and students.

Working with 10- to 14-year-olds in a classroom can be a challenge. In our university classes, our preservice teachers often tell us that their friends who are not middle school education majors often ask them: "Why do you want to teach in the middle school? Those kids are so obnoxious and poorly behaved. How can you hope to teach them anything?" While we agree that some young adolescents are difficult to work with, many are not—they are cooperative, respectful of authority, and models of good behavior. The challenge is for middle school teachers to understand individual young adolescents and to have classroom management plans ready to deal firmly and swiftly with behavior problems.

What, specifically do middle school educators want to achieve in their classrooms? According to C. M. Charles (1999) teachers are searching for a management system that prevents most misbehaviors; redirects misbehavior positively; promotes trusting relationships between teachers and students; engenders parental support and assistance; and is efficient, fair, and easy to use. Ideally, this management system would exist within a caring school environment that would foster learning and positive interpersonal relationships. Figure 6–3 shows how two middle schools have attempted to create a set of "community standards" for their schools.

There should be a balance between the needs of young adolescents and the demands of the school's curriculum. As Mack, a seventh grader, put it: "I know there have to be rules and that there are things I need to learn. But I need to have some space to do things my way or at least some options. I'm not some robot. I'm me!" Listening to Mack and other 10- to 14-year-olds, we believe that efforts to instill a positive classroom environment can be placed in two categories, as seen in Table 6–2. But remember, these two are not mutually exclusive.

Understanding Young Adolescents' Misbehaviors

What misbehaviors might young adolescents demonstrate, and what might be the underlying reasons for their misbehaviors? How can educators convince young adolescents to accept responsibility for their behaviors? Speaking of all levels of students rather than just young

Many schools have taken the work of classroom and behavior management theorists and developed a code of conduct for students. As you read about the theories in this chapter, refer to the management policies shown here and see if you can identify the management theories behind the guidelines.

Harriet Tubman Middle School, Portland, OR

Schoolwide Behavior Expectations:

The purpose of the schoolwide behavior expectations at Harriet Tubman Middle School is to provide a safe, positive, and orderly environment conducive to academic, social, and character development for our students. To accomplish this goal, students are expected to:

- Show respect for themselves, others, and all property
- Be responsible for their behavior
- Cooperate with others
- Put forth their best effort
- Solve conflicts and problems in a constructive manner
- Be actively involved and committed to their learning
- Be on time
- Bring all needed materials
- Attend school everyday
- Remain on school grounds at all times.

Source: Harriet Tubman Middle School. *Tubman Discipline Plan* at: http://www.tubman.pps.k12.or.us

Frank H. Harrison Middle School, Yarmouth, ME

Discipline Policy:

Like any community, we need to have guidelines about how we will work together, what we will be expected to do, and how we will treat each other. . . . We all will

- Respect the rights and property of others.
- Use common sense, good judgment, and self-discipline in our interactions with others.
- Apply ourselves, to the best of our abilities, to do the very best we can in school.
- Be a positive school citizen.
- Accept responsibility for our behavior and actions.

It is expected that the students and staff will treat each other with dignity and respect. . . .

Source: Frank H. Harrison Middle School. *Student/Parent Handbook* at: http://www.yarmouth.k12.me.us/YMS/handbook.htm

FIGURE 6–3 Student Conduct in Middle Schools

TABLE 6–2 *Young Adolescents and Management Procedures*

Young Adolescents	Management Procedures
Middle school educators should:	Middle school educators should:
Ensure a positive, caring, and humane school environment.	Make good use of the time in the school day.
Consider students' physical, psychosocial, and cognitive development to provide developmentally responsive educational experiences.	Consider classroom organization to allow opportunities for adequate socialization and collaborative learning.
Maximize student involvement in behavior and learning and in the decision-making processes of both.	Explain rules of student behaviors, model the procedures, and allow time before enforcing the rules.
	Communicate expectations for use of classroom materials and supplies.

adolescents, C. M. Charles (1999) reported five types of misbehaviors: aggression, immorality, defiance of authority, class disruptions, and goofing off. Teachers often dread dealing with aggression, immorality, and defiance, but, fortunately, these are not too prevalent. While these misbehaviors make the newspapers and the evening news, teachers most often deal with less serious offenses such as goofing off and talking. Although these may seem to be innocuous behaviors, they waste instructional time, interfere with learning, and challenge teachers to come up with strategies and techniques to control them (Charles, 1999).

Based upon Charles' beliefs and our own experiences in classrooms, we feel that, in most middle schools, the most significant problem is what Charles (1999) called goofing off. Students sit idly; they might talk to friends; they just do not do their work.

Consider this incident between Ms. Taylor and Patrick, an eighth grader. Ms. Taylor had finished the lesson and assigned written work; her plan was to meet with students in small groups. While most of the students enthusiastically started their assignment, Patrick sat quietly and did nothing. Ms. Taylor sat down beside Patrick, again explained the assignment, opened his book, put the pencil in his hand, and straightened his paper. As she walked away, Patrick put the pencil down and closed the book. There were no blatant or aggressive misbehaviors—Patrick just goofed off and did not do the assignment. After class, Ms. Taylor had an individual conference with Patrick about the work not being done. His only response was: "I just didn't feel like doing it."

Any number of reasons might cause students to goof off and fail to complete assignments. These range from lack of motivation and fatigue to serious physical or mental problems. Remember, 10- to 14-year-olds are very diverse. Each situation requires an individual decision based on the specific circumstances followed by appropriate actions. Although goofing off can pose quite a problem, in Patrick's case, Ms. Taylor could have taken several different approaches to dealing with it. She could have continually encouraged Patrick to complete the assignment, praised even minor efforts, varied her instructional strategies, given him smaller "chunks" of work so he would not feel overwhelmed, discussed the situation with his parents, sought assistance from the guidance counselor, and/or determined whether Patrick had any particular interests around which she could plan some activities.

Understanding Selected Classroom Management Theorists

Before we examine the theories of several classroom management experts, we need to share our beliefs with you. Call it, if you will, a disclaimer of our own personal prejudices.

Belief 1—We believe young adolescents should accept responsibility for their misbehaviors. There might be many reasons for the misbehaviors, but, still we believe that young adolescents should accept responsibility for their misbehaviors and accept responsibility for changing to appropriate behaviors. The teacher has the responsibility to help the student understand her or his behavior and to help the student change. Still, the ultimate responsibility rests with the young adolescent to demonstrate acceptable behavior at school, at home, and in the community.

Belief 2—We believe preservice and inservice educators should know the classroom management theories of experts. But we also feel that each teacher must determine what works for her or him and eventually develop a personal theory of classroom management. While some middle schools have developed whole-school approaches (e.g., Canter and Canter), each teacher should have the professional freedom (and obligation) to decide classroom management procedures that work for her or him.

Belief 3—We believe middle school educators should teach self-discipline. Classroom management systems should focus on teaching young adolescents "expected behaviors" and "how to achieve those behaviors." Constant punishment (or the fear of it) might serve as a temporary fix, but long-term changes in behaviors will only result when young adolescents learn acceptable behaviors and are convinced that their responsibility to the school, peers, and themselves requires acting in socially acceptable ways.

Belief 4—We believe that effective instruction is a key component in classroom management. Eight of the best students in seventh grade were assigned to Mr. Lovett, a first-year teacher, for an advanced math class. But Mr. Lovett did not know his subject and did not know how to teach. His lessons were poorly planned, and he complained of the difficulty he had "staying a few pages ahead" of the students in the textbook. In the face of inept instruction, these normally well-behaved students became, for that single class, some of the worst behavior problems in the school. What started as a result of boredom became a daily challenge to find a new way to torment Mr. Lovett. Fortunately, the seventh-grade team leader learned of the problem. When Mr. Lovett was replaced by another mathematics teacher, the students' behavior returned to normal. In chapter 9 of this book, you will learn about effective instructional strategies that might have helped Mr. Lovett. These work best when teamed with effective classroom management practices.

Because of our belief in the importance of effective instruction as part of classroom management, we support the work of Nancy Martin (1997). She maintained that many schools across the nation encourage student-focused instructional methods while they simultaneously adopt packaged approaches to classroom management, even though these approaches might not be designed to support student-centered instruction. In response to this dilemma, Martin offered several ideas about student-centered classroom management. For example, she advised teachers to "forget classroom management theory. If it works, do it" (p. 6). Also, she suggested using an eclectic philosophy in which the teacher applies a combination of models and classroom management techniques. Martin also reinforced the idea of creating a "learning environment" within the classroom. Changes in curriculum and instruction techniques must be linked to classroom management theory and models to create a student-centered environment. Educators need to build comprehensive student-focused classroom communities that develop independent, self-disciplined, and lifelong learners (Martin, 1997).

Finally, we believe that a good classroom manager needs to heed Tom Erb's (1997) assertion:

> In a world where kindergartners are treated like adult felons, and teenagers sometimes act like them, teachers and administrators have to resist the urge to make "controlling students" the foundation of classroom management. Acknowledging and validating student needs can result in a humane way to create orderly environments that provide structure and set limits. Listening to young people, rather than labeling them, is the place to start to recognize their needs. (p. 2)

With these beliefs and Erb's (1997) assertion clearly stated, we want to identify some major principles of several respected classroom management theorists, and then encourage you to develop a personal classroom management system. Table 6–3 provides an overview of selected theorists (listed alphabetically rather than any order of preference).

TABLE 6–3 *Models of Classroom Management*

Theorist	Principal Concepts
Lee Canter and Marlene Canter (1976, 1992)	Assertively taking charge Student and teacher rights in the class Consequences
Rudolf Dreikurs and P. Cassel (1972)	Teaching responsible behavior Democratic teaching Goals of belonging Mistaken goals Influence techniques
Haim Ginott (1971)	Congruent communication Sane messages Inviting cooperation Correcting by directing
Frederic Jones (1979, 1989)	Body language Efficient help Genuine incentives

Developed from: Charles, C. M. (1996). *Building classroom discipline* (5th ed.). White Plains, NY: Longman. p. 4.

Lee Canter and Marlene Canter

As Table 6–3 shows, Lee Canter and Marlene Canter (1976, 1992) as reported in Charles (1999), focus their attention on assertively taking charge to be sure that an orderly learning environment exists for both students and teachers. Students have the right to know the teacher's behavioral expectations, the right to receive specific instruction concerning how to behave, the right to positive recognition and support, and the right to have limits set on their behavior. Teacher rights include the right to establish an optimal learning environment that is consistent with the teacher's strengths and limitations, the right to expect behavior from students that contributes to optimal growth, and the right to backing from both administrators and parents.

The Canters offer teachers several suggestions such as identifying expectations clearly, setting specific limits, being persistent in stating expectations and feelings, maintaining eye contact, using nonverbal messages to support verbal statements, interacting with students concerning good and bad behavior, and following through on established consequences rather than threats. In all efforts to correct behavior, the Canters suggest an assertive style. They describe nonassertive responses such as "I have asked you so many times to stop that!" or "Will you two girls please stop talking!" Instead, an assertive response would be "It is against the rules to talk without permission during the lesson. This is a warning" (Charles, 1999).

What does the Canters' work say to middle school educators? First, young adolescents need to have limits set on their behavior—they need to know specific rules about talking without permission, walking around in the classroom, and handling conflict. Rather than students wondering "what to do" or "how much they can say," teachers should always be sure young adolescents know behavioral expectations. Second, middle school teachers should recognize and provide for young adolescents' need for socialization—the need to make friends, interact in meaningful ways with both students and adults, and engage in collaborative work. Third, middle school teachers often find young adolescents to be argumentative—some object to adult authority and some just like to argue (or that's the way it seems!). One example we have found is the "last worder," or the girl or boy who always wants to make the final statement in an argument. The solution of course, is to allow the student to have the last word, but still, the consequences of his or her behavior stay in force. The teacher does not have to have the last word, but he or she does have to assertively enforce the rule. Therefore, teachers should set limits, clearly explain behavior expectations, and strictly enforce expectations.

Rudolf Dreikurs

As shown in Table 6–3, Rudolf Dreikurs is a proponent of democratic teaching. We particularly like two aspects of Dreikurs' work: his types of teachers and his mistaken goals of misbehaviors.

In Dreikurs (1968) and Dreikurs and Cassel (1972), Rudolf Dreikurs proposed that teachers fall into three basic groups (Charles, 1999):

Autocratic: Those who boss, use a sharp voice, command, exercise power, demand cooperation, impose ideas and dominate.

Permissive: Those who put few if any limits on student behavior, nor do they invoke logical consequences when misbehavior disrupts the class.

Democratic: Those who demonstrate leadership, friendliness, inviting nature, stimulation, cooperation, guidance, encouragement, acknowledgment, and helpfulness.

Most teachers fall into one of these categories. But which type makes the most effective middle school teacher? We, of course, would say the *democratic* teacher. Such a teacher will respect young adolescents and understand their developmental needs. Democratic teachers are not "pushovers;" instead, they enforce clearly stated limits in a positive and caring manner. They promote cooperation, act friendly, and acknowledge students' interests and needs, without losing the professional relationship that should always separate teachers and students.

Considering the nature of young adolescents, the *permissive* teacher might experience behavior problems as young adolescents perceive a lack of limits set upon their behavior. Young adolescents might perceive this teacher as weak and unable to manage students on a daily basis. The result in all likelihood will be loss of teacher control, lack of respect for the teacher's authority, and outright pandemonium.

Last, the *autocratic* teacher fails to allow young adolescents to refine their decision-making skills (all decisions are made for them!). Students might feel resentful because the teacher commands, demands cooperation, and dominates the classroom. He or she fails to recognize young adolescents' individuality and diversity. Likewise, young adolescents are given few, if any, opportunities to exercise their developing judgment and increasing decision-making skills about appropriate and inappropriate behaviors.

Rudolf Dreikurs (1968) is also well-known for his proposal of mistaken goals of misbehavior. He proposed that all misbehaviors resulted from one (or a combination) of four goals: attention-getting, power-seeking, revenge, and inadequacy. These four can be defined as (Charles, 1999):

Attention-getting: Feeling neglected, the student feels she or he is not receiving attention needed for recognition and acknowledgment. Therefore, she or he misbehaves (such as disrupting, asking irrelevant questions, and asking for special favors) to get the teacher's attention.

Power-seeking: The student defies the teacher to get the recognition he or she wants. In essence, the student seeks power over the teacher by arguing, contradicting, lying, and behaving hostilely. The student does not have to "win" the battle; just provoking the conflict with the teacher (and thus interrupting the teaching-learning process) is sufficient for the student to feel the power he or she needs.

Revenge: The student has failed to gain status through attention or power, so now he or she will seek revenge. "I have been hurt," the student might say. Therefore, I will hurt." He or she will deliberately misbehave as revenge against the teacher.

Inadequacy: Sometimes students, especially young adolescents, feel inadequate to deal with situations, and thus feel compelled to misbehave to make up for and hide the inadequacy. "Leave me alone—I do not do school work—I will just sit here. It doesn't bother me to fail—I always have." Or perhaps, they know they cannot succeed with the school work and thus misbehave to "save face" with the other students.

What are some implications for Dreikurs' work on mistaken goals for middle school educators? It is imperative that middle school teachers understand both Dreikurs' four mistaken goals *and* understand the early adolescence developmental period. Educators need to remember that 10- to 14-year-olds might feel inadequate due to declining self-esteems or because of the increased difficulty of the middle school curricular content. Some students might consider it necessary to misbehave to maintain their self-image, especially those who excelled in the elementary school. Perceptive teachers need to address young adolescents' self-esteems and help them understand their many strengths. Young adolescents also engage in Dreikurs' other mistaken goals. Some middle school classes are large, and some middle school teachers are impersonal. Therefore, a few young adolescents might consider misbehaving in order to earn their teachers' attention. They might also engage in power-seeking and revenge to ward off their feelings of anonymity. Although they are older, they still lack control over situations. Thus, they seek power over situations that they previously would have taken for granted.

Haim Ginott

Haim Ginott (1971), as you can see in Table 6–3, proposes congruent communication that addresses the student's situation rather than the student's character and personality. For example, Ginott's principle concepts and teachings include using the present tense, understanding teachers at their best (and their worst), using sane messages, inviting cooperation, demonstrating acceptance and acknowledgment, and considering classroom management as a series of little victories. Ginott has a comprehensive classroom management system that would take too long to explain here. Therefore, we want to look primarily at three aspects: teachers at their best and worst, sane messages, and inviting cooperation. Then, as in the past, we will look at how middle school educators can take advantage of Ginott's principle concepts.

Teachers at their best use congruent communication in which they address situations rather than students' characters, confer dignity upon students, use brevity in correcting behavior, accept and acknowledge students' feelings, and express anger appropriately. Conversely, teachers at their worst name call, label students as slow and unmotivated, ask rhetorical questions, invade students' privacy, make sarcastic remarks, deny students' feelings, lose their tempers and self-control, and attack students' character (Charles, 1999).

Effective classroom managers use sane teacher messages. C. M. Charles gave the following examples of sane and insane messages of addressing the problem of two students talking during study time. An example of an insane message is "Stop that talking. You two are not only breaking rules, you are being very rude. You evidently have no consideration for others who are trying to work" (p. 66). Rather than destroying student self-concepts and personal relationships, the teacher should have used a sane message such as "This is quiet time. It needs to be absolutely quiet" (p. 66).

Ginott also encourages teachers to learn methods of inviting cooperation from students rather than demanding it. Teachers who do not encourage cooperation usually resort to demanding it by ordering, bossing, and commanding. Ginott urges teachers to avoid direct commands, which have the potential for provoking student resistance. Also, teachers should avoid long, drawn-out directions and explanations. Instead, he thinks teachers should describe the situation and allow students to decide what their course of action should be. For example, rather than giving step-by-step directions, teachers can say, "It is math time. The assignment is on page 60" (p. 67). With this kind of message, teachers show that they respect students' ability to behave autonomously. They invite cooperation, promote self-direction, and foster responsibility, all of which help students learn to function on their own (Charles, 1999).

What do Ginott's suggestions have to say to middle school educators? First, it is essential for young adolescents to develop a healthy self-esteem—hurtful comments can damage young adolescents' self-esteem. Therefore, middle school teachers should use only positive comments and classroom management practices that correct students' behavior problems. They should not lose their tempers or insult students' character. Second, middle school educators should model appropriate behavior and show by example how they want students to behave. Students will see how teachers model "sane messages" and, more specifically, how to demonstrate acceptable behavior and to handle conflicts in a harmonious manner. Third, middle school teachers need to encourage young adolescents to help set the standards of behavior and the actual classroom rules. Students who share in the decision-making process will be more likely to obey the rules. In general, middle school educators need to invite cooperation—this includes asking for students' cooperation, encouraging positive behavior without coercion, treating students in a way teachers want to be treated, and doing whatever possible to promote a positive school environment. Finally, middle school teachers need to remember Ginott's opinion that classroom discipline is attained gradually as a series of small victories in which the teacher, by using self-discipline and helpfulness, promotes humaneness and cooperation within students (Charles, 1999).

Frederic Jones

Frederic Jones (1979, 1987) provided some interesting thoughts about discipline problems that most of our preservice middle school teachers believe to be valid. For example, he concluded that approximately 99% of student misbehavior in most classrooms consists of talking without permission and generally goofing off, such as daydreaming, making noise, and being out of one's seat. In fact, teachers in typical classrooms lose 50% of their teaching time because students are off-task or otherwise disrupting learning (Charles, 1999). As Table 6–3 shows, Jones believes positive classroom discipline results from teachers using appropriate body language, providing incentive systems, and offering efficient help.

Frederic Jones (1979, 1987) offered two "firsts" for teachers to consider. He was the first person to place major emphasis on the importance of nonverbal communication or what he called body language. Also, he was the first to emphasize the importance of providing efficient help to students during independent activities or during other learning activities when students feel frustrated. Last, while not the first theorist to offer the suggestion, he also suggested that teachers provide genuine incentives for students to demonstrate appropriate behavior.

Body language refers to teachers' posture and movement such as teachers' facial expressions, gestures, eye contact, and physical proximity. For example, rather than making negative verbal comments that might actually escalate problems, teachers can address students' misbehaviors by walking toward the students and standing near them. Also, teachers should "carry themselves" in such a way that suggests strong leadership (i.e., teachers should hold themselves erect and move assertively). Frederic Jones thinks a drooping posture and lethargic movements suggest resignation or fearfulness—signs that students can quickly read. Teachers' facial expressions such as enthusiasm, seriousness, enjoyment, and appreciation tend to encourage positive behavior (Charles, 1999).

When teachers help students during times of frustration, they provide efficient help. For example, students often feel frustrated during group or individual work. With large classes and the teachers' limited amount of time, the key is for teachers to provide efficient help, such as the following:

1. Organize the classroom seating so that students are within easy reach of the teacher.
2. Use graphic reminders such as models or charts that provide clear examples and instructions.
3. Learn how to reduce to the bare minimum the time used for individual help (Charles, 1999).

Frederic Jones (1979, 1987) also believes genuine incentive systems can improve students' behavior. The key here is what Jones calls "genuine." For example, instead of teachers saying, "Let's all work in such a way that we will later be proud of what we do" (Charles, 1999, p. 113), teachers should make the request more genuine to the students, such as "If you complete your work on time, you can have five minutes of free time to talk with your friends" (Charles, 1999, p. 113). The latter statement will be more of an incentive for students. Other genuine incentives that Jones suggests include art, viewing a video, and having free time to pursue personal interests.

Middle school educators can take advantage of Jones' theories as they physically move toward young adolescents who begin talking or who begin to get off task. Just knowing that the teacher is aware of their talking or off-task behaviors might be sufficient to get some 10- to 14-year-olds back on task. Also, since many middle school teachers have large classes, they should give special attention to classroom organization. Students should always realize the teacher knows their progress and can respond promptly when they need assistance. Last, as we suggested in chapter 2, young adolescents are increasingly social beings and like to spend time with and talk to friends. Teachers who want to provide incentives that young adolescents consider genuine can provide time for students to socialize. Such an incentive system works—we observed a teacher who had high expectations for both student work and behavior. As many as two or three times a week, students knew the last 10 minutes of class time would be "free time," if they gave their best for the first 45 minutes. The teacher provided an incentive that they could understand and appreciate.

Other Respected Classroom Management Experts

Table 6–3 shows only selected classroom management theorists. There are a number of other respected models that readers might want to study. These include (but are not limited to) Fritz Redl's and William Wattenberg's group dynamics, William Glasser's discipline without coercion, Thomas Gordon's developing self-control, and Richard Curwin's and

Allen Mendler's dignity and hope—all discussed in C. M. Charles' *Building Classroom Discipline* (1999), listed in the Suggested Readings.

Developing a Personal Theory of Classroom Management

While we have professional respect for the classroom management theorists, we believe that most middle school teachers benefit when they thoughtfully consider the various classroom management models and, then, build their own personal theory of classroom management. You can find additional information to help you by visiting some of the Web sites listed in Keeping Current with Technology 6–1.

What should middle school educators consider when building a classroom management system that works for young adolescents? The classroom management system should:

1. reflect young adolescent development. It should show an understanding of young adolescents' physical development (i.e., the inability of some to sit for long periods of time); psychosocial development (i.e., the increasing need for socialization, which includes communicating with friends); and their cognitive development (i.e., the ability to think, consider their behavior, as well as understand reasons for demonstrating appropriate behavior).
2. reflect the teacher's beliefs of how classroom management should work (i.e., teach self-discipline rather than a series of punishments that might have little long-term consequences).
3. be workable and efficient. The classroom management system should not take an inordinate amount of time to administer and should contribute to and enhance learning experiences rather than take away from them.
4. be equitable. Students should not think it singles out selected students or misbehaviors. In other words, young adolescents, who are developing a strong sense of justice and fairness, should think the teacher has a "fair" system.
5. work in teacher advisories and exploratory programs as well as in regular instructional situations. In the more informal advisories and exploratory programs, young adolescents will be allowed (and encouraged) to talk more and move around the classroom. There might be action-based projects that require more noise than might be permitted in regular classroom settings. The classroom management system should take into account these differences and should continue to be workable, efficient, and equitable.
6. be professionally rewarding. Some middle school teachers might not view any classroom management system as rewarding; they might view it only as a necessity to be endured. We encourage teachers to build a system that makes a difference in their lives as well as young adolescents' lives, promotes a positive school environment, enhances interpersonal relationships between teachers and students, and teaches students self-discipline.
7. reflect the belief that building a personal model of classroom management evolves over time. We believe an attitude such as "I now have a model that works and I will never have to change" is a sure-fire way to failure since students and behavior situations constantly change.

Keeping Current with Technology 6–1

Look at the school environment statements found on the Web sites of the following middle schools:

Beck Middle School, Cherry Hill, N.J.
http://beck.cherryhill.k12.nj.us/mission.htm

Burbank Middle School, Boulder, CO–Neighborhood Program
http://bvsd.k12.co.us/schools/burbank/neighbor/neighbor_prog.html

Chaparral Middle School, Diamond Bar, CA
http://www.chaparral.wvusd.org/

William Annin Middle School, Basking Ridge, NJ
http://www.bernardsboe.com/wams/

For more information on the classroom management theories mentioned in this chapter, visit the following Internet sites:

Canter & Jones Models
http://www.humboldt.edu/~tha1/canter.html

Information on Canter's theory

Rudolf Dreikurs
http://www.alfredadler.edu/

The Alfred Adler Graduate School was founded by Rudolf Dreikurs.
http://www.redirectingbehavior.com

The International Network for Children and Families follows Dreikurs' principal concepts. Their Web site contains articles and advice for parents and teachers.

http://www.noogenesis.com/malama/discouragement/
mistaken_goals.html

Dreikurs mistaken goals are discussed.

Haim Ginott
http://www.onenet.net/~errw1/Ge_1.htm

The Great Expectations Teaching Model is based on Ginott's "teacher attitude and responsibility."

General information on school environment and classroom management can be found at these sites:

Classroom Management Resources.
http://www.nwrel.org/sky/Office/Teacher/Classroom_Related/Classroom_Management.html

Keeping Current with Technology 6–1 (cont.)

The Northwest Regional Educational Laboratory presents these resources.

Scottish Consultative Council on the Curriculum
http://www.sccc.ac.uk/docs/telclimate.htm

The Council presents its statement on the rights and responsibilities of the teacher to develop a positive classroom environment.

Behavioral Psychology
http://www.behavior.net

This is "the WWW gathering place for mental health professionals and applied behavioral scientists."

Closing Remarks

The classroom environment and classroom management strategies can have powerful effects on academic achievement, socialization, and interpersonal relationships between educators and students. Teachers' knowledge of the content and their ability to teach are undoubtedly essential; however, the classroom environment and management strategies will play major roles in determining their overall success and effectiveness.

We feel that middle school teachers who want to instill a positive classroom environment and classroom management practices should seriously consider Erb's (1997) belief that educators should acknowledge and validate student needs. Regardless of the classroom management model you select or the personal model you develop, you must also consider young adolescents' developmental needs. Developmental responsiveness is the key—only then will the environment and classroom management acknowledge and validate student needs.

Suggested Readings

Charles, C. M. (1999). *Building classroom discipline* (6th ed.). White Plains, NY: Longman. Examines the major classroom management theorists with examples of implementation.

Erb, T. (1997). Student-friendly classrooms in a not very child-friendly world. *Middle School Journal, 28*(4), 2. Suggests that acknowledging and validating student needs can result in an orderly and humane learning environment.

Managing student-friendly learning environments. *Middle School Journal, 28*(4). Theme issue—focuses on classroom management, secure environments, character development, and team approaches.

Manning, M. L. (1997, Fall). Building a middle school community. *Focus on the Middle School, 10,* 4–6. Offers suggestions for middle school educators wanting ideas for implementation.

Payne, M. J., Conroy, S., & Racine, L. (1998). Creating positive school climates. *Middle School Journal, 30*(2), 65–67. Provides keys to maintaining and promoting positive school climates, particularly high staff morale.

Sergiovanni, T. J. (1994). *Building community in schools.* San Francisco: Jossey-Bass. Includes topics such as teachers changing their theory of schooling, relationships in communities, emerging school communities, school curriculum, and school communities.

Part III

Planning, Implementing, and Assessing Instruction

As the title implies, chapter 7 gives you a look at planning considerations and the need to always consider young adolescents' development. Then, in chapter 8, the focus shifts to implementing effective instruction in middle schools through the use of strategies such as heterogeneous grouping; individual and group activities; collaboration; and selecting instructional methods and strategies.

Both practicing educators and teacher education students should find chapter 9 helpful since it describes actual proven teaching behaviors that should be used.

In chapter 10, you can read about assessment and evaluation. As one of our teacher education students said, "Controversial and often confusing—this is an area that troubles many teachers." You will be able to examine traditional and contemporary evaluative methods and read about the need for authentic assessments.

In these four chapters, you will be exploring the challenges faced by middle school educators on a day-to-day basis as they plan and provide direct instructional experiences to young adolescents and evaluate them.

Chapter 7

Planning Instruction—Appropriate and Interdisciplinary

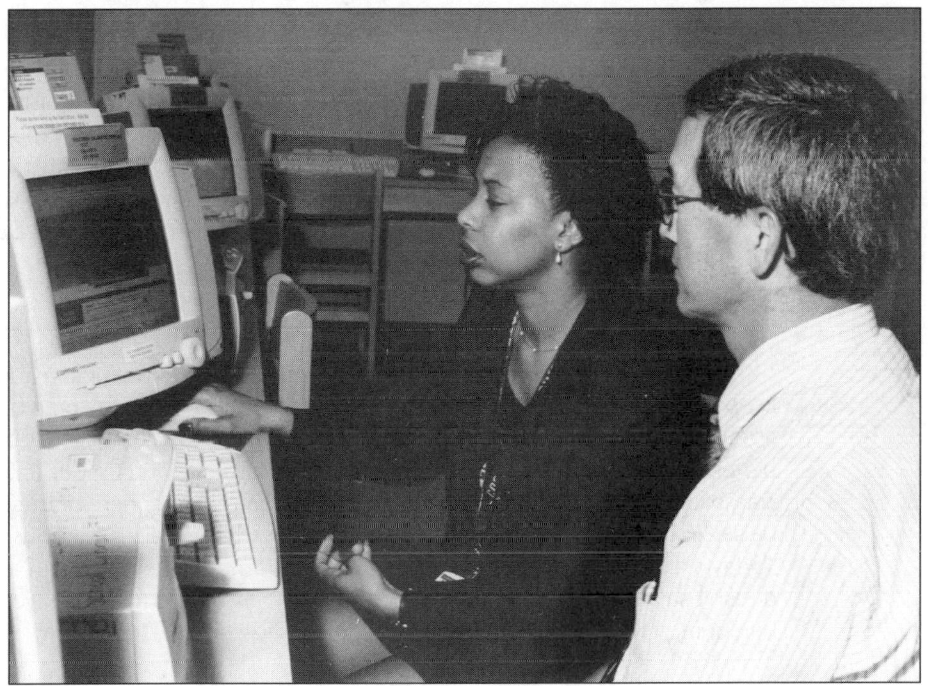

Scenario—Karyn Rothmer's Journal

Dear Diary, August 23

Gee, I haven't written those words since junior high school. I'm writing now because of this staff development project I'm in. It may seem strange, but Dr. Manningly, our consultant, suggested that we keep a journal or diary about the process we'll be going through this year at Washington Peaks Middle School. He told us just to pretend we're writing a letter to a friend.

I've been a teacher at WP, as we refer to it, for 6 years now. Five of them have been on the seventh-grade Osprey Team. Although we've been organized into interdisciplinary teams, we've never really done any interdisciplinary instruction (IDI). Now, there's a push for us to integrate our instruction and the school district hired Dr. M. to help us out. When I first started teaching, I was frustrated because nobody at WP was doing the kind of teaching that I had learned about in college. But now that I've been a successful language arts teacher for 6 years, I'm not sure I want to change. After all, I have all my lesson plans and I've worked hard to develop some really neat units. I've even involved the students in planning and evaluation. They seem to enjoy what we do and they score well on all the tests. I guess I don't see any need to change what we have. After all, "if it ain't broke, don't fix it" is my motto. Oh well, I'll at least listen to what Dr. M. says about IDI.

Dear Diary, August 25

This interdisciplinary teaching will not work! It would take a saint to try to teach with Deborah St. Johns. She might have been teaching science for 15 years, but she has no idea about what goes on in language arts. Furthermore, she's not about to learn!!!! Saying that she has to teach to the National Science Education Content Standards and that the rest of us could build something out of those if we wanted to was not a way to win friends. I may have to sit in these meetings, but I don't have to let Deborah dictate what I teach!!!!!!

Dear Diary, August 30

Now I understand what my students mean when they complain about having to keep a journal every day. With getting ready for the students to come back to school and attending these IDI meetings, I haven't been very faithful. Things are looking a little better. It seems we all have been very defensive about giving up our autonomy in the classroom. Dr. M. has been helping us build a team atmosphere of trust and respect and he's also trying to tie these new IDI concepts to what we already know about teaching. Today, Auggie Anderson spoke out for the first time. He teaches math and usually doesn't say much in team meetings. But today was different. Maybe we really are beginning to build that trust Dr. M. keeps mentioning.

Dear Diary, September 8

Today was my day to shadow a sixth-grade student. That meant I followed her from the time she came to school until she went home and observed what she did. I can see what Dr. M. means when he said our students need to see connections. Verlene has so much she has to remember that it's no wonder she seemed lost at times. She's got to remember a different assigned seat in each class and even a different way to put the heading on the paper for each teacher. I also saw lots of curriculum ties that could have been made but weren't. For example, I wanted to tell Mr. Gilbertson about some good novels that would tie into his social studies unit and Ms. Abi that she should consider combining her journal-writing activities with the journal the students were keeping in science. But I remembered that I was just to be a shadow, not a participant, and I kept quiet. Verlene was great and even liked the little thank-you present I gave her.

Overview

In chapters 3 and 4 of this book, you read about the curriculum of the middle school, while, in chapters 5 and 6, you read about organization and management. Now that you have an understanding of the structures of the school, you are ready to turn your attention to planning and implementing instruction. Entire books have been written about these topics, and our intent is not to try to cover them in depth in two chapters. Rather, we assume that you have had or will take a general course on teaching methodology or perhaps a "methods and materials" class related to a specific discipline.

In this chapter, we want you to look first at the reasons for planning instruction and then at the factors that affect planning in middle schools, including the developmental needs of young adolescents, curriculum standards and textbooks, as well as the characteristics of individual teachers. Then we will turn your attention to interdisciplinary instruction. While we discussed interdisciplinary team organization (ITO) in chapter 5 as an organizational feature of middle schools, in this chapter we want you to look at the interdisciplinary instruction (IDI) that is sometimes done by those teams. As Karyn Rothmer pointed out in this chapter's opening scenario, serving as a member of an interdisciplinary team does not necessarily mean engaging in interdisciplinary instruction. However, we hope to show you the benefits of IDI for both young adolescents and teachers.

Objectives

After reading and thinking about this chapter on planning interdisciplinary instruction in middle schools, you should be able to:

1. explain the importance of instructional planning;
2. identify the developmental characteristics of young adolescents that should be considered when planning instruction;
3. explain the role that curriculum guides, and state and national mandates, textbooks, and individual teachers play in instructional planning;
4. define *interdisciplinary teams* and explain their importance to interdisciplinary instruction;
5. discuss some of the problems of interdisciplinary teams that may impact on their ability to plan interdisciplinary instruction;
6. explain the relationships that exist among interdisciplinary team members and other educators throughout the school;
7. discuss the general process of instructional planning and the instructional pyramid of team involvement;
8. discuss the things to keep in mind during instructional planning; and
9. discuss planning for students at risk of failure.

Rationale for Detailed and Methodical Planning

A middle school teacher is responsible for designing authentic classroom instruction that allows students to construct knowledge, engage in disciplined inquiry, and gain knowledge they can use outside of school (Newmann, Wehlage, & Secada, 1995). This instruction must allow young adolescents to explain, explore, analyze, reflect, and apply learning (Beane, 1995; Zorfass & Copel, 1995, 1998). In addition, there must be opportunities for classroom learning to extend into advisory programs, exploratories, and student-community service projects (Ames & West, 1999). In order for these things to occur, instruction must be planned. It does not "just happen."

Planning provides continuity of instruction and efficient use of time. As one teacher told us, "planning eliminates the dead time in my classroom that becomes dread time. There's nothing worse in a class of seventh graders than having 15 minutes left and nothing to do." In addition to maintaining a realistic flow of instruction, planning also helps educators keep in mind the needs of their students, including their developmental needs, learning styles, ability levels (especially in reading), special learning needs, and cognitive skills. It also helps educators adhere to local, state, and national curricular guidelines and standards. On a more practical level, when teachers plan, they are able to identify and schedule resources such as library materials, computer labs, or additional help from other teachers and specialists. They can also identify possible links across disciplines.

One teacher we talked to had an interesting concept of planning. "My plan is my professional portrait. We have to turn in our plans each week so I use mine to show our assistant principal for instruction the things that happen in my classroom. Then, during parent-teacher conferences, I can show the parents what we've tried to accomplish and what I hope we can do for the rest of the term. I even let the students see the outline of my plans. They call it our road map because it lets all of us see what we've done and know where we're going."

Factors Affecting Middle School Instructional Planning

Young Adolescent Development, Needs, and Interests

All teachers engage in instructional planning. In the middle school, a primary difference is that the individual needs and the intelligences of each learner should be the basis of planning, teaching, and assessment (Reiff, 1997). While you read about the developmental characteristics of 10- to 14-year-olds in chapter 2, let us review a few things you must keep in mind in your quest to provide developmentally responsive instruction.

Young adolescents are diverse. As they begin to develop their individual identities, they may question their physical changes, challenge adult authority, and try to establish their own place in the communities in which they live. Cognitively, most arrive at the middle school as concrete thinkers and gradually gain the ability to engage in more abstract operations. Many become efficient problem solvers with the ability to analyze and evaluate information.

Turning Points (Carnegie Council on Adolescent Development, 1989) found no evidence that 10- to 14-year-olds can not "engage in critical and higher order thinking" (p. 42). Making connections between their prior knowledge and the new things that they are learning, young adolescents are developing their own learning strategies. Moving away from egocentrism, they also begin to accept the views of others and to evaluate their own views.

While teachers are often concerned with cognitive development when planning instruction, you must also keep in mind physical and psychosocial development. Physically, 10- to 14-year-olds want to move and be active. Psychosocially, they enjoy collaboration and cooperation. As one teacher said, "they really like to walk and talk." That is why small groups, collaborative learning projects, and peer tutors are frequently used instructional techniques.

All of these developmental changes are happening at the same time that young adolescents are going to a new school, meeting new friends, and adjusting to an entire team of new teachers instead of one familiar classroom teacher. Educators expect them to organize their lives at the same time that the only life they have ever known is vanishing or falling apart.

How do these characteristics relate to instructional planning? As Wood and Jones (1997) point out, while planning you must keep in mind the affective needs of middle school students for "freedom of choice, appropriate peer interactions, instructional diversity, personal expression, and a broadened perspective" (p. 292). You need to create a positive climate throughout the communities within the school. It is especially important that young adolescents have a sense of belonging and that they feel emotionally secure. Therefore, you need to design instruction so that students can be challenged yet feel successful in what they do. You should even involve the students in decision making, but it is your responsibility to provide structure and guidelines for the instructional process.

You should also help young adolescents feel free to take risks when investigating problems because they know that you and other adults in the school are there to help them, not ridicule them. They need a place where they can make mistakes and not be crushed by them; a place where risk is accepted, and it is okay to ask questions. As we heard one middle school language arts teacher say at the beginning of a book discussion: "It's fine to disagree with me as long as you can support your answers with information or passages from the novel we're discussing. Don't worry about trying to come up with the 'right answers,' I want your ideas."

District Curriculum Guides, and State and National Mandates

We have talked about the developmental needs of young adolescents, and these should become the basis for planning developmentally responsive instructional experiences. However, these developmental needs are not the only forces that affect instruction. As you read in chapter 3 of this book, there are national standards and guidelines that identify topics and concepts that should be taught for each of the core curriculum subjects as well as the related domains. Some states also have very specific curriculum documents such as the Standards of Learning developed by the Virginia State Department of Education. In the case of Virginia, not only are these documents provided to guide instruction throughout the state, students are tested on their knowledge of the designated content, and the results are to be used to determine the accreditation of the individual school.

In addition to the national and state curriculum guidelines and standards, individual school districts may develop their own curricula. While these may reinforce the state or national mandates, they may call for additional instruction in a number of areas. To make things even more complicated, school districts vary on the leeway that they give individual teachers in teaching the curricular content. We know of one school district in which the district social studies coordinator dictates the page in the district's social studies curriculum guide that each teacher should be on each week. This makes it difficult for the middle school social studies teachers to plan interdisciplinary instruction or to provide developmentally responsive instruction. When educators feel pressured to be at a certain place in the textbook or curriculum guide at a particular time, students can have too much material to learn. It is much better when teachers teach a developmentally responsive amount of material that reflects young adolescents' interests, motivation, and ability levels.

Textbooks

Why worry about planning? Why not just use the teacher's guide? Some of the worst experiences we have had in middle school classrooms have been the result of a teacher not planning ahead and trying blindly to follow a teacher's guide without making the necessary adjustments for his or her students and the school's curriculum. Teachers who "plan" by sticking strictly to the teacher's guide are usually not providing developmentally responsive instruction nor are they willing to make the modifications and adjustments required by interdisciplinary instruction. Problems also arise when the text does not match the state or local curriculum.

Individual Teachers

Individual teachers can influence middle school instructional planning. Depending on the background and professional training of a middle school teacher, he or she can be more interested in a discipline-specific approach to instruction than in integrated instruction or in teaching to the developmental needs of young adolescents. There are also teachers who fail to use the instructional resources of the total school and community and rely, instead, on only the resources in their individual classrooms. These teachers and their students miss the benefits that school library media specialists and other resource teachers can provide. Then too, there are some educators who do not use newer technologies such as computers or videodiscs because they are "just new gadgets." "I've been teaching for 10 years and never used a computer or the school library," remarked one social studies teacher. He thought he was boasting, while we could only think about the rich experiences that the young adolescents in his classroom were missing.

Thankfully, for each of the negative teachers, there are many other excellent middle school teachers who put the idea of developmentally responsive education for young adolescents first in their minds when planning instruction. These are the educators who take advantage of staff development opportunities and are willing to risk trying new techniques of instruction and assessment. They are willing to change and modify their instruction based on the learning styles of their students and feel comfortable working within the interdisciplinary team organization pattern of a middle school. Receptive to new ideas, they are ready to meet the challenges and rewards of working with 10- to 14-year-olds. We hope you will become this type of middle school teacher.

Interdisciplinary Team Organization and Interdisciplinary Instruction

As you read in chapter 5, the organization of teachers into interdisciplinary teams is integral to the middle school concept and is the most common type of middle school organization (McEwin, Dickinson, & Jenkins, 1996). Usually each team consists of one teacher from each of the core curriculum disciplines including language arts, science, math, and social studies. Erb (1997) has documented the influence of interdisciplinary teaming on both student and teachers. Easing the students' transition into middle schools, teams reduce the feelings of isolation, and they help create a more positive school climate that, in turn, fosters learning.

Students ultimately benefit from interdisciplinary teaming. Just the fact that students are on teams where teachers share common planning time increases the satisfaction that those students have toward school and towards doing class work (Warren & Muth, 1995). Felner et al. (1997) found that students in schools where interdisciplinary teaming is used have higher self-esteem, are less aggressive, and worry less than students in schools with other organizational patterns. Their teachers also use more interactive, hands-on instructional strategies. In many cases, successful interdisciplinary teams have changed how teachers teach and have increased students achievement in math, reading, and language arts as measured on state standardized tests (Felner et al., 1997).

Teams are very important to effective interdisciplinary instruction. When middle school educators use IDI (sometimes called interdisciplinary teaching, multidisciplinary instruction, interdisciplinary thematic instruction, or integrated instruction), two or more teachers on a team collaborate to plan, teach, and assess a group of students. In doing so, they use a number of instructional strategies and a variety of student-grouping patterns including large group, small group, and directed studies (Clark & Clark, 1987). These cooperating team members must maintain their relationships with other members of the team and must also develop successful relationships with teachers in the related domains of art, music, physical education, and library media/information skills to provide developmentally responsive educational experiences for the students on their teams. When a number of disciplines are integrated in a single interdisciplinary instructional unit, students can make connections across subjects (Clark & Clark, 1994).

But merely having a team organization does not guarantee that interdisciplinary instruction will take place. What is important is what is done within the team structure and because of it. Frequently, teams play only an incidental role in instruction while individual teachers make all of the decisions on their specific disciplines. Yet, as Erb (1999) and others have pointed out, one hint that teams are functioning is that they plan together and coordinate their teaching through the use of thematic units or similar instructional strategies.

Why are some interdisciplinary teams successful while others fail? There are many reasons, but one primary reason is that great teams do not just happen. They take time to develop and occur only when team members are prepared to invest both time and effort in their relationships and in building the team (Dickinson & Erb, 1997; Rottier, 1997). All of the team members must see the others as valuable contributors who will share the workload and the responsibilities of the team (Martin, 1999). While diversity is welcome, professional, philosophical, and personal diversity on a team can create stress as well as strengths (Martin, 1999) and can cause dysfunctional teams where personal preferences are at odds with team preferences (Schamber, 1999).

Even when individual teams function well, there can be problems. As Kain (1999) points out, each team has its own boundaries, but its members must frequently cross those boundaries to find resources and interact with others outside the team while individuals from outside the team must cross the boundaries into the team. Thus, while a team needs to be trained to work together, the members also need to be trained to develop good external relationships with others in the school (Kain, 1999) in a climate of mutual trust and respect.

On a school level, strong instructional teams may detract from the sense of community in the school and may alienate other teachers (Kain, 1999; Kruse, 1997). Problems also arise because everyone in a school belongs to a number of groups that may have conflicting goals. For example, a social studies teacher might belong to her sixth-grade Sharks interdisciplinary team, to the overall sixth-grade teachers group, to the group of all social studies teachers in the middle school, and to the whole middle school faculty. In one school, teachers meet with their grade level or house on Monday, with their instructional team on Tuesday, and with their discipline/curriculum area on Wednesday (Doughty, 1999).

Figure 7–1 shows some of the relationships between two teams on one grade level in a middle school. Remember, as you look at this drawing, that similar relationships exist among other teams in each grade and throughout the school. Notice that we have included the related domains in this figure. While the teachers in the related domains are not core members of the grade-level instructional teams, we believe that those teachers have a great deal to contribute to the instruction of young adolescents. Too many times we have seen those teachers left out of the instructional loop, and too many times we have heard those teachers explain how they could have helped with an instructional unit if they had only known about it.

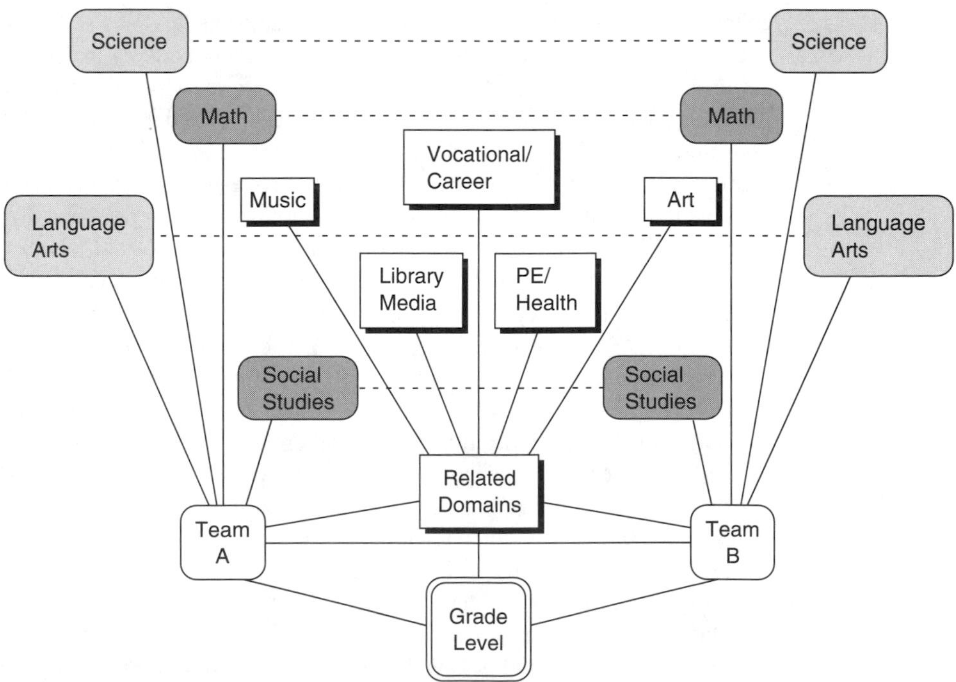

FIGURE 7–1 Instructional Relationships between Two Teams and the Related Domains

Without careful coordination and open communication, these groups can place conflicting pressures on individual team members. The key is to use all of the resources of the school and community to develop relationships that will improve the educational experiences for young adolescents.

Even when team members seem to be working well together and the team possesses most of the characteristics of an effective team, when they try to plan and implement IDI, problems can arise. Some teachers find that it is difficult to give up their autonomy. Isolated in their own classrooms, they were free to make their own plans and implement their own instructional practices. IDI asks teachers to give up some of that independence for the openness and vulnerability of cooperation and IDI. Many teachers, such as Deborah St. Johns in this chapter's opening scenario, find it difficult to do that.

Teacher attitudes toward IDI are very important and influence the effectiveness of the team (Schroth, Dunbar, Vaughan, & Seaborg, 1994). As one eighth-grade language arts teacher noted, "I like to cooperate, but not all the time. There are things in my curriculum that I need to emphasize. But that doesn't mean I don't support the team and the interdisciplinary teaching. And, even when I teach independently, I'm meeting with my team on a lot of things other than instruction."

Interdisciplinary Instructional Planning

Interdisciplinary instruction is one of a number of instructional methods for middle school teachers, but not the only one. Indeed, not even the most successful teams engage in IDI all the time. But the rewards of IDI are great, especially for young adolescents. With IDI, students can become involved in their learning, think globally, and can dissolve discipline lines (Brazee, 1995). They can become independent, confident students, "learn how to learn," and develop lifelong learning skills (Manning, 1993b). In fact, many people believe that IDI is one of the important characteristics that separate middle schools and junior high schools (Hough & St. Clair, 1995).

The development of young adolescents prepares them for IDI. Their cognitive development allows them to see relationships among content areas and understand principles that cross curricular lines. Their psychosocial development gives them the ability to understand people and to look at situations from various viewpoints. Successful curriculum integration and interdisciplinary instruction allow young adolescents to see wholeness rather than fragmentation. They can also confront questions and engage in experiences that are personally meaningful to them (Manning, 1993b). It is interesting to note that, while the problem-solving skills of all students can benefit from IDI, students who are at the formal operational stage of intellectual development may benefit the most (Hough & St. Clair, 1995).

Planning Instruction—An Overview

Before we examine the components of IDI in detail, we want to take a general look at the instructional planning process. As you read earlier in this chapter, effective instruction needs to be planned. Educators use factors such as curriculum mandates and national standards to determine what should be covered in a year in a specific grade. This amount is then broken down into units of study that may vary in length and depth and that consist of a series of lessons that

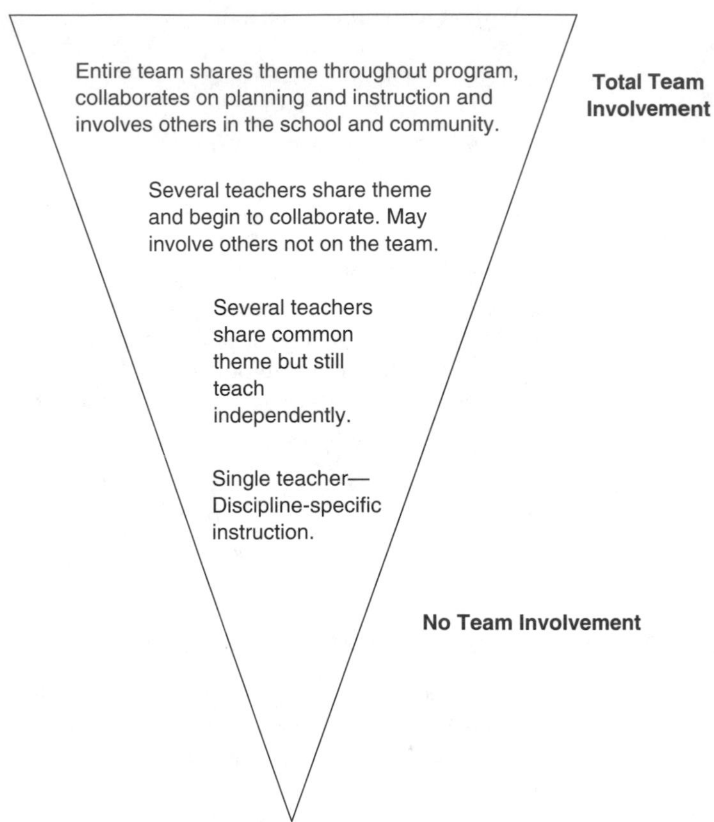

Entire team shares theme throughout program, collaborates on planning and instruction and involves others in the school and community.
Total Team Involvement
Several teachers share theme and begin to collaborate. May involve others not on the team.
Several teachers share common theme but still teach independently.
Single teacher— Discipline-specific instruction.
No Team Involvement

FIGURE 7–2 Team Involvement in Interdisciplinary Instruction

are based on the same topic or theme. Finally, each unit is divided into weekly and/or daily plans. Variations on this basic process are used by both individual teachers and interdisciplinary teams when planning instruction.

Figure 7–2 shows an instructional pyramid of team involvement in IDI. Remember, no team will function at the same level all of the time. Each teacher on a team may teach some units independently while pairs or even the entire team may combine for other units of instruction. The extent and frequency of interdisciplinary instruction will depend on the individual team.

Remaining Flexible When Planning

IDI planning begins with flexibility. Although we have worked with a number of teams, each team has established its own way of developing an IDI unit of study. Generally, however, the team must decide on the scope of the unit to be taught or an indication of the topic(s) that will be included and how much of each. Sometimes the team begins with a theme or several themes and then looks for ways to thread that theme throughout several disciplines. At other times, one teacher may present an idea for a unit, and the other teachers may look for relationships and build upon that. The process of writing, discussing, and revising instructional plans as a team strengthens the interdisciplinary instruction (Martin, 1995).

TABLE 7–1 ***Outline for Instructional Plan***

Checklist for Interdisciplinary Units
Have we:
Identified the topic or themes of the units?
Determined our instructional goals?
Determined the prior learning of our students?
Identified the skills we hope to reinforce?
Determined the new skills?
Written specific student behavioral objectives?
Checked to be sure our objectives are developmentally responsive?
Identified resources that we need for the unit?
Located sources for those resources and notified appropriate individuals?
Identified the instructional personnel who need to be involved?
Involved those instructional personnel in our planning?
Identified specific instructional responsibilities?
Determined developmentally responsive instructional methods?
Identified developmentally responsive activities that match our student objectives?
Identified possible student groupings?
Developed a sequence of activities?
Determined our desirable outcomes based on our objectives and activities?
Selected appropriate methods to assess student learning?
Planned for all educators involved in the unit to assess its success after it is over?

There are a number of planning guides that teachers use in designing instruction. Whichever guide you decide to use, be sure that it includes the items in Table 7–1.

No matter how the team arrives at its final plan, it is important that the team members agree upon when the final plans for the IDI unit will be presented to the students. Premature announcements by one teacher can result in frustrations and can undermine the cohesion of the team (Schamber, 1999). This "grandstanding" may make one teacher look good, but it can destroy a team.

Involving Young Adolescents in Planning

One effective way to motivate students is to involve them in planning instruction (Smith & Johnson, 1993). *Turning Points* (Carnegie Council on Adolescent Development, 1989) notes that young adolescents need to learn to make informed decisions. What better place is there for them to make these decisions than in the classroom? Here students can make decisions about many instructional practices. They can help determine the composition of small groups, set size limits on groups, determine and enforce class working rules, determine some of the guidelines for the content of class projects and some of the evaluation criteria, identify resources to use, and help set a schedule for assignments (Carroll & Taylor, 1998).

Keeping Current with Technology 7–1

For more information about IDI in general, visit:

Interdisciplinary Team Instruction (ITI) on the Web
http://www.ael.org/rel/iti/

Interdisciplinary Middle Years Multimedia Project, Manitoba, Canada
http://www.edu.gov.mb.ca/metks4/tech/currtech/imym/ovrview.html

Planning an Integrated Unit by Monroe 2-Orleans BOCES, New York State
http://www.monroe2boces.org/shared/instruct/interdisc/plan.htm

Tips for Beginners Interdisciplinary Instruction by Evelyn Alford, East Baton Rouge Parish Schools, LA
http://www.tec.nsula.edu/LMSA/tipsfor.htm

Using an Integrated and Interdisciplinary Approach
http://www.tiac.net/users/dfleming/resource/using.html

For IDI units and lesson plans, visit:

ART education network–art and ecology curriculum integration
http://artsednet.getty.edu/ArtsEdNet/Resources/Ecology/Curric/index.html

AskERIC Lesson Plan Collection
http://ericir.syr.edu/Virtual/Lessons/

The Collaborative Lesson Archive
http://faldo.atmos.uiuc.edu/CLA

East Grand Rapids Middle School, Grand Rapids, MI
http://www.remc8.k12.mi.us/eastgr/sixthgradeidu.html

Everitt Middle School, Wheat Ridge, CO
http://204.98.1.2/area_teams/team2/colodest.htm

Galveston Bay Curriculum for Middle School Students, TX
http://www.rice.edu/armadillo/Texas/galveston.html

The Gateway–Internet lesson plans, curriculum units, and other education resources
http://www.thegateway.org/

Immaculate Conception School, Ithaca, NY
http://www.clarityconnect.com/webpages3/immac/rainfrst.htm

Roosevelt Middle School, River Forest, IL
http://www.math.uic.edu/district90/roosevelt.html

School Library Media Activities monthly integrated lesson plans
http://ericir.syr.edu/Virtual/Lessons/SLMAM/index.html

Stark County, OH
http://www.stark.k12.oh.us:/Docs/units/

Keeping Current with Technology 7–1 (cont.)

Vital Power with VitaLinks.
http://chesterfield.k12.va.us/Admin/Instructional_Technology/Special_Projects/Vitalinks/

WebQuests made by the students in the Interdisciplinary Teaching with Technologies class at San Diego State University
http://edweb.sdsu.edu/courses/edtec596/ProjectsS98.html

West Greene School District, Green County, Waynesburg, PA
http://www.greenepa.net/~wgsd/Egypt.html

Selecting Topics and/or Themes

While IDI units can be based on a topic, they can also be developed around one or more themes. While a topic approach is usually subject-centered and may come directly from a curriculum guide of a single discipline (i.e., weather, the Great Depression, or creative writing), a theme may be either subject-centered or interdisciplinary. In contrast to topics, themes tend to be more dynamic and convey an underlying meaning or identify a problem. Teachers often select themes to reflect the interests of young adolescents.

One way to motivate students to learn is to make the learning interesting and relevant to their needs, interests, concerns, and experiences (Hootstein, 1994). Remember, we all learn more easily and enthusiastically when we are interested in the subject or enjoy the activity. Thus, some teams involve young adolescents in the selection of topics and themes that relate their concerns. A few of the popular topics and themes that we have discovered are "You Are What You Eat," "Surviving against the Odds," "The Face of AIDS" (Strobach, 1999), and "From Capture to Freedom: Slavery in America" (Doren, 1999).

Keeping Current with Technology 7–1 points you toward sources of additional information about IDI in general as well as to sources that have practical examples of specific IDI units that you can examine and evaluate. When you visit these sites, look for examples of team arrangements, and lesson plans, and compare these to traditional ones.

Determining Goals and Objectives

Usually an IDI unit has global goals for the entire unit as well as student-centered learning objectives. Clearly defined goals and objectives are essential to the success of IDI (Davis, 1992). While these objectives can describe the behaviors or learning outcomes that the students should exhibit by the end of the unit, some teachers find it helpful to identify the specific objectives for each week or day of instruction. These objectives should include each of the three instructional domains (cognitive or intellectual; affective or psychosocial; and psychomotor or physical) and should be developmentally responsive for young adolescents. The goals and objectives then become the basis for the criterion-referenced measurement, which we will describe in chapter 10. All middle schools can learn from high-performing middle schools that have high expectations for all of their students, not just the academically gifted (Ames & West, 1999).

Tying the Interdisciplinary Unit Together

There are a number of ways to tie an IDI together. Some educators suggest using language arts as a thread that can move across the disciplines (Smith & Johnson, 1993; Weber & Ingvarsson, 1996; Wood & Jones, 1996). Others begin with a focus on math (Hopkins, 1993; Mosca & Shmurak, 1995), science (Scarnati, 1994), social studies (Coate & White, 1996), or a combination of two of the disciplines (Lombard, 1994; Peltz, Powers, & Wycoff, 1994). Remember, IDI can occur at various levels on the interdisciplinary pyramid and can involve two or more teachers on the team. For example, the description of a science fair project can become an English writing assignment or a social studies report. Even math and English can be integrated when students are encouraged to use expressive writing techniques to write a letter to a younger student and explain how to solve a complex math problem (Weber & Ingvarsson, 1996). Theory into Practice 7–1 looks at IDI that was planned around a question of interest to students: Did their backpacks weigh too much?

Planning Instructional Strategies for Young Adolescents

> "Memorize, memorize, memorize. All Casy does is memorize lists of things. First the capitols, now the elements. I thought middle schools were supposed to be different. But that's the same kind of thing I did in junior high school." The parent of an eighth-grade student.

As we preach to our students, *memorize* is not a synonym for *understand.* Middle school teachers should build upon the natural curiosity of young adolescents and their exploratory nature and should try to integrate real-life experiences into their instruction (Beane, 1993a; Lounsbury, 1991; Wood & Jones, 1996). Developmentally responsive instruction includes learning how to learn, to think, and to cooperate (Irvin, 1995). In fact, collaborative learning projects and hands-on activities address many of the needs of 10- to 14-year-olds (Wood & Jones, 1997). That is why many middle school classrooms are student- or group-centered and project-oriented (Kellough & Kellough, 1999). In addition to improving social skills, cooperative learning activities help young adolescents develop higher-level thinking skills (Janssen-O'Leary, 1994).

While IDI asks teachers on a team to share common curricular goals, the instructional methods that they use to reach those goals do not have to be identical (Martin, 1999). What is important is that the instruction is planned so that students make connections across the disciplines. The holistic approach found in IDI helps students, especially those who are at risk of failure. This is true, in part, because the IDI unit examines a theme from a variety of viewpoints (Knight & Wadsworth, 1994).

Allowing for Individual Differences

When planning instruction, you must take into consideration the developmental and cultural differences of your students. Some of these differences will be the result of the diversity of adolescent development. In chapter 2, we discussed Gardner's theory of multiple intelligences as a part of cognitive diversity. It is important to identify these intelligences as strengths and use them as the basis for instruction (Reiff, 1997).

Theory into Practice 7-1

An Integrated Unit on Student Backpacks

Objective: Each student will weigh his/her backpack and determine whether the backpack is too heavy and/or whether it is being carried properly.

Discipline	Topics
Math	Ratio, proportion, graphing, measurement, percentages
Science	Human body, balanced forces, simple machines, skeletal systems
Language arts	Writing
Social studies	How different cultures carry loads

Developed from: Doughty, J. H. (1999). Class activities promote teamwork among staff members. *School in the Middle, 8*(4), 6–8.

As part of the developmental differences among your students, you will find a wide range of exceptionalities such as students with learning disabilities, attention-deficit/hyperactive disorder, limited English proficiency, and emotional disturbances. While it is beyond the scope of this book to discuss these exceptionalities, we want you to realize that, at times, you will be responsible for identifying specific exceptionalities. At other times, you will assist others in providing educational experience that address the exceptionalities, perhaps through the use of an Individualized Education Plan (IEP). When planning instruction, you will often need to plan appropriate educational experiences for students with a number of exceptional conditions and behaviors.

Young adolescents are also influenced by the cultural community in which they live. Sometimes the culture of the student and the culture of the school are radically different. However, culturally responsive teaching can lessen the resulting tensions and dissonance. You will need to use a wide variety of instructional styles to meet the needs of all learners (Manning & Baruth, 1996).

Selecting Resources for Interdisciplinary Instruction

One way to meet the diverse needs of young adolescents is to use a variety of instructional resources to appeal to visual, verbal, and auditory learners and to appeal to the multiple intelligences of young adolescents. These resources should also provide a multicultural and multidimensional look at the topics or themes that you teach. Photographs, videos, recordings, computer software, books, magazines, newspapers, realia, prints, games, sculpture, and even live animals are just a few of the resources that you can use in your instruction.

You should not, however, use resources just to use them. You must select resources carefully to be sure that they enrich the unit, not detract from it. The school library media specialist in your school is an excellent person to consult to determine appropriate resources. Your librarian can help you locate materials within the school library and point you to a number of sources that review instructional materials. Remember, never select instructional materials on the basis of a publisher's catalog. The materials you use must be

Theory into Practice 7–2

A Checklist for Evaluation of Instructional Materials

When selecting instructional materials, evaluate each item on the following criteria:

General Criteria

Content

Is the primary use instructional, informational, or recreational?
Are the frills (animation, pictures, etc.) more important than the educational content?
Does it contain accurate and up-to-date information?
Is the information organized and easy to find?
How in-depth is the information?
Is the material developmentally responsive for young adolescents?
Is the content free from stereotypes as well as cultural and gender bias?
How does the content of this item compare to others that have been selected for this unit?

Educational Suitability

What curriculum objectives or behavioral objectives does the material meet?
Would the material be used to introduce instruction, in direct instruction, or for reinforcement?
What thinking skills are involved in the use of this material?
Are there any accompanying teacher's guides or other supporting material? How readable is it?
Can the item be used by more than one student at a time?
Does the resource promote a commercial brand or a specific social cause?
Does the material contain proper grammar, spelling, and sentence structure?

Cost

How does the price of this material compare to similar items?

Additional Criteria for Computer Software (Including CD-ROMs)

Educational Suitability

Does the program follow accepted learning theories?
Does the item motivate learners to continue learning rather than simply transmit information?
How does this material keep the student engaged? On-screen questions or manipulatives? Workbook?
Will this software do any record keeping or track the progress of individual students?

Ease of Use

How easy is this item to use?
Can the user control the pacing?
Are there a variety of levels of interaction, such as novice and expert?

Technical Qualities

Is any text on the screen readable?
What is the quality of the audio?
If there is motion video, what is the quality?

Theory into Practice 7–2 (cont.)

Special Features

Are there any special features such as "hot links" between parts, video clips, audio clips, etc?
Can portions or passages be printed for use without the computer?

Installation and Maintenance

Can this software be used on existing hardware in your school? How accessible is this hardware?
Can this material be used on any network in the school?
Is technical support available? What is the cost?
Will it be necessary to purchase any additional hardware or software to use this material?

Developed from: Abramson, G. (1998). How to evaluate educational software. *Principal, 78*(1), 60–61; and Bucher, K. T. (1998). *Information technology for schools.* Worthington, OH: Linworth Publishing.

Diversity Perspectives 7–1

Selecting Resources on Women

Bucher and Manning (1998) examined current collective biographies of women that were written for young adults and noted that readers need to see women as human beings. The biographies should be accurate with controversial information and personal fallacies neither omitted nor glossed over. They also noted that writers should avoid placing women in stereotypical roles but should accurately portray the treatment that women have received over the decades, even though some of this treatment shows women as second-class citizens. While historical events cannot be changed, women should be shown as individuals with their own strengths and weaknesses.

In selecting collective biographies of women, the authors stressed the need to look for indicators of accuracy, "the worthiness of the subject, and the balance between the storyline and fact (p. 13)." They then went on to discuss 29 recent, recommended collective biographies of women in the categories of politicians and world leaders; scientists and inventors; artists, athletes, and professionals; and uncommon individuals.

Source: Bucher, K. T., & Manning, M. L. (1998). Telling our stories, sharing our lives: Collective biographies of women. *ALAN Review, 26*(1), 12–16.

developmentally responsive for your students and must coincide with your instructional objectives. Theory into Practice 7–2 contains a checklist that you can use to evaluate instructional materials in general, while Diversity Perspectives 7–1 provides some guidelines for selecting materials on women to use in your teaching.

Resources can often become the basis for collaboration. In fact the resources of the school library media center can become the foundation of interdisciplinary teaching (Bessant, 1997) and bring diversity into instruction. For example, when historical fiction books were used to teach medieval history and English, there were some interesting results. Not only did students learn history and practice their writing skills, they also improved their historical thinking skills (Hicks & Marlin, 1997). Thus, in any instructional planning, we encourage you to involve the school library media specialist. While this individual may not always be involved in the actual implementation of the instruction, he or she is invaluable in helping you select materials and identify resources both within your school as well as the community and, via the Internet, the world.

Scheduling for Interdisciplinary Instruction

Flexible organization structures such as block scheduling go hand-in-hand with interdisciplinary instruction (Felner et al., 1997). With flexible block schedules, teams can maximize instructional opportunities, use time more efficiently, and change student groupings to reflect students needs. When the individual team has control of large blocks of time, members can allocate the time to fit their instructional plans. While some teams make adjustments on a weekly basis, others may modify the schedule daily (Kasak, 1998).

By now you should have a general idea of the things that must be considered when planning instruction. There is still more to learn about implementing instruction and assessing students in other chapters of this book. However, before we leave the subject of overall instructional planning, we want to take a look at how one seventh-grade team planned an interdisciplinary instruction unit. In Case Study 7–1, we will revisit Karyn Rothmer from the opening scenario and her team a few years later.

Planning for Students at Risk of Failure

> "Failure is a vicious cycle of: 'Well, everyone says I'm dumb, so I may as well act dumb, because everyone says I'm dumb.' " Comments of a student in teacher education.

According to the Carnegie Council on Adolescent Development (1992) almost 25% of young adolescents have a high risk of failing in school, with another 25% having a moderate risk. John Lounsbury (1996a) explains that some students are in danger of failing "not because they can't learn but because the school has not adequately engaged them and provided experiences that are seen by those students as worth doing" (p. 212). How can middle school educators work with these students who have serious academic, health, social, or personal problems or who have just given up on education?

Students can be at risk of failing for many reasons. There is lack of confidence, fear, labeling, low self-esteem, constant reprimands, nagging, and punishments (Ciaccio, 1998). As a middle school teacher, your planning needs to consider the emotional stress exhibited by a growing number of young adolescents (Butte, 1993). That means you need to plan instruction that will ensure success, build a positive atmosphere, let students know you think they can succeed, encourage them, use positive comments, and provide genuine praise (Ciaccio, 1998). Build on your students' skills in art, music, drama, sports, dance, and technology, not

Case Study 7–1

The Osprey Team Plans a Unit

A few years ago, the teachers at Washington Peaks Middle School had begun work on interdisciplinary teaching. A consultant had even been hired by the central school administration to help with the effort. Of all the teams, the seventh-grade Osprey team had been very successful. That is not to say that things had been easy for them. One teacher, Deborah St. Johns, had not felt comfortable giving up the autonomy of her own classroom and had difficulty teaching with an interdisciplinary approach. As a result, she had asked for and received a transfer to the senior high school. Her position as a science teacher had been filled by Alysha McQueen, a new graduate, who was welcomed by Karyn Rothmer, language arts; Auggie Anderson, math; and Sandy Labyak, social studies.

The Osprey team members had worked hard to develop trust and mutual respect and had successfully taught two or three units each year using an interdisciplinary approach. At other times, one or two of the teachers would cooperate in planning joint activities or coordinate some of their instruction. Overall, they were pleased and thought both they and their students had benefited from the units.

Now they were ready to plan another interdisciplinary unit. They began by brainstorming ideas for possible themes and then asked their students during homeroom for ideas or issues they would like to explore. Over and over the word *survival* kept popping up, so the team members began to examine the existing curriculum, textbooks, and state guidelines to see if they could identify possible topics to tie into survival or any of the other suggested issues. Their plan was to look for commonalities and ideas related to survival that could be taught across the disciplines within their curricular framework. In addition, when the team members met with others in their disciplines across the grade levels, and during their semiweekly team meeting with the library media specialist and teachers from art, music, and physical education, they mentioned the theme and asked for suggestions. Finally they decided to call the unit "Surviving against the Odds" and to focus on the Holocaust.

Their next step was to identify individual teacher responsibilities for the unit. They came up with the following chart:

Teacher	Responsibilities
Social studies	World War II, Holocaust Geography of Scandinavia and Europe
Language arts	Novel: *Number the Stars* set in Denmark in WWII Writing: Creating a newspaper
Science	Chemicals and sense of smell Nutrition and the human body

Case Study 7–1 (cont.)

Teacher	Responsibilities
Math	Word problems based on novel use of percent, ratio, simple statistics
Librarian	Information skills, Internet searching resources on WWII, Danish culture
Art	Art as a way of healing after conflict
Music	Ethnic music
Health/physical education	Effects of a poor diet and lack of exercise

With some idea of their general responsibilities, the team developed individual and team goals and objectives for the unit, and came up with a scope and sequence timeline. After debating and refining their goals, they identified possible student outcomes and assessment procedures. At this point, the team decided to announce the theme to the students in each homeroom and get their input on the projects and the assessment. Naturally, there were some lively discussions, but, when the team met again, they modified their original plans based on some of the suggestions. After finalizing the student outcomes and the assessment, the team worked on developing specific lesson plans for the unit. Some of the plans were developed by the whole group, while others were done by individual teachers and then brought back to the group for discussion. As the plans were being finalized, the team also tried to see how they could best arrange their block schedule to fit the instructional plans.

Finally it was time to teach the unit. Throughout the teaching process, the team continued to meet with all of the participating teachers and specialists, to modify their plans as necessary, and to make adjustments in the block schedule. At the conclusion of the unit, the team held a final meeting with everyone who participated in the teaching or planning to discuss what happened, what they liked, and what they would change the next time they taught the unit.

just their academic skills. Since educators have found that ability grouping does not appear to improve academic achievement (George, 1993), you should strive for a task-focused rather than ability-focused learning environment by focusing on task mastery rather than on how students compare with their peers (Urdan, Midgley, & Wood, 1995).

Many educators argue against special programs for students at risk (Alexander, 1995; Lounsbury, 1996b; Siu-Runyan & Faircloth, 1995; Springer, 1994), citing teachers who have developed programs that meet the needs of all students rather than creating special programs for specific groups of students who might be "labeled" as different. In most cases, programs that are designed to meet the needs of middle school students who are at risk of failing are also the best programs for all middle school students. The difference is that while at-risk students need the same things that other middle school students need, they may need individualized help with academic work and with building self-esteem and achieving academic success (Ruff, 1993). Collaborative planning and interdisciplinary instruction can help, especially when teachers coordinate projects and homework assignments, use examples from young adolescent literature to focus on student problems and discuss coping strategies, or base problem-solving activities on historical situations. To help with stress, classroom discussions can be used to explore strong feelings and emotions about the social injustices and prejudices that young adolescents must often confront (Butte, 1993).

Closing Remarks

The instruction of young adolescents in middle schools is too important to be haphazard. For instruction to be developmentally responsive and effective, it must be systematically planned to meet the needs of the learners and the demands of the school's curriculum. Whether you are planning for your own classroom or for interdisciplinary instruction with other members of your middle school team, you need to keep in mind the principles that are contained in this chapter. In chapters 8, 9, 10 of this book, "Implementing Instruction—Methods and Materials," "Effective Instructional Behaviors—Research and Practice," and "Assessment—Methods and Issues," we will build upon this foundation. While you, as an educator, will benefit from good instructional planning, the ultimate benefits will go to the young adolescents whom you teach.

Suggested Readings

Bryant, M., & Land, S. (1998). Co-planning is the key to successful co-teaching. *Middle School Journal, 29*(5), 28–34. Defines co-teaching and explains how co-teachers can plan effectively.

Clark, S. N., & Clark, D. C. (1997). Exploring the possibilities of interdisciplinary teaming. *Childhood Education, 73*(5), 267–271. Explains how ITO makes better use of faculty skills and provides better strategies for dealing with diversified populations.

Dickinson, T. S., & Erb, T. O. (1997). *We gain more than we give: Teaming in middle schools.* Columbus, OH: National Middle School Association. Explores all aspects of teaming in the middle school and exemplifies the concept of "We gain more than we give."

Fuller, C., & Stone, M. E. (1998). Teaching social studies to diverse learners. *The Social Studies, 89*(4), 154–157. Uses the Planning Pyramid to meet the needs of all students.

Stephen, V., & Varble, M. E. (1995). Staff development model: Thematic units in the middle level school. *Schools in the Middle, 4*(4), 23–26. Describes a six-session staff development workshop.

Stevenson, C., & Carr, J. (Ed.). (1993). *Integrated studies in the middle grades: "Dancing through walls."* Williston, Vt: Teachers College Press. Discusses teaching units designed around topics of student interest.

Chapter 8

Implementing Instruction—Methods and Materials

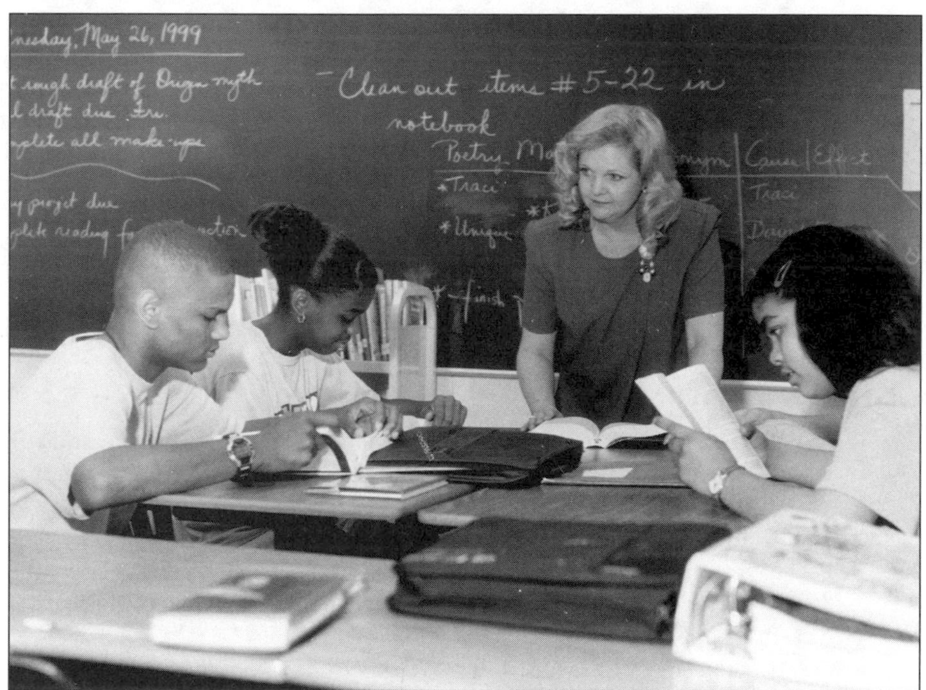

Scenario—A First Year Teacher Needs Help

It was 8:30 P.M. on a Wednesday evening in November when Jarrold Southworth, a first-year eighth-grade mathematics teacher at Long View Middle School, picked up the telephone and dialed the home telephone number of Bria Royster-Gregory. Bria had been Jarrold's cooperating teacher when he had done his student teaching the previous spring in an award-winning middle school in a neighboring district. As the telephone rang at Bria's house, Jarrold tried to focus on what he needed to tell her. He'd put this off as long as possible, but he had to face the facts. He just was not cut out to be a middle school teacher. Jarrold was about ready to hang up when Bria answered.

Her joy at hearing Jarrold's voice faded as Jarrold told her, "I'm leaving the teaching profession in December."

"But why?" was Bria's immediate response. "You did a great job in student teaching, and I've heard good things from my friends over at Long View Middle. What happened?"

Jarrold tried to keep his voice calm as he talked about the problems he was having with instruction. "I just can't seem to find a way to provide effective instruction to so many students, especially considering their tremendous diversity. On top of the cultural and gender differences, there are the really bright students and the ones who seem to take forever to learn something. How can I meet all of their needs all day, everyday? Sure, I coped with these things when I student taught, but that was sixth grade and I'm teaching eighth grade. I've tried some of the things you did, but they didn't work."

"Have you talked to anyone on your team, or in your school?" Bria asked.

"Yes, I shared my concerns with two teachers in the school. The first, Robbie Van Davier, the social studies teacher on my team, just shrugged off my concerns by saying, 'I'm sure you can do it!' The second teacher I talked to, Logan McCambridge on the seventh-grade Panther Team, was a little more sympathetic and offered encouraging advice."

"I know Logan—he's a good teacher. What did he tell you?"

"Oh, he gave me a pep talk about not working alone, sharing more of my concerns with other members of the team, talking to Rachel Benson in the library media center to locate a variety of instructional materials, and asking some of the other specialists for assistance," replied Jarrold. "He also mentioned something about planning differently for the block schedule, but I didn't get him to explain what he meant."

"Well," Bria responded, "what's wrong with that advice? What's happened that's so horrible that you're thinking about quitting? You're a good teacher, a little green, but that's expected in your first year. Why not take Logan's advice and get some help?"

"That's just it. I'm supposed to be a teacher now and I'm supposed to know how to handle these instructional problems. If I ask for help, I'll just show that I'm . . . I'm not a good teacher."

"Jarrold, listen to me! You are a good teacher. And you have the potential to be a great one, but all of us need advice at times. Yes, even with my experience, I rely on others for help with a lot of things including instruction. You saw that when you student taught. Now, I notice that you talked to Robbie and Logan but not to the others on your own team. Why?"

Jarrold hesitated and then replied, "Because I didn't want to appear stupid in front of the women on my team. They seem to expect so much from me, and they're so good themselves."

"Jarrold!" interjected Bria. "You didn't seem to have trouble talking to me last year. And you called me tonight. You know, I think you need some good old-fashioned motherly advice, so here it is. First, follow Logan's advice and talk to your team members and to Rachel in the library. You can't isolate yourself from people who can help you. Paige Faulk is your gifted specialist. Ask her for assistance with the faster students and ask your remedial resource teacher for help with the students experiencing difficulty. Now let's see, . . . it's here somewhere in this stack by my chair. Oh, here it is. Get the January 1998 issue of the *Middle School Journal* on teaching heterogeneous groups and read it! And, doesn't your school have a first-year mentor program?"

"Yes," Jarrold replied. "Mine's Logan McCambridge. That's why I talked to him."

"Go back to Logan and really talk to him. Tell him about your problems. I'll bet he had some of the same students in math last year in seventh grade. And don't even think of turning in your resignation. I never thought you were a quitter."

"Okay, you win." Jarrold said. "I'll try what you suggested, and I'll put my letter of resignation on hold for now."

Bria laughed, "Put that letter of resignation on hold for a long time, Jarrold. Teaching is a challenge, but it's one you can handle."

Overview

In chapter 7, you read about the process of planning instruction, especially interdisciplinary instruction, in the middle school. Now, in chapter 8, you will turn your attention to the actual implementation of instruction in middle schools. Hopefully, you have some familiarity with instructional practices from a general methodology of teaching class and can relate this information on teaching young adolescents to the general instructional practices that you already know.

This chapter is based on three premises that we hope will permeate all facets of instruction. First, we believe that the instructional methods that you use to teach middle school students should demonstrate an understanding of the early adolescence developmental period and should show your commitment to the education of young adolescents. In addition, your instruction should be implemented for heterogeneous groups, with accommodations made for the varying levels of student abilities. This means that you must keep in mind the unique abilities, interests, multiple intelligences, and cultural and gender differences of young adolescents. Third, we believe that effective instruction in middle schools must place emphasis on individual young adolescents' academic achievement and overall well-being, provide variable instructional group sizes, and ensure some degree of success for all young adolescents.

Objectives

After reading and thinking about this chapter on appropriate implementation of instruction, you should be able to:

1. identify the need to plan for young adolescents' varying abilities, interests, and cultural and gender differences;
2. explain the need for heterogeneous grouping in an effort to avoid the problems associated with students being grouped by ability;
3. identify a number of instructional methods and strategies;
4. explain how teaching in block schedules differs from the traditional five- or six-period day;

5. provide reasons for developmentally responsive teaching methods and strategies that reflect young adolescents' physical, psychosocial, and cognitive developmental characteristics (also discussed in chapters 2 and 7, and in Appendix A); and
6. discuss several methods of addressing the needs of students who need accelerative or remedial instruction.

Young Adolescents—Implementing Considerations

When you are trying to select appropriate instructional strategies that will increase the motivation and academic achievement of your students, you naturally must consider the tremendous developmental, socioeconomic, and cognitive diversity of young adolescents as well as the level of parental encouragement that each receives (Manning, 1993b). To help determine the strengths of individual learners, you can administer diagnostic tests, check school records (e.g., previous grades and teacher comments), interview each student, and request input from parents (Byrnes & Cortez, 1992; Crawford, 1993; Manning & Baruth, 1996). However, you must remember that a hallmark characteristic of young adolescents is their developmental diversity (Thornburg, 1982). As you will read later in this chapter, one way to meet individual differences and needs effectively is to use small-group instruction. Regardless of how conscientious you may be, young adolescents' wide range of developmental and individual differences usually makes whole-class teaching a very difficult task. That is one reason why Jarrold Southworth, in this chapter's opening scenario, seemed so despondent.

Abilities and Achievement

Whether due to lack of ability or lack of motivation (or a combination of these and other factors), significant numbers of young adolescents experience low academic achievement (Bruno & Adams, 1994; Carnegie Council on Adolescent Development, 1990; National Center for Educational Statistics, 1990, 1994). For example, a U.S. Bureau of the Census document (Bruno & Adams, 1994) reported that disturbing percentages of young adolescents scored below grade level (Table 8–1).

What does this mean for you as a middle school teacher? One reaction is to note that almost one-third of young adolescents have academic problems in school. Realize, too, that

TABLE 8–1 *Young Adolescents Scoring below Grade Level*

% of All 12- to 14-year-olds Scoring below Chronological Grade Level	% of 12- to 14-year-old Males Scoring below Chronological Grade Level	% of 12- to 14-year-old Females Scoring below Chronological Grade Level
30.8%	35.0%	26.2%

Source: Bruno & Adams, 1994.

a number of factors affect motivation and look for ways to improve motivation for learners of all abilities. You must also recognize the importance of including parents and families in the effort to build upon students' strengths and areas of expertise. In addition, you must understand the need for carefully planned instruction that emphasizes high expectations for all learners and accommodates a wide array of abilities. However, you should realize that not all learners will meet the same expectations. Finally, you should provide instruction that offers all students some degree of success in their educational attempts.

Interest and Relevance

> "I don't understand why we do some of the things we do in school. Like the math we're doing now. My dad says he doesn't know how to do it and he's pretty successful. So why do I have to learn it? I'll never use it once I get out of school." An eighth-grade student.

While it is impossible to make all educational experiences relevant to the needs, desires, and viewpoints of young adolescents, you should try to show learners how educational experiences relate to their lives. For example, teachers of language arts or communication skills such as reading, listening, speaking, and writing (as well as viewing and visually representing) can demonstrate how these are skills that young adolescents can use everyday. Let them practice those skills with topics they enjoy or are interested in. Mathematics teachers can explain how mathematics relates to everyday lives, from budgeting money to computing the percentage of discounts students should receive when shopping at sales. In social studies, teachers can have students study justice, equality, and democratic ideals, both from historical and contemporary perspectives. Let them examine contemporary causes in which they have an interest. While we could mention other curricular areas, the point remains: Teachers should attempt, whenever possible, to make the curriculum as relevant as possible to young adolescents' perspectives.

Culture and Gender

To provide effective middle school instruction, you must provide classroom organizational and instructional approaches that recognize the cultural and gender differences of your students. In order to do that, you must first learn about those cultural and gender characteristics and the perceptions of each group toward competition, group welfare, sharing, motivation, and success. While we can not provide detailed information on all gender preferences as well as racial, ethnic, religious, social, and other cultural groups, we can suggest, in Keeping Current with Technology 8–1, some Internet sites that you can visit to find multicultural information about a variety of cultural groups and to learn about gender differences.

If you visit a few of these Internet sites or do any reading about cultural and gender diversity, you will learn that not everyone responds the same way to things like competition. For example, some Native American learners may favor sharing and helping peers over competitive learning activities (Sanders, 1987), and some Puerto Ricans may not wish to excel or be set apart from the group as being different (Christensen, 1989). In terms of learning styles and preferences, some African Americans prefer to respond to things in terms of the whole picture rather than its parts and tend to approximate space, numbers, and time

Keeping Current with Technology 8–1

For more information about teaching young adolescents from a variety of cultural groups and to learn about gender differences, visit a few of these Internet sites.

Center for Multilingual Multicultural Research, University of Southern California
http://www.usc.edu/dept/education/CMMR/

Council of Great City Schools, an organization of the nation's largest urban public school systems
http://cgcs.org/

Hall of Multiculturalism
http://www.tenet.edu/academia/multi.html

Internet School Library Media Center (ISLMC) Multicultural page
http://falcon.jmu.edu/~ramseyil/multipub.htm

Multicultural Educational Resources page
http://peabody.vanderbilt.edu/ctrs/ltc/schulzeb/mcerhome.htm

Multicultural Pavilion, University of Virginia
http://curry.edschool.Virginia.EDU/curry/centers/multicultural/

MultiCultural Review, a quarterly journal for teachers at all grade levels
http://www.mcreview.com/

Pathways to School Improvement, a product of the North Central Regional Educational Laboratory in cooperation with the Regional Educational Laboratory network
http://www.ncrel.org/sdrs/pathways.htm

Tips for using multicultural students as resources in your classroom
http://www.cal.org/public/ilcdir/mcstrats.htm

World Cultures
http://www.wsu.edu:8080/~dee/

rather than strive for accuracy (Hale-Benson, 1986). To work with gender differences, you need to provide learning experiences such as peer tutoring and other small learning groups (Sadker, Sadker, & Long, 1993) and to encourage open dialogue and collaboration (Butler & Manning, 1998) rather than competition.

Implementing Effective Instruction in Middle Schools

"When I went to junior high school, we were grouped by ability. Although it was supposed to be a big secret, everyone knew who the fast-track students were. One thing I remember is that I didn't have too many friends outside my own track.

What's so different about the classes in middle schools today? Don't teachers still group by ability? And, if they don't, won't it hold my daughter back?" The parent of a sixth-grade student.

Committing to Heterogeneous Grouping

In the past, one way teachers have traditionally tried to deal with the diversity of 10- to 14-year-olds was to put them in homogeneous groups who likely stayed together throughout the day and throughout the years. Although, homogeneous grouping (often called ability grouping or tracking) of students based on their academic ability is used in some middle schools (as well as elementary and secondary schools), this is not the best grouping procedure (George, 1993). While there are a number of reasons for our statement, there are two primary ones. First, grouping homogeneously does not seem to promote overall achievement of learning (George, 1993). In addition, homogeneous grouping by ability results in inequitable educational experiences (George, 1993; Oakes, 1985) that produce discriminatory and damaging effects on students (Kellough & Kellough, 1999).

Even when teachers do group students homogeneously by some set of characteristics, there will still be a considerable range of cognitive, cultural, and gender diversities within the group (George, 1993). No set of criteria will produce a completely homogeneous group of young adolescents. Also, when young adolescents are grouped by ability, students in the "lower" groups often experience lower self-esteems as well as a host of other negative effects (Manning & Lucking, 1990). The result of ability grouping is that the grouping destroys rather than builds a sense of community in a middle school (George, 1993).

Varying the Composition and Size of Instructional Groups

When you group students for instruction, you do not have to group your students in the same way all day or even for extended periods of time. If you are teaching in a school that is organized into teams, you and the other educators on your team can cooperate to change the grouping throughout the day to meet your instructional needs. Even within your own classroom, you can use a variety of instructional groupings. For example, rather than grouping students by ability (i.e., achievement tests or reading scores), you can teach small heterogeneous groups or form groups based upon friendships or areas of interest. Theory into Practice 8–1 shows how one teacher used heterogeneous groupings for language arts instruction.

Collaborating with the School Library Media Specialist and Other Teachers in the Related Domains

In chapter 7, you read about the collaboration that occurs on interdisciplinary teams when they plan interdisciplinary instruction. However, collaboration should not take place just in planning and should not be limited to the members of a single team. In general, the term *collaboration* is used to define any direct interaction between at least two co-equal parties who voluntarily engage in shared decision making as they work toward a common goal

Theory into Practice 8–1

Heterogeneous Groups in Language Arts

For a study of the effects of war or conflict on people, a sixth-grade language arts teacher attempted to increase motivation and academic achievement by dividing her 25 students into five heterogeneous groups of five. These five "specific-conflict" groups selected one conflict in which the United States participated and read a novel about that conflict. Because of the diverse reading levels in each group, the teacher worked with the school library media specialist to select books on a variety of reading and comprehension levels.

The group reading about the Civil War selected books including *Shades of Gray, Nightjohn, Charlie Skedaddle, Pink and Say,* and *Mr. Lincoln's Drummer.* In the group reading about World War II, students read *Stepping on the Cracks, Under the Blood Red Sun, Foster's War, Summer of My German Soldier,* and *Lily's Crossing.* These books represented reading levels from second to seventh grade. After each student read his or her book, the specific-conflict groups met and discussed the following questions:

1. What effect does war have upon the basic needs of people?
2. What effects does war have upon a family and the lives of individuals? How and why does it differ from family to family?
3. What effects does war have on relationships between people from different families? What determines the effects?
4. What effect does war have on plans people have made for the future?
5. What effects does war have on a country?

Once the specific-conflict groups had finished their discussions, the teacher rearranged the groups into five different groups so that each group contained five students who had read about different conflicts. Now their task was to take the information about each of their specific conflicts and, through discussion, come up with a list of the things that conflicts in general have done to people and to the country.

Throughout the process, the more advanced students helped students needing assistance, and all group members engaged in social interaction with students of differing cultural and socioeconomic backgrounds. In addition, the teacher was able to give more attention to those students who needed her assistance.

Developed from: Bucher, K. T. (1998). Integrating children's/young adult literature into the social studies. In H. E. Taylor (Ed.), *What's goin' on? Trends and issues in American education* (pp. 207–214). Needham Heights, MA: Simon & Schuster Custom; and Sandmann, A., & Ahern, J. (1997). Using literature to study the Civil War and Reconstruction. *Middle School Journal 29*(2) 25–33.

(Cook & Friend, 1991). In other words, teachers should and do regularly collaborate with a number of other educators in the school. Through collaborative efforts, teachers can better serve a diverse group of students for whom they accept instructional responsibility (Gable, Friend, Laycock, & Hendrickson, 1990).

This collaboration can take many forms, with direct instruction being just one option. In addition to schoolwide collaboration on instructional and other committees or in cafeteria supervision, there is grade-level collaboration and subject-area collaboration. There is also multiclassroom, "cluster," or team collaboration; and the inclusive collaboration that allows core discipline teachers, faculty from the related domains, and also special educators to work together.

When we talked to middle school educators about collaboration, we got a variety of responses. As expected, we found that some teachers were more willing than others to collaborate. We also found that some of the teachers who were willing to collaborate while planning instruction felt less inclined to collaborate in the actual delivery of the instruction. As one teacher explained: "Sure, I collaborate with the library media specialist to locate resources that my students will need. But, no, I don't involve him in actually doing any of the teaching in the unit. That's my job."

To us, collaboration frequently goes beyond the planning stage. According to Cook and Friend (1991), teacher collaboration is predicated on several important qualities: voluntary participation, mutual respect, parity among participants, a shared sense of responsibility and accountability for decisions, and an equitable distribution of available resources. Unfortunately, some classroom teachers do not view the school library media specialist and other teachers in the related domains as equals. Rather than trying to enter into the "who is better than whom" battle, we like to think that the educators in a middle school are, in a way, just like the students. The educators, too, are a diverse group, each with his or her own strengths and weaknesses. Therefore, just as we believe in the use of heterogeneous groups to bring out the strengths of each of the students, we believe that heterogeneous groups of educators can provide a variety of rich learning experiences to all young adolescents. Furthermore, just as we advocate varying the mix in the groups of students, we advocate using a variety of groupings of educators throughout the year to best meet the needs of young adolescents.

In chapter 7, you read about some of the benefits of collaboration in planning instruction. Many of these same benefits also come as a result of collaboration during the implementation of instruction as educators learn from one another and establish long-lasting and trusting professional relationships (Lieberman, 1992). Teachers benefit from the diversity of philosophies toward instruction, the stimulation of new ideas, and the increased communication among professionals at all levels (Brookhart & Loadman, 1990). However, you must remember that, just as not every unit is planned cooperatively, not every unit is taught cooperatively. There are many topics that seem to work best when taught in an individual classroom.

While a number of professionals should be involved with implementing instruction in middle schools (e.g., teachers, special educators, resource teachers, and library media specialists), we want to focus, for a moment, on the role of the library media specialist. Although it is unrealistic to expect library media specialists to be involved with all implementation of instruction in a middle school, these professionals are trained to provide some basic skills that all young adolescents need. Specifically, they are trained to help students develop the information problem-solving skills that the students need to retrieve information, communicate effectively, and use that information to solve problems (American Association of School Librarians, 1998). In addition, they can provide different perspectives on curriculum and learners, how to incorporate technology in instruction, how to integrate literature into the curriculum, and how to use a variety of resources to meet the diverse needs of young adolescents.

Diversity Perspectives 8–1

A Gender-Equitable Project in Math

Realizing that the bulletin boards of most science and mathematics classrooms feature males, Gretchen R. Mosca, a seventh-grade teacher, planned a unit that, in addition to showing the contributions of mathematicians and scientists throughout history, showed that women have made many of those contributions. Her idea was to divide the students into groups and have each group produce a poster on a famous mathematician or scientist and to write a report providing information on that individual. Responsibilities for the unit were divided as follows:

Individual Teacher	Responsibility
Art	Making posters
Computer	Keyboarding skills
Health	Listening skills
Language arts	Writing and bibliography
Librarian	Teaching students to locate resources and to gather information
Math	Introducing unit, working with groups, evaluating work
Social studies	Historical background

Mosca and Shmurak (1995) reported that the project was successful and that students learned about group dynamics, developed language and listening skills, and gained an appreciation of the place of mathematics in society. Bulletin boards that had previously featured Thomas Edison and Albert Einstein now had pictures of Dian Fossey, Rachel Carson, and Grace Hopper. In addition, the authors reported that the project allowed for the use of six of the seven intelligences identified by Gardner (1983, 1993a) and gave everyone an appreciation for the talents of all the students, not just their academic abilities. Some unexpected results were improvement in the student's attitudes toward mathematics and an increase in the amount of mathematics homework that some students turned in. The authors felt that the project was an excellent way to get girls interested in both science and mathematics (Mosca & Shmurak, 1995).

Source: Mosca, G. F., & Shmurak, C. B. (1995). An interdisciplinary, gender-equitable mathematics project for the middle school. *Middle School Journal, 27*(1), 26–29.

Sometimes mathematics teachers find that it is difficult to cooperate with other teachers in implementing instruction. However, Diversity Perspective 8–1 shows what happened when teachers in art, computers, mathematics, social studies, health, and language arts teamed with a school librarian for a gender-equitable project in math (Mosca & Shmurak, 1995).

Focusing on Self-Exploration, Self-Directed Learning, and Student Selection of Activities Based on Personal Experiences

To help solve the problem of lack of motivation, you can give students reasons to be interested in their learning and can help them strive for academic success. One way is to determine students' special interests such as computers, debating, and drama and then utilize these in instruction (Allen, Splittgerber, & Manning, 1993; Hootstein, 1994). To identify special interests, you can use interest inventories or personal interviews. Then you can use the results to include these interests in your class or you can allow some students to engage in independent study in their areas of interests. Thus students can use their interest in television to write, edit, produce, and star in their own television news program for the entire school (Welsh, 1994). Take an interest in the Wild West and turn it into the production of "dime novel" westerns, researched and written by students (Chilcoat, 1993). Use drama, storytelling, pantomime, and panorama theater to bring social studies, language arts, and even science classes to life (Albert, 1994; Chilcoat, 1995). When the city council becomes engaged in a heated debate about financing a new public soccer complex for youth soccer leagues, take the students' interest and turn it into a lesson on city government that can show students how social studies topics do have relevance to their lives.

Collaborating with Special Educators

We have talked about the importance of core discipline teachers collaborating with teachers in the related domains. It is also important for all general-education teachers to collaborate with special educators in order to meet the diverse needs of young adolescents. Through mutual planning and goal setting, both general and special educators can gain ownership of the instructional process, place importance on mutually established goals, and, therefore, feel equally responsible for ensuring positive outcomes. In addition, through collaboration, educators can learn from one another, establish long-lasting and trusting professional relationships, and work to bring about school change (Gable & Manning, 1997, 1999).

Professional collaboration between general and special educators can take place before school, after school, or during a common teacher planning period. At that time, educators can meet to discuss learning and/or behavioral problems and to devise a plan of instruction (Chalfant & Pych, 1989). Together, they can explore possible explanations for the problem situation and then propose feasible program accommodations (e.g., classroom organization, curricular or instructional modifications).

Sometimes special and general educators engage in cooperative teaching. In this situation, both teachers share responsibility for planning and instructing a heterogeneous group of students in the regular classroom (Bauwens, Hourcade, & Friend, 1989; Cook & Friend, 1992). Selected cooperative teaching options include:

1. Shadow teaching—The general educator teachers specific subject matter, while the special educator works directly with one or two target students on academics and/or behavior.
2. One teach/one assist—The general educator teaches specific subject matter, while the special educator circulates around the classroom and offers individual students assistance.

3. Station teaching—The general educator and special educator teach different subject matter to groups of students who rotate from one learning station to another.
4. Complementary teaching—The general educator teaches specific subject matter, while the special educator assumes responsibility for teaching associated academic (e.g., note taking, test taking) or school survival skills (e.g., sharing, self-control).
5. Parallel teaching—The general educator and special educator divide the class into two smaller groups to provide more individualized instruction.
6. Supplementary teaching activities—The general educator teaches specific subject matter, while the special educator assumes responsibility for giving students content-specific assistance (Gable & Manning, 1997, 1999).

Selecting Instructional Methods and Strategies

In teaching, it is important that you develop a repertoire of instructional strategies that you can use. As Jarrold Southworth found out, what works with one group of students on a certain grade level might not be successful on another grade level or with another group of students, especially when you consider the diversity of young adolescents. Therefore, in this section, we want to focus on a number of instructional methods and strategies that have proven successful in middle schools. We have listed them alphabetically rather than by degree of effectiveness. They should provide you with a basic collection of strategies to which you can add.

Cooperative Learning

While competition motivates some learners, other young adolescents feel overwhelmed and unable to cope with the demands of competition (Manning & Lucking, 1991). Therefore, instructional methods that take advantage of cooperation and social interaction often prove effective with 10- to 14-year-olds. One of these methods is cooperative learning, which emphasizes cooperation rather than competition, and allows students to work in small groups (perhaps 4 to 6 students) and to help one another toward their learning goals. However, cooperative learning is more than putting students in groups and assuming they will stay "on task." To use cooperative learning, you must first teach your students a variety of cooperative learning procedures. A combination of peer evaluation (chapter 10 contains a sample peer evaluation form), assigned group roles, and careful monitoring and observation by the teacher will help the performance of cooperative learning groups (De Jong & Hawley, 1995).

Debate

> "When I was in middle school, I was reluctant to debate. Everyone told me I could think fast on my feet, but the idea of getting up in front of people was scary. I just couldn't seem to organize what I wanted to say. But now I'm glad they made me do it. I'm on the high school debate team and thinking about becoming a lawyer."
> Comments of a high school student.

When students debate, members of opposing teams make formal speeches on previously researched topics. Debates allow young adolescents to use their increasing verbal and thinking abilities and to build confidence in their ability to organize their thoughts and speak in a convincing manner. Teachers can either assign topics or allow students to choose their own. Either way, topics should be appropriate for the developmental period, such as the existence of the Loch Ness Monster, the need for a publicly funded soccer complex, or topics related to the school. While all students will not become proficient debaters (just as all students will not achieve excellence in sports), all students should have the opportunity to debate, perhaps only as an exploratory opportunity.

Demonstrations

Young adolescents enjoy demonstrations, and demonstrations can be used to teach any subject. While a social studies teacher can demonstrate proper role-playing for a simulation, a mathematics teacher can demonstrate the steps in solving a problem and a science teacher can show a chemical process. Demonstrations can introduce or close a lesson or unit, demonstrate a thinking skill, give students an opportunity to participate vicariously in active learning, grab attention, review a process, and save time and materials.

The success of any demonstration depends upon careful planning. It is important to decide who will conduct the demonstration (teacher, student, small group), if special arrangements (video or computer projection) need to be made so that everyone can see the demonstration, and exactly what supplies will be needed. When possible, let young adolescents do the demonstrations because students often know how to explain concepts effectively to other students. Plus, there is the added advantage that the student demonstrator gains confidence and develops speaking skills.

The reason for the demonstration should also be very clear. While a demonstration is an excellent attention-grabber, you should use one because is it the most effective means of presenting information. Do not become so involved in the special effects of a demonstration that students lose sight of the instructional objectives behind it.

Drill and Practice

Say the words "drill and practice" and most teachers respond with a negative comment. They often think only of "busy work" or young adolescents working endlessly on worksheets. However, this is *not* what we mean. Some learning tasks and concepts need to be practiced and reinforced again and again until the learner becomes proficient. The key is proficiency, not mindless repetition. For example, when learning equations in a mathematics class, students might need to practice a number of equations to gain confidence and for learning to occur. Thus one student might need to do five equations; another might need to do 15 equations; another might not need to do any; and one might need total reteaching. When drill and practice is used properly, students have a chance to gain confidence and practice what was supposedly taught; teachers know which students have mastered the concepts; and students know they are ready to proceed. To keep drill and practice from turning into endless worksheets, be sure that the drill and practice is closely related to the instructional objectives and that both you and your students know the exact reasons for the activity.

Exploratory Activities

"The whole class read *A Wrinkle in Time.* Shamir usually doesn't read, but he really seemed interested in science fiction. So the school librarian and I worked up an activity to let him read some additional science fiction books and keep a journal on them. He must have read 15 or 20 additional books." A seventh-grade teacher.

In chapter 4, you read about the exploratory programs that are found in many middle schools. Usually lasting a month, 6 weeks, or a semester, these programs (sometimes called minicourses) allow students to explore topics to determine whether interest suggests further study. However, this is not what we mean when we refer to "exploratory activities" as an instructional method.

In instructional exploratory activities, teachers give young adolescents, like Shamir, the opportunity to explore a particular interest *within the curricular areas*—not for a month, 6 weeks, or a semester, but for a more flexible length of time. For example, the young adolescent who sees a relationship between science and social studies should be encouraged to "explore" the interest; the student in the language arts class who wants to read more poetry should be given the opportunity to expand his or her knowledge through exploration.

Exploratory activities are particularly important for young adolescents as they are progressing from Piaget's concrete operational stage to the formal operational stage. Most are sufficiently mature to work independently, and most are forming opinions about what they like and do not like. Some young adolescents will give up a topic of exploration after only a short time; others might be so fascinated with the exploratory activity that it captures their attention for a longer time, perhaps well into their adult years.

Expository Teaching

In expository teaching, the teacher acts as a director of instruction through lectures, videos, reading from a textbook or tradebook, demonstrations, or using computer software (Jarolimek & Foster, 1989). Many teachers are most comfortable with expository teaching because they can plan precisely what they want to do and have more control over the teaching-learning situation. While many young adolescents have advanced cognitively to a point where they can concentrate on lessons for longer periods of time, expository teaching should be kept short and should provide opportunities for students to get involved. Even videos or other software can be "boring" and "get old" if students do not see the relationship between the media and instruction (Theobald, 1995).

Field Trips

"Don't mention the word *field trip* to me! The last one was a complete disaster." A seventh-grade teacher.

"I was really impressed with the students on last year's field trip. They proved to everyone that they were responsible young adolescents." A seventh-grade teacher.

TABLE 8–2 *Tips for Successful Field Trips*

1. Clarify behavior expectations up-front, a day or two prior to the trip.
2. Have three or four broad rules that young adolescents can understand.
3. Let the young adolescents help make the rules.
4. Clarify the learning objectives of the trip, so students will know the educational purposes of the trip.
5. Plan for student safety by thinking ahead to all possible problems and dangers and planning accordingly.
6. Make a preliminary trip to the location to determine if it is suitable for young adolescents and if it meets the objectives of the learning experience.
7. Give students enough time to make the visit worthwhile and to meet the learning objectives of the trip.
8. Make the field trip as "interdisciplinary" as possible.
9. Conduct follow-up discussions to determine whether objectives were met and to provide students with opportunities to share their thoughts and opinions.

Middle school teachers often view field trips with mixed emotions. While some enthusiastically see a genuine learning opportunity, others see a "nightmare." As with so many other instructional practices, planning is very important. Table 8–2 has a few suggestions to keep in mind when considering an instructional field trip.

Homework

For years, teachers have used homework to reinforce classroom learning. However, students, and sometimes parents, complain that middle school teachers require substantially more homework than elementary school teachers and more than the students can reasonably do. Their complaint is often valid because of the more difficult middle school content and the problems that may arise if teachers do not coordinate the amount of homework that they assign. We know of at least one school in which parental requests for their children to be moved to another instructional team because of homework and other academic differences resulted in the entire school looking at the use of homework (Holler et al., 1999). Still, homework plays a useful role, and we advise teachers to consider the reasons for and the amount of the homework assignment to decide its usefulness to student learning.

Individualized Instruction

Probably the most effective instruction occurs when middle school students receive personal attention or individualized instruction. With individualized instruction, learners assume responsibility for some aspects of their learning through study, practice, and reinforcement in a specially designed individual learning package. This instructional approach is effective if it assesses each young adolescent's individual strengths and weaknesses and provides developmentally responsive instruction designed for each student. Each student's progress must be monitored and evaluated in terms of his or her individual potential rather than in comparison to other students.

One major reason for the effectiveness of individualized instruction is that you can tailor instruction precisely to a student's needs. If the student learns quickly, you can move to other tasks; if not, you can determine the problem, try other methods and materials, or just spend more time on the task. Unfortunately, in the real world, providing every student with a teacher is impractical. However, for decades educational innovators have been trying to find ways to get as close as possible to one-to-one tutoring situations.

Inductive Discovery

In inductive discovery teaching, teachers use strategies that begin with specifics and move toward the development of a generalization. One example is an inductive lesson on the common characteristics of insects. First, students collect observations and gather information through their senses by observing ants, grasshoppers, butterflies, dragonflies, and beetles. Next, they classify the observations into categories or concepts that help explain the information they collected. Finally, students draw conclusions that describe the facts and observations, such as the observation that all insects have three body parts, wings, two antennae, and six legs (Jarolimek & Foster, 1989).

Many young adolescents like inductive discovery teaching because they can be actively involved and, if working in groups, can socialize. In addition, the cognitive development of 10- to 14-year-olds allows them to consider a number of characteristics simultaneously. However, teachers who use inductive discovery need to guide students away from wrong generalizations or inductions.

Learning Centers

At a classroom learning center, individuals or small groups of students can quietly work at their own pace to learn more about a topic or to improve specific skills. The center includes all materials and instructions, so students can work independently. Since the value of learning centers lies in their instructional diversity, you can design a number of centers, each accommodating particular student needs or learning styles. While centers can be geared to various readiness levels, interests, and learning profiles, they can also cross curricular boundaries, help students with special needs, provide opportunities for creative work and enrichment experiences, or be built around learning packages that use special equipment.

Lecture

A survey of seventh graders found that 72.2% disliked or really disliked lectures, calling them boring (Theobald, 1995). However, even with its faults, the lecture method still has two significant advantages: (1) it can convey information to a large number of students at one time; and (2) done correctly, a lecture can be a powerful motivating device, provided the lecturer is interesting to listen to and enthusiastic about the topic.

Even with these advantages, you should lecture only briefly. Some middle school students have relatively short attention spans, maybe only 8 to 12 minutes. Boring lectures, ones that are too long, and ones that "lose" the students will not be successful. Keep your lectures brief and address only a few clear points. Capture your students' interest at the beginning and encourage student participation through comments and questions. Pace your lecture so that students do not feel rushed or threatened, especially if you expect them to take notes. At the end, tie the lecture together with a clear summary.

Peer-Tutoring

> "I enjoy tutoring Cory and Jessie in math. But I had to learn not to be too hard on them and to be patient. I'm very competitive, but they aren't." A sixth-grade boy.

As the name implies, peer-tutoring is one student tutoring another and is one of the most cost-effective instructional practices (Martino, 1994). No matter what the subject, students can sometimes explain a concept or skill to another student better than an adult. However, for peer-tutoring to be effective, it requires far more than just, "Maria, will you help Bill with his math?" If you use peer-tutoring, you need to teach peer-tutors how to tutor, what attitudes to take, how to encourage, and how to motivate. One school district even offers an elective course for students who want to become peer-tutors (Martino, 1994).

Peer-tutoring frees up the teacher to work with other students, promotes socialization among cultures and both genders, and reinforces the tutor's skills. If you use peer-tutors, you must be sure that you are not taking the tutors away from their own learning so much that their own progress suffers. One eighth-grade teacher we know keeps a detailed chart of peer-tutors, with their expertises, and how much they have tutored, so she always knows the amount of time each tutor has spent away from her or his own studies.

Projects

Projects in which students produce a product, such as a paper, model, skit, report, hypermedia presentation, television spot, or a combination of these, are favorites of young adolescents. Remembering young adolescents' diversities in abilities and interests, you should encourage all students to participate in projects and let students use their imaginations, creativity, and individual areas of expertise to create projects such as computer slide shows, mobiles, models, short plays, and demonstrations. While projects should be approved in advance and should meet the objectives of the lesson or unit, they should also be the student's choice as much as possible. One way to avoid misunderstandings about projects is to provide a list of requirements and a grading rubric (discussed in chapter 10).

Role-Playing and Simulation

Role-playing and simulations can be effective ways for students to learn. Young adolescents can especially benefit from role-playing the resolution of problems and from working on computer simulations. Most middle school teachers we know feel that learning does not stop when the role-playing or simulation ends; they think students need some type of follow-up activity to understand feelings and emotions, both theirs and other participants.

Service Learning

Both *Turning Points* (Carnegie Council on Adolescent Development, 1990) and *Great Transitions: Preparing Adolescents for a New Century* (Carnegie Council on Adolescent Development, 1996) call for opportunities for youth service for young adolescents. Involvement with the community, whether in direct learning or service opportunities, can be a powerful learning tool. Not only does service learning address young adolescents' feelings of altruism and idealism, it reinforces the content that they learn in school and helps them develop the skills to be productive citizens (Dunlap, Drew, & Gibson, 1994; Hope, 1999). In essence, students become involved in activities related to the needs of the community while they are advancing academic goals and acquiring essential skills in real-life contexts (Hope, 1999; Kahne & Westheimer, 1996).

The idea behind service learning is not just to involve young adolescents in the community (which in and of itself is also a worthwhile idea) but also to *reinforce* or *refine* actual learning objectives from the classroom. For example, students can use science, math, social studies, and other subjects to develop a bird habitat in the community (Gadecki & McManus, 1996). They can practice reading, writing, and language skills in an Adopt-a-Grandparent program with a local retirement home (Wood & Jones, 1996) or participate in a Community Problems Solvers program to identify, examine, and suggest solutions to a community problem (Halsted, 1996). Young adolescents can tutor younger children or adults, organize a cleanup effort for environmental protection, or help preserve an endangered wildlife area. Rather than having a one-size-fits-all program, each middle school needs to consider its own individual student population and community to see how community learning projects can be tied into instructional objectives.

As we leave this brief overview of instructional strategies, we want to remind you, again, of the importance of using developmentally responsive educational experience with young adolescents. More examples of these experiences are shown in Appendix A.

Teaching in Block Schedules—Special Considerations

As you read in chapter 5, many middle schools are replacing the five- or six-period day with a block schedule. In addition to being an organizational strategy, block scheduling has changed the way many teachers think about and implement instruction.

With the five- or six-period school day, teachers had to plan instruction that they could teach in a class period of less than 1 hour, and they grew accustomed to these relatively short time periods. Most realized that the short time did not allow a variety of instructional strategies (e.g., demonstration, group work, and a video) and that the integration of curriculum content was difficult at best. Some felt frustrated when the class period ended just as the class was finally becoming actively involved or when class discussions had reached a point where learning was occurring. Other teachers, however, liked the five- or six-period day and felt students' attention spans made the short periods ideal.

The trend toward block scheduling has resulted in teachers voicing mixed feelings. Some teachers think block scheduling contributes to instruction by giving them more time

Case Study 8–1

Lost Lake Middle School Tries Block Scheduling

The faculty at Lost Lake Middle School, a school of about 600 students, was committed to instructional excellence. However some teachers were skeptical when the administration announced that it would implement block scheduling as a means of improving instruction and increasing academic achievement. Although the school district provided extensive inservice training with a consultant, and allowed teachers to visit schools with block schedules, some teachers were sure they would not like the changes.

Two years after the implementation of the block schedule, there were still mixed feelings on the faculty at Lost Lake Middle School. While some teachers liked block scheduling and thought the switch was a good move, others felt quite the opposite. When a group of team leaders sat down to discuss the situation, they all agreed that attitudes were the most influential factors in whether teachers felt successful.

Some teachers in the school readily adjusted. They realized that just using more of the same old instructional activities would not work with the longer time periods. These teachers changed their mindsets toward instruction as well as their actual practices. They did more detailed planning and used a broader repertoire of instructional methods and activities to maintain student interest in the longer blocks. After explaining block scheduling to their students and discussing how the change would affect their school day, they carefully observed their students to determine satiation, or the time when activities had to be changed in order to hold the students' attention. Some took advantage of technology and wove the use of a variety of information resources into their teaching. Many of the successful teachers used the block schedule to develop interdisciplinary units with others on their team.

With few exceptions, the unsuccessful teachers failed to change their instructional mindsets and tried to teach the same way they did with shorter periods. They only planned "more" to fill up the time. Students recognized their lack of enthusiasm or confidence and failed to help make block scheduling work.

for experiments, demonstrations, and simulations. Other teachers believe students need instruction and practice everyday.

Undoubtedly, teaching in the block schedule requires teachers to change *their instructional plans as well as their actual instructional methods.* Teachers who adopt the attitude of "I will do the same things I have always done—I will just cover more information" are likely to feel frustrated, as will their students! Case Study 8–1 looks at a school that adopted block scheduling and shows how some teachers experienced success while, unfortunately, others did not. See if you can identify the strategies teachers used to make their instruction successful in block scheduling.

INSTRUCTION FOR SPECIAL LEARNERS

Special Needs

Special-needs students (also referred to as exceptional students) include those with disabling conditions in any one or more of the following categories: mental retardation, hearing, speech or language, visual, emotional, orthopedic, autism, traumatic brain injury, other health impairment, or specific learning disabilities. To the maximum extent possible, students with special needs must be educated with their peers in the regular classroom whether for an entire day (full inclusion) or for part of the school day (partial inclusion). Earlier in this chapter, we listed some ways in which general and special educators can collaborate to provide instruction in the regular classroom. Providing effective instruction to special-needs students requires more attention to individual needs, better diagnosis of what the child already knows as well as his or her weaknesses, and an understanding of the child's characteristics, especially those that affect instruction. Table 8–3 shows some additional instructional practices that promote working with special needs students.

Gifted

Gifted young adolescents are sometimes neglected in the regular classrooms because there is no singular method to identify these students. Gifted students can be very diverse and may be antisocial, creative, high-achieving, divergent thinkers, or perfectionists. They can also have some special-needs characteristics such as attention deficit disorder, dyslexia, or other learning disorders (Kellough & Kellough, 1999). Undoubtedly, identifying gifted young adolescents can be a difficult task, and the best procedure is to ask advice of the specialist in gifted education or another professional educator trained in gifted education.

TABLE 8–3 ***Implementing Instruction for Special-Needs Students***

When working with special-needs students:

1. Learn about the young adolescent as a student and as a person.
2. Adapt instructional materials and procedures to meet individual needs.
3. Work from the concrete to the abstract.
4. Break complex learning into simpler components.
5. Check for understanding of procedures and instructions.
6. Provide sufficient drill and practice.
7. Help students maintain a record of assignments.
8. Plan questions and their sequences carefully.
9. Encourage and provide peer support and peer tutoring.
10. Provide opportunities and experience for some degree of success.

Based on Kellough & Kellough, 1999.

TABLE 8–4 ***Instructional Strategies for Gifted Students***

Instructional adaptations that are appropriate for gifted learners include:

1. Faster-paced instructional patterns
2. More frequent use of inquiry techniques
3. Use of varied questioning strategies including higher-level questions
4. Use of cooperative learning groups for problem solving
5. More frequent use of discussion
6. Greater use of independent learning contracts and individualized instruction
7. Use of advanced reading-level materials
8. Use of exploratory activities
9. Emphasis on critical thinking, problem solving, and inquiry

Source: Van Tassell-Baska, 1989; Erb, 1992; Kellough & Kellough, 1999.

Compared to the traditional elementary and secondary school, the middle school best meets the needs of gifted learners (Erb, 1992). Indeed, with the use of teams and the emphasis on problem solving in dynamic learning environments, many gifted students thrive in middle schools. Table 8–4 shows some instructional adaptations that are appropriate for gifted learners.

Closing Remarks

Middle school educations cannot rely on instructional strategies that have an elementary or secondary school focus. Young adolescents need instructional methods that are developmentally responsive—methods that reflect their increasing ability to work independently, their desire for socialization, and their increased concern with peer approval (and all the other characteristics mentioned in Appendix A). They also need instruction in heterogeneous groups by teachers who are willing to work collaboratively, to accommodate varying levels of abilities, and to place emphasis on individual young adolescents' academic achievement and overall well-being. We believe such instruction can become a reality, as middle school teachers learn about the early adolescence developmental period and about individual young adolescents, and as they make a commitment to provide effective middle school instruction.

Suggested Readings

Brodhagen, B. L. (1998). Varied teaching and learning approaches. *Middle School Journal, 29*(5), 49–52. Discusses strategies such as learning inventories, projects, interactive and reflective learning, and question-posing by young adolescents.

Carroll, P. S., & Taylor, A. (1998). Understanding the culture of a classroom. *Middle School Journal, 30*(1), 1998. Explores cultural diversity and individual class culture.

Ciaccio, J. (1998). Teach success to underachieving middle schoolers. *The Education Digest, 64*(3), 11–15. Explains how teachers can help students experience success despite their academic uncertainty.

Gable, R., A., & Manning, M. L. (1997). Teachers' roles in the collaborative efforts to reform education. *Childhood Education 73,* 219–223. Explains the process of effective collaboration.

Reiser, R. A., & Butzin, S. M. (1998). Project TEAMS: Integrating technology into middle school instruction. *TechTrends, 43*(7), 39–44. Explains Project TEAMS (Technology Enhancing Achievement in Middle Schools), which focuses on technology, active learning, and interdisciplinary instruction.

Weir, C. (1998). Using embedded questions to jump-start metacognition in middle school remedial readers. *Journal of Adolescent and Adult Literacy, 41,* 458–467. Describes embedded questions (and guidelines for writing embedded questions) that guide remedial readers toward metacognitive strategies.

Chapter 9

Effective Instructional Behaviors—Research and Practice

Scenario—Mr. Rodriguez, A Staff Development Specialist

"Carlos! Carlos Rodriguez! What are you doing here?"

Carlos Rodriguez, Staff Development Specialist for the Blazemore City Schools, a large urban system, paused in the middle of the busy hallway at the Capital Convention Center and tried to see who was calling him. Finally he located the speaker and moved through the crush of conference attendees until he stood beside a woman along one of the walls.

"Kenisha, I didn't realize you would be here. We could have flown up together."

Kenisha Harwood, the principal at Stony Brook Middle School in a suburban school system near Blazemore, just laughed. "I wasn't sure that I would be here. I didn't plan to attend the regional middle school conference unless I could take Dr. Jamison's postconference seminar and workshop on effective instructional behaviors. It was full and I had to go on a waiting list. Then they had a last-minute cancellation so I quickly rearranged my schedule and flew up yesterday."

"Hey, I'm here for the same seminar. Last year, everyone raved about Lee Jamison's workshop. Although no one from Blazemore attended, word got through to the superintendent. She decided someone from Blazemore needed to attend this year so I got the nod. The district administrative team wants me to see what I think about Jamison's ideas and whether the use of effective instructional behaviors will improve student behavior and achievement test scores. If I think it does, the team wants me to work with the teachers at P.S. 107."

"If Jamison's workshop is as good as his college classes were, you better start planning how you'll work with P.S. 107. You know, that's a tough middle school. Don't get me wrong, but I've had a few teachers on the faculty at Stony Brook Middle who worked at P.S. 107. They've mentioned . . ."

Carlos cut her off. "Spare me the horror stories. I know I'll have my work cut out for me."

"All I was going to say, Carlos, was that the school has a reputation for discipline problems and fairly low test scores. And I've been to meetings with Mike Landis, the principal. In the eight or so years that he's been at P.S. 107, Mike has tried hard but he seems a little reluctant to implement new ideas. My teachers also tell me that there is a core of teachers in the school who have been there a long time and have a great deal of influence. I'm sure some might feel threatened if they think they have to change their teaching style or even their lesson plan format."

"Yes, I know. Whatever I do will have to be done slowly with lots of interaction and time for teachers to digest new information. But, I know you don't have those kinds of problems at Stony Brook, Kenisha. Why are you so excited about this 3-day seminar?"

"Lee Jamison has a way of explaining research and theories so that you can understand them. And, frankly, I've been out of school for a while and need some new ideas. A teacher that I hired this year had attended one of Jamison's workshops. She's been throwing around names like Brophy, Walberg, Good, and Porter, and terms like *withitness*. My faculty is good, but teachers can always use help and ideas for improving instruction. So, I figured I needed to do some work." Glancing at her watch, Kenisha continued, "We'll have 3 days to talk. Right now, we better get to the seminar. I had Jamison for a college class and he likes people to be on time."

Overview

Like Carlos Rodriguez and Kenisha Harwood, most educators face the challenge of trying to determine the teaching behaviors that are most productive and effective for them. Unfortunately, this is not a problem that is limited to the middle grades; and finding a solution is not easy. In our opening scenario, Mr. Rodriguez knew presenting research and theories to the middle school teachers at P.S. 107 and asking them to change or modify their instructional methods would be a challenge. While some educators believe students learn more with direct instruction where the teacher conveys curricular content and students receive it, others believe students learn more when the teacher serves as a guide or allows students to work in small groups. Some educators base their ideas about effective instruction on their opinions, rather than on any documented research. Frequently, they believe that research says little about their everyday practices.

Too often we hear teachers express the belief that "research is for people who don't teach." We hope that you do not share their attitude because research on effective teaching does provide a great deal of useful, practical information on concepts such as how to teach, how to conduct oneself during instruction and teacher-student interactions, how to use time productively, and how to promote academic achievement. In this chapter, you will have an opportunity to look at the research on effective teaching and see how this research can be translated into middle school practice.

Objectives

After reading and thinking about this chapter on effective instructional behaviors, you should be able to:

1. list and explain several research studies that focus on effective teaching and discuss how teachers can become more effective in their teaching as well as their daily interaction with young adolescents;
2. explain Jere Brophy's (1983) concept of "withitness" (Kounin, 1970) and discuss how effective teachers demonstrate "withit" behaviors;
3. explain Herbert Walberg's (1988) research on effective teachers emphasizing productive time on task rather than only time on task;
4. list reasons for Porter's and Brophy's (1988) belief that effective teachers inform learners of intended objectives and help students progress toward those outcomes;
5. discuss several ways that Brophy and Good (1986) feel effective teachers can help students succeed;
6. identify the ways in which the research studies on effective teaching are relevant to middle school teaching and learning situations;
7. explain several characteristics that all effective middle school teachers need; and
8. explain how instructional experiences can be adapted according to young adolescents' intelligence and cognitive development, motivation, self-esteem, gender, and culture.

Contemporary Research on Effective Instructional Behaviors

Unfortunately, with only a few isolated exceptions, there have not been major studies focusing specifically on effective middle school teachers. This may be due, in part, to the mistaken idea that middle school is simply a grown-up elementary school or still a junior high school. It may also be because the middle school teaching license for grades 6 to 8 is often combined with either general elementary or secondary teaching credentials instead of standing on its own merits. However, regardless of the reasons, middle school teachers and their instructional behaviors have not been subjected to intense scrutiny.

Therefore, to learn about effective instructional behaviors, we must look at general research on effective teaching. Thankfully, during the last 10 to 15 years, the research on effective teaching has provided a great deal of insight into how teacher behaviors influence academic achievement and student attitudes toward school (Brophy, 1983, 1987; Brophy & Good 1986; Walberg, 1988). The challenge for you as a middle school educator is, first, to understand the research on effective teaching and, second, to determine how to change your own teaching practices to reflect the research findings. Throughout this process, you need to keep in mind the tremendous developmental diversity of 10- to 14-year-olds, the unique nature of the middle school culture and communities, and the increasingly more difficult and challenging middle school curricular content.

"Is teaching an art that someone is born with, or is it a science where people actually learn what to do in a classroom? It seems as if some people are just 'born to teach' while others don't seem to be able to teach and manage a classroom no matter what they do. Why does a born teacher need to take education classes? And will classes really help us regular people learn how to teach?" These comments came from an undergraduate college student in the middle school education program.

Indeed, it does seem that some people are born to teach. They seem to know what to do, how to handle transitions with ease, and how to deal successfully with discipline problems. But, just as artists or doctors need training and continuing education to improve their skills, even "born teachers" need to develop, modify, and perfect their teaching behaviors. Then, too, an individual with an interest in teaching and a sincere desire to become a teacher can, through hard work and practice, develop the skills to become an effective instructor. This is not to say that everyone can become a teacher. It takes more than subject knowledge and a grasp of teaching methods to be a teacher. Especially at the middle school level, a sincere knowledge of and desire to work with 10- to 14-year-olds and a willingness to help them through the turbulence of young adolescence are a must.

We believe that the research on effective teaching has much to offer both preservice and inservice teachers, especially those who are willing to experiment with new perspectives about how teachers should teach and about how young adolescents can be helped. Granted, some educators, due to their experience and personality, might have an advantage over others. However, regardless of their present capabilities, all teachers can benefit from learning about the researchers and theories shown in Table 9–1. While many researchers have studied instructional behavior, we want to focus on the work of these researchers because they pinpoint teaching behaviors that have the potential for improving the middle school experience and for helping both the person who was born to teach as well as the person who must learn to teach.

Although this chapter provides selected research findings on effective teaching, we recognize the need to respect and encourage teacher individuality, just as we suggested in chapter 6 on classroom management. Educators differ in many ways. Some teachers might be able to make use of all of the research on effective teaching; others, who are just as successful, might find that specific teaching techniques take away their freedom and individuality. We believe that teachers' individuality and spontaneity should be respected and encouraged.

TABLE 9–1 *Selected Research on Effective Teaching*

Researcher/Author	What Effective Teachers Do
Brophy (1983), Kounin (1970)	Effective teachers demonstrate "withitness"
Walberg (1988)	Effective teachers emphasize productive time on task
Porter and Brophy (1988)	Effective teachers inform learners of intended objectives
Brophy and Good (1986)	Effective teachers help provide opportunities for students to succeed
Brophy (1987)	Effective teachers seek academic success results from reasonable effort

Therefore, if you are successful as a teacher, we encourage you to continue with your instructional practices. However, we hope that you will explore the research on what makes teachers effective. You might find ideas to refine or expand your repertoire of instructional strategies. Also, as you select teaching strategies that have the most promise for helping young adolescents, remember that they must reflect both 10- to 14-year-olds' unique developmental needs and the middle school concept.

SELECTED STUDIES ON TEACHER EFFECTIVENESS

Jere Brophy: Effective Teachers Demonstrate a Sense of Withitness

Jere Brophy (1983) built on the term *withitness,* which was coined over 30 years ago by Kounin (1970). Brophy maintained that effective teachers were "withit" and demonstrated a sense of "withitness" by exhibiting specific "withit" behaviors, as described in Table 9–2.

Observing Jim Cardigan in his seventh-grade science classroom was like seeing Brophy's (1983) "withitness" in action. Jim was always aware of what was going on; in fact he could be working with a small group on an experiment and still be aware of what every other student was doing. Students accused him of having "eyes in the back of his head," but Jim credited it to his experience and to his ability to listen to several conversations at the same time. "When I'm working with one group, the conversations of the other groups seem to drift in and out of my hearing. What I'm doing is monitoring the class. Sure, I know the perennial troublemakers and keep an eye or ear out for them; but I also want to eliminate potential problems before they disrupt the entire class. I use a lot of small-group work in science and I need to keep on top of what's happening in each group. That doesn't mean I expect a quiet room. I know the science groups provide a needed time for the students to socialize. But the students know that I have limits and that I expect them to get the work done. When I work with the whole class, I want to be sure that I can see all the students. Sometimes I move around the room. And I never have my eyes buried in the teacher's manual like some teachers I know."

TABLE 9–2 *"Withitness"*

Teachers Who Demonstrate "Withitness":
Know all learners' behaviors
Know students' strengths, weaknesses, and learning needs
Eliminate problems before they become disruptive
Are where they can see all students at all times
Detect inappropriate learning behaviors early
Monitor the class and acknowledge requests for assistance
Handle disruptions and keep track of time
Listen to student answers
Observe other students for signs of comprehension or confusion
Formulate questions, determine the sequence of selecting students to answer, evaluate the quality of answers, and monitor the logical development of content
Provide small-group instruction rather than conventional whole-group instruction
Monitor several different activities at once

Jim Cardigan's actions demonstrate how Brophy's "withitness" relates to young adolescents and middle school teaching. First, teachers like Jim realize that young adolescents need both freedom and limits to their behavior and know when to give freedom and when to set limits. A wishy-washy teacher might fail to let students know limits or might let a science experiment degenerate into a social time. When a teacher allows certain behaviors one day and forbids the same behaviors the next day, students become confused. Second, teachers need to be confident enough to handle the routines of the day and to manage (without threat or coercion) young adolescents. Some students can occasionally test a teacher's confidence and determination. Third, middle school teachers who are "withit" realize their students' attention spans are somewhat short. Therefore, they frequently change instructional activities to avoid boredom. Finally, "withit" middle school teachers realize young adolescents need to socialize, and they provide teaching-learning activities that allow students to work collaboratively.

Lauren, a middle school student teacher complained: "Some days I demonstrate 'withitness,' while on other days, I don't. But my cooperating teacher always appears 'withit.' She knows the progress and behavior of all students; she always responds appropriately; she can eliminate behavior problems before they escalate; and she can monitor several different activities simultaneously. Will I ever be able to teach like that? Is 'withitness' something that can be learned?"

We explained to Lauren that understanding the concept of "withitness" and wanting to achieving this "withitness" were excellent first steps. However, it takes time and experience until you are able to gain confidence and develop all the nuances of "withitness." Unfortunately, not all teachers develop "withitness," but many teachers who work toward this goal become better teachers—more productive, more effective, and more humane and caring.

Herbert Walberg: Effective Teachers Demonstrate Productive Time on Task

How many times have you observed a teacher "who keeps students busy?" You might have heard a teacher say: "Never let them stop working." Whether the students are working on lab reports, worksheets, or exercises from the textbook, no time is lost in these teachers' classrooms because students are always busy. These teachers equate nonstop activity with learning, but research suggests that such a belief might not be true.

One key to effective teaching, suggests Herbert Walberg (1988), is to engage students in work that is "productive time on task," which is not the same as "time-on-task" (Walberg, 1988). Table 9–3 shows what Walberg had in mind.

"In my math classes, the students stay pretty busy," said Kim Vinsent, an eighth-grade teacher. "But that doesn't mean they're doing busy work. The challenge is for me to adapt my math lessons to the needs and interests of my students. I even try to use practical problems and examples that build on topics they are studying in their other classes, exploratories, and advisories. I have a lot of information to cover and I tried the total immersion, keep-their-noses-to-the-grindstone approach but it just didn't work. Now I use direct instruction interspersed with other teaching-learning activities as well as study times. Also, I've found that conventional 'whole-group' instruction can't always accommodate the vast differences in individual learning rates and prior knowledge of my students. So I use group work and individual work, too."

Walberg's (1988) theory indicates that teachers should engage learners in appropriate work that matches the individual learner's abilities and interests. However, as Kim Vinsent pointed out, it means much more than just keeping the students busy. Forcing students into nonproductive activities just for the sake of maintaining order and quiet in the classroom is counterproductive. Instead, students should engage in genuine activities that meet specific learning objectives.

Middle school teachers who want to refine their teaching behaviors to reflect Walberg's research can do several things. First, they can provide time-efficient, direct teaching during which they work directly with students. With this approach, they show students that they

TABLE 9–3 ***Productive Time on Task***

Teachers Who Demonstrate Productive Time on Task:
Prepare carefully planned lessons
Provide activities that meet specific learning objectives
Adapt lessons to learners' needs/interests rather than just keeping the students busy
Engage in direct teaching
Provide study interspersed with other learning activities
Provide appropriate work that matches individual learner's abilities and interests
Provide accurately paced learning activities that are appropriate and worthwhile
Ensure that learning goals and instructional activities accurately reflect prior achievement, developmental levels, motivational levels, and student self-esteem

are careful planners and methodical leaders. Second, teachers can plan accurately paced activities (whether curricular content, exploratory programs, or teacher advisories) that are combined with other school activities. Rather than expecting 10- to 14-year-olds to concentrate on learning for long periods of time, teachers can plan sequences of activities that provide variety and reduce students' frustration levels. Third, the instructional activities should be ones that learners consider appropriate and worthwhile and that address one or more specific learning objectives. In addition, these instructional activities need to reflect young adolescents' prior achievements, be age- and developmentally appropriate, and address students' motivational levels and their self-esteem. Finally, middle school educators need to ensure that, throughout the school environment, there is an appreciation for time being efficiently and effectively used. This means that all educators in the school share a professional commitment to ensure the most advantageous use of the school day. The effective use of learning time potentially reduces misbehavior in the classroom and throughout the school.

Andrew Porter and Jere Brophy: Theories on Objectives, Learning Strategies, and Learning Progress

In their research, Porter and Brophy (1988) stress how important it is for effective teachers to inform students about objectives, learning strategies, and learning progress. Table 9–4 provides a closer look at Porter's and Brophy's work.

"One reason I like Ms. Hanora is that she lets us know what we're supposed to do and then teaches us how do to it." Kevin, a seventh grader.

"Ms. Geerts can always tell when we don't understand or are having trouble with an assignment. I've had teachers who make an assignment and then forget about it until the day it's due. Ms. Geerts isn't like that." Phylisa, a sixth grader.

TABLE 9–4 ***Objectives, Strategies, and Progress***

Teachers Inform Students about Objectives, Strategies, and Progress by:
Being clear about instructional goals and activities
Teaching learners expected learning strategies
Monitoring learning progress and watching for frustration
Demonstrating expert use of instructional materials
Demonstrating an understanding of students
Addressing both low- and high-level cognitive objectives
Accepting responsibility for student outcomes
Communicating to students expectations for learning
Teaching metacognitive strategies
Reflecting about instructional and management practices
Providing appropriate feedback

"I like the way Mr. Minahan gives us our learning itinerary. That's what he calls the checklist he gives us for each big project. It's a step-by-step reminder of what we've got to do." Miquel, a seventh grader.

Each of these three middle school teachers demonstrate at least one of the characteristics identified by Porter's and Brophy's research. They were clear about their instructional goals and activities and communicated those expectations to their students. In doing so, they eliminated student confusion about teacher expectations. Ms. Geerts monitored her students' understanding by offering regular and appropriate feedback and let them know that she knew their actions, their frustrations, and their progress.

There are several other teaching behaviors identified by Porter and Brophy that can be used in middle schools. First, teachers need to remember the tremendous diversity (i.e., differing cognitive abilities) of young adolescents and know their strengths, weaknesses, and learning needs. Then they need to plan educational experiences that can address those learning needs. Working with the library media specialist and others, teachers can make expert use of curricular materials and can supplement the textbook with other information sources. When teachers use a variety of materials and instructional methods, they reduce the chance of students being confused about goals and outcomes. This, in turn, reduces off-task behaviors. Finally, educators can teach students metacognitive strategies and help students feel successful with school experiences.

Jere Brophy and Thomas Good: Theories on Momentum, Emphasis, Expectations, and Seatwork

Jere Brophy and Thomas Good (1986) reported several effective teacher behaviors that have potential for middle school educators. Table 9–5 summarizes their conclusions.

In Case Study 9–1, Amanda Brandon shows Brophy's and Good's theories on momentum, emphasis, expectations, and seatwork in action.

TABLE 9–5 *Momentum, Emphasis, Expectations, and Seatwork*

Teachers Who Gave Correct Momentum, Emphasis, Expectations, and Seatwork:
Provide instruction with the proper momentum—neither too fast nor too slow
Emphasize academic instruction
Expect all students to master the curriculum
Allocate most time to curriculum-related activities
Provide productive, meaningful learning activities at appropriate difficulty levels
Relate seatwork to specific objectives
Provide activities that result in high levels of success
Plan and establish clear rules and procedures in advance
Allow students to assume responsibility for behavior
Encourage teacher/student cooperation
Minimize disruptions and delays
Plan independent as well as organized lessons

Case Study 9–1

A Teacher's Efforts toward Student Success

Amanda Brandon was a seventh-grade language arts teacher at Varnay Middle School, which served a lower socioeconomic community. Although the building was old, dilapidated, and had high windows without shades, Amanda was very happy to work at Varnay. In addition to liking her fellow faculty members, she thought she could make a difference in some students' lives and she did. While she might not have consciously realized it, many of her attitudes and instructional methods reflected the research on effective teaching. For example, she had high expectations, both for her students and for herself. Although she realized that all students would not achieve equally, she always emphasized academic achievement and thought they all could achieve to some degree. Also, she took advantage of what she knew about momentum. She tried for an instructional pace that was neither too fast nor slow—one that would maximize productive time on task.

Her instructional techniques worked with several students of varying ability and motivational levels. Skip was a 12-year-old happy-go-lucky boy with average intelligence. In September, Skip had told Ms. Brandon, "I'm going to fail spelling this year—might make a D, but no higher. Always have. I can't spell; my Mom and Dad can't spell. Put me down for a D or F." When Ms. Brandon checked Skip's permanent records, she found that Skip was right. His spelling grade was either a D or an F. But Amanda Brandon was not ready to write off Skip that easily. So she made Skip a proposition. "Skip, I'll work with you and let's see if together we can't get you a higher grade in spelling." "No use trying, Ms. Brandon," Skip replied. "There's no way I'll ever make an A in spelling!" "Hey, I didn't say try for an A, Skip," Ms. Brandon explained. "Let's just work on bringing that F or D up to a C. What do you say?" It was not easy, but Skip really tried to meet Amanda Brandon's expectations. After lots of work, encouragement, and study, Skip earned a C for the year. While, to some students in the class, a C would have been a disaster, to Skip a C in spelling was a major success.

In the same class as Skip was Susan—bright, motivated, and destined for success. She did not study nearly as much as Skip, but she made all A's. Amanda Brandon saw a need to challenge Susan and gave her literature written for older adolescents and adults. However, in doing so, she worked with the school library media specialist to select the titles carefully. As an effective middle school teacher, she recognized that, while Susan could read and comprehend on an advanced level from other seventh graders, she might not be developmentally mature enough to handle the complex topics and adult situations found in some literature. With her insatiable appetite for reading and study, Susan read almost everything she suggested and asked for more. She wrote about the books, compared them, and changed endings. Gradually, her own writing began to take on sophisticated characteristics not usually found in the writing of seventh graders.

Case Study 9–1 (cont.)

Skip and Susan were as different as day and night, but Amanda Brandon challenged them both. She had conveyed high expectations, maximized the momentum for both (although Susan moved a great deal faster than Skip), encouraged and convinced them, and never let her students' self-doubts last long. Was she as successful with all students in the class? No, but she never quit trying. Her emphasis on academic achievement, self-esteem, challenging work, and maintaining momentum were keys to success for many of her seventh graders.

Good's and Brophy's conclusions can be divided into three broad categories. First, teachers like Amanda Brandon in Case Study 9–1, who have high expectations for students' academic achievement and behavior, "often get what they expect" as students work up to expectations. Students perceive that teachers expect them to do their best and that teachers are providing learning activities that are geared to the students' developmental and interest levels. Second, teachers who maintain an appropriate momentum and minimize disruptions and delays reduce student misbehaviors. When students are successful in their independent or cooperative group work, frustration and boredom are reduced. Finally, questioning strategies can have a significant effect on student behavior. Teachers who ask questions at the appropriate difficulty level, provide sufficient wait-times, and respond appropriately to incorrect answers can maintain students' attention and on-task behaviors. The teachers also show that they are aware of each student's progress and involvement with the lesson.

Jere Brophy and Thomas Good: Effective Teachers Help Students to Succeed

As you saw in Case Study 9–1, some students need more help than others to succeed. Some might not know how to study; others might wonder how to focus their efforts or make best use of their time. Teachers can use many of Jere Brophy's and Thomas Good's (1986) research findings to help students learn and succeed. We will see this when Carlos Rodriguez from the chapter's opening scenario returns in Case Study 9–2.

As a middle school educator, either presently teaching or preparing to teach, you, like the teachers at P.S. 107, should readily recognize the need to help students succeed. Rather than having a "student versus teacher" mentality, teachers actively need to help students, use instructional methods that capture students' interests, provide for student involvement, and engage students in meaningful activities. Similarly, effective middle school teachers must believe that all young adolescents can succeed to some degree; they might all not make A's or join honor groups, but they can all learn and succeed at some worthwhile task.

Case Study 9–2

Mr. Rodriguez Returns to Blazemore

Kenisha Harwood's prediction proved right. When she and Carlos Rodriguez finished Dr. Jamison's seminar, Carlos had to admit that he had found lots of research that he thought would help the middle school students and teachers at P.S. 107. Back in Blazemore, Carlos approached Mike Landis, the principal at P.S. 107. Carlos felt it might have been the pressure from the superintendent, but Mike agreed to give him six in-service slots of 3 hours each. Reflecting on all the research such as Brophy's "withitness" and Walberg's "productive time on task" that Dr. Jamison had presented, Carlos wondered how he could explain all the research and theories in an interesting nonthreatening way so that the teachers could translate theory into everyday practice.

Rather than lecture about the various research findings, Carlos came up with a program that he called "Teach for Success." His goal was to help each teacher find ways to give each student a successful learning experience in his or her class. Key ideas that he wanted to share with the teachers at P.S. 107 were the following:

Establish realistic expectations for your students
Help your students learn to set realistic goals that can be reached with reasonable effort
Provide curricular and instructional experiences that relate to the personal and social lives of your students
Match your learning objectives and activities to the developmental readiness levels of your students
Use teaching methods that are developmentally responsive
Provide cooperative learning and peer tutoring experiences that will meet 10- to 14-year-olds' desire to socialize
Recognize and value genuine student achievements
Avoid lecturing for long periods of time due to the limited attention spans of young adolescents
Realize the importance of self-esteem and how it affects learning and achievement in your classroom

Carlos drew on every technique he knew for conducting a successful in-service. Moving slowly, he wanted to involve the teachers in developing plans to incorporate his key ideas into the structure at P.S. 107. After the first in-service, although the teachers were generally positive, some were apprehensive. There were the expected questions about changing lesson plan format and trusting research that was "done by somebody who doesn't know our unique situation."

Most teachers, however, were willing to give Carlos a chance. As teacher Lou Parker told Carlos: "You've really opened my eyes about ways to reach our kids. In fact, the problem-solving exercise you had us do in small groups made me aware of how insecure some of my students feel." Lou's feelings were shared by Chandel Wilson, a seventh-grade teacher who told Carlos: "I liked the goal-setting exercise. You let me feel how frustrating it can be when someone sets goals that I know I can't reach!"

TABLE 9–6 *Academic Success through Reasonable Effort*

Teachers Who Foster Academic Success through Reasonable Effort:
Teach students to appreciate the value of classroom activities
Help students believe in their own ability to succeed
Provide incentives for learning
Provide motivation to learn the necessary knowledge and skills
Model and communicate their expectations and direct instruction
Help students set realistic expectations for themselves
Help students develop a commitment to work to their expectations

Jere Brophy: Effective Teachers Convince Learners to Believe Academic Success Will Result from Reasonable Effort

Students, especially those like Skip in Case Study 9–1, who have failed or underachieved for many years, need to be convinced that, with reasonable effort, they can succeed. When students enter the middle school, they often feel bewildered and frustrated with new demands, more powerful peer expectations, and a more rigorous curriculum. Sometimes they feel that there are too many pressures and that their efforts will only result in failure or at least lower grades than they received in the elementary school. In essence, they need, as Brophy (1987) and Good and Brophy (1994) suggested, to be reassured that academic success will result from reasonable effort. Table 9–6 summarizes what Brophy feels teachers should do.

Jere Brophy (1987) felt that "students are more likely to want to learn when they appreciate the value of classroom activities and when they believe they will succeed if they apply reasonable effort" (p. 40). This is what Carlos Rodriguez was trying to foster in his "Teach for Success" program.

Unfortunately, some middle school learners have lost faith in their ability to learn and to achieve academically. Either they establish unrealistic goals, or their teachers set unrealistically high standards. As a result, these students think academic pursuits result only in failure. Thus, it is easier not to try than to put forth effort and fail. Educators need to motivate learners and convince them to believe in their teacher and in themselves. Using motivation techniques, teachers can show young adolescents that their chances of accomplishing learning goals will increase when they establish realistic goals and work diligently and determinedly toward them. In addition to helping students select realistic short-term and long-term goals, effective middle school teachers also need to help young adolescents determine the most feasible means of achieving those goals. That means helping them acquire proper study habits, showing them how to maintain an assignment guide, reminding them to take books home, and modeling how to study for tests.

Keeping Current with Technology 9–1 provides some Internet sites where you can find additional information on some of the research we have presented. In addition, you will find sites that provide other resources that you can use to improve your instruction.

Keeping Current with Technology 9–1

American School Board Association: "Helping Students Learn: An Online Anthology on Student Achievement"
http://www.asbj.com/anthologies.html

Appalachia Educational Laboratory
http://www.ael.org/

College of Education at Michigan State University: "Research reports" contains several reports by Dr. Jere Brophy
http://ed-web3.educ.msu.edu/publications/researchrpt/default.htm

Educational Research Network
http://www.ernweb.com/

ERIC Clearinghouse on Elementary and Early Childhood Education: Jere Brophy's report on "Failure Syndrome Students"
http://ericeece.org/pubs/digests/1998/brophy98.html

Laboratory for Student Success at Temple University: Interactive Handbook on "Achieving Student Success," written, in part, by Herbert J. Walberg
http://www.reformhandbook-lss.org/

Middleweb: Discussions that occurred on the Middle-L listserve such as "failing grades for late assignments: teaching responsibility or giving permission to fail"
http://www.middleweb.com

National Resource Center for Middle Grades/High School Education
http://www.coedu.usf/edu/middlegrades/

The School Administrator on-line
http://www.aasa.org/SA/contents.htm

SPECIAL CHARACTERISTICS OF MIDDLE SCHOOL TEACHERS

At the beginning of their work in the college of education, some of our preservice middle school teachers argue that "teachers are teachers." They contend, quite forcefully, that no special qualifications are needed for teaching in the middle school. In fact, one teacher education student informed us that, "If a teacher knows the curriculum and basic instructional methods, she or he can teach any grade level." We usually smile at these students and ask to continue this discussion after their first practicum experience in the public schools. We agree with them to a point. The teacher whom they describe probably can teach the curricular content, but we believe that successful middle school teachers must also understand the age group that is being taught and the essential middle school concepts that have been identified

TABLE 9–7 ***Characteristics of Effective Middle School Teachers***

Successful Middle School Teachers Have:
A knowledge of and an ability to apply effective teaching methods for 10- to 14-year olds
A knowledge of and a belief in essential middle school concepts
A knowledge of and a respect for young adults and their unique developmental period
A desire to help young adolescents experience genuine success
A knowledge of and an ability to teach the content of the middle school curriculum
An awareness to evaluate periodically their own teaching methods

as being helpful to these students and their success in school. After their first practicum experience, there are always a few holdouts; however, most agree that middle school teachers need special skills and professional education.

In addition to the effective instructional behaviors already discussed in this chapter, effective middle school teachers need the characteristics shown in Table 9–7. Perhaps you can think of other characteristics, but all of them can probably be included in one of these categories. The basic characteristic is that effective middle school teachers perceive the school strictly as *middle school* and the students strictly as *young adolescents.* This means that you must understand the unique developmental needs of 10- to 14-year-olds and that you should plan your instruction with these needs in mind.

As a middle school teacher, you must also be able to relate effective teaching research to the essential middle school concepts, such as creating a positive school environment. A problem occurs because middle school teachers often do not receive professional training that is designed specifically for them. Rather, the training is part of an elementary (K–5) or secondary (9–12) program. Under those circumstances, middle school teachers need to work on their own to locate information about interdisciplinary teaming, teacher advisories, exploratory programs, developmentally responsive educational experiences, and integrated curriculum. They should also have field experiences in middle schools with teachers experienced in teaching young adolescents.

One concept that is especially important for effective middle school instruction is that of teacher collaboration. Through their work on interdisciplinary teams, teachers can help each other improve their instruction. Teachers, especially in middle schools with interdisciplinary teams, should not feel that they are working in isolation. Rather they should feel part of a school community that, on several levels, is working toward excellence in teaching. Collaboration, co-teaching, and peer evaluation all have potential for improving instruction in the classroom.

Having good instructional techniques is not enough. As an effective middle school teacher, you must modify and adapt those techniques to work with young adolescents. To do so, you must be familiar with young adolescent development (i.e., shorter attention spans and the relationship between cognitive and psychosocial development) and use this knowledge as a basis for instructional decisions. Effective middle school teachers know the challenges that 10- to 14-year-olds face: socialization, a widening world outside the immediate family, peer pressure, and developmental changes (or the concern that these changes are not occurring). Also, middle school educators need to understand that some middle schoolers have just left the supposedly safe confines of the elementary school and may feel intimidated, isolated, or threatened. Although we see the middle school as far more than just a "transitional school," we realize that some young adolescents view the middle school only as a bridge between the elementary school and the high school. We hope that you will view the school as having a greater purpose than just serving as a holding ground and that you will convey this feeling to young adolescents. One way to do this is by providing meaningful instructional activities and by setting realistic expectations for all students.

Middle school educators must provide opportunities for all students to succeed (Brophy & Good, 1986) with reasonable effort (Brophy, 1987). Unfortunately, many young adolescents experience lower academic achievement and declining self-esteems. Others may find that the middle school curriculum is difficult. Yet all of these 10- to 14-year-olds need to be given genuine opportunities to succeed. Notice that we said "genuine opportunities." We are not suggesting just "passing them on" or giving them busy work. Ten- to 14-year-olds need to be convinced that they can succeed when they apply reasonable effort.

Another component of a successful middle school teacher is a knowledge of the middle school curriculum. Only by knowing the curriculum can teachers provide experiences that are neither elementary nor secondary and that are designed especially for young adolescents. This is neither a "little more difficult" elementary curriculum nor is it a "watered-down" secondary curriculum.

How can you gain this knowledge of curriculum? You can enroll in a middle school curriculum course, participate in curriculum development workshops held by the school district, work collaboratively with other experienced middle school teachers, select curriculum improvement as a goal for an interdisciplinary team, and study teachers' manuals and district curriculum guides. As suggested in chapter 3, knowing the middle school curriculum (and the scope and sequence for your particular curricular area) is an essential teaching element that cannot be left to chance.

As a middle school educator, you must periodically examine your own teaching behaviors. It is too easy to keep teaching the same way, without taking any risks. Therefore, you routinely need to consider how effective you are, examine what you are doing right, and pinpoint what you are doing wrong. Only then can you decide on an agenda for improving your teaching performance.

Theory into Practice 9–1 presents a plan for a collaborative unit that incorporates a variety of effective instructional techniques and provides students with opportunities for success through reasonable effort. This unit also addresses an issue you will read about in the next section of this chapter: how using a variety of materials can meet the diverse needs and interests of 10- to 14-year-olds.

Adapting Instruction to Young Adolescents' Individual Characteristics

As we indicated before and in Table 9–7, one key to becoming an effective middle school teacher is the ability to provide educational experiences based on young adolescents'

Theory into Practice 9–1

Immigration to America

Grade: Sixth

Objectives:

Language Arts: Students will identify various elements of fiction and discuss each of them in relation to novels they have read.

Social Studies: Students will describe the immigrants who have come to America since World War II and explain reasons for their immigration.

Overview: A language arts and a social studies teacher should collaborate on this interdisciplinary unit. While students are studying recent immigrants in social studies, they will read realistic fiction books on the same topic and will use those books to explore each of the elements of fiction. Although the theme of immigration will run through all books, specific titles will be assigned based on the interests and reading abilities of the students.

Instructional Techniques: This unit will include both direct, large-group instruction as well as small-group work and independent reading assignments.

Planning: The language arts and social studies teachers will consult with the library media specialist and select a wide range of books that meet the students' varying motivational and cognitive levels and that contain both female and male characters. The books will also represent the diverse cultural background of recent American immigrants.

Prior to teaching the elements of fiction, the language arts teacher will assign each student to a book-group and will provide copies of the book that the group members will read. Each teacher will also give the students a grading rubric and a schedule of due dates for their work.

Language Arts Teaching: After the language arts teacher introduces an element of fiction to the whole class, he/she will divide the class into book-groups in which students will discuss that element of fiction in relation to the immigration book that they read. After all the elements have been presented and discussed, each group will present their book to the class by focusing on one element of fiction and highlighting the use of that element in their book.

Social Studies Teaching: The social studies teacher will help the students incorporate information from the realistic fiction books that they are reading into their discussion of immigration. Students will be encouraged to use geography skills to locate the home countries of "their" immigrants, and to trace the route that their immigrants took to America. In addition, students will be asked to identify the reasons why their immigrants left their home country and the hardships that they faced during the journey to America and after they arrived in this country. Students will be asked to complete comparison charts and to contrast the information from the fiction book to that contained in the textbook.

Evaluation: Students will be evaluated by the teachers based on the evaluation rubric that was given to students at the beginning of the unit.

Theory into Practice 9–1 (cont.)

Suggested Books for This Unit:

Bunting, Eve. *How Many Days to America?* HarperCollins, 1995.

Buss, Fran, and Cubias, Daisy. *Journey of the Sparrows.* Dutton, 1991.

Crew, Linda. *Children of the River.* Delacorte, 1984.

Lord, Bette Bao. *In the Year of the Boar and Jackie Robinson.* HarperCollins, 1984.

Temple, Francis. *Grab Hands and Run.* HarperCollins, 1995.

Whelan, Gloria. *Goodbye Vietnam.* Random, 1993.

Developed from: Bucher, K. T. (1998). Integrating children's/young adult literature into the social studies. In H. E. Taylor (Ed.), *What's goin' on? Trends and issues in American education* (pp. 207–214). Needham Heights, MA: Simon & Schuster Custom; and Hough, D. L. & Donlan, D. (1994). Achieving independent student responses through integrated instruction. *Middle School Journal, 25*(5), 35–42.

differences, whether these differences are in intelligence and cognitive development, motivation, self-esteem, gender, or culture. As chapter 2 pointed out, every difference affects learners' academic achievement and overall school success as well as their perceptions of school and their place in the school communities. Keeping a positive perspective toward young adolescents' differences and actually providing instructional practices that reflect your students' individuality requires hard work and planning. Although we discussed these differences in chapter 2, we would like to revisit some of these and examine a few representative examples and their impact upon instruction.

Respect for Diversity

Have you ever celebrated Fasnacht Day? Are you aware of the fasting requirements of Ramadan? Are you comfortable working with heterogeneous groups that include students of all abilities? Do your teaching strategies include ways to motivate students who have a history of goofing off? Are you aware of the ways to address gender-specific learning differences in your classroom?

While our middle school students are rich in diversity, this richness is not always welcome. One writer (Perez, 1994) maintained that American public schools have never offered an enthusiastic welcome to student differences. In fact, most of the time, educators have attempted to remove differences, especially those that they thought would be barriers to advancement in society in general. In order for schools to offer appropriate responses, Perez (1994) suggested that schools should demonstrate that diversity is not a problem. Instead, educators should use diversity as an opportunity for everyone to experience other peoples and their differences. Assuming Perez is correct, we feel strongly that middle school educators must recognize how young adolescents' diversity affects all aspects of the school day and must select instructional methods that reflect knowledge and understanding of that learner diversity.

Intelligence and Cognitive Diversity

Effective middle school teachers often have to figure out how they can match their instructional behaviors to the diverse intelligence and cognitive development of 10- to 14-year-olds. It is, perhaps, an oversimplification to state that a learner's degree of intelligence affects what will be learned, since intelligence can be defined in more than one way. Still, most educators agree that overall intelligence, abilities, or special expertise contribute to the degree to which learners process information.

An important part of intelligence is the ability to take new information and relate that to previously acquired knowledge or the learner's achievement level. Educators who provide effective instruction attest to the fact that what students already know affects their present and future achievement. The question should always be asked, "To what extent, and how, can previous learning contribute to new learning? And, how can I help students make those connections?"

Learners' cognitive development is, also, of particular importance in middle schools, because not all 10- to 14-year-olds process information in the same manner or at the same rate. Young adolescents vary widely in their abilities to use language, apply thinking strategies, make comparisons and hypotheses, and apply concepts and information. They have a wide range of learning styles and different attitudes toward achievement.

"I just don't understand it! Why do we have to learn algebra anyway?" This comment came from Celeste, an eighth grader who was accustomed to excelling in every subject. Unfortunately, she was hitting a stone wall in her prealgebra class, and her frustration was evident to everyone in the class. Although Ms. Cherry, her teacher, had gone over the problem several times, Celeste still could not understand the solution, which required more than the application of a memorized formula.

It is important to remember that learners, like Celeste, who are functioning at one developmental level simply cannot comprehend material that requires the thinking and cognitive skills of the next higher developmental level. Rather than assuming that Celeste could succeed by trying hard or doing more homework, Ms. Cherry needed to understand that development and readiness, not effort alone, affect what youngsters can learn. If Celeste is at the concrete operations stage, she cannot master intellectual challenges that demand formal, abstract thinking abilities. Although some memorization might occur, she will be unable to learn information that is beyond her cognitive ability at any given age. Teachers who assume that all learners can perform functions and master content at a level attained by a few precocious and intellectually advanced students ignore individual differences (Toepfer, 1988).

Motivation

Many young adolescents appear to lose interest or motivation during the middle school years. This decline in motivation may occur because of the growing difficulty of curricular content or because young adolescents are preoccupied with their widening social world. As one of our practicum students said, "We have to motivate students to listen and do the work—that's one of the most difficult parts of teaching. They just do not want to work. They don't complete the homework, and most will not read what they are supposed to read. How can we discuss a book in class that no one has read?" We understood her predicament and explained that while this behavior was characteristic of the age group, she had to change her instruction to try to motivate her students. While we did not expect her to motivate all students, we suggested that she use some of the techniques shown in Theory into Practice 9–1 and change from large-group work where she did most of the talking to small group where more students could become actively involved. We suggested that she try to incorporate or build on student interests as another way to motivate her students. As an example, we told her the story of Mike, a sixth grader who would not read until the library media specialist found a series of skateboarding books. Given books on a topic he loved, Mike began to read a book a week.

School learning requires active effort, and students like Mike often do not put forth the active effort if they do not see a relationship between their schoolwork and their own interests. While they may respond to their parents' or teachers' pressures, unless students have a personal motivation for completing school assignments, they are not likely to expend the effort to do the work. Educators need to understand the many dimensions of motivation, and then help learners see the qualities in their assignments that are either interesting or useful (Tyler, 1989). Once Mike saw that reading books could provide information on his hobby of skateboarding, he no longer viewed reading as a boring chore.

Self-Esteem

Throughout this book, we have talked about the importance of the 10- to 14-year-old's self-esteem and its effects on academic achievement. Self-esteem is an individual difference with the potential to enhance or destroy a student's chances at school success. Thus teachers should plan instructional experiences that help build young adolescents' self-esteem. The effective middle school teacher should provide positive reinforcement for students' accomplishments as well as their efforts and ensure a healthy and positive classroom environment.

Gender

Gender is a term used to describe xmasculine and feminine differences—the thoughts, feelings, and behaviors that are identified as being either male or female. While few psychological differences exist between the genders, learned behaviors can differ significantly (Gollnick & Chinn, 1998). The result is the need to provide gender-fair curriculum, instructional behaviors, and learning environments. Diversity Perspectives 9–1 provides a look at the Women's Educational Equity Act (WEEA) and the need for an equal chance for both genders.

How can educators address gender differences? How can females and males receive an education that shows both feminine and masculine perspectives? An obvious answer is to ensure that instructional behaviors as well as overall educational efforts are as nonsexist as

Diversity Perspectives 9–1

Gender Equity—Both Girls and Boys

The Women's Educational Equity Act (WEEA) (1997) defines gender equity as a set of actions, attitudes, and assumptions that provide opportunities and that create expectations about individuals, regardless of gender. Gender equity is an equal chance for females and males at:

- learning, regardless of the subject
- preparing for future education, jobs, and careers
- setting high expectations
- developing, achieving, and learning
- receiving equitable treatment and outcomes in school and beyond

Source: Women's Educational Equity Act. (1997). http://www.edc.org/Women'sequity.

possible. Similarly, all instructional materials should show females and males in nonsexist situations. Middle school educators can also help both genders by taking an active stance against discrimination and by fighting all forms of sexism and discrimination. Teachers can emphasize collaboration and cooperation over competition, involve both boys and girls in learning activities, pose equal numbers of questions (with equal difficulty) to both boys and girls, and expect both genders to achieve in traditionally stereotyped curricular areas. For example, girls should not be discouraged from taking math, science, and technology classes. Boys should not be ridiculed if they prefer to read or paint rather than participate in sports. Both boys and girls should be encouraged to accept the other gender as well as their own.

Culture

> "There's something sneaky about Randy. He'll never look me in the eye when I talk to him." An eighth-grade teacher.

> "I don't know what's wrong with Maria. She has a great voice but she refuses to sing a solo during our parent's night performance." A sixth-grade teacher.

As you saw in chapter 2, several different environments impact each young adolescent and help shape his or her actions, beliefs, attitudes, and values. Each young adolescent brings to school his or her cultural baggage, including prejudices, myths, and stereotypes. This baggage affects attitudes toward school, other learners, and actual learning achievement. The Asian American student may be taught to revere teachers; the African American child may listen, yet not look the speaker in the eye; the Native American learner may value cooperation and sharing as being more worthy than competition; or the Hispanic American adolescent may believe he or she should not stand out among peers.

The challenge for effective middle school teachers is to understand and to respect these personal aspects, and, whenever possible, to provide culturally appropriate instructional experiences. It is important that these instructional experiences and activities reflect the values, attitudes, and beliefs of learners' cultures while not requiring any learners to participate in actions that contradict their own cultural beliefs. For example, when working with students whose cultures focus on cooperation, teachers should use instructional methods that do not stress competition among peers.

Closing Remarks

Just as Mr. Rodriguez learned, the research on effective teaching has identified successful teaching practices. The challenge is for you to determine the specific teaching behaviors that will have positive effects on your students' academic achievement and their general perspectives toward schooling. In order to select appropriate instructional behaviors, you need to consider young adolescents' intelligence and cognitive development, motivation, self-esteem, gender, and culture. When teachers use the most effective instructional behaviors (both with respect to the research on effective teaching as well as young adolescents' tremendous diversity), they make effective use of teachers' and students' time, help learners improve their academic achievement and perspective toward school, and value the diversity of 10- to 14-year-olds.

Suggested Readings

Gordon, R. L. (1997). How novice teachers can succeed with adolescents. *Educational Leadership, 54*(7), 56–58. Maintains that educators should develop social insight by exposing themselves to adolescent culture and relating content to students' outside interests.

Jacobowitz, R. (1997). Thirty tips for effective teaching. *Science Scope, 21*(4), 22–25. Offers reminders for communicating with students and nurturing their interest in science.

Manning, M. L. (1989/1990). Contemporary studies of teaching behaviors and their implications for middle level teacher education. *Action in Teacher Education, 21,* 1–5. Summarizes the research on effective teaching behaviors.

Walberg, H. J. (1994). Educational productivity: Urgent needs and new remedies. *Theory into Practice, 33*(2), 75–82. Compares Japanese and American educational efforts and offers solutions to America's problems.

Walberg, H. J., & Greenberg, R. C. (1997). Using the Learning Environment Inventory. *Educational Leadership, 54*(8), 45–47. Discusses the importance of cohesion, challenge, and satisfaction in students' academic achievement, attitudes toward school, and involvement in nonrequired school activities.

Chapter 10

Assessment of Learning—Methods and Issues

Scenario—Changes at Longview Middle School

Standing by the frozen foods case in the Buy-Low grocery store, Shirella Reed was checking her shopping list when she heard someone calling her name. Turning around, she saw Debra Costino pushing her grocery cart down the aisle and heading directly for Shirella with a very determined look on her face. As a seventh-grade teacher at Longview Middle School, Shirella knew Ms. Costino. In the past, two of the Costino children had been in Shirella's homeroom, and it had not taken long to learn that Debra Costino liked to be involved with her children's education. In addition to being an active member of the local parent's organization, Debra Costino had volunteered in the classroom and in the school library. But, this year had been different. Although Matt, the youngest of the Costino children, was now a student in her team, Shirella had not seen Debra Costino at the school. Overhearing some of Matt's conversations, she gathered that his mother now had a full-time job.

"I'm so glad I saw you," Ms. Costino began when she reached Shirella. "Matt has been telling me about some things that are happening in the seventh grade. I've been meaning to talk to someone about it, but with my new job and everything I just haven't had time."

"Well, we're doing some really interesting projects this fall," Shirella began.

"No, it's not the projects," Ms. Costino interjected, "it's the way you're going to be grading the students. I believe Matt mentioned something about a portfolio and a rubric."

"Oh yes, we're . . ."

Before Shirella could say any more, Ms. Costino interrupted. "But don't we need more rigorous standards for students? And what about Matt's mastery of academics? What's wrong with multiple-choice and true-false tests? That's what they used when I was in school and they worked. I'd think you teachers would like them, too. It seems to me they would be fairly easy to make up and easy to grade. And will all these portfolios help raise our standardized test scores?"

Shirella Reed tried to explain that the problem was that those types of tests do not measure what was taught. She also tried to point out that some students do not do well on objective tests since their stress levels go up and all the answers look right.

Ms. Costino waited until Shirella took a breath. "Are you sure this isn't just some fad you educators came up with? Don't traditional tests have a place in school anymore? Do you have to throw away everything just because some new idea has come along? How are we parents supposed to know what this authentic assessment is? I remember that when I volunteered at the school, you teachers always complained about the superintendent coming up with new ideas and letting the teachers figure out how to do it. Are they teaching you how to design these authentic assessments for your students? How can you be sure that they are fair?"

"Well," Shirella replied "this time the superintendent is providing plenty of help. We're attending workshops that focus on the issues surrounding authentic assessment as well as the positive and negative aspects of more traditional forms of assessment. What we're trying to do is discover how our students can benefit from the various types of assessment and how to make them work in our classrooms."

As she looked at Ms. Costino, Shirella realized that it would take more than a conversation in the grocery store to explain authentic assessment. Glancing in her shopping cart, Shirella exclaimed, "Oh, the ice cream is melting. I've got to go, but I'll call you to schedule a time when you can drop by the school to see what we're doing. We have some evening parent/teacher conference times in 2 weeks. Let's plan on meeting then."

Overview

Like Shirella Reed, many middle school educators, who are trying new methods for developmentally responsive student assessment, find that they need to explain these measures and their rationale for using them. In recent decades, there have been increased calls for rigorous standards and more accountability for student mastery of academics. Following the lead of the accountability movement, legislators, concerned that public schools are ineffective, have mandated standardized tests to show whether students can demonstrate at least minimal competence in the three R's (Popham, 1993).

In light of these mandates, can assessment in the middle school be developmentally responsive and promote rather than hinder young adolescents' educational progress? In this chapter you will be able to explore the perceptions surrounding assessment, look at traditional and authentic assessment devices, discover ways of reporting results to parents and administrators, and examine the issues affecting the assessment process. Our goal is to provide an overview of assessment. For more in-depth information, we hope you will consult the references included at the end of this chapter.

One of our practicum students aptly summarized the assessment situation when she said, "Sometimes we place too little emphasis on real assessment—we want to know what students have learned, but we just grade a worksheet or quickly make out a test. Then, what they get is a letter grade or maybe just a percentage written on the paper. Very little thought goes into providing assessments that really let students, administrators, and parents see what the students know." We agree with the student. Furthermore, we also agree that assessment in the middle school should reflect the position stated in *This We Believe: Developmentally Responsive Middle Level Schools* (National Middle School Association, 1995)—assessment should be continuous, authentic, and developmentally responsive.

Objectives

After reading and thinking about this chapter on assessment and evaluation, you should be able to:

1. define *assessment, evaluation,* and *measurement;*
2. define *diagnostic, formative,* and *summative evaluations* and explain the roles of each;
3. state various perceptions about testing and explain how these perceptions affect middle school education;
4. discuss the role of assessment in contemporary middle schools;
5. define and explain the purposes and process of assessment, especially as they relate to middle school education;
6. list assessment instruments such as tests produced by teachers, state departments of education, and textbook publishers, as well as standardized tests;
7. discuss authentic assessments, including the key issues, characteristics, and various assessment formats;
8. discuss issues in assessment in the middle school such as criticisms and negative effects on young adolescent learning; the effects of culture, gender, and other forms of diversity; and learners' stress; and
9. list several guidelines for effective assessment that can be followed whether teachers employ traditional or alternative assessments.

ASSESSMENT TERMINOLOGY—DEFINITIONS

What exactly is assessment? James McMillan (1997) maintains that considerable confusion exists over the meaning and usage of the terms *assessment, evaluation,* and *measurement.* While some educators define the terms broadly, others give more narrow definitions (Gallagher, 1998). To further complicate the situation, some educators view the terms as being synonymous. We believe, however, that, if you look closely, you will find differences that are very important to teachers who are faced with determining and reporting student progress.

Classroom assessment can be regarded as both a process and a product. As a process, assessment is the collection, interpretation, and use of qualitative and quantitative information to assist educators in their decision-making processes (McMillan, 1997). But assessment is also a product. By this we mean that the term *assessment* is also used to refer to the instrument (set of questions or tasks) that is designed to elicit a predetermined behavior, unique performance, or product from a student (Gallagher, 1998). To keep these definitions separate, we will use the term *assessment* to refer to the entire process and the term *assessment instrument* for the specific product.

Measurement has traditionally been used to determine how much of a trait, attribute, or characteristic an individual possesses (McMillan, 1997). It can also be defined as the process of quantifying the degree to which someone or something possesses a given characteristic, quality, or feature (Gallagher, 1998). In other words, to create a ranking, educators use a systematic measurement process or set of rules to assign numbers (or letters) to the behavior, performance, or product of a student.

Evaluation is the process of making judgments about the quality of a product, or how good a behavior or performance is (McMillan, 1997). It includes using some basis to judge worth or value. For example, educators evaluate whether students have achieved specific instructional outcomes. Educators also use the evaluation process to determine whether students can be expected to do the next year's work (Gallagher, 1998).

Hopefully, these distinctions are clear to you. To review, let's use an example with which we are all familiar: a multiple-choice test. We like to think that, in the assessment process, educators design a test (the assessment instrument), administer it, grade it (measurement), and then determine how well students learned the objectives that were being tested (evaluation). Figure 10–1 shows this process.

Unfortunately, not all educators agree on these definitions. Richard Kellough and Noreen Kellough (1999) define both assessment *and* evaluation as the relatively neutral process of determining what students are learning or have learned as a result of instruction. Their definition of measurement, "the process of collecting and interpreting data" (p. 572), is similar to that of McMillan (1997) and Gallagher (1998).

The assessment process is often defined by when it is conducted. Most educators refer to three types of assessments: diagnostic, formative, and summative. Sometimes called a *preassessment,* a *diagnostic assessment* is used to help identify specific areas of deficiency or learning difficulty (Gallagher, 1998). With a diagnostic assessment, educators can identify specific causes of problems and plan appropriate instruction. Formative assessment happens during a lesson or unit to provide ongoing feedback to the

FIGURE 10–1 The Assessment Process

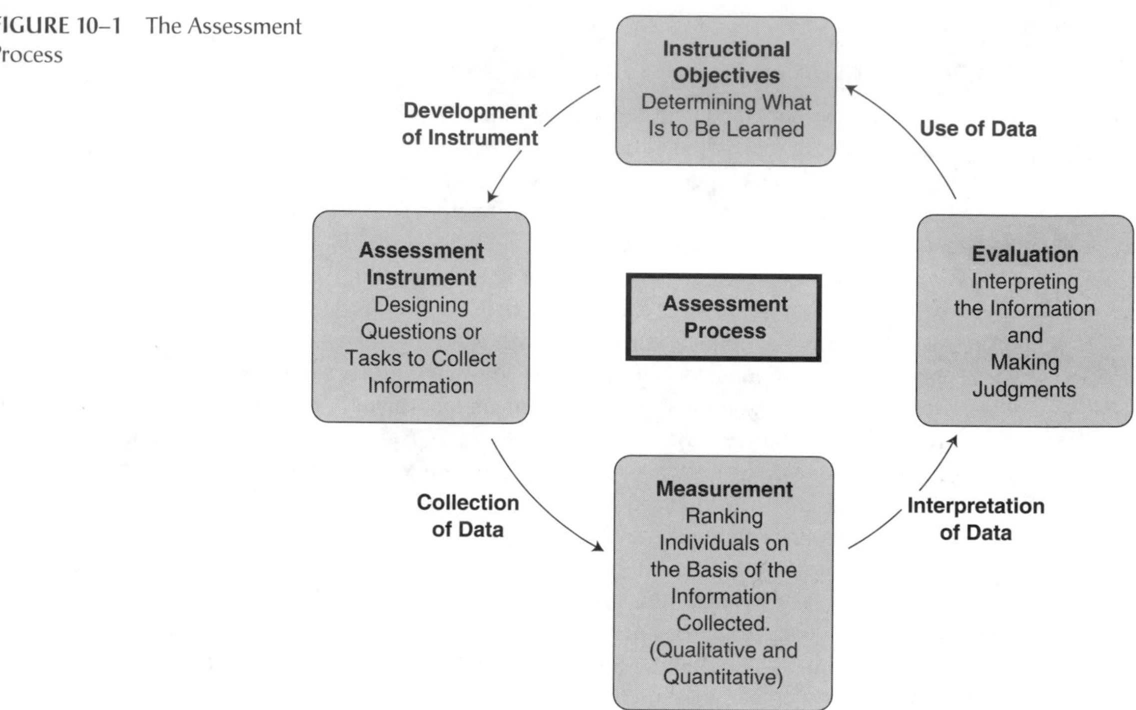

TABLE 10–1 *Diagnostic, Formative, and Summative Assessments*

	Diagnostic	Formative	Summative
Function of the assessment	To determine what needs to be learned	To determine what is being learned	To determine what has been learned as the result of the instruction
When given	Before instruction	During instruction	After completion of instruction
Purpose of the assessment	To plan instruction	To monitor progress toward objectives and plan additional instruction	To evaluate final student performance in relation to the objectives
Techniques of assessment	Tests, questioning, formal and informal observation	Informal observation, questioning, in-class work, homework	Papers, tests, projects, reports
Structure of the assessment	Either formal or informal	Generally informal	Generally formal

teacher and student. Occurring at the end of a unit of study, *summative assessment,* sometimes called *formal assessment,* documents student performance, measures overall achievement, and provides the basis for assigning grades. Table 10–1 shows the characteristics of diagnostic, formative, and summative assessments.

ASSESSMENT OF LEARNING—PERCEPTIONS

In teaching, we often use this common phrase: Perception is reality. By this we mean that people accept what they perceive as the truth, whether or not it actually is. Educators as well as members of society in general have several perceptions that affect how they react to the assessment process, especially to the use of standardized tests to measure achievement and excellence in middle schools. Ultimately, these perceptions, both individually and as a whole, influence the way that educators plan and implement essential middle school practices, such as the integrated curriculum and developmentally responsive instruction.

While most middle school educators know the value of effectively designed teacher-made tests and authentic assessments (such as portfolios), many community members, like Ms. Costino in our opening scenario, continue to believe that standardized tests are the most valid and reliable predictors of student learning. When newspapers give "objective" numbers that show "precisely" how students have scored, people pay attention. Looking to see how schools compare to each other, everyone wants to identify which school scores the highest, which scores the lowest, and which, therefore, is "the best." Unfortunately, people like to make comparisons and draw conclusions that realistically cannot and should not be reached on such limited data. It is difficult, if not impossible, to judge the effectiveness of one middle school compared to another middle school solely by examining the standardized test scores. Too many factors such as socioeconomic conditions, cultural backgrounds, and cognitive development of the students are not factored into the interpretation of many standardized tests.

One interesting observation to us, as university educators, is that often, when these same citizens decide to enter graduate school, many of them become concerned about the standardized tests they have to take. Now, however, instead of wanting to rely on these tests as objective measures of excellence, many people make the comment: "These test grades don't show what I really can do; I just don't do well on standardized tests." We believe that many middle school students would express the same concerns.

In response to some of the problems surrounding standardized tests, many middle school educators have begun to adopt authentic assessment procedures such as portfolios, exhibitions, demonstrations, rubrics, and observational checklists (all to be discussed later in this chapter). They believe that these nontraditional assessment procedures provide a clearer picture of what young adolescents can do. Unfortunately, critics often express concern and even outrage over such types of assessment or, in fact, any nontraditional assessment devices. These critics believe that authentic assessments, unlike standardized tests, lack objectivity; fail to offer sufficient comparisons; and fail to assess instructional objectives and procedures. This may happen because these individuals do not understand authentic assessments or because they are unwilling to accept newer assessment devices that measure a student's achievement gains in comparison to her or his potential. To them, any assessment that fails to compare a person with others in the class, school, state, or nation is not a valid assessment.

Some people also believe that middle school students are not successful on standardized tests because of flaws in the middle school education concept, not because of flaws in the testing system. People blame essential middle school practices such as advisor-advisee programs, exploratory programs, and the emphasis on positive school climates because they believe that these things do not directly affect academic achievement. However, these middle school efforts actually do influence both positive behavior and academic achievement.

There is also a perception that young adolescents do not do well on standardized tests because the middle school curriculum does not place sufficient emphasis on academics. In addition to belittling exploratories and advisor-advisee programs, some individuals think the middle school curriculum provides too much review work and not enough new information. Others feel the curriculum lacks academic rigor and fails to build a scholarly foundation for high school. In other words, these people believe that the middle school curriculum places too much emphasis on aspects other than scores and academic achievement.

Another curriculum-related assessment perception is that the integrated curriculum diminishes performance in academic subject areas. *A Middle School Curriculum: From Rhetoric to Reality* (Beane, 1993) and *This We Believe: Developmentally Responsive Middle Level Schools* (National Middle School Association, 1995) point clearly to the advantages of an integrated curriculum at the middle school. Still, many people believe that young adolescents learn too many relationships and cross-curricular perspectives at the expense of learning specific curricular areas. They think that only rigorous and intellectually demanding educational experiences in individual curricular areas lead to higher academic achievement.

Finally, *This We Believe* (National Middle School Association, 1995) calls for developmentally responsive or appropriate educational experiences. As you read in chapter 2, young adolescents differ greatly in their physical, psychosocial, and cognitive development. However, some people believe that assessment cannot reflect individual developmental characteristics *and* meet national standards. In other words, providing young adolescents with educational experiences (and the corresponding assessment) designed for individual students will not allow learners to be compared nationally. Similarly, they believe that standards cannot be maintained if a student's achievement is compared only to what he or she is developmentally capable of doing.

However, even with all of the misperceptions and problems surrounding assessment, the process is very important. Not only does it provide useful information to educators, parents, and students, it is a critical part of instruction. Our goal, as educators, must be to see that the assessment process is carried out fairly and that the purposes of the process, the results of the process, and the interpretations of those results are communicated clearly to all members of the communities served by the school. In order to do that, you need to understand what educators hope to accomplish with assessment.

Assessment—Rationale and Purposes

"The hardest part of teaching is testing and grading students. Some students try so hard, but they just don't do as well as others who seem to breeze through every assignment. And it really hurts me to assign letter grades when I know they only measure a part of what I see in a classroom." A seventh-grade teacher.

Assessment is a difficult, yet important, professional responsibility that needs to be taken seriously. W. James Popham (1998) maintained that educational tests, when designed with instruction in mind, represent an enormously potent tool in the hands of teachers. In the individual classroom and throughout the school, the assessment process serves several important purposes.

First, its basic function is to help educators determine the strengths, weaknesses, and overall academic progress of students. Educators can use assessment results to determine what students already know and what they need to learn. With appropriate assessments, educators can also diagnose learning problems and determine student progress, remediation, promotion, and retention. But the assessment is only a first step. It is important that educators use the assessment process to provide responsive educational experiences. As you have seen, young adolescents differ greatly in their development. By evaluating the results of an assessment instrument, educators can use instructional methods and materials that meet the individual needs of young adolescents.

We frequently hear middle-level teachers tell students that they need to be responsible or accountable for their actions. Similarly, educators face accountability demands on the national, state, and local level as well as from individual parents. They are often asked to explain the effectiveness of their efforts, why programs did or did not work, and why students did not meet expectations. Thus, a second purpose of the assessment process is to provide the documented results that teachers need to explain their actions.

Another purpose of assessment is to improve instruction. In Figure 10–1, you can see that the results of the assessment process feed directly into the instructional process. Herman (1997) believed that test performance and overall assessment can be influential in improving instruction. For example, assessments can communicate meaningful standards to which school systems, schools, teachers, and students can aspire. In turn, these standards can provide direction for teaching and learning. Assessment can promote instruction as students are increasingly motivated to learn and achieve, and teachers are motivated to provide more effective instruction (Herman, 1997).

Finally, a major reason for assessing young adolescents is to provide accurate reports to students, parents, and school officials. As an educator, you need to be able to identify strengths and weaknesses of individual students with some degree of certainty. Reaching the conclusion that a student needs remediation or retention is a serious decision and deserves a methodical process—one where both the decision and the process can be explained to students, parents, and administrators.

Assessment—Traditional Methods

Assessment Measurement Techniques

"I only got an 85% on the state test that we took last month, but Mrs. Reed says I scored at the 92nd percentile. Does that mean I made an A or a B on the test?" Leah, a sixth grader.

Assessment measurements can take various formats, each designed to achieve a specific purpose. When an assessment is measured on a norm-referenced basis, it judges an individual's performance, achievement, or ability relative to the overall performance of a group. Based on the bell-shaped curve, norm-referenced scores are statistical estimates that provide information on how well a student performs in comparison to other students in the norm group. This group can be on the local, state, regional, or national level. Because norm-referenced assessments often do not address a large portion of the content taught in the average middle school, they generally cannot be used to gauge the overall effectiveness of a local curriculum. Furthermore, since they usually involve paper-and-pencil tests, they are limited in their ability to assess process skills and higher order thinking (Reed, 1993).

Criterion-referenced assessment measurements judge behaviors, performance, or abilities against preestablished standards rather than against the behavior of others. They describe a student's attainment or mastery of specific skills or learning outcomes in relation to a predetermined criterion. Many teacher-made assessments (using instruments such as multiple-choice, true-false, or matching tests) fall into this category as well as some state-level exams and testing instruments constructed by textbook publishers. The accountability movement is prompting many school districts to utilize more criterion-referenced measures to determine whether they have met local and state objectives (Reed, 1993).

In Leah's case, she knew 85% of the material on a criterion-referenced basis. However, when measured against her peers throughout the state on a norm basis, she scored better than 91% of her peers.

Assessment Instruments

Middle school educators have many types of assessment instruments from which they can choose, including traditional tests as well as nontraditional assessments. We will look first at some traditional assessments before turning our attention to some alternative assessments.

In this chapter's opening scenario, Ms. Costino stressed "traditional tests." These can be teacher-made, standardized, state-produced, and textbook-specific (from the textbook publisher). Each has its unique function and purpose. However, you need to remember that the assessment instrument itself is just one part of the assessment process. Equally important are the measurement and evaluation of the data that the instrument produces.

As the name implies, a teacher-made instrument is designed, administered, and evaluated by an individual teacher to judge student behaviors, performance, or abilities. It is criterion-referenced rather than norm-referenced, meaning it measures specific teacher objectives rather than comparing students to other test-takers across the nation or state.

Standardized assessment instruments are norm-referenced and have precise directions for administration as well as uniform scoring procedures. Developed by subject-matter and assessment specialists, these instruments are field-tested under uniform administration procedures, revised to meet certain acceptability criteria, and scored and interpreted using uniform procedures and standards (Gallagher, 1998). Examples include the standardized tests that students take in the spring of selected school years that compare them with students across the state or nation. Since standardized tests are published by companies in the business of publishing and selling educational assessment instruments, these instruments are closely field-tested for validity and reliability.

As you have seen, there is widespread public and professional support for standardized assessment instruments. Their relative cost-efficiency in administration and reporting, usefulness in accountability, usefulness in placing students in special programs and ability groupings, and role in making curricular decisions add to their acceptance (Miller-Jones, 1989).

However, not everyone supports the unquestioned use of standardized assessment instruments. These individuals are concerned that the knowledge domain may not be understood well enough to be adequately represented in a sample of items. They also fear that the test items may be biased toward particular cultural or gender perspectives. Finally, they question whether the test items reflect the kind of subject matter likely to be encountered by most students (Miller-Jones, 1989).

State departments of education also produce various assessment instruments. While some are created by in-state experts under the auspices of a state department of education, others might be put out for bid. In some instances, the recent educational reform movement has even resulted in a few states shifting from a heavy reliance on multiple-choice, paper-and-pencil tests to more performance- and product-based assessments (Gallagher, 1998).

Many textbook publishers provide reproducible masters for assessment or databases of test items on computer disks. If a teacher uses a single textbook, teaches only to those instructional outcomes included in the text, and does not supplement the textbook with objectives and materials from other sources, the tests that accompany the textbook series may be adequate for assessment (Gallagher, 1998).

Types of Traditional Assessments

When we asked a few students what type of test they liked best, we received the following comments:

> "Multiple choice is best because the right answer is there—you don't need to remember it."
>
> "I like true-false tests because they're fast to take."
>
> "True-false can be tricky when the teacher throws in words like *never* and *always*."
>
> "Short essays are my favorite. They're easy to bluff. If you write enough, most teachers think you know the answer and give you credit."

Traditional assessment instruments usually include multiple-choice, true-false, matching, and essay tests. While each has distinct advantages and disadvantages, you can improve their design when you keep several suggestions in mind.

Multiple Choice. Multiple-choice tests are widely used as assessment instruments in schools, even though they may not provide the best method for assessing recall knowledge. They sample a broad array of knowledge, score easily and objectively, and provide students with an example of what they will see on standardized tests. Unfortunately, they take longer to answer than other types of objective items. Therefore, you often have to use a limited number of questions to test students' knowledge of a broad or complex topic. In addition, it is relatively difficult to design well-written multiple-choice questions (McMillan, 1997).

When you design multiple-choice test items, follow these guidelines: (1) keep the stem of the multiple-choice test item brief, concise, stated positively, and either a direct question or an incomplete sentence; (2) put as much as possible in a multiple-choice test stem itself so students do not have to reread the same information over and over again when determining alternatives; (3) include the best or most correct alternative as well as those that could be feasible responses to a student who is not prepared for the test; (4) use the correct grammar and punctuation between each stem and the corresponding alternatives; and (5) keep the alternatives of a multiple-choice test item of equal length, sequenced in random order, and free from statements such as "none of the above" or "all of the above" (Schurr, 1998).

True-False. Educators often ask students to select the correct answer from a choice of two answers. Such questions are termed binary-choice items and may include a number of forms such as true/false, right/wrong, correct/incorrect, yes/no, fact/opinion, and agree/disagree. Students can answer a large number of these test items in a short time, and most students are familiar with the format. Educators like binary items because they are relatively quick to write and also to grade. On the negative side, students often guess, particularly if test items are poorly constructed (McMillan, 1997).

In constructing true-false test items, be sure that the test items: (1) reflect only one major concept or idea; (2) are written with a positive rather than a negative focus; (3) avoid trick or trivial statements, double negatives, and determiners such as *all, never, entirely, absolutely,* and *only;* (4) contain approximately the same number of words in each item; (5) are totally true or false without qualification; and (6) are limited to 10 test items (Schurr, 1998).

While standardized test-makers often use multiple-choice and true-false formats, there are, however, several problems with using these formats. First, professional test-makers generally eliminate test items that a large proportion of the pilot population answered correctly. The overall goal of their tests is to discriminate among the students. Thus, those test items that fail to discriminate are deemed inappropriate and are deleted, even though the information may contribute to a broader understanding of student learning. A second problem with multiple choice and true-false test items on standardized tests is that they assume too much about the mind and background of the test-taker. Generally, test-makers are from white, middle-class, and suburban backgrounds and, therefore, they assume that certain cultural, social, and cognitive approaches represent the population as a whole. Third, true-false test items may lack meaningfulness and fail to reflect the complex environments in which learning occurs (Cheek, 1993).

Matching. Matching test items measure effectively and efficiently the extent to which students know related facts, associations, and relationships. Some examples of these associations include terms with definitions, persons with descriptions, dates with events, and symbols with names (McMillan, 1997).

Sandra Schurr (1998) offered three suggestions for educators preparing matching questions. First, limit the questions to 5 to 15 items. Second, use homogeneous test items—do not mix definitions and dates. Third, provide more choices than questions.

Short Answer and Essay. In short-answer items on tests, students supply an answer consisting of one word, a few words, or a sentence or two. In addition to being relatively easy to write, the short-answer format is similar to how many teachers phrase their questions during classroom instruction.

When writing short-answer test items, keep the following questions in mind (McMillan, 1997). Is there only one correct answer? Is it clear to students that the required answer is brief? Are questions based directly on sentences from the textbook avoided? Is the precision of a numerical answer specified? Is the item written as succinctly as possible? Is the space designated for answers consistent with the space required? Are the words used in the item too difficult for any students?

An extension of the short-answer item, essays serve as an excellent way to measure understanding and mastery of complex information. Most teachers think essays can tap complex thinking by requiring students to organize and integrate information, give arguments, provide explanations, evaluate the merit of ideas, and conduct other types of reasoning. When studying for essay tests, students usually look for themes, patterns, relationships, and the sequence and organization of information. While essay tests take less time to construct, can motivate better study habits, and ensure reasoning skills, they also take more time to grade, can produce different results from different graders, and can fail to provide a good sampling of content knowledge (McMillan, 1997).

Follow these suggestions to create essay tests. Use test questions that (1) require higher level thinking skills rather than simple recall of factual information and that highlight creative thought and problem-solving skills; (2) cover the key concepts of the course content; and (3) require information from the student that is sufficiently specific for common agreement by teachers on what constitutes an acceptable answer. In addition, when constructing essay tests, you should (1) have a suggested amount of time to be spent on each question; (2) provide a checklist of informational points and ideas that are important to include a satisfactory response; (3) inform students of the criteria for evaluation; and (4) avoid optional questions or opinion questions that can detract from the overall mission of the test and can detract from your ability to evaluate students in the same content areas (Schurr, 1998).

One teacher we know devises a list of points that students should include in their essay. Then, as she grades each essay, her list is at her fingertips. Such a practice undoubtedly contributes to consistency and fairness—either the students mentioned the information or they did not. Plus, during conferences with the students, she can pinpoint specific points they included or fail to include.

Points to Remember When Using Tests. Tests can be an excellent way to monitor student learning. Unfortunately, educators sometimes unknowingly teach one thing and then test another. Remember to match the assessment to the objectives being taught. Also, be sure to tell students the format and criteria of the test because students are likely to study and prepare differently for differing types of tests.

Authentic/Alternative Assessments

The Need for Authentic Assessments

How often have you memorized lists, filled in blanks, computed mathematical problems with predetermined formulas, and answered questions by rote? Did you ever question these assessment processes and wonder about their relationship to real learning? In recent years, middle school educators have also recognized several potential problems associated with traditional assessments, and have called for more authentic assessments of students' strengths, abilities, and progress. The goal is to provide assessments that have a real-world orientation and that are indicative of authentic learning rather than regurgitation or rote memorization.

In using authentic assessment, however, educators have had to deal with several issues. First, while performance standards have been around for several decades, the problem has been to develop appropriate and valid ways to assess the attainment of those standards. Still in its beginning stages, authentic assessment is imprecise, although efforts have been made to enhance its reliability and validity. In addition, authentic assessments can be time and labor intensive. Finally, two of the more difficult areas surrounding authentic assessment include (1) convincing teachers to participate and (2) coming up with a score that will satisfy parents and politicians looking for criteria for comparison (Clark & Clark, 1998). Still, even with the challenge of dealing with these issues, we agree with Popham (1993) that "authentic assessment is an idea whose time has clearly come" (p. 473).

Characteristics of Effective Alternative Assessment

What is authentic or alternative assessment? The idea behind authentic assessment is to allow students to demonstrate knowledge and skills, often from several topics, school subjects, or disciplines, by focusing on the student's ability to produce a quality product or performance, rather than a single right answer. Often authentic assessments attempt to simulate the challenges and constraints facing "professionals and citizens when they need to do something with their knowledge" (Nickell, 1992). As part of the assessment, teachers often provide the students with a set of evaluation criteria that are known, understood, and negotiated between the student and teacher before the assessment begins. However, like traditional assessments, an authentic assessment is also designed to produce results that can be reported and understood by students, parents, teachers, administrators, and the tax-paying public (Dana & Tippins, 1993). Figure 10–2 shows some other important characteristics of authentic assessments.

Alternative Assessment Formats

What does an authentic or alternative assessment look like? When middle school educators develop an assessment instrument, instead of relying on traditional tests, they often use one of the following formats: performance-based assessments, simulations and role-playing, portfolios, exhibitions, and demonstrations. Let's look briefly at each one of these.

Performance Assessment. Sometimes, in authentic assessment, the processes that the student uses are more important than the final product or outcome. Performance assessment relies on the professional judgment of assessors who observe the student performing a predetermined task such as researching a problem, giving an oral report, delivering a speech, demonstrating a scientific task, or reading poetry (Schurr, 1998). The idea is to develop situations that closely resemble real-world tasks and that require complex and challenging mental processes. Since there is often more than one approach or one right answer with per-

Effective authentic assessment tasks:

- are essential, "big ideas" rather than trivial microfacts or specialized skills;
- are in-depth in that they lead to other problems and questions;
- are feasible and can be done easily and safely within a school and classroom;
- typically include interactions between the teacher and the student and between students;
- provide multiple ways in which students can demonstrate they have met the criteria, allowing multiple points of view and multiple interpretations;
- allow for individual learning styles, aptitudes, and interests;
- involve cooperation, self-evaluation, and peer-evaluation;
- require scoring that focuses on the essence of the task and not what is easiest to score;
- call on the professional judgment of the assessor, who is usually the teacher;
- may involve an audience of some kind in addition to the teacher;
- call for different measurement techniques;
- identify strengths as well as weaknesses; and
- minimize needless and unfair comparisons.

FIGURE 10–2 Effective Authentic Assessment

formance assessment, the emphasis is on uncoached explanations and real products (Reed, 1993). According to Eisner (1999), performance assessment is a more accurate measure of learners' ability to achieve the aspirations we hold for them than are traditional measures of testing.

To use performance assessments, teachers usually give young adolescents a task or special project, or they ask them to investigate a routine or problematic situation in a real-world context. The teacher then uses the students' solutions and the processes they used to reach those solutions in order to assess what the students know and are able to do. In middle schools, performance assessments can: (1) reveal a student's understanding of processes associated with a particular discipline; (2) be used with individual students or with cooperative learning groups; (3) show special accomplishments and understandings not readily shown on other assessments; and (4) be used in conjunction with other assessment strategies to develop a comprehensive collection of evidence about the students (Dana, T. M. & Tippins, D.J., 1993).

Simulations and Role-Playing. In simulation assessments, students try to replicate real events, while, in role-playing, they assume the position of another person and, using their own knowledge and skill, act as that person might act. *Oregon Trail* is a computer simulation in which students take a trip west on the Oregon Trail and relive the hardships faced by pioneers. Role-playing assessments might ask students to play tour guides and design a tour featuring the architectural highlights of their community. Other students might become landscape architects as they design the school yard and construct a beautification plan (Dana & Tippins, 1993).

Portfolios. A popular approach to evaluation, student portfolios allow teachers to evaluate the work that students have completed and collected over a period of time rather than just on a few selected days (Collins & Dana, 1993). The idea is that the portfolio contains a systematic, purposeful, and meaningful collection of student work that exhibits the student's overall effort, progress, and achievements in one or more subject areas.

Portfolios include a wide variety of work samples selected by the student, parent, peer, and/or the teacher. These can include essays, reports, letters, creative writing, problem statements and solutions, journal entries, interviews, artistic media, collaborative works, workbook pages and tests, surveys and questionnaires, reading lists and reviews, self-assessment checklists and statements, teacher checklists and comments, peer reviews, or parent observations and comments (Schurr, 1998). An important element of all portfolios is the self-reflection piece, which requires the student to analyze his or her own work samples included in the portfolio.

Why has the use of portfolios as a popular assessment process grown so dramatically? In addition to providing opportunities for students to demonstrate what they know and what they do, portfolios are tools for discussion. They document student growth over a period of time and provide a vehicle for students to reflect on their work and to make decisions about what to include or exclude. Portfolios are ideal for assessing learning styles and multiple intelligence. Finally, portfolios help students make connections and transfers between prior knowledge and new learning (Schurr, 1998).

Exhibitions and Demonstrations. Most middle school students love to make or do something. Thus having students design and construct exhibitions, produce a videotape, write a manual, develop a hypermedia presentation, or demonstrate a process is an ideal way for young adolescents to prove their knowledge, skills, or competence. Exhibitions and demonstrations provide concrete evidence that some skill has been applied or some concept has been learned (Shurr, 1998).

Assessment—Evaluation of Traditional and Authentic Assessments

Effective Grading Methods

Sandra Schurr (1998), an authority on grading and assessment in middle schools, maintains that effective grading methods involve students in self-evaluation efforts; provide students and parents with sufficient information about students' needs, interests, and achievement levels; connect directly to what teachers teach and what students learn; integrate well with classroom assignments, activities, and instructional methods; and provide evidence of students' development of desired skills and behaviors.

Effective grading methods should be fair and objective. They should also be quantifiable, explicit, and precise. That means that everyone (students, teachers, parents, and administrators) knows exactly what the numbers or letters mean. This should minimize conflict over what grade a student should receive. Also, tests and class activities should be equitably weighted and cumulative so that final grades can be determined by a single computation at the end of the grading period (Schurr, 1998).

Rubrics

How many times have you said: "If I knew that was what the teacher wanted, I would have included that in my project?" Many teachers are now using rubrics to assist in determining how a product, performance, or portfolio is going to be judged or graded. Specifically, a rubric is a scoring tool (usually a matrix or list of narrative statements) that lists the criteria for a piece of work and the gradations of quality for each criterion (Goodrich, 1997/1998). Although teachers can create rubrics themselves, the most effective rubrics can be those created collaboratively by teachers and students. Analytic rubrics can be developed to analyze a list of specific criteria for a small piece or part of a project, while holistic rubrics can be used to evaluate a complete and final project (Schurr, 1998). Theory into Practice 10–1 provides an example of a portion of a rubric that was developed to evaluate student hypermedia projects in a social studies class. A simpler rubric for evaluating a student presentation is found in Theory into Practice 10–2.

Rubrics appeal to many teachers and students. By making teachers' expectations clear, rubrics often result in marked improvement in students' achievement and in the overall quality of student work and learning. Rubrics also help students learn how to evaluate their own work and to detect and solve problems on their own. Finally, because they are easy to use and easy to explain, rubrics reduce the time teachers spend on evaluating student work (Goodrich, 1997/1998). To be effective, a rubric should be organized around a skill, focus on a small number of evaluative criteria, and be sufficiently brief that a teacher will want to use it.

Observational Checklists

Similar to rubrics, observational checklists also provide a basis for determining and assigning grades. Teachers constantly observe students to determine what is happening in the class (i.e., student participation in class discussions, types of questions asked and responses given, interpersonal skills used in cooperative groups, students' reactions to assignments and to grades on tests, verbal skills demonstrated when expressing thoughts, need for additional examples, and students' interest levels) (McMillan, 1997). Theory into Practice 10–3 provides an example of an observational checklist that can be used by both students and teachers to evaluate a student's participation in a cooperative learning activity.

Theory into Practice 10–1

Rubric for a Hypermedia Project

Item	Requirements/ Guidelines	Rating Scale	Points Given by Student	Points Given by Teacher
Text	No more than two styles of type Type size between 24 and 36 points No more than six words in a line No more than six lines on a slide Upper- and lowercase letters Contain at least five text slides	0 Breaks all of the rules 1 Breaks three or more of the rules 2 Breaks only one or two of the rules 3 Follows all of the rules		
Use of color on text slides	One color for background No more than two colors for the text	0 Breaks both rules 1 Follows one of the rules most of the time 2 Follows both of the rules most of the time 3 Follows both rules all of the time		
Visuals	Images add and do not detract from the presentation Special effects are kept to a minimum	0 Breaks both rules 1 Follows one of the rules most of the time 2 Follows both of the rules most of the time 3 Follows both rules all of the time		
Grammar on text slides	Correct spelling Subject/verb agreement Correct punctuation	0 Serious errors throughout text in all three areas 1 Several errors in some or all areas 2 A few errors that do not detract from the presentation 3 No major errors		
Research	At least six sources Variety of sources including books, magazines, and at least one electronic resource Bibliography submitted at time of presentation Bibliography in correct format	0 No bibliography 1 Documentation is incomplete and/or sources are too limited 2 Meets requirements for sources and documentation 3 Exceeds requirements in number and variety of sources with correct documentation		

Developed from: Bucher, K. T. (1998a). *Information technology for schools.* Worthington, OH: Linworth Publishing; and Goodrich, H. (1997/1998). Understanding rubrics. *Educational Leadership, 54*(6), 14–18.

Theory into Practice 10–2

Simple Rubric for a Presentation

Points	Comment
15	Presentation is exemplary or exceptional and exceeds requirements.
14	Presentation is superior and exceeds requirements with only a few minor exceptions.
13	Presentation meets requirements in all areas.
12	Presentation meets requirements with only a few minor exceptions.
11	Presentation meets some requirements but has other areas needing improvement.
10–0	Presentation needs substantial work to meet minimal requirements.

Developed from: Goodrich, H. (1997/1998). Understanding rubrics. *Educational Leadership, 54*(6), 14–18.

Theory into Practice 10–3

An Observational Checklist

Item	Description	Points
Shared labor	Contributes to group discussions Contributes resources to project Contributes ideas to group Is willing to contribute	1 Never contributes 2 Little contribution 3 Adequate contribution 4 More than adequate 5 Outstanding contribution
Dependability	Completes assigned tasks Meets deadlines Brings books and supplies	1 Never 2 Once or twice 3 Sometimes 4 Usually 5 Always
Integration of personal and group work	Compromises with others Adapts work to group goals Revises personal work as needed	1 Never 2 Once or twice 3 Sometimes 4 Usually 5 Always
Collaboration	Keeps bickering to a minimum Accepts constructive comments Provides constructive comments tactfully Gives positive feedback to group	1 Never 2 Once or twice 3 Sometimes 4 Usually 5 Always

Developed from: Troutner, J. (1996). Yes, they put on quite a show, but what did they learn? *Technology Connection, 3*(1), 15–17.

ASSESSMENT—REPORTING

The assessment process does not exist for its own sake. At least at the end of the cycle, it is necessary to communicate the results to others. Most often this communication occurs through parent conferences; narrative systems, such as letters to parents; checklists; and letter grades. Most teachers who work with young adolescents must use letter grades for reporting performance and achievement (Oosterhof, 1999).

Even so, many teachers use their own reporting systems to supplement the required letter grade. At a minimum, they keep well-organized and comprehensive files on each student. As one seventh-grade teacher explained, "A few years ago I had to meet with a disgruntled parent who continued to question her son's language arts grade. She emphatically asked for proof—to see her son's tests and homework with the assigned grades. And she wanted an explanation of his D on his oral report. I had a folder that included all the student's work (chronologically organized), a copy of my rubric on the report, and my computation of the grade. It was a rough conference, but, with my records I was able to report on this student's progress and defend my actions."

Grade and Progress Reports

In addition to providing the required assessment information to school officials and to parents on a report card, many teachers use other methods to communicate with parents about assessment. For example, in one school, a parent of a relatively unmotivated student asked the teacher for a brief note each Friday. The student knew the teacher would send the note home on Friday; the parent asked her daughter for it each Friday. Some parents want monthly reports, while others are satisfied to wait for the 6- or 9-week grading report. Regardless of the schedule, you need to be prepared to provide parents with detailed reports of progress and behavior. These reports should give parents clear and meaningful information that they can understand, written comments that explain letter or number grades, a designated place for parents to offer comments, and a means for parents to request a parent conference.

Conferences with Parents

Some schools supplement grade reports with conferences between teachers and parents. In the conferences, teachers can show parents the student's work or ask the student to attend the conference to demonstrate what he or she had learned (Oosterhoff, 1999).

As opposed to written communication, a conference allows the teacher to use feedback from the parent to ensure that ideas are being communicated accurately and with appropriate emphasis. A conference can also increase parents' involvement in the child's schooling, both directly and psychologically (Oosterhoff, 1999). In addition to discussing individual assignments and assessments, you must be sure to provide an overall description of the student's progress.

Unfortunately, conferences take a great deal of time. In addition to the time needed for the conference itself, you will need to plan each one. Since it is often difficult for parents to come to regular conferences at times convenient for teachers, evening or weekend conferences are often necessary. Ideally you should follow each parent conference with a written documentation of what was discussed, and this, too, takes time (Oosterhoff, 1999).

Keeping Current with Technology 10–1

Awesomelibrary: Teacher link
http://www.awesomelibrary.org/

Colorado Department of Education: Standards and assessment
http://www.cde.state.co.us/index_assess.htm

Electronic Learning Marketplace: Old Orchard Beach Schools, Southern Maine Partnership and University of Southern Maine
http://www.elm.maine.edu/index.asp

FINE Foundation: Internet Resources on Student Achievement
http://www.iptv.org/FINELINK/hotlinks.html

Kentucky Department of Education
http://www.kde.state.ky.us

Long Beach, CA, Changing Schools in Long Beach
http://www.middleweb.com/Lngbchreform.html

Management and Evaluation Associates, Inc.
http://www.evaluator.com/links.htm

Mathematics, Science, and Technology Resource Guide (NY)
http://www.nysed.gov/mst/

Memorial Middle School in Sioux Falls, SD
http://inst.augie.edu/~crkock/homepage.htm

National Center for Research on Evaluation, Standards, and Student Testing (CRESST): U.S. Department of Education
http://cresst96.cse.ucla.edu/index.htm

National Council on Measurement in Education (NCME)
http://www.assessment.iupui.edu/NCME/NCME.html

School District #96 in Oak Park, IL: Authentic Assessment Resource Guide for the Essential, Transdiciplinary Qualities of Life-Long Learners
http://www.math.uic.edu/oakpark/district97/assessment/

For more information about assessment, including sample rubrics, information on standardized tests, and research on testing, visit some of the Internet sites listed in Keeping Current with Technology 10–1.

Assessment—Developmentally Responsive in Middle Schools

While effective assessment is a complex activity for all teachers, middle school educators need to keep a few special considerations in mind. *This We Believe: Developmentally Responsive Middle Level Schools* (National Middle School Association, 1995) maintained that the learning process should include continuous, authentic, and developmentally responsive evaluation. This means that assessment should deal with both the processes and the products of learning and should consider student differences.

In addition to academic content and skills, the middle school assessment process should address other aspects of a student's growth such as critical thinking, curiosity, and other desired personal attributes. This requires a variety of alternative assessment devices and procedures, such as checklists and observation scales. Young adolescents can assemble portfolios and conduct demonstrations that reveal growth in many dimensions and categories (National Middle School Association, 1995). In middle schools, students need to participate in all phases of assessment by helping to set individual and group goals and by evaluating their own accomplishments.

In developmentally responsive middle-level schools, assessment and evaluation procedures must reflect the characteristics and uniqueness of young adolescents. Since early adolescence is a crucial period in establishing a clear self-concept and self-esteem, assessment and evaluation should emphasize individual progress rather than comparison with other students and should help young adolescents discover and understand their strengths, weaknesses, interests, values, and personalities (National Middle School Association, 1995).

Assessment—Issues

Criticisms and Negative Effects on Student Learning

The assessment process often receives harsh criticism, especially from those who believe that grading is inaccurate and unfair and from those who feel students and learning achievement are negatively affected by too much emphasis on assessment. These individuals contend that young adolescents experience too much pressure and stress, assessment takes a toll on their self-esteem, and assessment fails to take into account cultural, racial, gender, and ethnic differences. While all these criticisms may indeed be true to some extent, middle school educators will continue to assess students in order to make instructional decisions as well to report student progress. The key, then, is to understand the criticisms and to try to minimize the negative effects.

Culture, Gender, and Other Forms of Diversity

As a middle school educator, you need to recognize the wide range of diversity (i.e., young adolescents' developmental, cultural, racial, and gender differences) in your classroom and to design instruction and assessments to meet the needs of this diverse student population (Manning, 1993b, Manning & Hager, 1995). Demographic shifts in the general population, along with the regular-class inclusion of students with learning and/or behavior problems, have spawned classroom differences that pose tremendous challenges to teachers (Arllen, Gable, & Hendrickson, 1996). The study in Diversity Perspectives 10–1 raises some issues that must be addressed in assessing our increasingly diverse student populations.

Diversity Perspectives 10–1

Diversity and Authentic Assessments

Garcia (1994) made the following recommendations regarding assessment:

- Educators in low-income schools should adopt authentic classroom assessments.
- Classroom teachers should recognize the ways in which their own cultural values and upbringing influence their choice of teaching-learning activities and assessment procedures.
- Performance-based assessment should result in improved instruction offered to low-income students.
- The expenditures involved in developing and implementing performance-based assessment should not result in the reduction of monies for other necessary services.
- The changes in instruction and assessment should lead to increased engagement and learning of students from diverse backgrounds.

Garcia (1994) stressed that all students deserve to be treated fairly and equitably when schools implement authentic assessments–one group of learners cannot benefit from authentic assessments while another group suffers. To do so, educators should determine how students from poverty and differing cultural and linguistic backgrounds perceive and respond to authentic assessments and should determine whether these assessments are compatible with cultural backgrounds and perspectives.

Source: Garcia, G. E. (1994). Equity challenges in authentically assessing students from diverse backgrounds. *The Educational Forum, 59,* 64–73.

The assessment process can have negative effects on all learners, especially in multicultural settings. Traditional teacher-made and commercial tests do not provide objective information about atypical students. Follow these guidelines to help minimize problems:

1. Closely monitor the effects of testing to determine whether learners from differing cultural and gender backgrounds experience undue stress or confusion with directions, perhaps resulting from second-language problems.
2. Explain testing purposes and procedures to both young adolescents and their parents and families and help them understand how test results will be used.
3. Be sure assessment constructs or concepts are universally valid.
4. Be sure assessment instruments are culturally appropriate and reflect learners' cultural and gender values and perspectives.

Case Study 10–1 tells of a middle school teacher's dilemma and challenge as she tried to provide assessment devices for young adolescents from differing cultural, gender, and socioeconomic backgrounds.

Case Study 10–1

Young Adolescent Differences and Assessment

Shirella Reed wanted to provide an assessment process that the diverse group of young adolescents on her team could understand. This year's Hawk Team, about half boys and half girls, came from all socioecomonic groups and were a cultural mix of European, African, Asian, and Hispanic Americans. Like most young adolescents, some liked to compete; others did not. Some demonstrated high levels of motivation; others "appeared" unmotivated. While a few seemed to take her assessment efforts seriously, others "appeared" to view assessment as an unimportant aspect of school.

Teaching such a "mixed" group of students was a challenge. At team meetings, some of the teachers expressed a longing for the old days when all students supposedly had the same perspectives toward tests and testing–all students conscientiously took tests, wanted to score high, and perceived the importance of tests. But, Shirella wondered if classrooms were really like that. "Maybe," she thought, "culture, gender, and social class have always affected test-takers. We just haven't been aware of it."

It was while she was attending a district workshop that she began to see a way to use authentic assessments in her classroom. Presenting the workshops were a school librarian and two classroom teachers who were using a model called "The Big Six" (Eisenberg & Johnson, 1996) to teach research and organizational skills to students. Shirella could see that the six steps in the model could help all of her students by providing a basic structure that all of them could use and modify to fit their own individual needs. The presenters made the assessment process seem easy when they talked about their use of rubrics and observational checklists. In fact, they stressed that their students had even learned how to evaluate their own work before they turned it in for a grade. Shirella also noted that the presenters discussed how they involved parents by providing a column on the rubric for parents to check off that they had seen the completed work.

Shirella left the meeting with handouts and the determination to try to implement "The Big Six" and authentic assessment. Maybe, if she could demonstrate their use with the Hawk Team students in her classes, some of the other teachers would try it too. She also planned to talk to her school's library media specialist to see if they could team up like the presenters in the workshop. Using a variety of resources to locate information instead of just relying on printed encyclopedias would help the diverse learning styles of her students. And, letting the students decide how to present information, even using multimedia presentations, would help, too. She could already imagine the excitement on her students' faces when she explained her new approach to assessment.

Multiple Grading Systems

Faced with a diverse and inclusive student population, some schools have used multiple grading systems in which separate scales or special notations are used for students with diverse needs. However, it seems that this only contributes to confusion for teachers, parents, and students. There is a growing awareness that alternative grading practices are appropriate for students with special learning needs only to the extent that they are nondiscriminatory ("Grading," 1997). That is, grading systems available to students with special learning needs should be available to other students as well. In this way, a special symbol recorded on a report card does not single out a student as receiving special education ("Grading," 1997).

Closing Remarks

Recent developments in assessment have given middle school educators exciting new ways to determine young adolescents' achievement as well as their own teaching effectiveness. While some traditional assessment devices still can be used effectively (especially when properly constructed), the newer authentic assessments hold considerable promise. Your challenge is to develop an assessment process that allows students to demonstrate what they know and that provides you with a more reliable basis for making diagnostic decisions, assigning grades, and improving instruction.

Suggested Readings

Clark, S., & Clark, D. (1998). Authentic assessments: Key issues, concerns, guidelines. *Schools in the Middle, 6*(5), 50–51. Contains six guidelines for implementing authentic assessment.

Danielson, C., & Abrutyn, L. (1997). *An introduction to using portfolios in the classroom.* Alexandria, VA: ASCD. Provides an overview of basic types of portfolios, steps in portfolio development, and the most effective ways to use this means of assessment.

Eisner, E. (1999). The uses and limits of performance assessment. *Phi Delta Kappan, 80*(9), 658–660. Looks at performance assessment in its broad educational and social contexts.

Herman, J. (1997). Assessing new assessments: How do they measure up? *Theory into Practice, 36*(4), 196–204. Discusses the role of assessment in instruction, the promise of alternative assessments, and various issues surrounding assessment such as fairness, bias, and alignment with standards.

Lustig, K. (1996). *Portfolio assessment: A handbook for middle level teachers.* Columbus, OH: NMSA. Examines portfolio assessment with specific guidance, examples, and forms.

Madaus, G. F., & O'Dwyer, L. M. (1999). A short history of performance assessment. *Phi Delta Kappan, 80*(9), 688–695. Offers an interesting historical look at performance assessment.

Marzano, R. J., & Kendall, J. S. (1996). *A comprehensive guide to designing standards-based districts, schools, and classrooms.* Alexandria, VA: ASCD/McREL. Provides strategies needed for organizing curriculum, instruction, and assessment around standards.

Middle School Journal, 25(2), 1993. The November 1993 issue of the *Middle School Journal* focused on alternative assessment, including portfolios, rubrics, and linking assessment and instruction.

Oosterhoff, A. (1999). *Developing and using classroom assessments* (2nd ed.). Columbus, OH: Merrill/Prentice-Hall. Provides a practical look at assessment issues as well as appropriate means of assessment.

Part IV

Guiding Students and Working with External Communities

With its focus on guidance in middle schools, chapter 11 gives you suggestions for team and collaborative approaches to guidance. You will also read about the advisor-advisee program, an essential program in effective middle schools. Because middle school guidance programs cannot address all the challenges faced by young adolescents, you will also find information about the need for specialized services.

In chapter 12, you will find information about reengaging parents and families as partners and resources. Parents' roles in schools can be strengthened through parent involvement, parent-teacher conferences, and parent education programs. We encourage you to view communities as resources as well as opportunities for young adolescents to provide service.

The Epilogue looks at the present status of middle schools as well as the future. In it, we call for developmentally responsive educational experiences and suggest that teaching in the middle school can be both challenging and rewarding.

After you read *Teaching in the Middle School,* we hope you will have a better understanding of middle schools and will be prepared to make the commitment to work toward the education and well-being of young adolescents.

Chapter 11

Guiding Young Adolescents—Teachers and Counselors

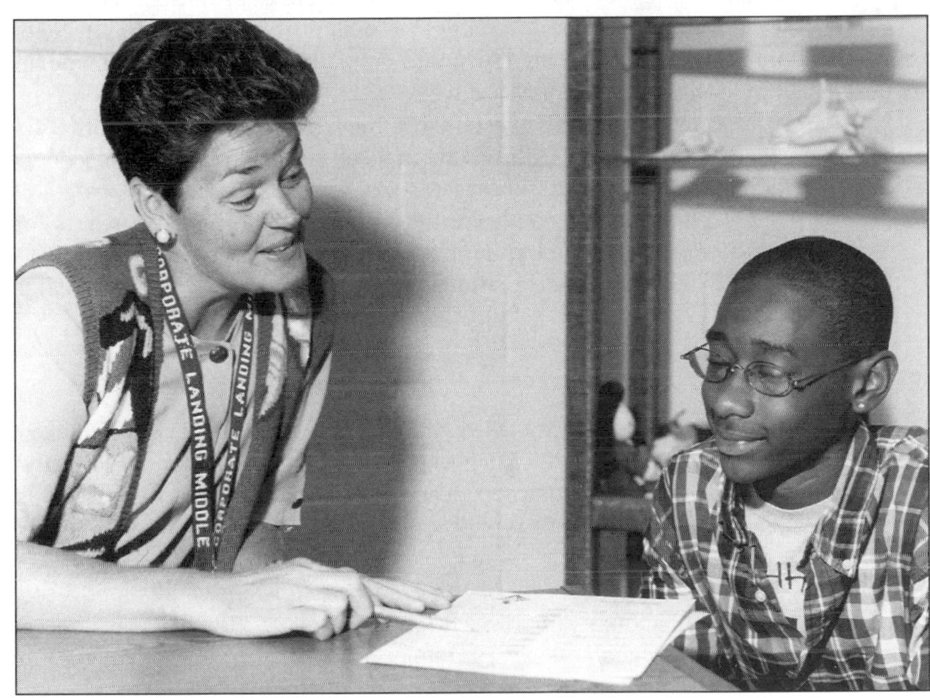

Scenario—Kim Matusi and the Guidance Team

Although Kim Matusi, a guidance counselor at Lost Lake Middle School, had asked the teachers in her school to help her compile a list of problems faced by their students, she certainly was not prepared for the results. Glancing through the lists that had been placed in her mailbox, she was flabbergasted at the concerns—pressures from parents, underachievement, a suspected case of anorexia, three seventh graders caught smoking, at least two pregnancies in the eighth grade, peer pressure, gangs, and violence near the school and at home.

Her thoughts were interrupted by Ted Canon as he dropped off another list for her growing pile. "So you thought you'd like to get an idea about where to focus your guidance efforts, did you? Well, how are we doing?"

Glancing at Ted's list, Kim sighed. "We have just about every young adolescent problem here at Lost Lake that the experts write about. And I'm not sure that we're doing all we can to address these problems. If only I could find some teachers willing to work with me—maybe even one whole team willing to try a new collaborative team approach to guidance."

"Hey, how about us?" Ted asked. "You know the Lion Team is the most innovative one in the school. And we sure have our share of problems. Why not start with us or even with the entire sixth grade? We could plan this spring and have things ready to implement in the fall. If you want to give it a try, I can give you some time at the sixth grade in-service meeting next week."

"You bet!" was Kim's response. "I think we all agree that, in order to meet the special needs of our students, this needs to be a team approach with teachers and counselors, administrators, parents, and even social service agencies all playing a part. The problems are too great for any counselor to handle alone, but together we can make a difference!"

"Hey, save some of your enthusiasm for next week's meeting. I'll e-mail you the time and place. Got to run; class is waiting," Ted called as he headed down the hall.

Overview

Like most contemporary young adolescents, the students at Lost Lake Middle School face a number of challenges and problems that are as diverse as young adolescents themselves. In previous years, teachers taught their subject areas and left counseling and advisement to guidance professionals who often accepted too many roles and counseled hundreds of students.

Kim Matusi's concept of comprehensive guidance and support services is found in many contemporary middle schools that provide a team approach to guidance. In these schools, teachers, counselors, administrators, and sometime parents and families all work together to provide for the welfare of young adolescents. Through advisor-advisee programs and daily interactions, middle school teachers play major roles in the overall counseling efforts. When student problems grow acute or extend beyond the domains of the school, the guidance team seeks the help of social service agencies and mental health professionals trained to work with 10- to 14-year-olds. This chapter looks at guidance in the middle school and at this collaborative process for helping young adolescents.

Objectives

After reading and thinking about this chapter on guiding young adolescents, you should be able to:

1. explain how middle school guidance efforts differ from guidance in elementary and secondary schools;
2. explain teachers' roles in providing comprehensive guidance and support services and how teachers' efforts neither undermine or replace the roles of trained guidance professionals;
3. list several needs of 10- to 14-year-olds that developmentally responsive middle school guidance programs can address;
4. explain the functions of middle school guidance programs;
5. provide a rationale for a team approach–teachers, counselors, administrators, and parents–to guidance for young adolescents;
6. define advisor-advisee programs (sometimes called *teacher advisories*) and explain how they address the needs of young adolescents;
7. offer guidelines for implementing advisor-advisee programs and suggest developmentally responsive topics; and
8. explain why some young adolescent problems require specialized help and offer suggestions for appropriate referral agencies.

Guidance in Middle Schools

> "I don't understand why some teachers act as if they don't like kids. I mean, the kids are what make middle school teaching interesting, fun, and challenging. Sure it can be frustrating at times, but we all can remember how lost we felt at that age. This is our opportunity as adults to make a real difference. I want to show middle school kids that there are adults who care about them. And I want to make a difference in their lives. When my supervising teacher and I took his "advisory" kids to the zoo last week, you would have thought we had taken them to Disney World. I mean, all we did was take a school bus and ride across town. But those kids are still talking about it. For some of them, it was probably the most attention any adult had paid to them in a long time. All I had to do was look at their faces and I realized that's why I want to be a middle school teacher." University teacher education practicum student.

Caught "in the middle" between childhood and adulthood, young adolescents are going through a difficult period of their lives. Therefore, an essential characteristic of effective middle schools must be the existence of a comprehensive and developmentally responsive guidance program that addresses the needs of young adolescents. Some 10- to 14-year-olds have unique problems, challenges, and concerns that can interfere with their academic achievement, social development, and attitudes toward life and school. Others have strengths and assets that deserve to be cultivated and nurtured. With the support of administrators and parents, both teachers and counselors can play vital roles in helping young adolescents cope with problems as well as with the ordinary trials and tribulations of growing up. While these problems will be as diverse as the young adolescents themselves, they can include dealing with peer pressure, understanding growing bodies, dealing with expanding social worlds, engaging in at-risk behaviors, and understanding parental expectations. No longer children and not yet adults, young adolescents need advocates who understand their problems and concerns and who will provide developmentally responsive guidance efforts.

Differences from Elementary and Secondary Schools

Guidance efforts in a middle school can neither be a slightly revised elementary school program nor be a watered-down version of the secondary program. While elementary school guidance programs address the needs of younger children such as learning about school and dealing with friends, secondary school programs address the needs of adolescents finishing school and preparing to find their place in life and society. Rather than adopting a "one-program-fits-all" philosophy, middle school guidance programs need to offer activities that reflect the needs of 10- to 14-year-olds, the middle school concept, a knowledge of the early adolescence developmental period, and the challenges facing young adolescents.

As Kim Matusi pointed out in this chapter's opening scenario, classroom teachers provide a major part of the middle school guidance effort. This is not meant to belittle the work done by elementary and secondary teachers; however, middle school teachers play major guidance roles in both planned programs as well as in their daily interaction with young adolescents. No longer is guidance limited to one hour a week or when a student requests an appointment with the counselor.

Guidance in a middle school is unique because middle school students differ significantly from elementary and secondary students and also from each other. As we mentioned in chapter 2, young adolescents are so diverse that it is difficult to describe a typical student. They deserve educators and counselors who are willing to provide guidance services that meet their unique developmental needs.

Unfortunately, while many middle school teachers have readily accepted these guidance and advisory roles, others have been reluctant to become involved. One teacher we visited candidly stated, "That is not what I was trained to do; some teachers feel alright with that touchy-feely stuff, but I don't and I'm not." While staff development activities and other professional training might improve both the skills and attitudes of some teachers, others continue to be reluctant to engage in any guidance and advisory activities. Unfortunately, those who suffer most are young adolescents.

Functions of Middle School Guidance Programs

Effective middle school guidance programs have a number of developmentally responsive functions that usually complement one another. While it would be an impossible task to list all guidance functions, we can suggest several that reflect the middle school concept and that allow teachers and counselors to work together for the welfare and betterment of 10- to 14-year-olds.

First, counselors and teachers serve as advocates for young adolescents. Serving as advocates means educators foster compassion, a workable set of values, and the skills of cooperation, decision making, and goal setting (National Middle School Association, 1995). It is important for young adolescents to know they have a source of support in the school—someone to talk to, to confide in, and to turn to for help. Being an advocate does not mean that educators take sides or lose their sense of objectivity; it does mean that young adolescents feel they know a caring adult in the school who is willing to help them. The advocate agrees to talk with other teachers and with parents when problems arise, again not taking a student's side, but acting as a helpful and caring adult working for the young adolescent's overall welfare. Similarly, the advocate helps the student make decisions about friends, goals, and behavior. The young adolescent realizes educators working in advocacy roles want to help, support, and nurture. In middle schools today where young adolescents often feel anonymous, there is a significant need for educators to serve as advocates and for overall guidance activities to reflect this sense of advocacy.

For example, through Kim Matusi's efforts, the Lion Team at Lost Lake Middle School took deliberate steps to make students feel they each had an advocate. Each of the 70 students on the team was assigned to a teacher-advisor. In some cases, it was one of the four core teachers; in other cases it was the library media specialist, a specialty teacher, or Kim. The teacher did not have any special duties except to keep an eye on the student and possibly to discuss topics of interest. In addition, the teacher tried to speak to the student (and call him or her by name) several times a week, preferably every day. The overall goal was for students to feel some caring adult knew them and cared sufficiently to speak to them.

A second function of middle school guidance activities is to have teachers and counselors address the special needs of 10- to 14-year-olds. We know that young adolescents face an array of problems related to physical, psychosocial, and cognitive development; school pressures (both academic and social); at-risk conditions and behaviors; general health, diet, and eating disorders; alcohol, drugs, and tobacco; AIDS and STDS; teenage pregnancy; peer pressure; physical and psychological violence; and other problems. In order to help 10- to 14-year-olds, educators can address these problems through the advocacy roles, advisor-advisee programs, and individual and group counseling. Will guidance teams be able to address all these problems? Unfortunately, they will not; however, they will be able to make referrals to health care providers and mental health counseling centers.

Third and closely related to the second, middle school guidance programs prepare young adolescents to make sound choices and decisions. Due to peer pressure and the media glorification of growing up and engaging in adult behaviors, young adolescents must make challenging decisions. For example, it is difficult for a 13-year-old not to smoke marijuana when all his friends do. A seventh-grade girl might not want to be the only one who cannot wear blue jeans in spite of the dictates of her religion. It might be easier for an eighth-grade boy to cut his hair in the latest style and face the wrath of his parents than face the stigma of being different. Educators must understand this intense and often troublesome pressure and help young adolescents. This does not mean that they dictate young adolescents' behavior and attitudes. Instead, true professionals help 10- to 14-year-olds think through situations, engage in a sound decision-making process, and reach sound decisions. This is not easy. Anyone who has worked with 10- to 14-year-olds realizes the difficulty of preparing some young adolescents to make sound decisions. However, teachers and counselors still have a responsibility to work diligently toward this goal.

Fourth, middle school educators serving in guidance capacities help further the development of young adolescents' cognitive and academic goals. Students often need direction in making realistic goals. While students should never be discouraged from setting and pursuing lofty goals, they need to be guided toward the accomplishment of their goals. Most teachers remember a student who they thought would not be successful, yet who, through determination and motivation, prevailed and achieved a seemingly insurmountable task. It might take years for some guidance efforts to be realized; however, the guidance team should never underestimate its influence and power in helping young adolescents in the formation of both short-term and long-term goals.

A fifth guidance function addresses psychosocial needs. Making and keeping friends, coping with widening social worlds, experiencing a declining self-esteem, dealing with peer pressure, and resolving interpersonal conflicts can take a toll on young adolescents. All these problems and issues can be addressed with some degree of success by adult advocates, advisor-advisee programs, and individual and both small- and large-group counseling. While middle school professionals should not and cannot "make friends for students," they can, through individual advisement and advisor-advisee sessions, discuss topics such as "Characteristics I Want in Friends," "Maintaining Friendships," and "How I Can Keep from Doing What My Friends Want Me To." As students go through self-esteem–building exercises and cooperative learning and peer-tutoring sessions, they learn to work together and perhaps form friendships.

Finally, the effective middle school guidance program promotes and articulates roles between elementary and secondary schools. As we previously noted, elementary and secondary school guidance programs have their respective roles, goals, and responsibilities. Similarly, the middle school guidance program functions to help 10- to 14-year-olds. However, instead of the middle school working in isolation as a separate entity, there needs to be close articulation with other levels of schooling. The middle school guidance counselor should know (and communicate to teachers in the school) the goals of both the elementary and secondary school guidance programs.

At one large middle school that we visited, one of the counselors felt that her school was doing a good job. However, she also felt that she and the advisors did not know what was actually going on at the feeder elementary and secondary schools. In response, she formed a committee of counselors from all three levels. At their meetings, the counselors discussed what each school was doing and what each school saw as its and the others' mission. "We want less duplication and fewer gaps in the guidance efforts," she explained.

Guidance for a Diverse Population

One special challenge to all educators is how to provide guidance activities that acknowledge and respect the cultural diversity of their students and the community. A greater challenge for middle school educators is to find ways to use the strengths of that diversity throughout the guidance program. While one approach is to attempt to hire counselors and teachers from diverse cultural backgrounds, that may be difficult in some areas.

One school that we visited decided to provide multicultural counseling training to all guidance professionals as well as most team leaders. Among the topics explored in the training sessions were cultural characteristics, worldviews, perceptions held by cultural groups about teachers and school success, and motivation. As a result of the training, the counselors and team leaders learned that all students do not perceive events through a Euro-centric lens.

Another principal tried a unique way to help her staff learn about the increasing Vietnamese community near the school. She told her teachers that, on one of the teacher preparation days at the beginning of school, they would be taking a field trip. But she did not say where they were going. Throughout the summer, this principal had been working with the leaders of the local Vietnamese community to plan some activities that would highlight parts of their culture, including music, dance, and food. On the appointed day, the teachers, still in the dark about where they were going, climbed on the buses. When they arrived at their destination, they were warmly greeted by parents, students, and community members. Without the formality of the school setting, people felt free to talk with each other, and students delighted in "educating" their teachers about the Vietnamese culture. In turn, the teachers were able to meet parents and to see where their students lived. Everyone we talked to told us how much that simple "field trip" had meant to them.

While we cannot hope to identify all cultural differences that middle school educators should take into consideration when planning guidance activities, we do want to mention some of them. Diversity Perspectives 11–1 examines how teachers and counselors should consider cultural differences when counseling students and when planning advisory experiences.

Team and Collaborative Approaches to Guidance

Advantages of Teachers and Counselors Working Collaboratively

In previous chapters, we have discussed the general concept of teaming and the benefits that accrue from working collaboratively toward common instructional goals. These qualities naturally carry over into the guidance program where teachers, counselors, administrators, and parents work for the benefit of young adolescents. At Lost Lake Middle School, Kim Matusi, in the chapter's opening scenario, saw the benefits of a team approach to guidance. First, teams are better able to address young adolescents' broad array of needs because they share responsibility for students. Kim knew that teaming increases communication among professionals and often serves the collateral function of enhancing their knowledge of the students under their guidance. In addition, teachers and counselors who work together are more likely to establish rewarding and long-lasting professional relationships. If the members of the teams come from diverse backgrounds, they can also model intercultural cooperation for their students.

Second, a team approach to guidance allows young adolescents to receive on-going assistance throughout the school day. Kim Matusi realized that guidance can no longer be limited to a specific period every week or so or when the student can schedule an appointment with the guidance counselor. Her approach at Lost Lake was to have teachers and specialists serve as advisors as they teach and interact with students. While they are not expected to solve all problems or to be trained as guidance professionals, they are readily available to listen and to offer advice; they also constantly consider students' problems to determine whether a meeting with the counselor is warranted.

Members of guidance teams also work collaboratively to help young adolescents develop respect for themselves and others. Young adolescents often lose respect for themselves and others during the early adolescence developmental period and during the transition from a smaller elementary to a usually larger school. Adopting a team approach to guidance, teachers and counselors are in a prime position to recognize when young adolescents lose their sense of respect. Before the situation grows acute, they can address the problem by

Diversity Perspectives 11-1

Counseling Students of Differing Cultural Backgrounds

With the steadily increasing number of young adolescents from diverse cultural backgrounds, educators should understand students' cultural orientations and worldviews and use culturally appropriate counseling strategies.

Don Locke (1989) suggests that counselors and teachers working with African American students should be open and honest, respect and appreciate cultural differences, participate in activities of the African American community, reject prejudice and racism, ask questions about the African American culture, and hold high expectations for African American young adolescents.

J. S. Hartman and A. C. Askounis (1989) maintained that Asian American students might feel conflict with respect to their cultural background and the Western values advocated in school since the American emphasis on spontaneity, assertiveness, and independence often conflicts with Asian American values. Many Asian immigrants are not accustomed to seeing counseling professionals and feel reluctant to admit they need help in handling personal problems. In addition, many Asian families teach their children that problems are to be kept within the confines of the family to avoid bringing shame and embarrassment to the family. Counselors and teachers working with Asian American students should determine individual strengths and weaknesses; be aware of the students and their families' degree of acculturation; understand Asian Americans' difficulty in being self-disclosing and open; understand that confrontational, emotionally intense approaches may cause additional problems and turmoil; and learn about individuals and their respective cultures to avoid stereotypical labels.

Roger Herring (1996) maintained that schools often ask Native American students to adopt unfamiliar ways of acting and thinking and to reject their traditional ways of storytelling and their participation in healing rituals and ceremonies. When counseling Native American students, educators should be sure the counseling intervention is highly individualized, includes assessment with minimal socioeconomic or cultural bias, reflects learning styles and life purposes, places value on the child's culture, and places high value on self-worth.

Sources: Hartman, J. S., & Askounis, A. C. (1989). Asian-American students: Are they really a "model minority"? *The School Counselor, 37,* 109–111; Herring, R. D. (1996) Synergetic counseling and Native American Indian students. *Journal of Counseling and Development, 74,* 542–547; and Locke, D. C. (1989). Fostering the self-esteem of African American children. *Elementary School Guidance and Counseling, 23,* 254–259.

having the teacher work daily in an advisory capacity with the advice and assistance of the counselor. If the situation arises where a number of students seem to be losing respect for a particular person or a group of people, the counselor might elect to provide a class guidance experience or small group or individual counseling.

Fourth, working collaboratively as a guidance team, teachers and counselors can develop and model skills of cooperation, decision making, and goal setting. Young adolescents are at a crucial stage of life for developing values, perspectives toward others, respect for cooperation, and decision-making skills. By working together, teachers and counselors can model these crucial skills.

Coordinating Professionals' and Parents' Efforts

In most instances, teachers and counselors will be responsible for most of the middle school guidance services. However, guidance programs should also be based on a coordinated effort of administrators, counselors, teachers, specialists, school nurses, social service agencies, and parents. The nature and severity of some young adolescents' problems are too serious to leave to chance or only to one or two professionals. While the teacher might be among the first to identify a potential problem, other educational professionals should also accept responsibility for identifying problems and for working with teachers. School personnel should also be well-acquainted with social-service agencies, which can provide specialized services. Likewise, parents and families should play major roles, both in identifying problems and in helping young adolescents.

Roles and responsibilities of school personnel, social-service agencies, and parents may include, but are not limited to, the following:

Teachers

- maintain constant observation for indicators of problems and conditions suggesting the need for guidance efforts;
- make appropriate referrals in a timely and professional manner based on accurate, factual, and objective information;
- communicate with parents and families and request their input and assistance in efforts to help young adolescents; and
- insist on coordinated approaches and shared efforts of all school personnel in providing comprehensive guidance efforts.

Guidance Counselors

- understand the unique developmental needs of young adolescents and how development might contribute to problems warranting counseling;
- know appropriate individual and group counseling strategies that work with 10- to 14-year-olds;
- know appropriate tests and assessment instruments for making objective and accurate identification decisions; and
- suggest to teachers and/or students appropriate strategies to eliminate or reduce problems and provide counseling to individual students.

Library Media Specialist

- purchase professional materials on young adolescent development and contemporary problems and share these with school personnel and parents;
- purchase nonfiction and realistic fiction materials for young adolescents that discuss contemporary problems and make them accessible to students through displays and book talks; and
- use the strategies of bibliotherapy to help students cope with specific problems.

Administrators

- provide leadership in the effort to help young adolescents, especially in coordinating efforts of all professionals;
- communicate effectively with teachers, social-service agencies, and parents;
- provide school personnel with appropriate in-service activities on identifying and working with young adolescents; and
- insist on objectivity and accuracy in identification procedures either to avoid labeling or to minimize its effects.

Parents and Families

- provide assistance in the identification of young adolescents' problems by providing information and insight about the girl or boy in the home environment;
- provide support and encouragement for educator's efforts and programs;
- take advantage of the powerful influence of immediate and extended families; and
- change home and family situations that might be contributing to conditions (i.e., older brothers and sisters experimenting with drugs).

Social-Service Agencies

- serve as a resource agency to provide expertise and services not available in the school setting;
- serve as an impetus to influence community and home standards (i.e., poverty situations in the home) that educators are powerless to change;
- monitor progress away from school or situations where school officials lack jurisdiction; and
- provide educators with information about home and family conditions that otherwise would not be known.

Advisor-Advisee Programs

Definitions and Goals

When we asked some middle school students to describe their advisor-advisee programs, they gave a wide range of responses. Here are a few of their comments:

"It's a time to be yourself."
"Mr. Canon treats me like a real person, not like I'm just a kid."
"I can tell Ms. Ortega anything I want and I know she won't tell anybody else."
"Mrs. Walker seems to know when things aren't right. I feel like she really cares, not like my parents."
"It's not phony. Some kids say their advisor doesn't like them and tries to hide it. But I don't feel that way about Ms. Matusi."
"I got a chance to see the real Mr. Soto. Like, we've done some awesome things together."

FIGURE 11–1 Student within the School Communities

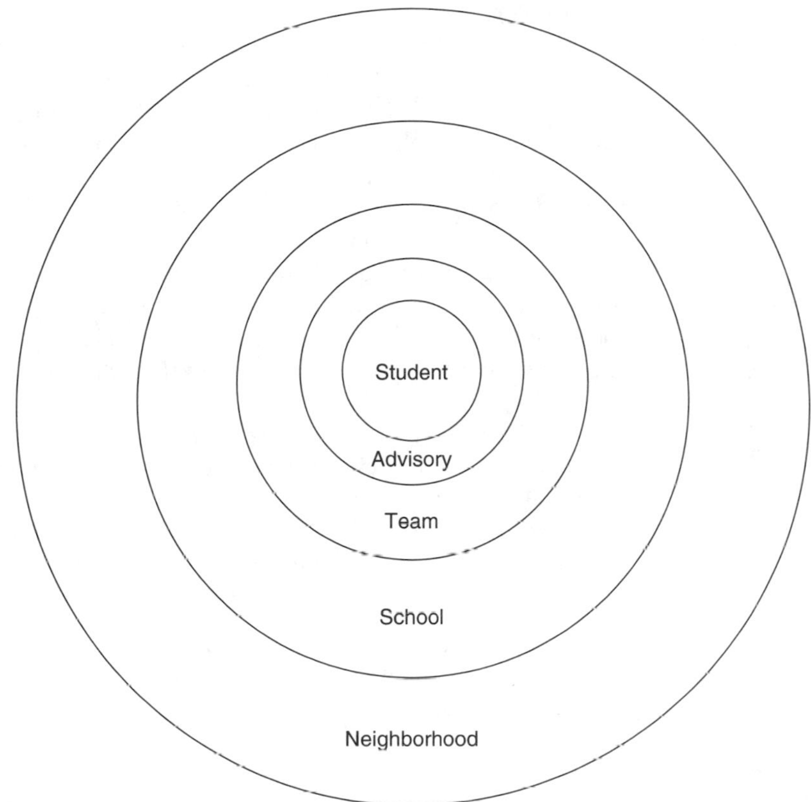

One of the most powerful and successful ways for educators to provide guidance to young adolescents is through advisor-advisee programs. The advisor-advisee program (also called advisories, teacher advisories, or home-based guidance) is a planned effort in which each student has the opportunity to participate in a small interactive group with peers and school staff to discuss school, personal, and societal concerns. The advisory program helps each student develop a meaningful relationship with at least one significant adult in the middle school (Allen, Splittgerber, & Manning, 1993) while providing personal and academic guidance. To reduce the student-teacher ratio, all faculty, including specialists, serve as advisors.

Advisors serve advisees as friend, advocate, guide, group leader, community builder, liaison with parents, and evaluation coordinator. They also provide a warm, caring environment; plan and implement advisory programs; assist advisees in monitoring academic progress; provide times for students to share concerns; refer advisees to appropriate resources; communicate with parents and families; maintain appropriate records, and encourage advisees' cognitive and psychosocial growth (James, 1986).

Depending on the school, advisories meet every day or two or three times a week with most successful advisories occurring at the beginning of the day and lasting at least 25 minutes (Arnold, 1991). The teacher plans advisory sessions, preferably with the help of other team members and the guidance counselor (if needed). Here are some topics for advisor-advisee sessions along with some titles that have been used in schools: peer pressure (How to be an individual and still be part of the group), substance abuse (Knowing when to say NO), friendships (Making new friends and keeping your old ones), health-related issues (Can you be too thin?), career exploration (Set your goals high), development (Who said growing up was easy?), school rules (Staying out of the principal's office), understanding parents (How to talk to your parents), contemporary issues (Slime on the lake doesn't bother me, does it?), and leisure-time activities (When you're bored, try this). In addition, young adolescents might want to discuss topics such as those in the advisory scope and sequence in Case Study 11–1. Other activities that take place during advisor-advisee sessions include meeting with individual students about problems; offering career information and guidance; discussing academic, personal, and family problems; addressing moral or ethical issues; discussing multicultural and intergroup relations; and helping students develop self-confidence and leadership skills (Epstein & MacIver, 1990).

At Shoreham-Wading River Middle School (Long Island, NY), advisors meet daily with 8 to 10 students. Reinforcing the advisor-advisee programs are a psychologist, a guidance counselor, and a social worker. These professionals not only work with the students, but also provide in-service activities for the school's advisory staff (Maeroff, 1990).

While specific goals of advisor-advisee programs should reflect each middle school's overall philosophy and young adolescents' needs and concerns, examples of goals include:

1. ensure all students feel known by at least one caring adult;
2. provide opportunities for students and educators to learn about one another on a personal adult-student basis;
3. improve young adolescent-teacher relations;
4. promote an atmosphere of equality for all cultures, social classes, and both genders;
5. provide opportunity for group work and collaboration;
6. improve the sharing of feelings; and
7. make teachers more aware of students' attitudes and behavior.

Roles of Teachers, Counselors, and Administrators

A number of publications discuss the importance of advisor-advisee programs and how effective programs operate (Cole, 1992; James, 1986; MacLaury, 1995; Manning, 1993b). In the program, there are specific roles for teachers, counselors, and administrators. We believe that the ultimate success and overall effectiveness of the program depend upon the degree of commitment these guidance team members bring to the advisory effort. While each has a designated role that will vary somewhat, according to the respective school and with individual advisory programs, they must work in a complementary fashion in order for young adolescents to have effective advisory experiences.

In effective advisory programs, teachers plan advisory experiences with their interdisciplinary team, preferably with the direction of the guidance counselor. While the number of teams and team meetings will not allow the counselor to attend all team-planning sessions, she or he can attend and offer assistance when special expertise is needed. While planning and implementing advisory activities are primary roles of teachers, teachers are also responsible for providing warm, caring overall classroom environments where young adolescents feel known by an adult and where they feel physically and psychologically safe. Since many young adolescents need a caring and attentive adult to listen to their concerns, teachers must also serve as active listeners. Also, they can monitor young adolescents' social and academic progress and help them attain a realistic perspective of such progress. Finally, teachers must communicate with parents and families about their child's progress in school and must work with the guidance counselor to prevent and solve both short-term and long-term problems.

Diversity plays a part in the development of effective advisor-advisee programs. Often that means teachers make a special effort to learn about the cultural backgrounds of their students. At one middle school, Wendy Lee, a bright and enthusiastic first-year teacher, voiced a concern to her mentoring teacher, Jennifer Milbury, about working with students from other cultural groups. "As you know, I am a second-generation Asian American and I'm not sure I can develop advisories for students of differing cultures." While Jennifer wanted to say, "No problem, you can do it!" she realized that there really might be a problem. Jennifer received Wendy's permission to discuss the situation with the guidance team. The team agreed that, while cultural perspectives and worldviews differ, Wendy could be taught to handle an advisory group composed of 10- to 14-year-olds from other cultures. However, rather than just put Wendy with her own group, the team decided that she should sit in with an experienced advisor who was a member of a different cultural group to see what the school expected of advisors. The team also arranged for Wendy to work with one of the guidance counselors and the school library media specialist to learn more about the cultural backgrounds of the students.

Sometimes people think teachers are usurping the counselors' roles and counselors are no longer needed. We believe that teacher participation in advisory efforts does not negate the role of the counselor. In effective middle schools where guidance is a team and collaborative effort, counselors support teachers in guidance efforts and assist with both advisory programs and daily interactions; offer individual, small- and large-group counseling; sponsor and coordinate programs in peer mediation and peer tutoring; and place priority on meeting with individual teachers and teams.

Administrators also play major roles. Their commitment to the advisory concept and daily support of advisory efforts can either "make or break" the program. Both teachers and counselors will develop a sense of the priority administrators place on advisement efforts. Other administrator roles include establishing and allocating funds fairly and equitably, assuming responsibility for making advisor-advisee programs a major part of the master schedule, voicing support for advisories in the community, coordinating school-community-home relations, and possibly agreeing to conduct their own advisory group.

Guidelines for Effective Advisory Programs

"Are advisory programs worth the effort? Sure. But like anything else, they take time and planning. We developed a detailed scope and sequence chart and listed goals, roles, guidelines, and procedures for the program. It's almost like planning a unit. The difference is that with the unit, I'm in my teacher role; with the advisory, I'm in my guidance role. Yes, guidance spills over into my entire day, but the advisory is a special time and my students know it too." Seventh-grade teacher.

Case Study 11-1

Lost Lake Develops an Advisor-Advisee Program

While Lost Lake Middle School had been a middle school for several years, realistically speaking, little had changed in the way the guidance program operated. However, after Kim Matusi and Ted Canon met with the sixth-grade teachers, they decided to implement an advisor-advisee program. When they talked to Louise Henzel, the principal, she suggested that the whole school make guidance its focus for the next year. Thus Kim's original plan spread throughout the school. As a result, an Advisor-Advisee Planning (AAP) Committee, with representatives from all three grades as well as counselors, specialists, and administrators, went to work. Using books and guides such as *This We Believe* (National Middle School Association, 1995) and *Advisor-Advisee Programs: Why, What, and How* (James, 1986), the AAP Committee decided to (1) define the advisory program in terms of the needs of the 10- to 14-year-olds at Lost Lake, (2) outline implementation procedures, and (3) develop a tentative scope and sequence. To help the committee reach educationally sound decisions, Mrs. Henzel appointed an Advisory Review Committee consisting of a consultant, three parents, two students, several teachers, school counselors, a mental health specialist trained to work with 10- to 14-year-olds, and an administrator. They would review the AAP Committee's report and offer suggestions.

The AAP Committee identified three purposes of their advisory program: (1) to ensure that all students have at least one adult who knows them well, (2) to be sure all students belong to a small interactive group, and (3) to provide opportunities for students and educators to learn about one another on a personal adult-student basis. In the scheduled advisor-advisee sessions, the educators wanted to promote students' social, emotional, and moral growth, while providing personal and academic guidance. Advisory sessions would meet five times every 2 weeks (on an ABABA and BABAB block schedule) with sessions lasting 35 minutes. Kim Matusi and the other guidance counselors would continue to play a crucial role in the advisory program by providing services to individual students and small groups and by assisting advisors as needed.

To implement the plan, the group decided to (1) design an advisory scope and sequence showing monthly topics; (2) list ways teacher advisors and guidance counselors can work collaboratively toward agreed-upon goals; (3) write a letter to parents describing the purposes of the newly implemented advisory program; (4) determine a means of evaluating the advisory effort; and (5) plan an on-going professional development program to prepare all educators for participation in the advisory program.

The development of the scope and sequence included (1) considering the special challenges students faced at Lost Lake, (2) deciding how to effectively use faculty strengths and interests, and (3) ensuring comprehensive coverage of topics without needless repetition. Everyone stressed that, although the guidance program needed a scope and sequence, it should be sufficiently flexible to meet the needs of 10- to 14-year-olds. The following scope and sequence was a *preliminary* effort developed with the understanding that it would be revised throughout the year.

Case Study 11-1 (cont.)

Advisory Scope and Sequence

Month	Grade 6	Grade 7	Grade 8
September	Get acquainted/ School spirit	Get acquainted/ School spirit	Get acquainted/ School spirit
October	Study skills	Study skills	Study skills
November	Friendships	Substance abuse	Decision making
December	Getting along/ Social skills	Understanding diversity	Understanding diversity
January	Community service	Community service	Community service
February	Family relationships	Family relationships	Substance abuse
March	Test taking/ Time management	Creativity/ Problem solving	Creativity/ Problem solving
April	Substance abuse	Accepting responsibility	Communication
May	Development	Caring/Manners	Preparing for high school

What the Advisory Review Committee Suggested

The Advisory Review Committee reviewed the AAP Committee's report. After praising the work done by the committee, they made the following suggestions:

1. Provide sufficient planning time prior to implementation and include opportunities for staff development and training.
2. Include teachers from a broad array of academic areas, specialists, guidance counselors, administrators, and, whenever possible, students and parents in identifying topics and planning sessions.
3. Continue to refine the scope and sequence, remembering that such a document needs to evolve as student concerns and needs change;
4. Place the advisory program at a specified day and time, so students will perceive it as more than an activity to be conducted upon completion of other regular activities.
5. Notify parents of the advisory program and provide an orientation session that explains its goals and limitations.

Building an effective advisory program takes time; however, you need to remember that advisory programs should reflect young adolescents' needs as well as the organization (e.g., schedules, teaming) of the individual middle school.

Advisory sessions should:

1. Begin *only after* advisors have received sufficient staff development to know the goals of the program, the needs of young adolescents, and how to plan and implement effective sessions.
2. Be smaller than average academic classes, so participants will feel that they are well-known and that they are comfortable sharing information.
3. Meet 25 to 35 minutes per day or several days each week at a regularly scheduled time, so students will perceive advisories as an integral part of the school day.
4. Allow advisors to have considerable freedom and flexibility to design their own programs.
5. Include counselors serving as collaborative team members and playing vital roles in initiating and maintaining advisory programs.
6. Reflect the concerns, issues, and problems faced by young adolescents.
7. Be open to administrators, other professional educators, and parents.
8. Be carefully planned (e.g., a scope and sequence) so young adolescents will have specific experiences during designated months and grades.
9. Undergo comprehensive and objective evaluation to determine the strengths and areas needing improvement.

In Case Study 11–1, let's revisit Kim Matusi at Lost Lake Middle School to see how Lost Lake planned their advisor-advisee program.

Advisory Plans

As a teacher, you will want to help design an advisory format that reflects your individual approach and overall advisory concept, that actively involves students, and that addresses issues that are relevant to young adolescents. To help you, in Theory into Practice 11–1 and 11–2, we provide examples of advisory plans dealing with peer pressure and with making and maintaining friendships.

Need for Specialized Services

The guidance team can hardly be expected to meet all of young adolescents' wide array of needs since problems are greater than educators and parents can address. Therefore, teachers and counselors should be on constant surveillance for problems and concerns that extend beyond the purview of the middle school and call for more specialized mental health attention. By suggesting that the school cannot address more acute problems, we do not want to downplay the middle school's guidance and counseling roles. However, in some situations, responsible educators and counselors must be prepared to suggest community organizations and social-services agencies that can provide assistance.

Theory into Practice 11-1

Peer Pressure Advisory Plan

Topic: Dealing with Peer Pressure
Grade: 7 (12 students)
Time: 25 minutes
Objectives: The students will:

1. Name at least three types of peer pressure they have experienced during the past week.
2. Suggest a positive response to each.

Materials: None (for this introductory session)

Interest Builder: Tell students that all people are subject to peer pressure at some time, but 10- to 14-year-olds are particularly vulnerable. Peer pressure can take many forms, such as wearing a certain kind of shoe or having a particular backpack. It can also be more serious such as believing that, to be accepted by others, you need to engage in a forbidden behavior such as smoking. Ask such questions as: Can you name an example of peer pressure? How has peer pressure caused you to do something that you normally would not have done? Then explain that peer pressure is the topic for the next 8 to 10 advisory sessions and that this introductory discussion will provide a general overview. Future advisory sessions will focus on specific areas in more detail.

Procedures:

1. Ask students to work in three groups of four each to (a) name three types of peer pressure they have experienced in the past week, (b) name one or two types they have observed on television or read about in a book or short story, (c) describe how feeling pressured made them feel, and (d) suggest a positive response to peer pressure.
2. Have each group choose a spokesperson to report the group's types of peer pressures and the accompanying feelings.
3. Ask each group to plan a brief (no more than 2 minutes) role-playing situation in which they experience peer pressure and in which they offer a positive response.
4. Explain again that peer pressure will be the topic for the next 8 to 10 advisory sessions and that students need to continue to think of positive responses when they feel pressured to engage in certain behaviors.

Evaluation: Due to the nature of advisory sessions, formal evaluation such as a written test will not occur; however, the teacher-advisor should evaluate his or her overall performance and the degree of interest in the topic. Also, observe students to determine whether they have a better understanding of peer pressure and whether they demonstrate increased resistance to being pressured by others.

Developed from: James, M. (1986). *Advisor-advisee program: Why, what, and how.* Columbus, OH: National Middle School Association.

Theory into Practice 11–2

Friendships Advisory Plan

Topic: Making and Keeping Friends
Grade: 6 (16 students)
Time: 25 minutes
Objectives: The students will:

1. Name three problems associated with making and keeping friends.
2. Name three ways they can better understand friends.
3. Name three qualities they look for in friends.

Materials: None (for this introductory session)

Interest Builder: Making and keeping friends are important parts of growing up, especially for people your age. When I was about your age, I had several good friends whom I saw a lot both at home and at school. In fact, we went almost everywhere together. Making and keeping friends, however, can be difficult. What qualities do you look for in a friend, Lamont? How about you, Lori? Friends are sometimes difficult to understand, aren't they? What can we do to better understand why a friend acts as she or he does, Cole? For the next month in our advisory sessions, we will discuss making and keeping friends. Today, we will have a general discussion about friends, what we look for in a friend, how we can be a friend, and how we can understand why our friends act as they do.

Procedures:

1. Have students work alone and list four or five characteristics they want in a friend. Also, list four or five of their personal characteristics that make them good friends. Tell students it is not necessary to sign their names to their lists.
2. Collect all the lists and read them to the class. Make few comments, so students will consider the lists from their own perspectives.
3. Have students work in four groups of four to name several problems associated with making friends—such as friends not having similar friends, friends having different interests, and friends who live so far apart that they can only be friends at school. Next, ask students how they can remedy these problems.
4. Have a spokesperson from each group report to the class. Ask students to brainstorm ways they can better understand friends.

Evaluation: After the advisory sessions on making and keeping friends are over, students could complete a checklist (not for a grade) on topics such as what we should look for in a friend, how we should act as a friend, and how we can understand why our friends act as they do.

Developed from: James, M. (1986). *Advisor-advisee program: Why, what, and how.* Columbus, OH: National Middle School Association.

Keeping Current with Technology 11–1

American Academy of Child and Adolescent Psychiatry
http://www.aacap.org/

American Counseling Association
http://www.counseling.org/

American Mental Health Counselors Association
http://www.amhca.org/home2.html

Broughal Middle School Guidance: Guidance links
http://www.users.fast.net/~wfeigley/home.html

CyberPsych
http://www.cyberpsych.org

Fall Creek Valley Middle School, Indianapolis, IN
http://www.msdlt.k12.in.us/msdlt/fallcreekvalley/guidance/index.html

Maternal and Child Health Bureau
http://www.mchb.hrsa.gov/index.html

Mental Health.Com: On-line encyclopedia
http://www.mentalhealth.com

Petersons Education & Career Center
http://www.petersons.com/

Psych Web
http://www.psychwww.com/

While you will want to learn about the organizations and agencies in your own communities, selected sources of help include area health departments, mental health professionals, social-service agencies, Tough Love, AIDS information hotlines, Urban Leagues, Departments of Social Services, area mental health centers, Share Self-Help Support Groups, Big Sister, Big Brother, YMCA and YWCA, Quest International, Planned Parenthood, and Crisis Pregnancy Centers. In fact, we encourage the guidance team to make a list (addresses, telephone numbers, and resources provided) of social-service agencies, referral services, and community organizations. This list could be modified for distribution to parents and families. Visit some of the Internet sites in Keeping Current with Technology 11–1 to locate additional information on issues related to guidance in middle schools.

Closing Remarks

Rather than guidance being only the domain of the guidance counselor, guidance and counseling in effective middle schools take a team approach of teachers, counselors, specialists, administrators, parents and families, and sometimes social-service agencies. Working with guidance professionals, teachers plan daily (or at least several times a week) advisor-advisee sessions and advise on a daily basis, as they teach and interact with students.

This comprehensive approach to guidance requires commitment and dedication. It also means that middle school educators must develop an advisory scope and sequence to meet specific young adolescent needs. While the diversity of young adolescents and their problems suggests meeting all needs is an unrealistic goal, through cooperation and collaboration, the middle school guidance team should be able to address many of the concerns and issues faced by 10- to 14-year-olds.

Suggested Readings

Burkhart, R. M. (1999). Advisory: Advocacy for every student. *Middle School Journal, 30*(3), 51–54. Maintains that too many advisory programs do not achieve success because they are seen as curriculum rather than nurturing relationships.

Cole, C. (1992). *Nurturing a teacher advisory program.* Columbus, OH: National Middle School Association. Explains how advisory programs can deal with changing demographics, new family patterns, and at-risk behaviors.

Galassi, J. P., Gulledge, S. A., & Cox, N. D. (1997). Middle school advisories: Retrospect and prospect. *Review of Educational Research, 67*(3), 301–338. Presents a critical analysis of middle school advisor-advisee programs and offers alternative educational practices.

Galassi, J. P., Gulledge, S. A., & Cox, N. D. (1998). *Advisory: Definitions, descriptions, decisions, directions.* Columbus, OH: National Middle School Association. Defines advisory programs and provides educations with critical information for designing effective programs.

Johnston, H. (1997). What's going on? From advisory programs to adult-student relationships: Restoring purpose to the guidance program. *Schools in the Middle, 6*(4), 8–15. Describes changes in children, schooling, and behavior during the twentieth century and how comprehensive advisory programs should be connected to the central mission of the school.

Reese, S. (1998). The counselor's conundrum: Provide triage or full-service programs. *Middle Ground: The Magazine of Middle Level Education, 2*(2), 17–19, 24. Explores whether middle-level school counselors should provide triage (the sorting and allocation of guidance services) or full-service guidance programs.

Vars, G. F. (1997). Getting closer to middle level students: Options for teacher-advisor guidance programs. *Schools in the Middle, 6*(4), 16–22. Argues that middle school students need a variety of advisory techniques used by competent and committee advisors.

Wilson, C. (1998). The real meaning of middle school advisory programs. *Contemporary Education, 69*(2), 100–102. Planning and the participation of teachers who will serve as advisors are necessary for effective advisory programs.

Chapter 12

Parents, Families, and Community Members—Partners and Resources

Scenario—Encouraging Community Involvement

"So what do you miss most about Lakeside Elementary now that you teach at the middle school?" It seemed like an innocent question coming from her friend Briana Mayes, a fourth-grade teacher. But Lyvonne Miller paused to think before she answered.

Last fall, with the reorganization of the schools in East Point, Lyvonne had moved from teaching sixth grade at Lakeside Elementary School to teaching sixth grade in the new Seldon Way Middle School. Academically, the change had not been that dramatic. For several years while they were still housed in the elementary school, the sixth-grade teachers had been organized into interdisciplinary teams and had begun to implement some of the programs like exploratories and advisories that they hoped to use in the middle school. In fact, when construction at Seldon Way was held up by the hurricane, the teachers had another year to prepare for the transition.

Now, however, as she reflected on her first year as a middle school teacher, Lyvonne thought about the things she missed. Really, there were not many. Her fears of having the sixth graders with the older students had not materialized, and she was surprised at the sense of community that had developed among the students and teachers at the new school. But there was one thing lacking.

"Well, Briana, what I miss most will probably surprise you. It seems strange not to have the parents and other family members involved at the school like they were at Lakeside Elementary. Lakeside feeds directly into Seldon Way, but the parents just aren't active there."

"Gee, Lyvonne, I'm really surprised. We've always had an active parent and community volunteer group at Lakeside, and the parent-teacher organization is very supportive, too. What do you think happened?"

"I don't know. Maybe they figure that, because their children are older, we don't need their help as much as we did. Maybe they're intimidated by the advanced curriculum and even the strangeness of the new building. Many parents attended Lakeside themselves, and everything about the school was familiar to them." Lyvonne shrugged her shoulders.

Briana thought for a moment before asking, "What have you folks done to encourage parents to get involved? Have you developed any school-community relations programs? You know the parental and community involvement with Lakeside didn't happen overnight. We worked a long time to develop a sense of trust and good lines of communication. What have you done at Seldon Way?"

"Good question. And I'm afraid the answer is that we haven't done very much this first year. What with getting adjusted to the new building and trying to get the integrated curriculum, advisories, and exploratories operational, we just haven't had time."

"What do you mean, you haven't had time? You sixth-grade teachers wouldn't have had time for your cooperative planning if the school volunteers hadn't made it possible for you to leave your classrooms. Volunteers help make time!"

"You know you're right, Briana. But it isn't just the volunteers. I miss the chance to work with parents. There's so much about the middle school concept they don't know. But, maybe the blame isn't just with the parents. If a few of us teachers really make a concerted effort to improve our own involvement and relationships with parents and the community, the rest of the faculty might follow. If you ask that same question next year, my answer might be: 'Nothing, Seldon Way has it all.'"

Overview

For a long time, all educators have recognized how important it is to involve parents, families, and community members in the education of children. Thus, they have encouraged parents and other adults to volunteer in the schools, attend parent-teacher conferences, join parents' organizations, volunteer for school programs, and form community partnerships. However, while many individuals are involved in programs in elementary schools, adult involvement drops drastically once children enter middle school. For example, although 75% of elementary school parents are moderately or highly involved in their children's education, the number drops to about 50% when children reach middle school (Seline, 1997). Participation by other community members declines as well. We believe that you and other middle school educators will need to work to recapture the interest and commitment of parents and other community members and to "reengage" them in the education of young adolescents.

While most writers use the term *parental involvement,* a more inclusive term might be *adult involvement.* In this chapter, we will talk about families and community members as well as parents and the involvement of all of these groups in middle schools. You will discover some suggestions for maintaining and strengthening relationships and communication throughout the community. In addition, we encourage you to read the articles that we cite for more complete information. Your goal should be to use all of the strengths of a community to improve the educational experiences of young adolescents.

Objectives

After reading and thinking about this chapter on parents and community as partners and resources, you should be able to:

1. name several factors that suggest the need for including parents and families in the education of their young adolescents;
2. offer explanations for parents and families disengaging themselves from middle schools;
3. list cultural considerations to remember when reengaging parents and families from varying cultural backgrounds;
4. explain parents' concerns about middle schools and how to turn parents from critics to allies;
5. explain parent involvement—ways to increase it, and essential elements of effective programs;
6. explain *Turning Points'* recommendations for reengaging parents and *Great Transitions'* suggestions for strengthening parents' roles;
7. explain how to implement parent education programs for parents of young adolescents and identify some appropriate topics; and
8. define *community service* and offer a rationale for involving young adolescents in the community.

Reengaging Parents and Families in Middle Schools

Rationale for Including Parents, Families, and Community Members

Why, you might wonder, would Lyvonne Miller, in the chapter's opening scenario, say that the thing she missed most in the middle school was the lack of parental or community involvement? Like many teachers we talk to, Lyvonne knows the value of having parents, family members, and other citizens involved in the education of young adolescents. Here are a few comments other teachers had when we asked them about community involvement:

> "I've found that students of interested and involved parents are usually more motivated and serious about education."
>
> "When I get to know parents and other family members, we can work as a team and can assist each other in the education of the child."
>
> "When parents get more involved in school activities and homework, they learn about the middle school curriculum and the various purposes of middle school education. They're less likely to question the things we do or put down the middle school concept. They also make the transition from elementary school a little easier."
>
> "Having adult role models for our students is wonderful. Some of our students don't have very good role models where they live. Since the Halton Corporation has become our community partner and helped with some of our exploratories, I've noticed a real change in the outlook and the behavior of some students."

These informal comments of teachers have been echoed by others. Hazel Loucks and Jan Waggoner (1995) found that parents who were involved in well-planned, systematic programs at a school had more positive attitudes about schools and teachers. In addition, family involvement in education increases student attendance, decreases the dropout rate, and improves student attitudes and behavior (Loucks & Waggoner, 1995). When parents are "educated" in the middle school concept, parents can be turned from critics into allies (Giannetti & Sagarese, 1998).

In chapter 2, we talked about the communities that affect the young adolescent, including the family, neighborhood, and ethnic/racial/religious communities, as well as society in general. We noted that these communities can, in some instances, place conflicting demands upon young adolescents. But we also believe that the power and influence of these communities can help in the education of young adolescents.

Disengagement and Reengagement

Turning Points (Carnegie Council on Adolescent Development, 1989) called for middle school educators to reengage parents in the education of their children. Notice the use of the word *reengage* rather than *engage.* Although many parents participate actively in educational activities when their children are in elementary school, by the time their children go to middle school, these same parents disengage themselves from many educational activities.

Perhaps because parents feel that they are not needed or that their children can take care of educational matters themselves, many parents of middle school students do not take an active role in their children's education. A survey of eighth graders and their parents revealed:

- Two-thirds of the students never or rarely discussed classes or school programs with parents.
- One-third of the parents never or rarely checked homework.

- Half of the parents had not attended a school meeting since the beginning of the year.
- Two-thirds of the parents had never talked to school officials about the academic program.
- Only one-third of the parents belonged to a parent-teacher organization (Parents Key to Classroom Experience, 1991).

As you read in chapter 2, as a part of natural developmental changes, the social behaviors of young adolescents are changing with their social networks expanding, and their allegiances shifting from adults to peers. While parents do need to allow young adolescents greater freedom and autonomy, the middle school years are not the time for parents to make a complete break. Although young adolescents are moving toward independence, they are still strongly connected to their families, and they need to have their parents involved in the educational process. Surveys reveal that they want parental attention and guidance in making educational and career decisions, in forming values, and in assuming adult roles. In essence, they do want supportive guidance from both parents and other adults (Carnegie Council on Adolescent Development, 1996).

Adults benefit, too, from the continued relationship with the school. They learn about the academic program, the school curriculum, the class and school rules and expectations, and a host of other aspects that contribute to their child's behavior, academic achievement, and overall development. The school also provides a neutral ground, where parents can work with their children away from the emotional struggles that are often found at home. As one eighth grader told us, "My mom's a different person here at school than she is at home. At home she's always nagging me to do things. But here, when she helped with the career exploratory, even my friends thought she was okay."

Obstacles to Reengagement

Unfortunately, there are many reasons why parental involvement decreases when children become young adolescents. Being a parent of an adolescent can be a tough job and a great responsibility, and many families with adolescent children may be experiencing difficulties dealing with them. These families may welcome the "distance" created when a young adolescent goes to school and may believe that trying to work with young adolescents at school would only highlight their own feelings of inadequacy. Unfortunately, families with adolescents have been neglected in many professional services, community programs, and public policies with more information provided for families of younger children than is provided for parents of adolescents (Carnegie Council on Adolescent Development, 1996).

Many parents who want to remain closely involved in their adolescent's life are sometimes prevented from doing so by their own job and career demands. Often, we find that when children enter middle school, mothers or fathers, who had previously stayed home, now return to the workforce. Unless their place of employment has a school partnership program, it is difficult for them to keep the close connection to the school that they were able to maintain when they were not employed outside the home.

Sometimes, the obstacle is the school itself. Existing school policies and teacher attitudes in some middle schools have discouraged the involvement of parents or other adults. According to *Turning Points,* "Many middle schools do not encourage, and some actively discourage, parental involvement at school" (Carnegie Council on Adolescent Development, 1989, p. 22). If this assertion is true, no programs to reengage parents will have significant effects if the parents continue to believe that the teachers do not want their participation and involvement.

Cultural Considerations–Reengaging Parents and Families from Varying Cultural Backgrounds

It can be tempting to lump all parents into a single category and to try to make general statements about them or try to develop one single program to meet the needs of all families. However, it is important to recognize the differences among families from differing cultural backgrounds and even among families who are in the cultural majority. Remember, parents and families from diverse cultures and social classes might think and act differently from middle-class, majority culture parents.

In working with individuals from some cultures, you will probably need to redefine the meaning of the term *family.* Traditionally, most educators have only felt comfortable sharing confidential information (such as a student's progress or learning problems) with the parents. However, in some cultures, family members in addition to parents feel responsible for the child's behavior and school performance. Some parents may visit the school with extended family members such as aunts, uncles, and grandparents. Also, in today's society, stepparents or even stepgrandparents might attend meetings in lieu of the student's biological parents. As an educator, you need to recognize the importance of working with a variety of family organization patterns, including both immediate and extended families.

Although you will need to work with all families, those from differing cultural backgrounds might be in even greater need of assistance. Some parents and families may not understand middle school expectations. While some families expect high achievement in all areas from their children and adolescents (Yao, 1988), others may have difficulties communicating with the school or may not even understand how the American school systems "work." Unfortunately, educators sometimes misunderstand parents' differing attitudes, behavior, and mannerisms and assume that they do not care about their children's progress in schools. Such an assumption can have serious consequences for young adolescents, especially when this assumption results in lower expectations for the children. With well-planned parent education programs and other educational experiences, families can learn about U.S. schools and can help their children benefit from school experiences.

Sometimes, it is also difficult to accept the decisions of families from other cultures. In one middle school, Sam was a bright, talented sixth grader. Yet Sam was shunned by many of his peers because of a facial scar. A group of concerned teachers was able to find money, through a local program, for Sam to have the cosmetic surgery that he needed. The only thing lacking was the permission of his parents. Unfortunately, Sam's father would not give his permission. To him, if Sam had the surgery, it would be admitting that something was "wrong" with his son, a cultural taboo. Accepting the father's decision was very difficult. It was even more difficult for those teachers to continue to respect and work with Sam's father. However, Sam's situation was unusual. In most cases, if educators accept the challenge of understanding the diversity of parents and families, the results will include improved overall school achievement and a stronger partnership between families and teachers.

Suggestions for Reengagement

Two influential documents, *Turning Points* (Carnegie Council on Adolescent Development, 1989) and *Great Transitions* (Carnegie Council on Adolescent Development, 1996), offered recommendations for reengaging parents in the education of their middle school children. Table 12–1 and Table 12–2 provide an overview of these recommendations.

Calling for reengagement is one thing—actually reengaging parents and community members is another. In the next section of this chapter, we will explore parental involvement in more detail. In doing so, we want to identify the things parents want from schools and the things that schools can do to establish better communication with parents.

TABLE 12–1 ***Turning Points' Recommendations for Reengaging Parents***

Recommendation	Implementation
Offer parents meaningful roles in school governance	Join parents in the decision-making process concerning building wide issues and problems.
Keep parents informed	Use parent conferences and involvement activities to inform parents about school rules and policies.
Encourage parents to support learning	Offer families opportunities to tutor children, monitor homework, and encourage children to apply themselves, maintain good health, and engage in youth service.

Developed from: *Turning Points: Preparing American youth for the 21st century.* (1989). Washington, DC: Carnegie Council on Adolescent Development.

TABLE 12–2 ***Great Transitions' Recommendations for Strengthening Parent Roles***

Recommendation	Implementation
Sustain parent involvement in middle school	Provide family resource centers that teach about young adolescence development, counseling, health promotion, and family life.
Provide guidance to parents of young adolescents	Provide parents with guidance about diseases, distress, healthy adjustment, and how to prevent problems.
Reassess public and private work	Reassess policies and procedures so that professionals can work with families as well as with students.
Create parent peer support	Teach families how to show warmth and mutual respect, to have sustained interest in young adolescents, and to communicate high expectations for behavior and achievement.

Developed from: *Great transitions: Preparing adolescents for a new century.* (1996). Washington, DC: Carnegie Council on Adolescent Development.

Parents and Middle Schools

Parent Involvement Yesterday and Today

Involving parents in the education of their children and providing "parenting education" programs are not new concepts. While parents have been their children's first educators since prehistoric times, the first formal parent education classes began in 1815. However, the recent focus on parent collaboration emerged during the 1960s with federal programs such as Head Start, Home Start, and Follow Through and continued during the 1980s and 1990s in programs such as Parents as School Partners and the National Parent Information Network. The emerging alliance between homes and schools came from the recognition that not only are schools important to parents and families but that parents are also important to schools (Berger, 1991). As Goal 8 of the National Education Goals states: "Every school will promote partnerships that will increase parental involvement and participation in promoting the social, emotional, and academic growth of children (Goals 2000)."

Levels and Types of Parent Involvement

What exactly do educators mean when they talk about parental involvement in education? Is attending a parent-teacher conference enough? Or is something more required?

Eugenia Berger (1991) maintained that parent participation in the schools includes at least five levels of involvement. At the highest level, the parent is an active partner and educational leader both at home and school. This is followed by the parent as an education decision maker, the parent as a school volunteer or paid employee, and the parent as a liaison between home and school to support homework. At the lowest level of involvement, the parent is a passive supporter of the educational goals of the school (Berger, 1991).

What Do Parents Want from Schools?

"Since Ben entered middle school, I've gone back to work full time. I can't volunteer anymore."

"I've only been in this country a few years, and my English isn't too good."

"They don't need me at the middle school do they? After all, kids are grown up by the time they're in seventh grade these days."

These are a few of the comments we've heard from parents who were not involved in their young adolescent's school.

You may be tempted to write off the lack of parent involvement as a general lack of interest in education. However, that is not true. In researching the question "What do parents want from teachers?" Dorothy Rich (1998) identified three consistent parent concerns: how well teachers know and care (1) about teaching, (2) about their children, and (3) about communicating with parents. She then listed questions about each concern. Table 12–3 provides examples of questions selected from Rich's suggestions.

TABLE 12–3 ***Questions Parents Might Want Answered from Teachers***

With regard to teaching:

Does the teacher appear to enjoy teaching and believe in what he or she does?

Does the teacher set high expectations and help children reach them?

Does the teacher know the subject matter and how to teach it?

Does the teacher create a safe classroom where children are encouraged to pay attention, participate in class, and learn?

With regard to their children:

Does the teacher understand how our child learns and try to meet these needs?

Does the teacher treat my child fairly and with respect?

Does the teacher provide helpful information during conferences?

With regard to communicating with parents:

Does the teacher provide clear information about class expectations?

Is my child's teacher accessible and responsive when I want to meet?

Does the teacher work with me to develop a cooperative strategy to help my child?

Developed from: Rich, D. (1998). What parents want from teachers. *Educational Leadership, 55*(8), 37–39.

Parents' Concerns about Middle Schools

Many parents have questions about teaching, evaluation, classroom climate, and other items that Rich (1998) listed. Also, they might have attended a more traditional junior high school and might not understand essential middle school concepts such as advisor-advisee, exploratory programs, and interdisciplinary teaching. As J. Howard Johnston and Ronald Williamson (1998) found, middle schools are sometimes controversial places due to the dynamic nature of young adolescents and the transitional nature of the school. There is strong public opinion about what middle schools do and how they do it.

Johnston and Williamson (1998) investigated the parent and public concerns about middle schools. While they found many positive aspects, they also identified seven major categories of concern:

1. *Anonymity*—Concern that the larger size of the middle school (in contrast to the elementary school their child had attended) results in a sense of anonymity for their child and for themselves.
2. *Curriculum*—Confusion about the middle-level curriculum content and format, such as the actual focus of the curriculum, the "trivial" and "disjointed" (p. 48) middle-level school curriculum, and how interdisciplinary units fit into the overall curriculum.
3. *Rigor and Challenge*—Concern that the middle-level programs lack rigor, and that teachers had low expectations, trivial assignments, and vast quantities of mindless exercises.
4. *Safety, Sociability, and Civility*—Concern over the level of civility, unkindness, and rudeness in the schools.

5. *Responsiveness*—Concern over the lack of responsiveness to their needs, inquiries, and requests or to those of their children.
6. *Instruction*—Concern that instruction may be dull, boring, and lacking in the use of technology (i.e., too much lecturing, student seatwork, and paper-and-pencil testing).
7. *Parent and Public Relations*—Complain that the school lacks effective ways of dealing with routine problems and that they did not know who to contact with their concerns.

We, too, have heard similar comments. While we cannot discount these concerns, we do believe that the criticism often comes from misunderstandings and a lack of communication. Middle schools can build on these concerns and take the initiative to explain their programs, to implement a systematic public information campaign, and to encourage parent, family, and community participation in the school. One thing you need to keep in mind: Parental involvement is more than getting parents or other community members to provide volunteer labor for a school. It is also a means to educate individuals outside the school community about the middle school concept and the exciting, if somewhat nontraditional, things that happen there.

Parent-Teacher Conferences

One of the most familiar ways to increase parental involvement is the parent-teacher conference. This formal meeting provides an opportunity for parents and teachers to exchange information and allows educators to involve parents in planning and implementing their child's educational program.

In attempting to lessen the parent's anxiety about the conference, you might explain the purpose of the conference in advance and provide parents with a written agenda (Shea & Bauer, 1985). You should also make the conference as comfortable as possible and end the conference on a positive note. Some educators suggest having young adolescents join in the conference to offer their opinions. While some parents might welcome this, others might experience difficulty with these suggestions because some cultures place value on children being "seen and not heard" (Spaulding, 1994).

At the parent-teacher conference, you and the parents might discuss the student's test scores or assessment results. It might even be necessary to explain the terms normally associated with measurement and evaluation. Test results are often a concern for parents, and they may react strongly to results that indicate their young adolescent is functioning at a lower level than most learners. You should ask parents to restate the information in their own words and make sure they understand the results and conclusions. Also, make a sincere effort to alleviate any anxiety expressed by parents over possible misuse of test results (Shea & Bauer, 1985). If parents leave a meeting feeling confident that their children will succeed academically and emotionally, then the meeting builds a strong foundation for positive parent-teachers relationships throughout the year. Unfortunately, the reverse situation is also true (Ribas, 1998).

Effective and Ongoing Communication

Going one step beyond the formal parent-teacher conference, middle school educators need to develop positive, ongoing communications with parents and families. One study

(Upham, Cheney, & Manning, 1998) revealed that both parents and teachers considered communication a key to developing positive working relationships. The teachers felt that meeting with parents face-to-face was the best way to communicate; writing notes was less desirable due to problems with interpretation. To promote good communication with parents, Upham et al. (1998) suggested (1) meeting early, perhaps during the first month of the school year; (2) updating progress regularly; (3) scheduling meetings in advance, so both parents and teachers can be prepared; (4) listening to parents' knowledge of the child and possible techniques for working with the young adolescent; (5) using nonjudgmental language; (6) using a strengths-based approach; and (7) allowing for flexible meeting times due to work schedules. They also suggested designating an advisor for each student, so parents can call her or him when needed and using e-mail wherever possible to reinforce and expand face-to-face meetings (Upham et al., 1998).

> "I call all the parents at the beginning of the year to let them know I'm willing to help, to see whether they have questions, to see how their child feels about beginning the middle school, and, to show that I feel parents should be involved in the middle school just as they probably were in the elementary school. This telephone call gets the year off to a good start. The students know I called their home; the parents know I'm interested; and I get a better perspective of parents' commitment to the education process. Unfortunately, the parents receive my calls with different degrees of enthusiasm, but I continue the calls and try to focus on the benefits for my students." A sixth-grade teacher.

No matter how diligently you work at developing good channels of communications with parents and families, differences in opinions will surface sooner or later. There may even be problems when a young adolescent conveys erroneous (perhaps unconsciously) information to parents or teachers. These differences need to be resolved professionally and quickly, since unresolved differences can escalate. That can harm the young adolescent, decrease your chances of educational success with the student, and encourage parents to develop negative feelings about you as a teacher and the school.

As a teacher, you also need to realize that parents might be anxious or fearful of encounters with educators. Some parents may be reluctant to express their concerns about their child's education for fear of possible negative repercussions for their child, or they may not know how to verbalize their concerns. In spite of that, you should convey to parents, perhaps subtly, the need to express their concerns directly to you and to avoid destructive criticism of teachers and schools in front of their children (Katz, Aidman, Reese, & Clark, 1996).

To build positive relationships between teachers and parents, keep in mind the following:

1. Talk regularly with parents to tell them about accomplishments and concerns, and to ask for their advice and suggestions. Extra efforts might be needed to convince parents to become active participants, especially since some cultures place teachers in high regard and are reluctant to question them or offer advice (Spaulding, 1994).
2. Inform parents that they can contact teachers to discuss issues they consider important.
3. Invite parents to observe in the classroom so they can see what really happens.
4. Ask parents about their main concerns and interests early in the school year.

5. Know the school policy for addressing parent-teacher disagreements.
6. Involve parents in classroom activities.
7. Be discreet about discussing children and their families (Katz et al., 1996).

Widening the Scope of Parental Involvement

While parent-teacher conferences and effective communications with individual parents are first steps in increasing overall parental involvement in middle schools, much more can be done. Perhaps the first step may seem like an oversimplification, but middle school educators need to let parents and community members know that teachers and young adolescents still need the help that other adults can provide. Some parents and community members, quite frankly, do not realize that educators would welcome their involvement in middle schools. After that initial awareness building, the next step is to develop specific ways to get adults into the middle school, to get them to accept the involvement necessary to the education of young adolescents, and to maintain the momentum once efforts are begun. Table 12–4 shows 14 ways educators can involve parents in school activities. You can probably add your own suggestions to the list.

TABLE 12–4 *Ways to Increase Parent Involvement*

To increase parental involvement:

1. Recognize students and parents as important aspects of the education process;
2. Provide parents with sufficient information about involvement activities;
3. Make parent involvement a school-wide effort–one emphasized by all teachers and administrators;
4. Involve students in the parent involvement recruitment process;
5. Conduct participatory projects that include the entire family;
6. Recruit community members–people who are not parents, but who are still interested in being involved in schools;
7. Make the classroom and school a comfortable place for parents, a place where they feel welcome and at ease;
8. Use the telephone to convey good news;
9. Learn why parents are not involved;
10. Have a variety of scheduling plans that meet a number of parent scheduling needs;
11. Implement a parent hotline that tells parents of ways to get involved;
12. Solicit community members to endorse the involvement program;
13. Provide videotapes of educational programs for parents; and
14. Provide support services such as babysitting for parents.

Developed from: Jesse, D. (1997). Increasing parental involvement. *Schools in the Middle, 7*(1), 21–24; and Fredericks, A. D., & Rasinski, T. V. (1990). Conferencing with parents: Successful approaches. *The Reading Teacher, 44*(2), 174–176.

Essential Elements of Effective Programs

Offering a program for parents and other adults and hoping they will show up is not enough. To be effective and to contribute to the positive image of the middle school, the program must be well-planned and well-organized. Most successful programs are based on a partnership approach and provide two-way communication between the home and the school on a frequent, regular basis. Administrators should support the effort and provide a budget for implementing programs, purchasing materials and other resources, and paying personnel costs. Everyone should work together to identify additional resources and to encourage others to share their information, resources, and expertise. Use regular evaluations during key stages and at the end of each program to monitor its effectiveness (Jesse, 1997; Williams & Chavkin, 1989).

While there are many programs that could be used to involve parents and other adults in middle schools, we would like to look at a few examples. In one middle school, parents agreed to supervise weekly 50-minute silent reading and study sessions, patrol the halls, and work in the office while teachers met to explore school reforms. Another middle school arranged for parents to teach sign language and computer skills for 2 hours while teachers met to plan and study (Seline, 1997).

Many middle schools encourage parents and other adults to work as homework helpers. Sometimes this is done on an informal basis, while other times it is a more formal program held before or after regular school hours. In some cases, the school works with a local community agency to offer the help at nonschool locations, such as libraries and recreation centers or clubs. Sandra Balli (1998) studied middle school students' perceptions about parental involvement with homework and found a significant number of students believe they do better in school when their parents help them with homework. Interestingly, however, some middle-grade students felt parents sometimes confused them. That points to the need to provide training for the homework helpers.

Adults working as homework helpers need to have some understanding of the development of young adolescents and must be trained to provide developmentally appropriate instruction. This includes matching concepts to be learned to the learning and thinking abilities of the students and using vocabulary the children can understand (Balli, 1995; Hoover-Dempsey & Sandler, 1995).

Having parents or other adults involved in homework activities can enhance a young adolescent's education. In addition to reinforcing concepts learned in school, adult homework helpers provide opportunities for direct one-on-one instruction and can lead to better understanding. When an adult volunteers his or her time to help with homework, it can show young adolescents that school-related activities are worth the time and effort (Balli, 1998; Hoover-Dempsey & Sandler, 1995). When parents serve as the helpers at home, the activity provides a common ground for more effective communication between parents and children and often improves the attitudes of both parents and students toward school (Epstein, Simon, & Salinas, 1997).

Some middle schools use parent advisory councils to provide parents and families with an opportunity to voice their opinions and to influence the overall operation of the school. In addition to serving as a liaison between school and community, the council can function as a permanent parent-to-parent communications committee to announce meetings, special events, personnel changes, and other items of interest. It can also assume responsibility for organizing and directing ad hoc or temporary committees (Shea & Bauer, 1985). Advisory council representatives (or parents who make suggestions and comments through their representatives) can make specific suggestions for things, such as improving the middle school curriculum, the overall school environment, or testing. Orientation sessions can be held for parents who might not understand the purpose of the council, might feel that parents are meddling in schools' business, or might not understand the procedures by which meetings work (Jennings, 1989).

In one middle school, parents established an advisory council and formed committees to address specific areas of change and reform. The security committee brought to school a number of fathers who served as role models while the communications committee established a telephone tree to pass on important information about school issues and events. The advocacy committee attended all school board meetings and served as an advocate for the middle school. The success of these parent-educator partnerships depends significantly on strong leadership inside and outside the school (Seline, 1997).

Involving Special Groups: Limited English-Speaking Skills; Single Parents and Nontraditional Families; and Fathers

All levels of schools now face the challenges of working with "new" groups of parents. At one time in history, the mother stayed home (and perhaps the father), visited the school, and became involved with school activities. However, with the vanishing of the traditional nuclear family, there have been significant cultural and family changes. Increasingly, you will work with families with limited English-speaking skills, single parents and nontraditional families, and fathers visiting the school without the mother. We would like to look at these three special groups, and offer some suggestions for making them significant partners in the effort to educate young adolescents.

According to Anita Seline (1997), middle schools, especially in urban areas, may encounter an increasing number of parents who are recent immigrants and might be unable to speak English with the proficiency necessary for effective communication. These parents may be intimidated by or unfamiliar with the school and its culture. In some cases, their children, who have attended U.S. schools, might speak better English than the parents. As a result, the parents may feel unable to deal with teachers and other educators. Diversity Perspective 12–1 presents some strategies you can use to help parents with limited English proficiency.

An increasing number of children live in single-parent and stepfamilies, while some live in foster families and other nontraditional families. It can be difficult to involve members of these families in schools. However, that does not mean that you should not try. Diversity Perspectives 12–2 has some suggestions for effective communication with nontraditional families.

When working with parents, do not forget fathers. Too often fathers are left out of family-oriented programs, especially since mothers have traditionally been more involved

Diversity Perspectives 12–1

Working with Parents with Limited English Proficiency

The number of parents with limited English skills is increasing in many localities. The following are some strategies that may help teachers work with these parents:

- translate letters, notices, progress reports, school handbooks, newsletters, and information packets into the languages of all parents.
- have individuals who speak the languages of parents available to answer the school telephone.
- record phone messages in other languages so non-English-speaking parents can also keep track of their children's coursework and school events.
- use school newsletters to announce cultural and other events sponsored by other language groups represented in the school.
- integrate bilingual and multicultural materials in school displays, publications, libraries, and classrooms.
- use paid or volunteer interpreters to promote communication with limited English parents.
- hire bilingual parent coordinators or find volunteers to meet with parents in their homes and at parent centers, churches, and other gathering places to talk about school-related issues.
- recruit, train, and hire bilingual parents to be paraprofessionals in the schools.
- make special efforts to welcome limited English-proficient parents who visit the schools.

Source: Office of Educational Research and Improvement (1996). *Reaching all families: Creating family-friendly schools.* Washington, DC: U.S. Department of Education.

in the schools. However, with more mothers in the labor force and a growing recognition of the father's importance for child development, there is more interest in involving fathers in their children's education.

In all forms of communication to families, be sure to mention fathers as well as mothers, assume that both will be interested, and encourage both to participate in school-sponsored activities. Schedule meetings at times when all parents can attend, such as before school, in the evenings, or on weekends. You can also develop special programs such as father-child breakfasts or dinners, and career days. Your goal should be to seek a balance of fathers and mothers in school leadership positions, as volunteers, and as assistants at special events and contests (Office of Educational Research and Improvement, 1996).

Keeping Current with Technology 12–1 provides readers with Internet sources that provide additional information on working with parents.

Diversity Perspectives 12–2

Working with Nontraditional Families

Use different and more sensitive ways of communicating with nontraditional families by trying to:

- avoid making the assumption that students live with both biological parents;
- avoid the traditional "Dear Parents" greeting in letters and other messages, and instead use "Dear Parent," "Dear Family," "Friends," or some other form of greeting;
- develop a system of keeping noncustodial parents informed of their children's school progress;
- demonstrate sensitivity to the rights of noncustodial parents by informing parents that schools may not withhold information from noncustodial parents who have the legal right to see their children's records;
- develop a simple unobtrusive system to track family changes, such as asking for the names and addresses of individuals to be informed about each child; and
- place flyers about school events on bulletin boards of major companies in the community that are family-friendly to learning.

Source: Office of Educational Research and Improvement (1996). *Reaching all families: Creating family-friendly schools.* Washington, DC: U.S. Department of Education.

Parent Education Programs for Parents of Young Adolescents

The term *parent education* has evolved to denote "organized activities that have been developed in order to further parents' abilities to raise their children successfully" (Mitzel, 1982, p. 1379). Although parent education programs have become routine aspects of many primary schools, they are not part of many middle school programs. However, we believe that parents and families of young adolescents need carefully designed and implemented parent education programs that teach parents about 10- to 14-year-olds and the middle school.

There are several reasons for this. Many parents need help (1) understanding the early adolescence developmental period; (2) responding appropriately to young adolescents' behavior; and (3) understanding the middle school concept. Many parents may not understand the complex changes their child is going through and how these changes affect things like self-esteem, body image, and behavior. Rather than allowing parents to assume that they have failed in parenting roles, or allowing parents to absolve themselves of responsibility for behavior, parent programs can help parents understand the developmental changes and act appropriately.

Keeping Current with Technology 12–1

America Goes Back to School
http://www.ed.gov/Family/agbts_old/

Building Community Partnerships
http://eric-web.tc.columbia.edu/families/strong/
Information based on *Strong Families, Strong Schools*

Carnegie Foundation–Great Transitions
http://www.carnegie.org//sub/pubs/reports/great_transitions/gr_intro.html

Colorado Parent Information & Resources Center
http://www.cpirc.org/

National Parent Information Network
http://www.npin.org/

National PTA
http://www.pta.org

North Central Regional Educational Laboratory
http://www.ncrel.org/sdrs/pidata/pi0over.htm

Parent Power
http://www.parentpower.org/confcue.html
Information on being prepared for parent-teacher conferences.

Parents as School Partners
http://eric-web.tc.columbia.edu/families/NCJW_child/

Principals Best Ten Tips to Increase Parental Involvement
http://eric-web.tc.columbia.edu/guides/tentips1.html

Project Appleseed, the National Campaign for Public School Improvement
http://www.projectappleseed.org/appleframe2.html

Middle school parent education programs can also teach parents about unique middle school programs and efforts such as advisor-advisee, integrated units, and exploratory programs that can help their children. In all likelihood, parents may not understand these programs or they might even have misconceptions about middle schools. If a parent education program teaches middle school concepts and their purposes, it is likely to improve parents' attitudes about the middle school and can help them feel more comfortable helping their children. Case Study 12–1 looks at the development of a parent education program at one middle school.

Case Study 12–1

Seldon Way Implements Parent Education

It had taken a lot of hard work, but the Parent/Community Advisory Council at Seldon Way Middle School was now meeting twice a month to discuss parent and community involvement at Seldon Way and how to increase and improve relationships between the school and the community that it served. One of the first things the Council had done was to use *Reaching All Families: Creating Family-Friendly Schools* from the U.S. Department of Education as a guide and develop a list of ideas to implement at Seldon Way.

On their list were the following items:

1. Implement grade-level sessions where teachers invite parents to an educational event planned especially for them.
2. Schedule monthly meetings where parents can engage in informal conversations with the principal.
3. Start a "Breakfast with the Teacher," which includes parents coming to school on a selected day and having a potluck breakfast.
4. Consider neighborhood coffees organized jointly by school staff and parents and held in homes, community centers, and other convenient locations.
5. Study school-based literacy and family nights during which literacy and other adult education services are provided to parents (and special activities planned for the children).
6. Hold parent-teacher conferences and other school events in the evening.
7. Work with local businesses to arrange for released time from work so parents can attend conferences and participate in other involvement activities.
8. Create support groups for parents with difficult or disabled children, alienated teenagers, and other traumatic events related to teenagers.
9. Begin a parent resource center that provides training, information, and support to parents and those who work with young adolescents.
10. Provide parent education classes and workshops that teach parents about the early adolescence developmental period, young adolescent behavior, and middle school programs and efforts.

On one Wednesday in April, the Advisory Council listened as Joan Baker, one of the guidance counselors, discussed item number 10 on the list, parent education programs. Joan talked about why Seldon Way might want to implement one, what topics might be appropriate, how to publicize the meetings, and who would lead the discussions. Following her presentation, the council members debated the time and commitment the program would take. When Kate Kincade, one of the parents, commented on the success of the parent program at the primary school, her comments were echoed by Cecilia Martinez who explained how the program at the primary school had helped her whole family. Cecilia's remark that she was sometimes willing to try anything to help her get her two boys through the early adolescence years brought a laugh from the

Case Study 12–1 (cont.)

teachers and a lot of nodding heads from the parents. Lyvonne Miller, a teacher member of the council, mentioned how parents often ask her for advice and suggestions on how to effectively handle situations. After much discussion, the Council decided to ask Dr. Deliese, the principal, for funding outside the council's regular budget to offer a short parent education program. If Dr. Deliese would agree to finance the program, Joan Baker volunteered to chair a committee of teachers and parents to explore possible alternatives.

At the next Advisory Council meeting, Joan Baker reported that Dr. Deliese would provide a modest amount of funding for the parent education program. As a result, her committee had met and come up with two plans for a parent education program. In one plan, the teachers and parents at Seldon Way would develop their own program while the other plan relied on a prepackaged program that was available commercially. Following a lively debate, the Advisory Council recommended that Joan's committee develop their own program based on the needs of the local community as expressed on surveys and comments from parents and teachers. Several Advisory Council members stressed the need to provide lots of time for questions and comments during the education sessions. Joan indicated that her group had already discussed the idea of using a panel discussion with one teacher from each grade level on the panel and then breaking into small discussion groups with a teacher and parent as coleaders of each group. The committee was given approval to continue with the planning for a 3-week program to be held in the fall of the next school year.

As they closed the meeting, the Chair reminded the Advisory Council members to continue thinking about the Parent Education Program and also to consider the community service option that they still needed to discuss.

Publicity

Publicity is a key to most successful programs, with flyers sent home by teachers, leaflets distributed by churches and synagogues, free public service announcements on radio and television, and postings to the school's home page on the Internet. Theory into Practice 12–1 provides an example of a publicity effort designed for the 3-week parent education program at Seldon Way Middle School.

Topics

Topics for the middle school parent education program should focus on interests of parents and families of *middle school students.* Generic programs that are too broad rarely work. Parents of young adolescents want to hear about topics that they deal with on a daily

Theory into Practice 12–1

Publicity

THOSE "TWEEN" YEARS: A FREE PROGRAM FOR PARENTS

Sponsored by the Parent Advisory Council of
Seldon Way Middle School

A 3-week program (every Tuesday) designed to help parents live with young adolescents, ages 10 to 14.

Time: 7:00–9:00 PM
Location: Seldon Way Middle School
First floor: Parenting Center
789 Elm Street, East Point, VA

Week 1 What's Happening to My Child–Young Adolescent Development
Tuesday, October 9, 2000

Week 2 Why Do They Act That Way–Young Adolescent Behavior
Tuesday, October 17, 2000

Week 3 What Are Middle Schools All About–Purposes, Goals, and Concepts
Tuesday, October 24, 2000

The program leaders will be Mrs. Christina Rodriquez, Mrs. Lyvonne Miller, and Ms. Christy Dyar

To preregister, please call:
Mrs. Joan Baker, Guidance Counselor
Seldon Way Middle School
767-6226

Developed from: Manning, M. L. (1992). Parent education programs at the middle level. *NASSP Bulletin, 76*(543), 24–29.

basis instead of those of younger children or older adolescents. Theory into Practice 12–2 provides an example of a 3-week parent education program developed by Seldon Way Middle School.

Communities and Young Adolescents

We have talked about involving parents and other community members in the education of middle school students. However, there is another aspect that must be considered. Young adolescents want and need to be involved in the communities in which they live and attend school. They accomplish this both through school-sponsored community-service activities and by belonging to service-based community organizations.

Theory into Practice 12–2

A Three-Week Parent Education Program

MIDDLE SCHOOL PARENT EDUCATION PROGRAM

Week 1: What's Happening to My Child–Young Adolescent Development
- Introductions of leaders and attendees
- Purpose of the three-week parent education program
- Changes during the early adolescence developmental period
  - Physical development
  - Psychosocial development
  - Intellectual development
- How these changes affect young adolescents
  - Relationships with others
  - Feelings toward themselves
  - Lower grades and changing behavior
- Constancies–Responding appropriately
  - The need for acceptance, security, and successful experiences
  - Parent guidance

Week 2: Why Do They Act That Way–Young Adolescent Behavior
- Changing behavior
  - Seek more independence
  - Engage in more "adult" behaviors
- At-risk conditions and behaviors
  - Drugs and alcohol
  - Pregnancy and sexually transmitted diseases
  - Eating disorders
  - Delinquent behaviors
- Responding appropriately to young adolescent behavior

Week 3: What Are Middle Schools All About–Transition to Middle Schools
- The middle school–Its purpose
- Middle school programs
  - Advisor-advisee
  - Exploratory curriculum
  - Integrated curriculum
  - Intramural sports
- How you can get involved
  - Working with the teachers
  - Involving yourself in class and school
- Parent evaluation of the 3-week program

Developed from: Manning, M. L. (1992). Parent education programs at the middle level. *NASSP Bulletin, 76,*(543), 24–29.

Young Adolescents Serving Communities

As young adolescents develop a sense of belonging to a community larger than their school, family, and peer groups, it is natural that they turn to community service. In performing community service, they discover new skills, develop a sense of competence, try out socialization skills, take part in the adult world, and test value systems and make decisions, all supported and guided by caring adults (Schine, 1987, 1989). The best programs are developed locally with teachers and students having a great deal of latitude in selecting service projects. Ideally, the service project will strengthen and reflect the school curriculum, including the sciences, the humanities, and the arts (Allen, Splittgerber & Manning, 1993).

At Shoreham-Wading River Middle School (Long Island, NY), almost every student performs some community service. As part of a curriculum unit, groups of students received training from two community agencies. Then they left the building for a double period once a week for 6 to 8 weeks under the supervision of a teacher and four part-time aides to perform community service. Groups worked with special-needs children in a hospital and with elderly residents of retirement homes (Maeroff, 1990).

Other community-service projects occur at Whittier Middle School (Sioux Falls, SD), a school known for its community service and volunteerism. The school's principal considers the following conditions essential for a successful community project: short-term projects with specific beginning and ending dates; action-oriented projects reflecting the nature of young adolescent learners; participation of a large number of students; student involvement in planning; faculty support and guidance; emphasis on intrinsic incentives; communication between school and community agencies; and opportunities to celebrate community projects (Kiner, 1993).

Other examples of community-service projects include (1) the Magic Me program (Baltimore, MD), which pairs middle school youth for the school year with nursing home residents; (2) Challenger Middle School's (Colorado Spring, CO) HUGSS (Help Us Grow through Services and Smiles), which provides numerous services to the community; and (3) the Governor's Summer Citizenship School, which focuses on work with middle school students at-risk (Scales, 1991).

Communities Serving Young Adolescents

More than 17,000 youth-serving organizations presently operate in the United States. They include such national groups as the Boy Scouts, 4-H clubs, the YMCA and YWCA, and thousands of small, independent grassroots organizations. Many of them offer just what young adolescents need: safe havens where they can relax, be with their friends, and learn useful skills in the crucial after-school, weekend, and summer hours when neither parents nor schools provide supervision and support. Such programs often offer adult mentoring, drop-in activities, and opportunities for community service, for learning about careers and the world of work, and for discovering places beyond the neighborhood. They help young people build self-worth, get along in groups, make durable friendships, and generally prepare for lives as responsible, inquiring, and vigorous adults. Table 12–5 shows a few characteristics to look for in community programs that are responsive to the needs of young adolescents.

TABLE 12–5 *Characteristics of Community Programs*

Community programs that are responsive to the needs of young adolescents:

1. are safe and accessible to all youth;
2. base their content and methods on a systematic assessment of community needs and existing services;
3. work with a variety of other community and government agencies to extend their reach to the most vulnerable adolescents;
4. have staff who are knowledgeable about young adolescent development and trained to work with young people;
5. regard young people as resources in planning and program development and involve them in meaningful roles;
6. reach out to families, schools, and other community partners to create a strong social support system for young adolescents;
7. have clear objectives and criteria for evaluation of success;
8. have strong advocates for and with youths to improve their opportunities to become well-educated and healthy; and
9. have active, committed community leadership on their boards (Carnegie Council on Adolescent Development, 1996).

Closing Remarks

We hope that you realize the benefits of parent involvement and that you will make every attempt to reengage parents and other adults in the education of young adolescents. The benefits are clear: Young adolescents will see their parents and other adults working as partners with their teachers; teachers will gain much-needed support for their many efforts; and parents and community members will gain a better perspective of teachers' efforts and the purposes of middle school education. The timing is right—the research explains the benefits, and *Turning Points* and *Great Transitions* offer specific recommendations for reengaging parents. Strengthening the bonds between middle schools and communities will not be an easy task; however, we do believe the rich dividends for young adolescents, parents, and teachers are well worth the time and the risks.

Suggested Readings

Epstein, J. L., Simon, B. S., & Salinas, K. C. (1997). Involving parents in homework in the middle grades. *Research Bulletin 18,* 1–4. Explains the Teachers Involve Parents in Schoolwork (TIPS) program and how it has been extended into the middle grades.

Hatch, T. (1998). How community action contributes to achievement. *Educational Leadership, 55*(8), 16–19. Discusses attitudes, expectations, and learning experiences.

Upham, D. A., Cheney, D., & Manning, B. (1998). What do teacher and parents want in their communication patterns? *Middle School Journal, 29*(5), 48–55. Identifies strategies for overcoming communication barriers.

Williams, C. (1997). Families + schools = learning. *Schools in the Middle, 7*(1), 39–41. Describes workshops that help parents participate in the education of their children.

Epilogue

Middle Schools of the Future

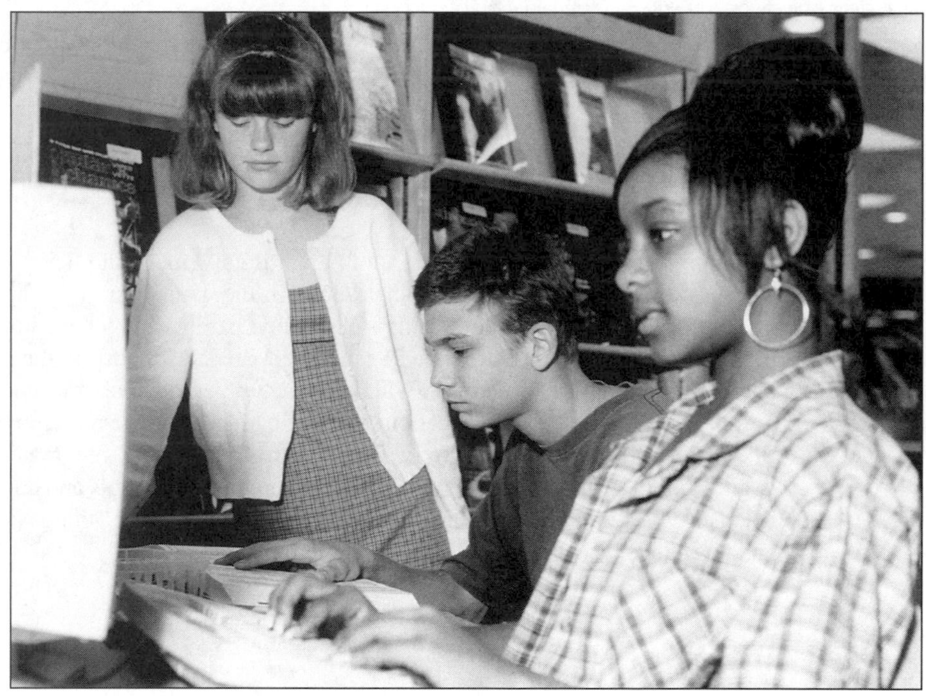

Are you ready for the challenges of teaching in a middle school? Let's take a few moments to think back over the concepts presented in this book—concepts dealing with middle school education as well as the development of young adolescents.

Middle Schools

The Beginning and Rationale

As you have read in this book, schools "in the middle" realized that elementary and secondary schools were not meeting the needs of students in the middle grades. To accommodate student needs, educators tried various grade organizations in the elementary and secondary school. Eventually, the intermediate school and the junior high school grew in popularity. Unfortunately, while the junior high school was supposed to be the ideal transition school between the elementary and secondary school, it became more like the high school and, thus, did not meet the needs of young adolescents.

Then, the middle school came into being as an extension of the elementary school. As research and scholarly writing provided more information on "what schools in the middle should be" and "what young adolescents are like," educators and proponents of middle schools reached an agreement that the middle school should be more than a copy of the elementary school. Undoubtedly, young adolescents differ from children and deserve a school that addresses the needs of 10- to 14-year-olds rather than 5- to 9-year-olds. Gradually, a middle school way of thinking emerged, and essential middle school concepts developed. No longer was the middle school supposed to be an upward extension of the elementary school or a downward extension of the secondary school—it was a school with its own mission: To address the unique physical, psychosocial, and cognitive developmental needs of 10- to 14-year-olds in an academic setting.

Documents, Position Papers, and Reports

As we said in chapter 1, in the past 15 years, a number of important publications have paved the way for effective middle schools: California's *Caught in the Middle* (1987), Florida's *The Forgotten Years* (1984), Maryland's *What Matters in the Middle Grades* (1989), Virginia's *Restructuring Education in the Middle School Grades* (1989), the Carnegie Council on Adolescent Development's *Great Transitions: Preparing Adolescents for a New Century* (1996) and *Turning Points: Preparing American Youth for the 21st Century* (1989), the National Middle School Association's *This We Believe: Developmentally Responsive Middle Level Schools* (1995), the National Association of Secondary School Principals' *An Agenda for Excellence at the Middle Level* (1985), and the Association for Childhood Education International's *Developmentally Appropriate Middle Level Schools* (1993).

Directions

While all of these publications offered different perspectives, they also called for reform and improvements in middle school education; and all promoted the idea that middle schools should develop their own structures and programs designed to address the developmental and academic needs of young adolescents. For example, the curriculum should be designed specifically for middle school students (rather than being a rehash of what was learned in the elementary school or a preview of secondary curriculum); school and class organization should be flexible; all schools should provide strong guidance and counseling components; and young adolescents' developmental needs should be considered and addressed. The list could go on and on. The good news is that middle school educators now have the knowledge base to provide effective middle schools. The challenge will be to continue the momentum and use these suggestions and recommendations to improve middle school education, and eventually, the educational experiences and lives of all young adolescents.

Present Status

The future of middle school education looks bright. We have the National Middle School Association (as well as its state affiliates), the National Association of Secondary School Principals, the Association for Childhood Education International, and various other associations calling for and providing directions for effective middle school education. In addition, the number of researchers, authors, and scholars has continuously grown from the earliest days, and the research base on both middle school education and young adolescents has steadily increased in quantity and quality. Several textbooks now tell both preservice and in-service teachers what they need to know to become effective teachers of young adolescents. The middle school has grown beyond its infancy stage. It is a school in and of itself, has developed its own identity, and has "come of age."

Young Adolescents

Recognition of the Developmental Period

In this book you have read about the legitimacy of early adolescence, a developmental period between childhood and adolescence that has only been accepted during the past 30 or 40 years. Just as childhood and adolescence received slow acceptance in some circles, the early adolescence developmental period struggled to justify its legitimacy. Robert Havighurst (1968) gave credibility to early adolescence when he suggested developmental tasks for the age group, as did Thornburg (1983b) when he described 10- to 14-year-olds' physical, psychosocial, and cognitive developmental characteristics.

As the recognition of early adolescence increased, perceptive educators began calling attention to the need to base teaching and learning experiences on 10- to 14-year-olds' developmental characteristics. Eichhorn (1966) brought attention to the middle school and the importance of considering learners' development when planning and implementing instruction. During the 1980s, Thornburg's contributions as a researcher and leader in the movement to understand the early adolescence developmental period added credibility to the study of this developmental stage. In 1981, he founded the *Journal of Early Adolescence,* designed as a forum for researchers and writers interested in early adolescence. During the 1990s, books and other publications indicated a growing acceptance of the early adolescence developmental period, the age range 10 to 14 years, and the designation "young adolescent." Just as educators no longer view children as miniature adults, they realize that they cannot perceive young adolescents as functioning "somewhere in between" elementary and secondary schools.

Increasing Research Base

Fortunately for young adolescents and middle school educators, the research base on early adolescence and young adolescents continues to improve. The *Journal of Early Adolescence* continues to publish research, the *Middle School Journal* makes excellent contributions, and the Association for Childhood Education International publishes *Childhood Education* and *Journal of Research in Childhood Education,* both of which focus on children from birth through early adolescence. While it would be difficult to list all journals that publish research and scholarly work on early adolescence and young adolescents, we hope you can see that the research base continues to grow in quantity and quality and provides information upon which middle school educators can base their decisions.

Contemporary Perspectives

Today, most educators view young adolescents as unique—too old to be considered children and too young to be considered adolescents. As a result, they are recognized as a special group, a recognition that children and adolescents have enjoyed for many decades. However, even though they are recognized as a group, they are a diverse group. Some forms of their diversity can be readily detected (e.g., their physical changes) while others (e.g., their cognitive readiness) are more difficult to determine. Cultural, gender, and social class differences also contribute to the difficulty of making generalizations about these students.

Stereotypes about young adolescents are beginning to disappear. Prior to her practicum, we overheard Kincsha, one of our university students remark: "Middle schoolers are such behavior problems; I am not sure I want to teach them." After her practicum, when we were discussing how perceptions can change after a classroom experience, Kincsha confided that "The students were not as bad I had thought; most, in fact, are pretty good." We think young adolescents are a pretty good group, too. While some are behavior problems, most behave appropriately, especially for teachers who have a good understanding of their unique state of life, who provide effective middle school educational experiences, and who have a well-planned and developmentally responsive classroom management system. Still, we have to admit that some of our teacher education students will go to almost any length to avoid the middle school because they continue to believe the "bad behavior" stereotype.

Teaching in the Middle School—Challenges

Can teaching in the middle school be a challenge? Sure, but it can be exciting and enjoyable. If you are willing to accept this challenge, you have made the first step toward providing young adolescents with developmentally responsive educational experiences. These and other challenges that you face should not be considered hurdles that you can accomplish and then basically forget. Instead, these challenges are part of a process, whereby you will continue to seek knowledge and to improve professionally.

Seeking Professional Preparation: Young Adolescents and Middle School Education

Professional preparation in understanding and teaching young adolescents and in essential middle school concepts is essential for teaching in the middle school. We realize that some middle school teachers are and will continue to be trained in either elementary or secondary education. In fact, we know some of these teachers who are doing an excellent job in the classroom, and we respect their work with young adolescents. However, we stand by our position that educators working in middle schools need professional preparation (either preservice or in-service training, or both) in understanding young adolescents and teaching in the middle school. Teaching middle schoolers from elementary or secondary perspectives can be difficult for teachers and can do an injustice to young adolescents.

How can you obtain that professional preparation? You can complete college coursework and a supervised practicum, participate in in-service training at the middle school, develop a planned reading agenda for personal and professional improvement, and/or attend and participate in professional conferences such the National Middle School Association's annual meeting. You can also work with master teachers who have taught at the middle school level long enough to know essential middle school concepts.

Never think or say, "I have my training; now all I have to do is teach." Professional training should be an ongoing process that never ends. Young adolescents are changing, middle school practices are changing, technology is making many new activities possible, and the research base continues to increase and improve. Regardless of your education and experience, you have a professional responsibility to engage in a continuous process of professional development.

Committing to Teach Middle Schoolers

One challenge about which we feel strongly is that you, as a middle school educator, should be committed to teaching young adolescents. We worry about a teacher who says, "I will teach here until I can find another job, but to be honest, I never wanted to teach in the middle school." Young adolescents need teachers who care for them, want to teach them, want to serve in advising and guidance roles, and strive daily to provide developmentally responsive educational experiences for this age group. *This We Believe: Developmentally Responsive Middle Level Schools* (National Middle School Association, 1995) states in its discussion of educators committed to young adolescents:

> By blending vision and commitment they make a positive difference in the lives of young adolescents. The clear challenge is to provide a rigorous and relevant education based on the developmental needs of young adolescent learners. We need educators committed to young adolescents who can meet that challenge. (p. 14)

Serving as Advocates for Young Adolescents

As an effective middle school educator, you should be willing to be an advocate for young adolescents. Young adolescents need teachers (whether in teaching or advising roles) who want what is best for middle school students. Such teachers support both young adolescents and the middle school concept and believe that their efforts influence young peoples' lives. Serving in an advocacy role does not mean that you can disregard misbehavior, lack of motivation, or learner mistakes—such a teacher would not be an advocate. However, it does mean that you will help young adolescents learn from their mistakes and help them realize that they have a caring adult in the school who will listen to them and help whenever possible. Young adolescents should never feel neglected or anonymous; instead, every student in the middle school should feel that he or she has an advocate to talk with about personal and academic problems.

Providing Developmentally Responsive Educational Experiences

Another challenge that you will face as a middle school educator is to use developmentally responsive educational practices. Education theorists have suggested that learners' development should provide the basis for school curricular, instructional, and organizational practices as well as for the overall teaching and learning environment. While insightful theories have been offered regarding physical, psychosocial, and cognitive development, the process of translating theories into practice has been somewhat slow, especially beyond the elementary school years. For guidance, you should look to publications, such as *This We Believe: Developmentally Responsive Middle Level Schools* (National Middle School Association, 1995) and *Developmentally Appropriate Middle Level Schools* (Manning, 1993b), which call for educational practices that are based on young adolescents' development.

Engaging in Research to Determine What Works

Denny Wolfe and Lee Manning (1997) challenged teachers to be researchers. They maintained that teachers needed to redefine their roles to include responsibilities for conducting their own research with the students they teach. Conducting research takes time and effort, but you can determine what works most effectively. This is not meant to disparage research published by someone else; rather, it is meant to acknowledge the efficacy of your own research. Often, classroom-based research requires nothing more than (1) being more attentive to what students are doing and how they are doing it, (2) recording observations about students and their learning, (3) trying to make sense of recordings and observations, and (4) making adjustments to what is taught and how it is taught. It is not necessary for you to be formally trained in research methods, but it is essential that you are disciplined and determined to conduct research to determine best practices.

The Future

Push for Excellence

During the twenty-first century and beyond, middle school educators will need to continue their push for excellence. Some middle schools have effective programs such as interdisciplinary teams, exploratory programs, teacher advisories, and a positive school climate, but, unfortunately, some do not. Barely half of the middle-level schools in the country even claim to engage in interdisciplinary teaming (Erb, 1999). The same is true with middle school teachers—some are expertly trained and understand both young adolescents and essential middle school concepts, but again, some do not. Throughout this book you have seen evidence that the push for excellence in middle school education has begun. Look at the emphasis in the professional literature on improving middle schools and understanding young adolescents, the many reports and publications calling for middle school reform, the increased number of teachers receiving professional training in middle school education, and the middle schools that are examining their educational program to determine what works, what does not work, and what can be improved. It is your personal professional responsibility to participate in that strive toward excellence.

Collaborative Efforts–Administrators, Teachers, Teacher Educators, Parents, State Departments of Education, and the Community

We believe the momentum and push for excellence will continue and that you, as a professional educator, must be part of it. However, we also believe that the movement must be a collaborative effort of administrators, teachers, teacher educators, parents, state departments of education, and the community. You as a middle school teacher, who is committed to young adolescents and serving as an advocate, will be the determining factor and will be the key to lasting reform and improvements. As an individual teacher, you cannot, however, do this alone. You will need support from other teachers and from administrators and teacher educators. We all need support from the state departments of education, parents, and the community. Collaboration means helping each other, engaging in team decision making, and sharing in the process of setting goals as well as implementing a change plan. It means sharing the heartaches as well as the success in providing the best educational experiences for young adolescents.

A Time for Responsive Action

The twenty-first century will be a time for responsive action. We have a sound research base on young adolescents and effective middle school practices, and the momentum to improve middle school has started. We can see the challenges ahead of us—to provide young adolescents with effective middle schools, to understand young adolescents, and to serve as advocates, both for young adolescents as well as middle schools. As a middle school educator, you have a responsibility to the profession and to young adolescents to try to meet these challenges.

Appendix

Physical Developmental Characteristics	Implications for Middle Level School Educators	For Additional Information:
Young adolescents experience a rapid growth spurt (girls around age 12 and boys around age 14) during which typical growth increases may be 7″ in girls and 9″–10″ in boys. Between ages 11 to 13, girls are usually taller, heavier, and overall more physically advanced than boys.	1. Understand physical diversity and its effects on self-concept and other psychosocial developmental areas. 2. Understand gender differences. 3. Provide developmentally appropriate physical activities. 4. Avoid competition between early and late maturers. 5. Provide educational experiences (direct instruction, exploratory programs, and adviser-advisee programs), which teach young adolescents about their changing bodies.	Tanner (1971, 1973) conducted the most comprehensive studies of development during early adolescence. Lawrence (1980) provided a detailed look at how educators can address physical development.
Young adolescents experience visible skeletal and structural changes; accelerated growth in limb length, chest breadth and depth, muscles, heart, and lungs; bones often develop faster than muscles; and changes occur in body contours such as nose, ears, and long arms. Generally speaking, legs develop adult size first; then, hands, feet, and head, and last, shoulders.	1. Teach young adolescents that development occurs at varying rates, and slow or late development should not cause alarm. 2. Provide educational experiences in nutrition, healthful living, proper exercise, and adequate health. 3. Teach young adolescents that bones and muscles do not develop at the same rate, which often leads to awkwardness and a gangly appearance. 4. Teach self-understanding and positive attitudes about body changes. 5. Provide educational experiences that allow active participation rather than long periods of passive sitting.	Tanner (1971) provided specifics, such as diagrams and actual pictures. Alexander (1989) focused on gender differences and health concerns.

Physical Developmental Characteristics	Implications for Middle Level School Educators	For Additional Information:
Young adolescents experience considerable diversity in development rates (i.e., ranges of 6″–8″ and 40–60 pounds are common). Greater variability occurs in girls ages 11, 12, and 13 and in boys ages 13 and 14.	1. Emphasize that diversity in development is normal and expected. 2. Plan educational experiences that reflect gender differences. 3. Avoid competitive activities between early and late maturers. 4. Understand and respond to the relationship between self-esteem and developmental differences.	Schuster and Ashburn (1986) emphasized diversity in development.
Young adolescents experience distinct gender differences (i.e., girls' hips widen, pubic hair appears, and breast development begins around age 10). Likewise, boys' voices deepen, shoulders grow wider, and facial and pubic hair appears.	1. Provide accurate and objective information about development. 2. Plan educational experiences that reflect gender differences. 3. Address the problems of both early and late maturers and encourage both groups to understand the normalcy of development. 4. Encourage young adolescents to consult parents, teachers, counselors, and school nurses for accurate answers to questions.	Dorman and Lipsitz (1984) suggested middle-grades assessment programs should include how well middle schools address development. Butler and Manning (1998) examined gender differences in young adolescents.
Young adolescents experience the onset of puberty or the development of the sexual reproductive system. While considerable diversity exists in age range, menarche in girls usually begins ages 11 to 14, and the first ejaculation in boys usually occurs ages 11 to 15.	1. Provide developmentally appropriate educational experiences focusing on puberty. 2. Emphasize healthful living and positive attitudes. 3. Emphasize puberty as a normal development phase yet a stage resulting in significant changes. 4. Provide developmentally appropriate instruction on AIDS, pregnancy, and sexually transmitted diseases.	Tanner (1968, 1971) provided detailed "specifics" on pubertal development. *Turning Points* (Carnegie Council, 1989) and *Great Transitions* (Carnegie Council, 1996) provided disturbing statistics on the problems facing young adolescents. Martin (1996) in *Puberty, Sexuality, and the Self* explored implications of sexual development. Hamburg (1997) discussed healthy development in today's society.

Psychosocial Developmental Characteristics	Implications for Middle Level School Educators	For Additional Information:
Young adolescents make friends and interact socially, which are crucial to psychosocial development. Developing friendships allow relationships and conversations, which boost self-esteem, reduce anxiety as trust and respect develop, help in the development of identities, contribute to positive interpersonal skills, and help 10- to 14-year-olds adjust to the physical and emotional changes associated with puberty.	1. Understand that friendships and social networks are crucial to proper development. 2. Encourage friendships and social networks and provide in-class opportunities (i.e., cooperative learning) for young adolescents to make friends. 3. Understand the difficulty of competing with peers; peers' opinions will be more powerful than parents' and teachers' opinions. 4. Understand the relationship between physical development and psychosocial development. 5. Provide educational experiences that boost self-esteem, emphasize trust, help in building personal identities, and teach socialization skills.	Manning and Lucking (1993, 1991) provided a comprehensive examination of cooperative learning. Manning and Allen (1987) looked at social development and its implications for educators of young adolescents.
Young adolescents experience gender differences in their socialization patterns (i.e., boys tend to have larger social networks, and girls tend to have a smaller number of close friendships). Also, boys and girls follow same-sex friendship patterns since both perceive themselves as having similar interests and concerns. Then, cross-sex friendships usually begin around middle adolescence.	1. Recognize gender differences and sex roles, yet avoid stereotyping. 2. Understand gender differences in social networks and overall socialization and plan gender-responsive social opportunities. 3. Provide educational experiences that encourage positive self-esteem and positive perceptions of one's gender.	Benenson (1990) examined gender differences in social networks and friendships. Deegan (1992) provided an excellent look at friendships among fifth graders. AAUW (1996) proposed directions for educating young adolescent girls. Butler and Manning (1998) examined gender differences in young adolescents.

Psychosocial Developmental Characteristics	Implications for Middle Level School Educators	For Additional Information:
Young adolescents shift their allegiance and affiliation from parents and teachers toward the peer group, which becomes the prime source for standards and models of behavior. In fact, some young adolescents feel maintaining an allegiance to parents and teachers can result in decreased peer approval and acceptance.	1. Recognize the powerful effects of peers and the difficulty of competing with peers. 2. Take advantage, whenever possible, of positive peer pressure. 3. Understand that shifting allegiance and affiliation are normal developmental occurrences, and avoid making young adolescents feel guilty or uncomfortable.	Manning and Allen (1987) looked at peer pressure and its consequences in considerable detail.
Young adolescents increasingly seek freedom and independence from adult authority and seek to handle social tasks and situations without adult supervision. This request for freedom results in scrutiny of long-held beliefs and assumptions and may result in young adolescents engaging in activities that, ordinarily, they would not participate in.	1. Provide significant opportunities for freedom and to make genuine choices. 2. Provide educational experiences that teach young adolescents how to handle social tasks. 3. Encourage young adolescents to understand that the pursuit of freedom is normal and expected yet should not include engaging in dangerous or unsafe practices (i.e., freedom requires responsibility). 4. Understand that young adolescents scrutinizing long-held assumptions may be dependent on their cognitive growth and overall ability to think.	Thornburg (1983), a leader in the movement to accept early adolescence as a developmental period, wrote extensively about development during early adolescence and how middle-level schools can provide developmentally appropriate instruction. Manning (1988) related young adolescents' social development to Erikson's psychosocial theories.
Young adolescents experience a changing self-esteem, which is influenced by all aspects of their lives—both at home and at school. Several factors affecting self-esteem may include: changing from the elementary school to the middle school or preparing to move to the secondary school, and seeking independence yet being dependent on adults.	1. Provide direct opportunities through curricular experiences, organizational patterns, instructional approaches, exploratory programs, and adviser-advisee programs to build self-esteem. 2. Work toward making the move from the elementary school a positive and rewarding experience.	Koff, Rierdan, and Stubbs (1990) provided readers with a useful look at gender differences. Galassi, Gulledge, and Cox (1997) provided a comprehensive examination of middle school advisory programs.

Psychosocial Developmental Characteristics	Implications for Middle Level School Educators	For Additional Information:
	3. Understand how physical changes affect self-esteem and provide educational experiences that emphasize the normalcy of development and the interconnectedness of developmental areas.	
Young adolescents' preoccupations with themselves lead to critical self-examination and subsequently, to the formation of self-perceptions of all developmental areas such as height, weight, and bodily features. These perceptions significantly influence young adolescents' self-esteem, their decision to interact socially, and their close self-examination when developmental characteristics appear unlike their peers.	1. Help young adolescents to view themselves objectively and accurately and to realize height, weight, and bodily features might be only temporary. 2. Help young adolescents through science classes, health classes, exploratory programs, and adviser-advisee programs to understand the harmful effects of overly critical self-examination. 3. Promote self-esteem in all educational experiences. 4. Help young adolescents to understand the nature of their developmental period and the tremendous diversity characterizing the period.	Roberts, Sarigiani, Peterson, and Newman (1990) examined the relationship between self-image and gender differences.
Young adolescents demonstrate behaviors (argumentative, aggressive, and daring) that may appear "disturbing" to parents and teachers. Such inconsistent behaviors may result from a feeling of newfound freedom, bravado resulting from too rapid or too slow development, or feelings of frustration or lack of ability to handle social situations.	1. Understand and accept young adolescents' newfound desire to be aggressive, argumentative, and daring. 2. Help young adolescents to understand feelings of frustration resulting from early and late development. 3. Help young adolescents to understand that feelings of bravado might be dangerous and might result in situations they are unable to handle. 4. Provide educational experiences that encourage debates and other outlets to be argumentative in a socialized manner.	Milgram (1992) examined considerable research in his chapter on development.

Cognitive Developmental Characteristics	Implications for Middle Level School Educators	For Additional Information:
Young adolescents *begin* to develop from Piaget's concrete operations stage to the formal operations stage, which allows the ability to think abstractly, to form mental classes and relationships, to exhibit seriation, and to understand weight and volume. Not all young adolescents function in the formal operations stage—some 10- to 14-year-olds continue to function in the concrete operations stage and may be unable to handle higher-order thinking skills.	1. Use great *caution*. Diversity must be remembered! All young adolescents do not reach the formal operations stage at the same time—avoid over-challenging late developers to think beyond their capacity. 2. Provide formal operations thinkers with challenging activities (i.e., higher-order thinking skills and cause-and-effect relationships). 3. Provide concrete operational thinkers with developmentally appropriate activities (i.e., manipulatives and nonabstract learnings). 4. Encourage students to think on appropriate levels—neither under- nor over-challenging.	Allen, Splittgerber, and Manning (1993) cautioned educators to avoid assuming all young adolescents function in Piaget's formal operations stage. Manning and Lucking (1990) looked at the realities of ability grouping and suggested alternatives. Ginsburg and Opper (1988) provided the most detailed and comprehensive discussion of Piaget's theories of intellectual development.
Young adolescents begin to analyze and synthesize data; to pose questions; to explore, experiment, and reason; and to apply various problem-solving strategies. As a result, young adolescents may question school and home rules, think about their future, and experience diminishing egocentrism.	1. Provide "real-life" thinking exercises in which young adolescents analyze and synthesize data. 2. Allow considerable experimentation and problem solving. 3. Allow young adolescents to question school and home rules and to understand reasons for rules. 4. Adapt educational experiences to changing interests (i.e., exploratory programs).	*Caught in the Middle* (California Department of Education, 1987) explained why and how educators should provide higher-order thinking opportunities.

Cognitive Developmental Characteristics	Implications for Middle Level School Educators	For Additional Information:
Young adolescents begin to develop the ability to make reasoned moral and ethical choices. The close relationship between intellectual and moral development allows young adolescents to consider the morality of a situation and to think through the moral and ethical validity of ideas.	1. Encourage young adolescents to consider the ethics and morality of social and personal situations. 2. Explore concepts of justice and equality and such social issues as sexism, racism, and discrimination. 3. Understand and capitalize on the relationship between cognitive and moral development (i.e., higher-order thinking skills allow higher levels of moral reasoning).	Bergman (1992) provided readers with a detailed examination of exploratory programs.
Young adolescents' diversity in cognitive development results in varying levels of intellectual growth, varying degrees of creativity, a wide range of reading abilities, and varying attention spans.	1. Provide individual or at least small-group instruction designed to meet learners' developmental levels. 2. Provide instructional materials for various reading and interest levels to involve as many learners as possible. 3. Encourage creativity, but accept individual efforts. 4. Adapt educational experiences to varying attention spans, learning styles, multiple intelligence, and left brain/right brain capacities.	Reiff (1997) examined multiple intelligence and the effects of culture. Gardner (1987) explained the spectrum of multiple intelligence and showed how educators can provide appropriate instruction. Springer and Deutsch (1985) wrote a comprehensive book called *Left Brain, Right Brain.*
Young adolescents' cognitive development is affected by social development and overall socialization as they interact with peers, parents, teachers, and other significant people in their lives. For example, a 10- to 14-year-old who is unable to master a concept might, through social contact and verbal interaction, understand the concept after social interaction with a peer.	1. Understand the relationship between cognitive and social development and provide opportunities that address both types of development (i.e., cooperative learning). 2. Allow friends to work together, so one learner can help another or one's strength can complement another's weakness.	Manning (1993) provided readers with a detailed explanation of opportunities to enhance cognitive development through social development.

Cognitive Developmental Characteristics	Implications for Middle Level School Educators	For Additional Information:
	3. Provide opportunities whereby teachers and young adolescents (and perhaps parents) can work together. 4. Implement peer-tutoring sessions to help other students, perhaps providing different perspectives and social interactions.	
Young adolescents develop the ability to understand time perspectives, such as past, present, and future.	1. Teach young adolescents to place and perceive events in historical relation to one another. 2. Help young adolescents to understand the past and its effects on contemporary events and perspectives. 3. Provide opportunities for young adolescents to engage in problem-solving activities about present problems in an attempt to influence the future.	Manning (1994/1995) provided a detailed account of educational practices that address cognitive characteristics.
Young adolescents develop increased language skills and a better grasp of vocabulary and word meanings.	1. Provide communication opportunities in which young adolescents can speak and listen in language-rich environments. 2. Take advantage of students' enhanced language by teaching words and meanings such as similes, idioms, and metaphors. 3. Provide opportunities for young adolescents to engage in debates, purposeful conversations, interviews, and dramatic activities.	Irvin (1997) suggested ways to create literacy learning programs for young adolescents. The January 1997 issue of the *Middle School Journal* focuses on literate environments. Myers and Hilliard (1997) suggest students' language needs can be addressed through holistic language learning.

For Additional Information

Alexander, C. (1989). Gender differences in adolescent health concerns and self-assessed health. *Journal of Early Adolescence, 9*(4), 467–479.

Allen, H. A., Splittgerber, F., & Manning, M. L. (1993). *Teaching and learning in the middle level school.* Columbus, OH: Merrill.

American Association of University Women (AAUW). (1996). *Girls in the middle: Working to succeed.* Annapolis Junction, MD: Author.

Benenson, J. F. (1990). Gender differences in social networks. *Journal of Early Adolescence, 10*(4), 472–495.

Bergman, S. (1992). Exploratory programs in the middle level schools: A responsive idea. In J. L. Irvin (Ed.), *Transforming middle level education: Perspectives and possibilities* (pp. 179–192). Boston: Allyn and Bacon.

Butler, D. A., & Manning, M. L. (1998). *Gender differences in young adolescents.* Olney, MD: Association for Childhood Education International.

California Department of Education. (1987). *Caught in the middle.* Sacramento, CA: Author.

Carnegie Council on Adolescent Development. (1989). *Turning points: Preparing American youth for the 21st century.* Washington, DC: Author.

Carnegie Council on Adolescent Development. (1996). *Great transitions: Preparing adolescents for a new century.* Washington, DC: Author.

Deegan, J. G. (1992). Understanding vulnerable friendships in fifth grade culturally diverse classrooms. *Middle School Journal, 23*(4), 21–25.

Dorman, G., & Lipsitz, J. (1984). Early adolescent development. In G. Dorman, *Middle Grades Assessment Program* (pp. 3–8). UNC-Chapel Hill, NC: Center for Early Adolescence.

Galassi, J. P., Gulledge, S. A., & Cox, N. D. (1997). Middle school advisories: Retrospect and prospect. *Review of Educational Research, 67*(3), 301–308.

Gardner, H. (1987). Developing the spectrum of human intelligence. *Harvard Education Review, 57,* 187–193.

Ginsburg, H. P., & Opper, S. (1988). *Piaget's theory of intellectual development.* Englewood Cliffs, NJ: Prentice-Hall.

Hamburg, D. A. (1997). Toward a strategy of adolescent development. *American Journal of Psychiatry, 154*(6), 7–12.

Irvin, J. (1997). Creating a middle school culture of literacy. *Middle School Journal, 28*(3), 4–9.

Koff, E., Rierdan, J., & Stubbs, M. L. (1990). Gender, body image, and self-concept in early adolescence. *Journal of Early Adolescence, 10,* 56–68.

Lawrence, G. (1980). Do programs reflect what research says about physical development? *Middle School Journal, 11*(2), 12–14.

Manning, M. L. (1988). Erikson's psychosocial theories help explain early adolescence. *NASSP Bulletin, 72*(509), 95–100.

Manning, M. L. (1993). *Developmentally appropriate middle level schools.* Olney, MD: Association for Childhood Education International.

Manning, M. L. (1994/1995). Addressing young adolescents' cognitive development. *The High School Journal, 78,* 98–104.

Manning, M. L., & Allen, M. G. (1987). Social development in early adolescence: Implications for middle school educators. *Childhood Education, 63,* 172–176.

Manning, M. L., & Lucking, R. (1990). Ability grouping: Realities and alternatives. *Childhood Education, 66,* 254–258.

Manning, M. L., & Lucking, R. (1991). The what, why, and how of cooperative learning. *The Clearing House, 64,* 152–156.

Manning, M. L., & Lucking, R. (1993). Cooperative learning and multicultural classrooms. *The Clearing House, 67*(1), 12–16.

Martin, K. A. (1996). *Puberty, sexuality, and the self.* New York: Routledge.

Milgram, J. (1992). A portrait of diversity: The middle level student. In J. L. Irvin (Ed.), *Transforming middle level education: Perspectives and possibilities* (pp. 16–27). Boston: Allyn and Bacon.

Myers, J. W., & Hilliard, R. D. (1997). Holistic language learning at the middle level: Our last, best chance. *Childhood Education, 73*(5), 286–289.

Reiff, J. (1997). Multiple intelligences, culture, and equitable learning. *Childhood Education, 73*(5), 301–304.

Roberts, L. R., Sarigiani, P. A., Peterson, A. C., & Newman, J. L. (1990). Gender differences in the relationship between achievement and self-image during early adolescence. *Journal of Early Adolescence, 10,* 159–175.

Schuster, C., & Ashburn, S. (1986). *The process of human development.* Boston: Little, Brown.

Springer, S. P., & Deutsch, G. (1985). *Left brain, right brain* (Rev. ed.). New York: W. H. Freeman.

Tanner, J. M. (1968). Earlier maturation in man. *Scientific American, 218*(1), 21–27.

Tanner, J. M. (1971). Sequence, tempo, and individual variation in the growth and development of boys and girls aged twelve to sixteen. *Daedalus, 100,* 907–930.

Tanner, J. M. (1973). Growing up. *Scientific American, 229*(3), 35–43.

Thornburg, H. (1983). Can educational systems respond to the needs of early adolescents? *Journal of Early Adolescence, 3,* 32–36.

Glossary

ability grouping: students are assigned to different classes or different groups within a class based on their academic abilities, such as achievement in a subject, reading scores, or overall academic standing

accountability: the movement or philosophy that holds educators responsible for their behavior as well as for demonstrating they have fulfilled all their job responsibilities or contractual obligations

advanced organizer: an effort (i.e., a story, brainteaser, or short activity) prior to actual instruction that captures or promotes learners' attention and prepares them for the learning experiences that follow

advisor-advisee programs: sometimes called home-based guidance or teacher advisories, these are advisement efforts conducted by classroom teachers, sometimes spontaneous and other times reflecting a carefully prepared scope and sequence

alternative assessment: assessment that differs from traditional paper-and-pencil tests—assessment that actually assesses students' achievement such as performance-based assessment, portfolios, exhibitions, demonstrations, and journals

analytic rubrics: assessment devices developed to analyze a list of specific criteria for a small project

anorexia nervosa: a severe eating disorder in which a person starves herself or himself, exercises compulsively, and develops an unrealistic view of her or his body

assessment: collection, interpretation, and use of qualitative and quantitative data designed to elicit some predetermined behavior from the student

at-risk: presumed factors or conditions that place learners in danger of negative future events, such as substance abuse, underachievement, or other risky behaviors that might prevent them from reaching their potential

authentic assessment: the direct examination of students' ability to use knowledge to perform a real-life task (i.e., students plan, construct, and deliver a project or other form of evidence that demonstrates their learning)

behavioral objective: a statement of learning expectation that tells what the learner should be able to do upon completion of learning or a lesson

Big Six: a model for developing information/problem-solving skills consisting of the following steps: task definition, information-seeking strategies, location and access of sources and information, use of information, synthesis and organization of information, and evaluation of the results and the process

block scheduling: a school organizational scheme that allows large blocks of time (perhaps 1 hour and 45 minutes in contrast to a 50- or 55-minute period) in which a teacher or a team of teachers provide instruction for varied periods of time

bulimia: a psychological and physical disturbance in which a person tries to lose weight by vomiting—the bulimic fears being unable to stop eating, experiences depression, and self-induces vomiting so weight will not be gained

CD-ROM: (*c*ompact *d*isc, *r*ead-*o*nly *m*emory) digitally encoded information permanently recorded on a compact disc

character education: refers to moral training, one that reflects and teaches particular values as well as particular assumptions about the nature of children and how they should behave and live

classroom management: methods of maintaining order in the classroom; the techniques for changing student misbehaviors and for teaching self-discipline as well as ensuring an orderly progression of events during the school day

cognitive development: the changes and advancements that occur in intellectual (ability to learn, think, and reason) skills during the course of development

cognitively appropriate seatwork: written or oral work that matches young adolescents' cognitive skills and abilities—challenging work that is neither too easy nor too difficult and that results in learning rather than frustration

collaboration: cooperative efforts among professionals (and parents and young adolescents) where all parties share expertise and work toward a common goal

community-based learning: learning that takes advantage of community resources or allows students to leave the school and learn in the community, thus addressing real-life problems

community service: students provide direct individual or group services by participating in community-assistance projects, such as providing service to homeless shelters, environmental projects, or other service opportunities

complementary teaching: the general educator teaches specific subject matter, while the special educator assumes responsibility for teaching associated academic (e.g., note taking, test taking) or school survival skills (e.g., sharing, self-control)

continuous progress: instructional procedures whereby students work and progress at their own pace through a carefully planned curriculum that avoids lapses in learning or gaps in learning sequences

cooperative learning: instructional techniques that emphasize cooperation rather than competition and allow students to work in small groups (perhaps four to six students) and help one another toward learning goals

core curriculum: the subject areas generally considered essential for all students in the middle school: language arts, social sciences, mathematics, and science

criterion-referenced tests: assessment designed to assess or judge behaviors, performance, or abilities against preestablished standards rather than against the behavior of others

curriculum: program of study that includes all the planned and unplanned experiences available to young adolescents throughout the school day

departmentalized classroom: an instructional and organizational pattern that organizes subjects by discipline where teachers are usually subject-matter specialists and teach only one or two subjects during the school day (in contrast to interdisciplinary teaming or interdisciplinary instruction)

detracking: efforts to avoid or minimize the effects of ability grouping by grouping students (or not grouping students at all) on some basis or criterion other than their ability

developmentally responsive: educational experiences that reflect and respond to individual young adolescents' developmental needs and interests rather than providing the same educational experiences for all students, regardless of their development

developmental needs: learning, social, and other needs that are appropriate to the developmental characteristics of the age (i.e., the developmental needs specific for the early adolescence developmental period)

developmental tasks: challenges in a person's life that are unique to that stage of development, such as young adolescents seeking freedom and independence

diagnostic assessment: sometimes called "preassessment," these efforts identify specific areas of deficiency of learning difficulty and allow educators to identify specific causes of problems and to plan appropriate instruction

discipline-based art education: a movement to teach the arts as content in programs that provide systematic, sequential teaching experiences that involve all students—rather than just a talented few—in creating, studying, and experiencing arts (making art, appreciating art, understanding art, and making judgments about art)

early adolescence: the period of physical, psychosocial, and cognitive development of 10- to 14- (or 15)-year-olds, commonly thought to be between the childhood years and adolescence

equal access: the belief that all young adolescents should have equal access to middle school programs, facilities, and activities rather than having some criteria, either overt or covert, that prohibits some young adolescents participation or "access"

evaluation: making judgments about quality (e.g., its worth or value) or how good a behavior or performance is, such as educators evaluating students' achievement of instructional outcomes

exhibitions: often called "demonstrations," this assessment device provides a means for young adolescents to prove knowledge, skills, or competence by allowing them to make or do something

exploratory activities: an instructional method for young adolescents to explore a specific interest within the curricular areas for a flexible length of time

exploratory programs/exploratory curriculum: a series of carefully planned 6 weeks, 8 weeks, or semester courses (sometimes called "mini-courses") that provide young adolescents with opportunities to explore their needs, interests, and aptitudes

expository teaching: in this traditional method of teaching, the teacher acts as a director of instruction—she or he conveys content information to learners in a direct, concise, and time-efficient and predetermined sequence and on predetermined schedules

flexible scheduling: organizational patterns of classes and activities that allow variation from day to day as opposed to traditional periods of equal or near-equal length each day

formative assessment: assessment efforts (e.g., informal observation, questioning, in-class work, homework, and teacher feedback) that determine students' progress during a lesson or unit to provide ongoing (rather than at the end) feedback to the teacher and student

growth spurt: a time of growth (usually around age 12 for girls and around age 14 for boys) during which young adolescents experience rapid increases in body size as well as readily apparent skeletal and structural changes

guidance: program or services provided by middle school professionals that focus on young adolescents' adjustment to middle school, at-risk behaviors, and any problems that have the potential for affecting academic achievement or overall development

heterogeneous grouping: grouping students to different classes, grades, or schools on the basis of random selection rather than specific criteria, such as academic abilities or achievement in a subject, reading scores, or overall academic standing

hidden curriculum: intentional or unintentional curricular aspects that students experience or perceive, such as students learning from educators' actions, expectations, and behaviors, and their feelings toward social issues, groups, and individuals

holistic rubrics: rubrics developed to analyze a list of specific criteria for complete and final project

homogeneous grouping: *see* ability grouping

house: sometimes called a "pod," "cluster," or "school-within-a-school," this form of organization remedies or addresses the problems (e.g., feelings of anonymity) associated with large schools by placing one team of teachers with about 100 to 125 students for the same block of time for the entire day

I-search: an instructional research strategy in which students move from building background knowledge through developing a search plan, gathering information, and analyzing and synthesizing information to developing a report on their findings

inclusion: the policy of educating a special-needs learner in the school, and whenever possible, in the class that the child would have attended if she or he did not have a disability

individualized instruction: an instructional method in which learners assume responsibility for some aspects of their learning through study, practice, and reinforcement in specially designed individual learning packages

inductive discovery: an instructional method whereby teachers use strategies that begin with specifics and move toward the development of a generalization

informational literacy: the ability to identify, locate, evaluate, organize, and use information effectively

inquiry learning: the young adolescent designs the processes to be used in solving a problem or learning a particular assignment

integrated: a curricular approach that uses themes, topics, or other efforts to integrate subject matter across curricular lines in an attempt to avoid the single-subject curriculum

integrated curriculum: the curriculum is integrated using topics, themes, and subject areas to promote interdisciplinary learning, which allows students to connect learning from one subject area to another, to real-world situations, and to their own experiences

interdisciplinary teaming: working on a collaborative team, three or four teachers representing different curricular areas plan and implement "interdisciplinary units" as opposed to teachers working in isolation or teachers being organized solely by curricular area; although two or more teachers may teach in the same room, teaching in the same room is not required

interdisciplinary team organization: an organization that combines curricular areas (perhaps using a common theme) that traditionally have been taught separately, so learners will see relationships between and among curricular areas

interdisciplinary thematic unit: a thematic or problems lesson of study that crosses curricular lines, usually using a common theme that all teachers on the interdisciplinary team teach at the same time

intermediate school: a school organization approach for students between elementary school and secondary school, usually including grades 5 to 7 or 7 to 8

junior high school: a precursor of the middle school, this school usually included grades 7 to 9 and addressed the educational and developmental needs of students between the elementary school and the secondary school

learning center: a special station located in the classroom where one or two students (perhaps more, depending on the design of the center) can quietly work and learn more about a topic or improve specific skills at his or her own pace

learning community: *see* sense of community

learning style: patterns of how students learn or respond to learning stimuli or strategies or the personal and school conditions under which students learn more effectively

library media center: the location in a school where a wide range of information resources and related technologies are housed and where a professional library media staff including a school library media specialist provides instruction on information literacy and other services to students and teachers

looping: multigrade programs in which teachers and students remain together for more than one year (i.e., seventh-grade teachers teach the eighth grade the next year with the same group of students)

measurement: systematic process of assigning numbers to performance and used to determine how much of a quality, feature, trait, attribute, or characteristic a student possesses

middle school: a school organizational approach, usually grades 6 to 8 and sometimes grade 5, that addresses the educational and developmental needs of 10- to 14- (and sometimes 15-) year-olds, commonly known as "young adolescents"

minicourses: *see* exploratory programs/exploratory curriculum

multicultural education: a concept and deliberate process designed to teach young adolescents to recognize, accept, and appreciate cultural, ethnic, social class, religious, and gender differences among people, and instill in young adolescents during their crucial psychosocial and cognitive developmental period a sense of responsibility and a commitment to work toward the democratic ideals of justice, equality, and democracy

multidisciplinary curriculum: a curricular approach that brings the perspectives of different disciplines to the unified study of problems, topics, and themes; relationships and connections between and among disciplines are explored, but the disciplines are kept distinct and separate

multiple grading system: alternative grading practices for students with special learning needs; an asterisk on a report card of a student with a disability or special need

multiple intelligences: the theory that instead of people having just one intelligence, they have a number of intelligences, such as linguistic, logical-mathematical, spatial, interpersonal, intrapersonal, musical, and kinesthetic

norm-referenced test: assessment that determines an individual's performance, ability, or achievement relative to the overall performance of the group in relation to a local, regional, or national norm group

observational checklists: a basis for determining and assigning grades (i.e., teachers observe students to determine student class participation, types of questions asked/responses given, interpersonal skills, verbal skills, need for additional examples, and students' interest levels)

overlapping: an effective teacher behavior whereby the teacher attends to or takes care of more than one aspect of teaching at one time

parallel teaching: the general educator and special educator divide the class into two smaller groups to provide more individualized instruction

parent advisory council: a committee of parents, representative of the school's diversity, who volunteer to serve in an advisory capacity to advise administrators and teachers on issues and problems facing the school

parent education: consisting of one session on a particular topic or a series of topics over several weeks, these classes or workshops are designed to educate parents about young adolescents, middle schools, or topics suggested by the parents

peer-tutoring: a situation where one (or more) young adolescent helps or tutors another student or small group of students with a topic, skill, or concept

performance-based: assessment is based more on the processes the student uses than on the final product or outcome and relies on the professional judgment of assessors who observe the student performing a predetermined task

personal concerns: concerns specifically related to young adolescents, their schooling, family issues, or development

physical development: the growth and development of the physique or the skeletal, structural, and muscular system

portfolios: students collect various types of work over a period of time (e.g., 6 or 9 weeks) and select work they consider best represents their ability, achievement, and motivation

productive time on task: in contrast to "time-on-task," which often results in students being involved in "busy work," this term emphasizes "productive," the actual time students are working productively on learning tasks

project: a form of study in which students produce something, such as a paper, an investigation, a model, a skit, a report, or a combination of these

psychosocial development: the growth and development of young adolescents' psychological, social, and emotional domains such as increased socialization, changing self-esteem, desire to make friends, and shifting allegiance from parents to friends

reliability: the consistency, stability, and dependability of the results; a reliable result shows similar performance at different times or under different conditions

revolving schedules: schedules that revolve on a daily or weekly basis—one example is science and mathematics being taught in the morning one day and then revolving to the afternoon the next, so students can learn at different times of the day

role-playing: often called "simulations," teachers assess students' active participation, such as assuming another's perspective and using one's own knowledge and skill to act as another person might act

rubrics: assessment that determines how a product, performance, or portfolio artifact is to be judged or graded

school-within-a-school: *see* house

self-contained classroom: a classroom where students stay with one teacher all day—the teacher provides instruction in all subjects (with the possible exception of art and music)

self-esteem: how one feels about herself or himself; one's ability to succeed in specific situations, and how she or he judges her or his worth

sense of community: young adolescents should perceive a feeling of togetherness where students and teachers know each other sufficiently well to create a climate for intellectual development and shared educational purpose

service learning: students work in the community to provide service to individuals or groups such as nursing homes, homeless shelters, animal protection agencies, and environmental efforts to teach a sense of volunteerism and duty to the community

sexually transmitted diseases (STDs): diseases that are transmitted through sexual experimentation or activity

shadow teaching: the general educator teaches specific subject matter, while the special educator works directly with one or two target students on academics and/or behavior

single-subject curriculum: single subjects are taught without any attempt at thematic units or other efforts to achieve curricular integration and to teach young adolescents relationships between and among curricular areas

site-based management: a policy of school districts allowing individual schools to make decisions that affect their daily operation, based upon the belief that those professional educators working directly with students are in the best position to make educational decisions

social issues: issues such as democracy, equality, and justice that concern many young adolescents and can serve as themes in integrated curriculum

special-needs student: a student who differs from other students in ways such as mental characteristics, sensory ability, physical abilities, or multiple handicaps and who deserves specialized services from educators

station teaching: the general educator and special educator teach different subject matter to groups of students who rotate from one learning station to another

summative assessment: sometimes called "formal assessment" and conducted at the end of a unit of study, summative assessment (e.g., term papers, chapter achievement tests, final examinations, and research projects) documents student performance, measures overall achievement, and provides the basis for assigning grades

team planning: in contrast to teachers planning in isolation, team planning includes teams of three to four teachers, each representing a different curricular area and planning as a team, thus trying to build upon each others' strengths as well as teaching students to see relationships between and among curricular areas

thematic unit: teaching unit that crosses two or more subject areas as compared to a unit that focuses entirely on one curricular area

tracking: the policy of placing students in different programs or courses, based on their abilities or previous achievement

traditional assessments: assessment devices such as multiple choice, true-false, and matching that teachers have relied upon for many years

transescence: another term for early adolescence or the 10- to 14- (or sometimes 15-) year-old developmental period

transescents: another term for young adolescents or 10- to 14- (or sometimes 15-) year-olds

validity: the appropriateness of the inferences, uses, and consequences that result from the test or other method of gathering information and reliability

"withitness": a term or descriptor indicating an effective teaching behavior whereby the teacher simultaneously knows what is occurring in all areas of the classroom and is able to manage a number of tasks with a degree of competence and confidence

young adolescents: girls and boys commonly between the ages of 10 and 14, sometimes considered the ages of 9 and 15, who are progressing through the early adolescence developmental period and its accompanying physical, psychosocial, and cognitive developmental changes

References

Abramson, G. (1998). How to evaluate educational software. *Principal, 78*(1), 60–61.

Alam, D., & Seick, R. E. (1994). A block schedule with a twist. *Phi Delta Kappan, 75,* 732–733.

Alaniz, M. L., Cartmill, R. S., & Parker, R. N. (1998). Immigrants and violence: The importance of neighborhood context. *Hispanic Journal of Behavioral Sciences, 20*(2), 155–174.

Albert, E. (1994). Drama in the classroom. *Middle School Journal, 25*(5), 20–24.

Alexander, W. (1995). *Student-oriented curriculum: Asking the right questions.* Columbus, OH: National Middle School Association.

Alexander, W. M. (1968). *A survey of organizational patterns of reorganized middle schools.* Washington, DC: United States Department of Health, Education, and Welfare.

Alexander, W. M., & McEwin, C. K. (1989a). *Schools in the middle: A research report.* Boone, NC: Appalachian State University. (ERIC Document Reproduction Service No. ED 312312).

Alexander, W. M., & McEwin, C. K. (1989b). *Schools in the middle: Status and progress.* Columbus, OH: National Middle School Association.

Alexander, W. M., & Williams, E. (1968). *The emergent middle school.* New York: Holt, Rinehart, and Winston.

Alexander, W. M., Williams, E. L., Compton, M., Hines, V. A., Prescott, D., & Kealy, R. (1969). *The emergent middle school* (2nd ed). New York: Holt, Rinehart, and Winston.

Allen, H. A. (1992). Middle grade education: A one hundred year perspective. *Education Report, 32*(2), 1–2, 4.

Allen, H. A., Splittgerber, F. L., & Manning, M. L. (1993). *Teaching and learning in the middle level school.* Upper Saddle River, NJ: Merrill/Prentice-Hall.

Allen, M. G., & Stevens, R. L. (1994). *Middle grades social studies: Teaching and learning for active and responsible citizenship.* Boston: Allyn and Bacon.

American Association for Health Education. (n.d.). *Responsibilities and competencies for teachers of young adolescents in coordinated school health programs for middle level classroom teachers.* Reston, VA: Author.

American Association for the Advancement of Science (AAAS). (1990). *Science for all Americans.* Washington, DC: Author.

American Association of School Librarians. (1994). *Information literacy: A position paper on informational problem solving.* Chicago, IL: Author.

American Association of School Librarians. (1998). *Information power: Building partnerships for learning.* Chicago: Author.

Ames, N., & West, T. (1999). Practices and strategies: Helping all middle level students achieve at high levels. *Schools in the Middle, 8*(4), 19–45.

Arllen, N., Gable, R. A., & Hendrickson, J. M. (1996). Accommodating students with special needs in the general classroom. *Preventing School Failure, 41,* 7–13.

Arnold, D. E. (1998). Action research in action: Curricular articulation and integrated instruction. *NASSP Bulletin, 82*(596), 74–78.

Arnold, J. (1991). The revolution in middle school organization. *Momentum, 22*(2), 20–25.

Arnold, J. (1993). A curriculum to empower young adolescents. *Midpoints Occasional Papers, 4*(10), 1–11.

Atwater, E. (1988). *Adolescence.* Englewood Cliffs, NJ: Prentice-Hall.

Bailey, N. J., & Phariss, T. (1996). Breaking the wall of silence: Gay, lesbian, and bisexual issues for middle level educators. *Middle School Journal, 27*(3), 38–46.

Balli, S. J. (1998). When mom and dad help: Student reflections on parent involvement with homework. *Journal of Research and Development in Education, 31*(3), 142–146.

Barth, R. P., Middleton, K., & Wagman, E. (1989). A skill building approach to preventing teenage pregnancy. *Theory into Practice, 28*(3), 183–190.

Baruth, L. G., & Manning, M. L. (1992). *Multicultural education of children and adolescents.* Boston: Allyn and Bacon.

Bauwens, J., Hourcade, J. J., & Friend, M. (1989). Cooperative teaching: A model for general and special education integration. *Remedial and Special Education, 10,* 17–22.

Beane, J. (1990). *Middle school curriculum: From rhetoric to reality.* Columbus, OH: National Middle School Association.

Beane, J. (1993a). *Middle school curriculum: From rhetoric to reality* (2nd ed.). Columbus, OH: National Middle School Association.

Beane, J. (1993b). Problems and possibilities for an integrative curriculum. *Middle School Journal, 25*(1), 18–23.

Beane, J. (1995). *Toward a coherent curriculum.* Alexandria, VA: Association for Supervision and Curriculum Development.

Beane, J. (1996). On the shoulders of giants! The case for curriculum integration. *Middle School Journal, 28*(1), 6–11.

Beane, J. A. (1999a). Middle schools under siege: Points of attack. *Middle School Journal, 30*(4), 3–9.

Beane, J. A. (1999b). Middle schools under siege: Responding to the attack. *Middle School Journal, 30*(5), 3–6.

Berger, E. H. (1991). Parent involvement: Yesterday and today. *Elementary School Journal, 91*(3), 209–219.

Bessant, D. (1997). Collaborating to connect good literature to middle school readers. *Middle School Journal, 29*(2), 8–12.

Blasewitz, M. R., & Taylor, R. T. (1999). Attacking literacy with technology in an urban setting. *Middle School Journal, 30*(3), 33–39.

Bossing, N., & Cramer, R. (1964). *The junior high school.* Boston: Houghton-Mifflin Company.

Brandt, R. (1987/1988). On discipline-based art education: A conversation with Elliot Eisner. *Educational Leadership, 45*(4), 6–9.

Brazee, E. (1995). An integrated curriculum supports young adolescent development. In Y. Siu-Runyan & C. V. Faircloth, (Eds.), *Beyond separate subjects: Integrative learning at the middle level* (pp. 5–24). Norwood, MA: Christopher-Gordon.

Brodhagen, B. L. (1998). Varied teaching and learning approaches. *Middle School Journal, 29*(5), 49–52.

Brookhart, S. M., & Loadman, W. E. (1990). School-university collaboration: Different workplace cultures. *Contemporary Education, 61,* 125–128.

Brooks, M., Fusco, E., & Glennon, J. (1983). Cognitive levels matching. *Educational Leadership, 40*(8), 4–8.

Brophy, J. E. (1983). Classroom organization and management. *The Elementary School Journal, 83*(4), 265–285.

Brophy, J. E. (1987). Synthesis of research on strategies for motivating students to learn. *Educational Leadership 45*(2), 40–48.

Brophy, J. E., & Good, T. L. (1986). Teacher behavior and student achievement. In M. C. Wittock (Ed.), *Handbook of research on teaching* (3rd ed., pp. 328–375). New York: Macmillan.

Brown, L. M., & Gilligan, C. (1990, April). *The psychology of women and the development of girls.* Paper presented at the Laurel-Harvard Conference on the Psychology of Women and the Education of Girls, Cleveland, OH.

Bruno, R. R., & Adams, A. (1994). *School enrollment—social and economic characteristics of students: October 1993.* (U.S. Bureau of the Census, Current Population Reports, P20-479.) Washington, DC: U.S. Government Printing Office.

Bryant, M., & Land, S. (1998). Co-planning is the key to successful co-teaching. *Middle School Journal, 29*(5), 28–34.

Bucher, K., & Fravel, M. (1993). Social studies: The roaring twenties. *School Library Media Activities Monthly, 10*(3), 27–29.

Bucher, K. T. (1998a). *Information technology for schools.* Worthington, OH: Linworth Publishing.

Bucher, K. T. (1998b). Integrating children's/young adult literature into the social studies. In H.E. Taylor (Ed.), *What's goin' on? Trends and issues in American education* (pp. 207–214). Needham Heights, MA: Simon & Schuster Custom.

Bucher, K. T., & Manning, M. L. (1998). Telling our stories, sharing our lives: Collective biographies of women. *ALAN Review, 26*(1), 12–16.

Buie, J. (1987). Teen pregnancy: It's time for the schools to tackle the problem. *Phi Delta Kappan, 68,* 737–740.

Burkhardt, R. (1997). Teaming: Sharing the experience. In T. S. Dickinson & T. O. Erb (Eds.), *We gain more than we give: Teaming in the middle school* (pp. 163–184). Columbus, OH: National Middle School Association.

Burkhart, R. M. (1999a). Advisory: An advocate for every student. *Middle School Journal, 30*(3), 51–54.

Burkhart, R. M. (1999b). Advisory: Advocacy for every student. *Middle School Journal, 30*(3), 51–54.

Butler, D. A., & Manning, M. L. (1998). *Addressing gender differences in young adolescents.* Olney, MD: Association for Childhood Education International.

Butler, D. A., & Manning, M. L. (1999). Helping middle schools address gender differences. *Focus on Middle School, 11*(3), 1–6.

Butte, H. P. (1993). Developing curriculum to reduce emotional stress in middle schoolers. *Middle School Journal, 24*(4), 41–46.

Byrnes, D. A., & Cortez, D. (1992). Language diversity in the classroom. In D. A. Byrnes & G. Kiger (Eds.), *Common bonds: Anti-bias teaching in a diverse society* (pp. 71–85). Olney, MD: Association for Childhood Education International.

California State Department of Education. (1987). *Caught in the middle.* Sacramento, CA: Author.

Canady, R. L., & Rettig, M. D. (1995). The power of innovative scheduling. *Educational Leadership, 53*(3), 4–10.

Canfield, J. (1990). Improving students' self-esteem. *Educational Leadership, 48*(1), 48–50.

Canning, C. (1993). Preparing for diversity: A social technology for multicultural community building. *The Educational Forum, 57,* 371–385.

Canter, L., & Canter, M. (1976). *Assertive discipline: A take-charge approach for today's educator.* Seal Beach, CA: Lee Canter & Associates.

Canter, L., & Canter, M. (1992). *Assertive discipline: A take-charge approach for today's educator* (2nd ed.). Seal Beach, CA: Lee Canter & Associates.

Carnegie Council on Adolescent Development. (1989). *Turning points: Preparing American youth for the 21st century.* Washington: Author.

Carnegie Council on Adolescent Development. (1990). *Turning points: Preparing American youth for the 21st century* (abridged version). Washington, DC: Author.

Carnegie Council on Adolescent Development. (1992). *A matter of time: Risk and opportunity in the nonschool hours.* New York: Author.

Carnegie Council on Adolescent Development. (1996). *Great transitions: Preparing adolescents for a new century.* Washington, DC: Author.

Carroll, J. M. (1989). *The Copernican plan: Restructuring the American high school.* Andover, MA: The Regional Laboratory for Educational Improvement of the Northeast and Islands.

Carroll, P. S., & Taylor, A. (1998). Understanding the culture of the classroom. *Middle School Journal, 30*(1), 9–17.

Cauley, K. M., & Seyfarth, J. T. (1995). Curriculum reform in middle level and high school mathematics. *NASSP Bulletin, 79*(567), 22–30.

Chalfant, J., & Pych, M.V. (1989). Teacher assistance teams: Five descriptive studies on 96 teams. *Remedial and Special Education, 10,* 49–58.

Charles, C. M. (1996). *Building classroom discipline* (5th ed.). White Plains, NY: Longman.

Charles, C. M. (1999). *Building classroom discipline* (6th ed.). White Plains, NY: Longman.

Chavkin, N. F. (1989). Debunking the myth about minority parents. *Educational Horizons, 67(4),* 119–123.

Cheek, D. W. (1993). Plain talk about alternative assessments. *Middle School Journal, 25*(2), 6–10.

Chilcoat, G.W. (1993). The dime novel western: Studying the American/Canadian West. *Middle School Journal, 24*(4), 66–67.

Chilcoat, G.W. (1995). Using panorama theater to teach middle school social studies. *Middle School Journal, 26*(4), 52–56.

Children's Defense Fund. (1991). *Making the middle grades work.* Washington, DC: Author.

Christensen, E. W. (1989). Counseling Puerto Ricans: Some cultural considerations. In D. R. Atkinson, G. Morten, & D. W. Sue (Eds.), *Counseling American minorities: A cross-cultural perspective* (3rd ed., pp. 205–212). Dubuque, IA: W. C. Brown.

Ciaccio, J. (1998). Teach success to underachieving middle-schoolers. *Schools in the Middle, 7*(4), 18–20.

Clark, G., & Zimmerman, E. (1998). Nurturing the arts in programs for the gifted and talented. *Phi Delta Kappan, 79*(10), 747–751.

Clark, S. N., & Clark, D. C. (1987). Interdisciplinary teaming program: Organization, rationale, and implementation. *Schools in the middle: A report on trends and practices.* Reston, VA: National Association of Secondary School Principals.

Clark, S. N., & Clark, D. C. (1994). *Restructuring the middle level school: Implications for school leaders.* New York: State University of New York Press.

Clark, S. N., & Clark, D. C. (1997). Exploring the possibilities of interdisciplinary teaming. *Childhood Education, 73*(5), 267–271.

Clark, S. N., & Clark, D. C. (1998). Authentic assessments: Key issues, concerns, guidelines. *Schools in the Middle, 6*(5), 50–51.

Coate, J., & White, N. (1996). History/English core. *Social Studies Review, 34*(3), 12–15.

Cole, C. (1992). *Nurturing a teacher advisory program.* Columbus, OH: National Middle School Association.

Collins, A., & Dana, T. M. (1993). Using portfolios with middle grades students. *Middle School Journal, 25*(2), 14–19.

Collins, R. P. (1994). Middle school mathematics: Student empowerment through quality innovations. *The Clearing House, 67*(4), 180–181.

Colvin, C., & Schlosser, L. K. (1998). Developing academic confidence to build literacy: What teachers can do. *Journal of Adolescent & Adult Literacy, 41*(4), 272–281.

Cook, L., & Friend, M. (1991). Principles for the practice of collaboration in the schools. *Preventing School Failure, 35,* 6–9.

Cooke, L. B., & Adams, V. M. (1998). Encouraging "Math talk" in the classroom. *Middle School Journal, 29*(5), 35–40.

Cornett, C. E. (1983). *What should you know about teaching and learning styles?* Bloomington, IN: Phi Delta Kappa Education Foundation.

Crawford, L. W. (1993). *Language and literacy in multicultural classrooms.* Boston: Allyn and Bacon.

Crockett, L., Losoff, M., & Peterson, A. (1984). Perceptions of the peer group and friendship in early adolescence. *Journal of Early Adolescence, 4*(2), 155–181.

Curtis, T., & Bidwell, W. (1977). *Curriculum and instruction for emerging adolescents.* Reading, MA: Addison-Wesley.

Daley, D. (1991, January 9). Little girls lose their self-esteem on way to adolescence, study finds. *The New York Times,* p. B6.

Dana, T. M., & Collins, D. J. (1993). Considering alternative assessments for middle level learners. *Middle School Journal, 25*(2), 3–5.

Danielson, C., & Abrutyn, L. (1997). *An introduction to using portfolios in the classroom.* Alexandria, VA: Association of Supervision and Curriculum Development.

Darst, P. W., Pangrazi, R., & Stillwell, B. (1995). Middle school physical education: Make it more exciting. *Journal of Physical Education, Recreation, and Dance, 66*(8), 8–9.

Davis, M. A. (1992). Are interdisciplinary units worthwhile? Ask students. In J. H. Lounsbury (Ed.), *Connecting the curriculum through interdisciplinary instruction* (pp. 37–41). Columbus, OH: National Middle School Association.

Dawson, M. M. (1987). Beyond ability grouping: A review of the effectiveness of ability grouping and its alternatives. *School Psychology Review, 16,* 348–369.

De Jong, C., & Hawley, J. (1995). Making cooperative learning groups work. *Middle School Journal, 26*(4), 45–48.

Derman-Sparks, L. (1993/1994). Empowering children to create a caring culture in a world of differences. *Childhood Education 70,* 66–71.

Dickinson, T. S., & Erb, T. O. (1997). *We gain more than we give: Teaming in middle schools.* Columbus, OH: National Middle School Association.

Diem, R. A. (1992). Dealing with the tip of the iceberg: School responses to at risk behaviors. *The High School Journal, 75*(2), 119–125.

Doda, N. M., & George, P. S. (1999). Building whole middle school communities: Closing the gap between exploratory and core. *Middle School Journal, 30*(5), 32–39.

Doren, K. (1999). From capture to freedom: Slavery in America. *School Library Media Activities Monthly, 15*(6), 22–24.

Dorman, G., & Lipsitz, J. (1984). Early adolescent development. In G. Dorman (Ed.), *Middle grades assessment program* (pp. 3–8). Chapel Hill, NC: Center for Early Adolescence.

Doughty, J. H. (1999). Class activities promote teamwork among staff members. *Schools in the Middle, 8*(4), 6–8.

Drake, T. L., & Roe, W. H. (1999). *The principalship* (5th ed.). Upper Saddle River, NJ: Merrill/Prentice-Hall.

Dreikurs, R. (1968). *Psychology in the classroom* (2nd ed.). New York: Harper & Row.

Dreikurs, R., & Cassel, P. (1972). *Discipline without tears.* New York: Hawthorn.

Dunlap, N. S., Drew, S. F., & Gibson, K. (1994). *Serving to learn: K–8 manual.* Columbia, SC: South Carolina State Department of Education.

Dunn, R. S., & Dunn, K. J. (1979). Learning styles/teaching styles: Should they . . . can they . . . be matched? *Educational Leadership, 36,* 238–244.

Education and gender. (1994). *Congressional Quarterly Researcher, 4*(21), 481–504.

Edwards, C. M., Jr. (1995). The 4 × 4 plan. *Educational Leadership, 53*(3), 16–19.

Eichhorn, D. (1966). *The middle school.* New York: Center for Applied Research in Education.

Eisenberg, M., & Berkowitz, R. E. (1992). Information problem-solving: The big six skills approach. *School Library Media Activities Monthly, 8*(5), 27–29.

Eisenberg, M., & Johnson, D. (1996). *Computer skills for information problem-solving: Learning and teaching technology in context.* (ERIC Clearinghouse on Information & Technology Document Reproduction No. ED 392463.)

Eisner, E. (1999). The uses and limits of performamce assessment. *Phi Delta Kappan, 80*(9), 658–660.

Elkind, D. (1991). *The hurried child.* Reading, MA: Addison-Wesley.

Elkind, D. (1993). What ever happened to childhood? *Momentum, 24*(2), 18–19.

Epstein, J. L., & MacIver, D. J. (1990). *Education in the middle grades: An overview of trends and practices.* Columbus, OH: National Middle School Association.

Epstein, J. L., Simon, B. S., & Salinas, K. C. (1997). Involving parents in homework in the middle grades. *Research Bulletin, 18,* 1–4.

Erb, T. O. (1987). What team organization can do for teachers. *Middle School Journal, 18,* 3–6.

Erb, T. O. (1992). Encouraging gifted performance in middle schools. *Midpoints, 3*(1), 1–24.

Erb, T. O. (1997). Meeting the needs of young adolescents on interdisciplinary teams. *Childhood Education, 73*(5), 309–311.

Erb, T. O. (1999). Team organization reconsidered. *Middle School Journal, 30*(3), 2.

Erickson, L. G. (1998). Informational literacy in the middle grades. *The Clearing House, 71*(3), 165–168.

Erikson, E. (1963). *Childhood and society* (Rev. ed.). New York: Norton.

Felner, R. D., Jackson, A. W., Kasak, D., Mulhall, P., Brand, S., & Flowers, N. (1997). The impact of school reform for the middle years: A longitudinal study of a network engaged in *Turning Points*-based comprehensive school transformation. *Phi Delta Kappan, 78,* 528–532, 541–550.

Finn, J. D. (1998). Parental engagement that makes a difference. *Educational Leadership, 55*(8), 20–24.

Florida State Department of Education. (1984). *The forgotten years: PRIME.* Tallahassee, FL: Author.

Francka, I., & Lindsey, M. (1995). Your answers to block scheduling. *American Secondary Education, 24*(1), 21–28.

Fredericks, A. D., & Rasinski, T. V. (1990). Conferencing with parents: Successful approaches. *The Reading Teacher, 44*(2), 174–176.

Fullan, M. G. (1995). The school as a learning organization: Distant dreams. *Theory into Practice, 34*(4), 230–235.

Fullan, M. G. (1998). Breaking the bonds of dependency. *Educational Leadership, 55*(7), 6–10.

Fullan, M. G., & Miles, M. B. (1992). Getting reform right: What works and what doesn't. *Phi Delta Kappan, 73*(10), 745–752.

Gable, R. A. (1994). *An ecological analysis of aggression: Implications for prevention and treatment.* Paper presented at the American ReEducation Association Conference, Nashville, TN.

Gable, R. A., Friend, M. Laycock, V., & Hendrickson, J. M. (1990). Interview skills for problem identification in school consultation: "Separating the forest from the trees." *Preventing School Failure, 35,* 5–10.

Gable, R. A., & Hendrickson, J. M. (1997). Teaching all the students: A mandate for educators. In J. Choate (Ed.), *Successful inclusive teaching: Detecting and correcting special needs* (2nd ed., pp. 2–17). Boston: Allyn and Bacon.

Gable, R. A., & Manning, M. L. (1996). Facing the challenge of aggressive behaviors in young adolescents. *Middle School Journal, 27*(3), 19–25.

Gable, R. A., & Manning, M. L. (1997). Teachers' roles in the collaborative efforts to reform education. *Childhood Education, 73,* 219–223.

Gable, R. A., & Manning, M. L. (1999). Interdisciplinary teaming: Solution to instructing heterogeneous groups of students. *The Clearing House, 72*(3), 182–185.

Gadecki, V. L., & McManus, T. D. (1996). Then there are the birds: Getting and giving in the community. *Middle School Journal, 28*(2), 34–38.

Gajar, A., Goodman, L., & McAfee, J. (1993). *Secondary schools and beyond: Transition of individuals with mild disabilities.* Upper Saddle River, NJ: Merrill/Prentice-Hall.

Galassi, J. P., Gulledge, S. A., & Cox, N. D. (1997). Middle school advisories: Retrospect and prospect. *Review of Educational Research, 67*(3), 301–338.

Galassi, J. P., Gulledge, S. A., & Cox, N. D. (1998). *Advisory: Definitions, descriptions, decisions, directions.* Columbus, OH: National Middle School Association.

Gallagher, H. (1999). Teaching in the block. *Middle Ground, 2*(3), 10–15.

Gallagher, J. D. (1998). *Classroom assessment for teachers.* Upper Saddle River, NJ: Merrill/Prentice-Hall.

Gamoran, A. (1992). Is ability grouping equitable? *Educational Leadership, 49*(2), 11–17.

Garcia, G. E. (1994). Equity challenges in authentically assessing students from diverse backgrounds. *The Educational Forum, 59,* 64–73.

Gardner, H. (1983). *Frames of mind.* (Rev. 1993). New York: Basic Books.

Gardner, H. (1993a). Educating for understanding. *American School Board Journal, 180*(7), 20–24.

Gardner, H. (1993b). *Multiple intelligences: The theory in practice.* New York: Basic Books.

Gardner, H. (1995). Reflections on multiple intelligences. *Phi Delta Kappan, 77*(3), 200–209.

Gardner, H. (1997). Multiple intelligences as a partner in school improvement. *Educational Leadership, 55*(1), 20–21.

Gatewood, T. (1998). How valid is the integrated curriculum in today's middle school? *Middle School Journal, 29*(4), 38–41.

Gega, P. C., & Peters, J. M. (1998). *Science in elementary education* (8th ed.). Upper Saddle River, NJ: Merrill/Prentice-Hall.

George, P., Lawrence, G., & Bushnell, D. (1998). *Handbook for middle school teaching* (2nd ed.). New York: Longman.

George, P. S. (1982). Interdisciplinary team organization: Four operational phases. *Middle School Journal, 13*(3), 10–13.

George, P. S. (1993). Tracking and ability grouping in the middle school: Ten tentative truths. *Middle School Journal, 24*(4), 17–24.

George, P. S. (1996). The integrated curriculum: A reality check. *Middle School Journal, 28*(1), 12–19.

George, P. S., & Alexander, W. M. (1993). *The exemplary middle school* (2nd ed.). New York: Harcourt Brace Jovanovich.

George, V. D. (1986). Talented adolescent women and the motivation to avoid success. *Journal of Multicultural Counseling and Development, 14*(3), 132–139.

Gerber, T. (1992). Meeting the challenge of middle school teaching. *Music Educators' Journal, 78*(5), 37–41.

Gerking, J. L. (1995). Building block schedules. *The Science Teacher, 62*(4), 23–27.

Giannetti, C. C., & Sagarese, M. M. (1998). Turning parents from critics to allies. *Educational Leadership, 55*(8), 40–42.

Ginott, H. (1971). *Teacher and child.* New York: Macmillan.

Ginsburg, H. P., & Opper, S. (1988). *Piaget's theory of intellectual development.* Englewood Cliffs, NJ: Prentice-Hall.

Glasser, W. (1992). The quality school curriculum. *Phi Delta Kappan, 73*(9), 690–694.

Glasser, W. (1997). A new look at school failure and school success. *Phi Delta Kappan, 78*(6), 597–602.

Gollnick, D. M., & Chinn, P. C. (1998). *Multicultural education in a pluralistic society* (5th ed.). Upper Saddle River, NJ: Merrill/Prentice-Hall.

Good, T. L., & Brophy, J. E. (1994). *Looking in classrooms* (6th ed.). NewYork: HarperCollins.

Goodrich, H. (1997/1998). Understanding rubrics. *Educational Leadership, 54*(6), 14–18.

Grading. (1997, March). *LRP Publications, 4,* 4–5.

Graves, L. N. (1992). Cooperative learning communities: Context for a new vision of education and society. *Journal of Education, 174,* 57–79.

Grineski, S. (1995). Do you believe competitive activities should be used in middle and secondary school physical education classes? *Journal of Physical Education, Recreation, and Dance, 66*(7), 7.

Grossman, H., & Grossman, S. H. (1994). *Gender issues in education.* Boston: Allyn and Bacon.

Hackmann, D. G. (1995a). Improving the middle school climate: Alternating-day block schedule. *Schools in the Middle, 5*(1), 28–34.

Hackmann, D. G. (1995b). Ten guidelines for implementing block scheduling. *Educational Leadership, 53*(3), 24–27.

Hackmann, D. G., & Valentine, J. W. (1998). Designing an effective middle level schedule. *Middle School Journal, 29*(5), 3– 13.

Haladyna, T., Hass, N., & Allison, J. (1998). Continuing tensions in standardized testing. *Childhood Education, 74*(5), 262–273.

Hale-Benson, J. (1986). *Black children: Their roots and their culture* (Rev. ed.). Baltimore: Johns Hopkins.

Halsted, A. (1996). Community problem solvers: Working "as one body." *Middle School Journal, 28*(2), 19–23.

Hancock, V. (1993). *Informational literacy for lifelong learning.* Syracuse, NY: (ERIC Document Reproduction Service No. ED 358870).

Harrison, E. R. (1996). The nature of the middle school learner: Implications for art instruction. In C. Henry (Ed.), *Middle school art: Issues of curriculum and instruction* (pp. 1– 10). Reston, VA: National Art Education Association.

Hartman, J. S., & Askounis, A. C. (1989). Asian-American students: Are they really a "model minority"? *The School Counselor, 37,* 109–111.

Hastings, C. (1992). Ending ability grouping is a moral imperative. *Educational Leadership, 49(2),* 1.

Hatch, T. (1998). How community action contributes to achievement. *Educational Leadership, 55*(8), 16–19.

Havighurst, R. J. (1968). The middle school child in contemporary society. *Theory into Practice, 7,* 120–122.

Havighurst, R. J. (1972). *Developmental tasks and education.* New York: McKay.

Hendrickson, J. M., & Gable, R. A. (1997). Collaborative assessment of students with diverse needs: Equitable, accountable, and effective grading. *Preventing School Failure, 41,* 159–163.

Herman, J. (1997). Assessing new assessments: How do they measure up? *Theory into Practice, 36*(4), 196–204.

Herring, R. D. (1989). Counseling Native-American children: Implications for elementary school educators. *Elementary School Guidance and Counseling, 23,* 272–281.

Herring, R. D. (1996). Synergetic counseling and Native American Indian students. *Journal of Counseling and Development, 74,* 542–547.

Hicks, A., & Marlin, D. (1997). Teaching English and history through historical fiction. *Children's Literature in Education, 28*(2), 49–59.

Hinckley, J. (1992). Blocks, wheels, and teams: Building a middle school schedule. *Music Educators' Journal, 78*(5), 26–30.

Hinton, N. K., & Orlich, L. (1996). Perfect partners: Technology and integrated instruction. *Technology Connection, 2*(9), 23–24.

Holler, E., Brooks, S., Haskins, K., Hastings, J., Riva, J., & White, R. (1999). Standardizing practices: Presenting a uniform set of expectations for academic success at the middle level. *Schools in the Middle, 8*(4), 26–30.

Hootstein, E. W. (1994). Motivating middle school students to learn. *Middle School Journal, 25*(5), 31–34.

Hoover-Dempsey, K. V., Bassler, O. C., & Brissie, J. S. (1987). Parent involvement: Contributions of teacher efficacy, school socioeconomic status, and other school characteristics. *American Education Research Journal, 24,* 417–435.

Hoover-Dempsey, K. V., & Sandler, H. M. (1995). Parental involvement in children's education: Why does it make a difference? *Teachers College Record, 97*(2), 310–331.

Hope, W. C. (1999). Service learning: A reform initiative for middle level curriculum. *The Clearing House, 72*(4), 236–238.

Hopkins, H. J., & Canady, R. L. (1997). Integrating the curriculum with parallel block scheduling. *National Elementary Principal, 76*(4), 28–31.

Hopkins, M. H. (1993). Ideas. *Arithmetic Teacher, 40,* 512–519.

Hough, D. L., & Donlan, D. (1994). Achieving independent student responses through integrated instruction. *Middle School Journal, 25*(5), 35–42.

Hough, D. L., & St. Clair, B. (1995). The effects of integrated curricula on young adolescent problem solving. *Research in middle level education quarterly, 19*(1), 1–25.

Howe, A. C., & Jones, L. (1998). *Engaging children in science* (2nd ed.). Upper Saddle River, NJ: Merrill/Prentice-Hall.

Howe, E. (1998). Integrating information technology into and across the curriculum. *Knowledge Quest, 26*(2), 32–39.

Irvin, J. L. (1995). Cognitive growth during early adolescence: The regulator of developmental tasks. *Middle School Journal, 27*(1), 54–55.

Irvin, J. L. (1997). Using social proclivity to enhance literacy learning for young adolescents. *Childhood Education, 73*(5), 290–291.

Irvin, J. L. (1998). *Reading and the middle-school student: Strategies to enhance literacy* (2nd ed.). Boston: Allyn and Bacon.

Jackson, L. A., Hodge, C. N., & Ingram, J. M. (1994). Gender and self-concept: A reexamination of stereotypic differences and the role of gender attitudes. *Sex Roles, 30*(9/10), 615–630.

James, M. (1986). *Advisor-advisee programs: Why, what, and how.* Columbus, OH: National Middle School Association.

Janssen-O'Leary, S. (1994). Interdisciplinary teaching and cooperative learning: A perfect combination for the middle school. *Social Science Record, 31*(1), 28–33.

Jarolimek, J., & Foster, C. D. (1997). *Teaching and learning in the elementary school* (6th ed.). Upper Saddle River, NJ: Merrill/Prentice-Hall.

Jennings, W. B. (1989). How to organize successful parent involvement advisory committees. *Educational Leadership, 47*(2), 42–45.

Jesse, D. (1997). Increasing parental involvement. *Schools in the Middle, 7*(1), 21–24.

Johnston, H. (1997). What's going on? From advisory programs to adult-student relationships: Restoring purpose to the guidance program. *Schools in the Middle, 6*(4), 8–15.

Johnston, J. H., & Williamson, R. (1998). Listening to four communities: Parent and public concerns about middle level schools. *NASSP Bulletin, 82*(597), 44–52.

Jones, F. H. (1979). The gentle art of classroom discipline. *National Elementary Principal, 58,* 26–32.

Jones, F. H. (1987). *Positive classroom discipline.* New York: McGraw-Hill.

Jones, J. P. (1997). Mature teams at work: Benchmarks and obstacles. In T. S. Dickinson & T. O. Erb (Eds.), *We gain more than we give: Teaming in the middle school* (pp. 205–228). Columbus, OH: National Middle School Association.

Kagan, J. W., & Coles, C. (1972). *Twelve to sixteen: Early adolescence.* New York: Norton.

Kahne, J., & Westheimer, J. (1996). In the service of what? The politics of service learning. *Phi Delta Kappan, 77*(7), 593– 599.

Kain, D. L. (1996). Recipes or dialogue? A middle school team conceptualizes "curricular integration." *Journal of Curriculum and Supervision, 11*(2), 163–187.

Kain, D. L. (1999). We all fall down: Boundary relations for teams. *Middle Schools Journal, 30*(3), 3–9.

Kasak, D. (1998). Flexible organizational patterns. *Middle School Journal, 29*(5), 56–59.

Katz, L. G., Aidman, A., Reese, D. A., & Clark, A. M. (1996). Resolving differences between teachers and parents. *ERIC/EECE Newsletter, 8*(1), 1–4.

Keefe, J. W. (1987). *Learning style: Theory and practice.* Reston, VA: National Association of Secondary School Principals.

Keefe, J. W. (1990). Learning style: Where are we going? *Momentum, 21*(1), 44–48.

Kellough, R. D., & Kellough, N. G. (1996). *Middle school teaching: A guide to methods and resources* (2nd ed.). Upper Saddle River, NJ: Merrill/Prentice-Hall.

Kellough, R. D., & Kellough, N. G. (1999). *Middle school teaching: A guide to methods and resources* (3rd ed.). Upper Saddle River, NJ: Merrill/Prentice-Hall.

Kenny, A. M. (1987). Teen pregnancy: An issue for schools. *Phi Delta Kappan, 68*(10), 728–736.

Kiner, R. W. (1993). Community service: A middle school success story. *The Clearing House, 66*(3), 139–140.

Knight, D., & Wadsworth, D. (1994). Accommodating the at risk student in the middle school classroom. *Middle School Journal, 25*(5), 25–30.

Kohn, A. (1997). How not to teach values: A critical look at character education. *Phi Delta Kappan, 78*(6), 429–439.

Kommer, D. (1999). Is it time to revisit multiage teams in the middle grades? *Middle School Journal, 30*(3), 28–32.

Kostelnik, M. J., Stein, L. C., Whiren, A. P., & Soderman, A. K. (1988). *Guiding children's social development.* Cincinnati, OH: Brooks/Cole.

Kounin, J. (1970). *Discipline and group management in classrooms.* New York: Holt, Rinehart, and Winston.

Kruse, S. D., & Louis, K. S. (1997). Teacher teaming in middle schools: Dilemmas for a schoolwide community. *Educational Administration Quarterly, 33*(3), 261–289.

Kurth, B. (1995). Learning through caring: Using service learning as a foundation for a middle school advisory program. *Middle School Journal, 27*(1), 35–41.

Lapp, D., & Flood, J. (1992). *Teaching reading to every child* (3rd ed.). New York: Merrill/Prentice-Hall.

Lasley, T. J., Matczynski, T. J., & Williams, J. A. (1992). Collaborative and collaborative partnership structures in teacher education. *Journal of Teacher Education, 43*(4), 257–261.

Lawton, E. (1994). Integrating curriculum: A slow but positive process. *Schools in the Middle, 4*(2), 27–30.

Lieberman, A. (1992). The meaning of scholarly activity and the building of community. *Educational Researcher, 21*(6), 5–12.

Lincoln, R. D. (1997). Multi-year instruction: Establishing student-teacher relationships. *Schools in the Middle, 6*(3), 50– 52.

Lipsitz, J. (1977). *Growing up forgotten.* Lexington, MA: D. C. Heath.

Locke, D. C. (1989). Fostering the self-esteem of African-American children. *Elementary School Guidance and Counseling, 23,* 254–259.

Loeb, R. C., & Horst, L. (1978). Sex differences in self- and teachers' reports of self-esteem in preadolescents. *Sex Roles, 4,* 779–788.

Loertscher, D., & Woolls, B. (1998). Information literacy: Teaching the research process vs. mastery of content. *Knowledge Quest 26*(2), 48–49.

Lombard, R. (Ed.). (1994). Social education as the curriculum integrator: The case of the environment. *Social Studies and the Young Learner, 6*(3), 20–22.

Loucks, H., & Waggoner, J. (1995). *Keys to reengaging families in the education of young adolescents.* Unpublished manuscript.

Lounsbury, J. (1996a). Curriculum integration: Problems and prospects. *Middle School Journal, 28*(1), 3–4.

Lounsbury, J. H. (1991). A fresh start for the middle school curriculum. *Middle School Journal, 23*(2), 3–7.

Lounsbury, J. H. (1996b). Please, not another program. *Clearing House, 69*(4), 211–213.

Love, C. (1998). On middle schools and middle level education. A conversation with John H. Lounsbury. *Current Issues in Middle Level Education, 7*(1), 5–12.

Lundeberg, M. A., Fox, P. W., & Puncochar, J. (1994). Highly confident but wrong: Gender differences and similarities in confidence judgments. *Journal of Educational Psychology, 86,* 114–121.

Lustig, K. (1996). *Portfolio assessment: A handbook for middle level teachers.* Columbus, OH: National Middle School Association.

MacLaury, S. (1995). Establishing an urban advisory program throughout a community school district. *Middle School Journal, 27*(1), 42–49.

Madaus, G. F., & O'Dwyer, L. M. (1999). A short history of performance assessment. *Phi Delta Kappan, 80*(9), 688–695.

Maeroff, G. I. (1990). Getting to know a good middle school: Shoreham-Wading River. *Phi Delta Kappan, 71,* 505–511.

Manning, M. L. (1988). Erikson's psychosocial theories help explain early adolescence. *NASSP Bulletin, 72*(509), 95–100.

Manning, M. L. (1992). Parent education programs at the middle level. *NASSP Bulletin, 76*(543), 24–29.

Manning, M. L. (1993a). Cultural and gender differences in young adolescents. *Middle School Journal, 25,* 13–17.

Manning, M. L. (1993b). *Developmentally appropriate middle level schools.* Olney, MD: Association for Childhood Education International.

Manning, M. L. (1994/1995). Addressing young adolescents' cognitive development. *The High School Journal, 78,* 98–104.

Manning, M. L. (1995). Understanding culturally diverse parents and families. *Equity and Excellence in Education, 27*(3), 52–57.

Manning, M. L. (1997). An interview with John Lounsbury. *Childhood Education, 73,* 262–266.

Manning, M. L. (1999). Developmentally responsive multicultural education for young adolescents. *Childhood Education, 76*(2), 82–87.

Manning, M. L. (1999). Building a sense of community in middle schools. In C. W Walley & W. G. Gerrick. (Eds.), *Affirming middle grades education.* (pp. 93–108). Boston, MA: Allyn and Bacon.

Manning, M. L., & Allen, M. G. (1987). Social development in early adolescence: Implications for middle school educators. *Childhood Education, 63,* 172–176.

Manning, M. L., & Baruth, L. G. (1995). *Students at risk.* Boston: Allyn and Bacon.

Manning, M. L., & Baruth, L. G. (1996). *Multicultural education of children and adolescents* (2nd ed.). Boston: Allyn and Bacon.

Manning, M. L., & Hager, J. (1995). Gender differences in young adolescents: Research findings and directions. *American Secondary Education, 73*(4), 17–22.

Manning, M. L., & Lucking, R. (1990). Homogeneous ability grouping: Realities and alternatives. *Childhood Education, 66,* 254–258.

Manning, M. L., & Lucking, R. (1991). The what, why and how of cooperative learning. *The Clearing House, 64,* 152–156.

Manning, M. L., & Lucking, R. (1993). Cooperative learning and multicultural classrooms. *The Clearing House, 67*(1), 12–16.

Marcell, A. V. (1994). Understanding ethnicity, identity formation, and risk behavior among adolescents of Mexican descent. *Journal of School Health, 64,* 323–327.

Marinoble, R. M. (1998). Counseling and supporting our gay students. *The Education Digest, 64*(3), 54–59.

Martin, K. M. (1999). Building and nurturing strong teams. *Middle School Journal, 30*(3), 15–20.

Martin, N. K. (1997). Connecting instruction and management in a student-centered classroom. *Middle School Journal, 28*(4), 3– 9.

Martin, P. L. (1995). Creating lesson blocks: A multi-discipline team effort. *Schools in the Middle, 5*(1), 22–24.

Martino, L.R. (1994). Peer tutoring classes for young adolescents: A cost-effective strategy. *Middle School Journal, 26*(4), 55–58.

Maryland State Department of Education. (1989). *What matters in the middle grades.* Annapolis, MD: Author.

Marzano, R. J., & Kendall, J. S. (1996). *A comprehensive guide to designing standards-based districts, schools, and classrooms.* Alexandria, VA: ASCD/McREL.

McCadden, J., & Swendseid, R. (1997). Providing a secure environment for students with emotional problems. *Middle School Journal, 28*(4), 10–17.

McEwin, C. K. (1997). Trends in the utilization of interdisciplinary team organization in middle schools. In T. S. Dickinson & T. O. Erb (Eds.), *We gain more than we give: Teaming in the middle school* (pp. 313–324). Columbus, OH: National Middle School Association.

McEwin, C. K., Dickinson, T. S., & Jenkins, D. M. (1996). *America's middle schools: Practices and progress—A 25 year perspective.* Columbus, OH: National Middle School Association.

McEwin, C. K., & Thomason, J. (1991). Curriculum: The next frontier. *Momentum, 22*(2), 34–37.

McMillan, J. H. (1997). *Classroom assessment: Principles and practice for effective instruction.* Boston: Allyn and Bacon.

Merenbloom, E. (1991). *The team process: A handbook for teachers.* Columbus, OH: National Middle School Association.

Messick, R. G., & Reynolds, K. E. (1992). *Middle level curriculum in action.* New York: Longman.

Milgram, J. (1992). A portrait of diversity: The middle level student. In J. L. Irvin (Ed.), *Transforming middle level education: Perspectives and possibilities* (pp. 16–27). Boston: Allyn and Bacon.

Miller-Jones, D. (1989). Culture and testing. *American Psychologist, 44*(2), 360–366.

Mitzel, H. E. (1982). Parent education. *Encyclopedia of Educational Research* (5th ed., vol. 3, pp. 1379–1382). New York: The Free Press.

Mosca, G. F., & Shmurak, C. B. (1995). An interdisciplinary, gender-equitable mathematics project for the middle school. *Middle School Journal, 27*(1), 26–29.

Mullins, S. L. (1990, November). *Social studies for the 21st century: Recommendations of the National Commission on social studies in the schools.* Bloomington, IN. (ERIC Document Reproduction Service No. EDO-SO-90-9).

Murdock, L. A., Hansen, M. J., & Kraemer, J. P. (1995). Horace's Fridays. *Educational Leadership, 53,* 37–40.

Murphy, J. (1993). What's in? What's out? American education in the nineties. *Phi Delta Kappan, 74,* 647–650.

Murray, N., Kelder, S., Parcel, G., & Orphinas, P. (1998). Development of an intervention map for a parent education intervention violence to prevent violence among Hispanic middle school students. *Journal of School Health, 68*(2), 46–52.

Music Educators National Conference. (1994). *The school music program: A new vision.* Reston, VA: Author.

Music Educators National Consortium. (1994). *What every young American should know and be able to do in the arts.* Reston, VA: Author.

Muth, K. D., & Alvermann, D. E. (1992). *Teaching and learning in the middle grades.* Boston: Allyn and Bacon.

Myers, J., & Hilliard, R. D. (1997). Holistic language learning at the middle level: Our last, best chance. *Childhood Education, 73*(5), 286–289.

National Arts Educators Association. (1994). *What every young American should know and be able to do in the arts.* Reston, VA: Author.

National Association of Secondary School Principals. (1985). *An agenda for excellence at the middle level.* Reston, VA: Author.

National Association of Secondary School Principals. (1989). *Middle level education's responsibility for intellectual development.* Reston, VA: Author.

National Association of Secondary School Principals. (1993). *Achieving excellence through the middle level curriculum.* Reston, VA: Author.

National Center for Education Statistics. (1990). *A profile of the American eighth grader.* Washington, DC: U.S. Department of Education.

National Center for Education Statistics. (1994). *The pocket condition of education, 1994.* Washington, DC: U.S. Department of Education.

National Council for the Social Studies. (1994). Expectations of excellence: Curriculum standards for social studies. http://www.ncss.org/standards/stitle.html

National Council of Teachers of English. (1996). *Standards for the English language.* Urbana, IL: Author.

National Council of Teachers of Mathematics (NCTM). (1989). *Curriculum and evaluation standards for school mathematics.* Reston, VA: Author.

National Council of Teachers of Mathematics (NCTM). (1991). *Professional standards for teaching mathematics.* Reston, VA: Author.

National Council of Teachers of Mathematics (NCTM). (1993). *Assessment standards for school mathematics: Working draft.* Reston, VA: Author.

National Middle School Association. (1995). *This we believe: Developmentally responsive middle level schools.* Columbus, OH: Author.

National Research Council. (1989). *Everybody counts: A report to the nation on the future of mathematics education.* Washington, DC: National Academy Press.

National Science Foundation. (1996). *The learning curve: What we are discovering about U.S. science and mathematics education.* Arlington, VA: Author.

Newmann, F. M., Wehlage, G. G., & Secada, W. G. (1995). *A guide to authentic instruction and assessment: Vision standards and scoring.* Madison, WI: Wisconsin Center for Educational Research.

Nickell, P. (1992). Doing the stuff of social studies: A conversation with Grant Wiggins. *Social Education, 56*(2), 91–94.

Nixon, J. L. (1987). *A family apart.* New York. Bantam.

Nolan, F. (1998). Ability grouping plus heterogeneous grouping: Win-win schedules. *Middle School Journal, 29*(5), 14–19.

Nystrand, M., & Himley, M. (1984). Written text as social interaction. *Theory into Practice, 18*(3), 198–207.

Oakes, J. (1985). *Keeping track: How schools structure equality.* New Haven, CT: Yale University.

Office of Educational Research and Improvement (1996). *Reaching all families: Creating family-friendly schools.* Washington, DC: U.S. Department of Education.

Oosterhoff, A. (1999). *Developing and using classroom assessments* (2nd ed.). Upper Saddle River, NJ: Merrill/Prentice-Hall.

Parents key to classroom experience. (1991). *Middle Ground, 18*(4), 1–2.

Payne, M. J., Conroy, S., & Racine, L. (1998). Creating positive school climates. *Middle School Journal, 30*(2), 65–67.

Peltz, C., Powers, M., & Wycoff, B. (1994). Teaching world economics: An interdisciplinary approach for the middle level classroom. *Middle School Journal, 26*(4), 23–25.

Peressini, D. (1997). Parental involvement in the reform of mathematics education. *The Mathematics Teacher, 90*(6), 421–427.

Perez, S. A. (1994). Responding differently to diversity. *Childhood Education, 70,* 151–153.

Perlstein, D., & Tobin, W. (1988). *The history of the junior high school: A study of conflicting aims and institutional patterns.* Washington, DC: Carnegie Council on Adolescent Development.

Perrone, V. (1991). On standardized testing. *Childhood Education, 67*(3), 131–142.

Peters, J. (1998). *A sampler of National Science Educational Standards.* Upper Saddle River, NJ: Prentice-Hall.

Petty, W. T., Petty, D. C., & Becking, M. L. (1989). *Experiences in language: Tools and techniques for the language arts* (5th ed.). Boston: Allyn and Bacon.

Pikulski, J. J. (1991). The transition years: Middle school. In J. Flood, J. M. Jensen, D. Lapp, & J. R. Squire (Eds.), *Handbook of research on teaching the English language arts* (pp. 303–319). New York: Macmillan.

Pinar, W. F. (1992). "Dreamt into existence by others": Curriculum theory and school reform. *Theory into Practice, 31*(3), 228–235.

Pitts, J. (1994). *Personal understanding and mental models of information: A qualitative study of factors associated with information seeking and the use of adolescents.* Unpublished doctoral dissertation, Florida State University.

Plodzik, K. T., & George, P. S. (1989). Interdisciplinary team organization. *Middle School Journal, 20*(5), 15–17.

Popham, W. J. (1993a). Circumventing the high costs of authentic assessment. *Phi Delta Kappan, 74*(6), 470–473.

Popham, W. J. (1993b). *Educational evaluation* (3rd ed). Columbus, OH: Prentice-Hall.

Popham, W. J. (1997). The standards movement and the emperor's new clothes. *NASSP Bulletin, 81*(590), 21–25.

Popham, W. J. (1998). Farewell, curriculum. *Phi Delta Kappan, 79*(5), 380–384.

Porter, A. C., & Brophy, J. E. (1988). Synthesis of research on good teaching: Insights from the work of the Institute of Research on Teaching. *Educational Leadership, 45*(8), 74–85.

Powell, R., Fussell, L., Troutman, P., Smith, M., & Skoog, G. (1998). Toward an integrative multicultural learning environment. *Middle School Journal, 29*(4), 3–13.

Purkey, W. W. (1970). *Self-concept and school achievement.* Englewood Cliffs, NJ: Prentice-Hall.

Purkey, W. W., & Novak, J. M. (1984). *Inviting school success.* Belmont, CA: Wadsworth.

Redl, F., & Wattenberg, W. (1951). *Mental hygiene in teaching* (Rev. ed.). New York: Harcourt, Brace and World.

Reed, L. C. (1993). Achieving the aims and purposes of schooling through authentic assessment. *Middle School Journal, 25*(2), 11–13.

Reese, S. (1998). The counselor's conundrum: Provide triage or full-service programs. *Middle ground: The magazine of middle level education, 2*(2), 17–19, 24.

Reiff, J. (1997). Multiple intelligences, culture, and equitable learning. *Childhood Education, 73*(5), 301–304.

Reimer, B. (1997). Music education in the 21st century. *Music Educators' Journal, 84*(3), 33–38.

Reiser, R. A., & Butzin, S. M. (1998). Project TEAMS: Integrating technology into middle school instruction. *TechTrends, 43*(7), 39–44.

Rettig, M. D., & Canady, R. L. (1996). All around the block: The benefits and challenges of a nontraditional school schedule. *School Administrator, 53*(8), 8–14.

Reul, D. (1992). The middle school revolution: Coping with a new reality. *Music Educators' Journal, 78*(6), 31–36.

Ribas, W. B. (1998). Tips for reaching parents. *Educational Leadership, 56*(1), 83–85.

Rich, D. (1998). What parents want from teachers. *Educational Leadership, 55*(8), 37–39.

Rikard, G. L., & Woods, A. M. (1993). Curriculum and pedagogy in middle school physical education. *Middle School Journal, 24*(4), 51–55.

Risinger, C. F. (1992, October). Trends in K–12 social studies. Bloomington, IN: (ERIC Document Reproduction Service No. EDO-SO-92-8).

Rosenberg, P. S., Biggar, R. J., & Goedert, J. J. (1994). Declining age in HIV infections in the United States. *New England Journal of Medicine, 330*(11), 789–790.

Rottier, J. (1997). *Implementing and improving teaming: A handbook for middle level leaders.* Columbus, OH: National Middle School Association.

Ruff, T. P. (1993). Middle school students at risk: What do we do with the most vulnerable children in American education? *Middle School Journal, 24*(5), 10–12.

Saddlemire, R., & Manning, M. L. (1999). Five solutions for a humane and respectful learning environment: A case study. *American Secondary Education, 27*(3), 47–52.

Sadker, M., Sadker, D., & Long, L. (1993). Gender and educational equality. In J. A. Banks & C. A. McGee Banks (Eds.), *Multicultural education: Issues and perspectives* (2nd ed., pp. 111–128). Boston: Allyn and Bacon.

Sanders, D. (1987). Cultural conflicts: An important factor in the academic failures of American Indian students. *Journal of Multicultural Counseling and Development, 15,* 81–90.

Sandmann, A., & Ahern, J. (1997). Using literature to study the Civil War and Reconstruction. *Middle School Journal, 29*(2), 25–33.

Saravia-Shore, M., & Garcia, E. (1995). Diverse teaching strategies for diverse learners. In *Educating everybody's children* (pp. 47–74). Alexandria, VA: Association of Supervision and Curriculum Development.

Sautter, R. C. (1995). Standing up to violence. *Phi Delta Kappan, 76,* K1–K12.

Scales, P. C. (1991). *A portrait of young adolescents in the 1990s.* Chapel Hill, NC: Center for Early Adolescence.

Scarnati, J. T. (1994). Interview with a wild animal: Integrating science and language arts. *Middle School Journal, 25*(4), 3–6.

Schamber, S. (1999). Ten practices for undermining the effectiveness of teaming. *Middle School Journal, 30*(3), 10–14.

Schine, J. G. (1987). Learning through serving. In B. Hatcher (Ed.), *Learning opportunities beyond the school* (pp. 55– 60). Olney, MD; Association for Childhood Education International.

Schine, J. G. (1989). Adolescents help themselves by helping others: The early adolescent helper program. *Children Today, 18*(10), 10–15.

Schmuck, P. A., & Schmuck, R. A. (1994). Gender equity: A critical democratic component of America's high schools. *NASSP Bulletin, 78,* 22–31.

Schroth, G., Dunbar, B., Vaughan, J. L., & Seaborg, M. B. (1994). Do you really known what you're getting into with interdisciplinary instruction? *Middle School Journal, 26*(4), 32–34.

Schurr, S. L. (1998). Teaching, enlightening: A guide to student assessment. *Schools in the Middle, 6*(5), 22–31.

Schurr, S., Thomason, J., & Thompson, M. (1995). *Teaching at the middle level: A professional's handbook.* Lexington, MA: D. C. Heath.

Seed, A. (1998). Free at last: Making the most of the flexible block schedule. *Middle School Journal, 29*(5), 20–21.

Seifert, K. L., & Hoffnung, R. J. (1991). *Child and adolescent development* (2nd ed.). Boston: Houghton-Mifflin.

Seline, A. M. (1997). Parents as partners; Schools seek to build better relationships with families. *High Strides: The Bimonthly Report on Urban Middle Grades, 9*(5), 1, 2–5.

Sergiovanni, T. J. (1994a). *Building community in schools.* San Francisco: Jossey-Bass.

Sergiovanni, T. J. (1994b). Organizations or communities? Changing the metaphor changes the theory. *Educational Administration Quarterly, 30*(2), 214–226.

Shea, T. M., & Bauer, A. M. (1985). *Parents and teachers of exceptional children: A handbook for involvement.* Boston: Allyn and Bacon.

Simmons, S. L., & El-Hindi, A. E. (1998). Six transformations for thinking about integrative curriculum. *Middle School Journal, 30*(2), 32–36.

Siu-Runyan, Y., & Faircloth, V. (1995). *Beyond separate subjects: Integrative learning at the middle level.* Norwood, MA: Christopher-Gordon Publishers.

Slavin, R. E. (1988). Cooperative learning and student achievement. *Educational Leadership, 47*(4), 31–33.

Slavin, R. E. (1996). Cooperative learning in middle and secondary schools. *The Clearing House, 69*(4), 200–204.

Smith, J. L., & Johnson, J. (1993). Bringing it together: Literature in an integrative curriculum. *Middle School Journal, 25*(1), 3–7.

Smith, J. M. (1996). Giving students the creative edge. *Electronic Learning, 15*(6), 47–49.

Spaulding, S. (1994). 4 steps to effective parent conferences. *Learning, 23*(2), 36.

Sperry, R. W. (1974). Lateral specialization in the surgically specialized hemispheres. In F. O. Schmitt & F. G. Warden (Eds.), *The neuro-sciences third study program* (pp. 5–19). Cambridge, MA: MIT Press.

Springer, M. (1994). *Watershed: A successful voyage into integrative learning.* Columbus, OH: National Middle School Association.

Steele, D. F., & Arth, A. A. (1998). Math instruction and assessment: Preventing anxiety. promoting confidence. *Schools in the Middle, 6*(5), 44–48.

Stevenson, C., & Carr, J. F. (1993). *Integrated studies in the middle grades: Dancing through walls.* New York: Teachers College Press.

Stevenson, C., & Erb, T. (1998). How implementing *Turning Points* improves student outcomes. *Middle School Journal, 30*(1), 49–52.

Stokrocki, M. (1997). Rites of passage for middle school students. *Art Education, 50*(23), 48–55.

Strobach, S. (1999). The face of AIDS in realistic fiction. *School Library Media Activities Monthly 15*(6), 12–14.

Strother, D. B. (1986). Suicide among the young. *Phi Delta Kappan, 67,* 756–759.

Sue, D. W., & Sue, S. (1983). Counseling Chinese-Americans. In D. W. Atkinson, G. Morten, & D. W. Sue (Eds.), *Counseling American minorities: A cross-cultural perspective* (2nd ed., pp. 97–106). Dubuque, IA: William C. Brown.

Tallman, J. (1995). Connecting writing and research through the I-search paper: A teaching partnership between the library program and classroom. *Emergency Librarian, 23*(1), 20–23.

Tanner, J. M. (1962). *Growth at adolescence.* Oxford: Blackwell Scientific Publications.

Tanner, J. M. (1968). Earlier maturation in man. *Scientific American, 229*(1), 21–27.

Tanner, J. M. (1971). Sequence, tempo, and individual variation in the growth and development of boys and girls aged twelve to sixteen. *Daedalus, 100,* 907–930.

Taylor-Dunlop, K., & Norton, M. M. (1997). Out of the mouths of babes: Voices of at-risk adolescents. *The Clearing House, 70*(5), 274–278.

Teele, S. (1990). *Teaching and assessment strategies appropriate for the multiple intelligences* (Rev. 1992). Riverside, CA: University of California.

Terwilliger, J. S., & Titus, J. C. (1995). Gender differences in attitudes and attitude changes among mathematically talented youth. *Gifted Child Quarterly, 39*(1), 29–35.

Theobald, M. (1995). What students say about common teaching practices. *Middle School Journal, 26*(4), 18–22.

Thomas, D. (1997). "It's not like we have good models to follow. We're learning as we're doing it.": A case study of the Dolphin team. In T. S. Dickinson & T. O. Erb (Eds.), *We gain more than we give: Teaming in the middle school* (pp. 93–118). Columbus, OH: National Middle School Association.

Thomson, J., & Lenzini, C. (1996). Middle school is where I belong: An interview with Nancy Plantinga. *The Instrumentalist, 50*(9), 11–14.

Thornburg, H. (1982). The total early adolescent in contemporary society. *High School Journal, 65,* 272–278.

Thornburg, H. (1983a). Can educational systems respond to the needs of early adolescents? *Journal of Early Adolescence, 3,* 32–36.

Thornburg, H. (1983b). Is early adolescence really a stage of development? *Theory into Practice, 22,* 70–84.

Thornburg, H., & Glider, P. (1984). Dimensions of early adolescent social perceptions and preferences. *Journal of Early Adolescence, 4,* 387–406.

Titus, T. G., Bergandi, T. A., & Shryock, M. (1990). Adolescent learning styles. *Journal of Research and Development in Education, 23,* 165–170.

Toepfer, C. F. (1985). Suggestions of neurological data for middle level education: A review of research and its implications. *Transescence: The Journal of Emerging Adolescence, 13*(2), 12–38.

Toepfer, C. F. (1988). What to know about young adolescents. *Social Education, 52,* 110–112.

Toepfer, C. F. (1996). Caring for young adolescents in an ethically divided, violent, and poverty-stricken society. *Middle School Journal, 27*(5), 42–48.

Tomlinson, C. A. (1998). For integration and differentiation choose concepts over topics. *Middle School Journal, 30*(2), 3–8.

Tomlinson, C. A., Moon, T. R., & Callahan, C. M. (1998). How well are we addressing academic diversity in the middle school? *Middle School Journal, 29*(3), 3–11.

Tompkins, G. E. (1998). *Language arts: Content and strategies* (4th ed.). Columbus, OH: Merrill.

Troutner, J. (1996). Yes, they put on quite a show, but what did they learn? *Technology Connection, 3*(1), 15–17.

Tyler, R. W. (1989). Educating children from minority families. *Educational Horizons, 67*(4), 114–118.

Unks, G. (1996). Will schools risk teaching about the risk of AIDS? *The Clearing House, 69*(4), 205–211.

Upham, D. A., Cheney, D., & Manning, B. (1998). What do teachers and parents want in their communication patterns? *Middle School Journal, 29*(5), 48–55.

Urdan, T., Midgley, C., & Wood, S. (1995). Special issues in reforming middle level schools. *Journal of Early Adolescence, 15*(1), 9–37.

U.S. Bureau of the Census. (1992). *Statistical abstracts of the United States 1992* (112th ed.). Washington, DC: Author.

U.S. Bureau of the Census. (1993). *Statistical abstracts of the United States 1992* (113th ed.). Washington, DC: Author.

U.S. Bureau of the Census. (1996). *Statistical abstracts of the United States,* (116th ed.). Washington, DC: Author.

U.S. Bureau of the Census. (1998). *Statistical abstracts of the United States,* (118th ed.). Washington, DC: Author.

Valentine, J. W., Clark, D. C., Irvin, J. L., & Melton, G. (1993). *Leadership in middle level education: Vol. 1: A national survey of middle level leaders and schools.* Reston, VA: National Association of Secondary School Principals.

Van Hoose, J., & Strahan, D. (1988). *Young adolescent development and school practices: Promoting harmony.* Columbus, OH: National Middle School Association.

Van Tassell-Baska, J. (1989). Appropriate curriculum for gifted learners. *Educational Leadership 46*(6), 13–15.

Vare, J. W., & Norton, T. L. (1998). Understanding gay and lesbian youth: Sticks, stones, and silence. *The Clearing House, 71*(6), 327–331.

Vars, G. F. (1997). Getting closer to middle level students: Options for teacher-advisor guidance programs. *Schools in the Middle, 6*(4), 16–22.

Vaughn, S., Bos, C. S., & Schumm, J. S. (1997). *Teaching mainstreamed, diverse, and at-risk students in the general education classroom.* Boston: Allyn and Bacon.

Virginia Department of Education. (1990). *Framework for education in the middle school grades in Virginia.* Richmond, VA: Author.

Virginia State Department of Education. (1989). *Restructuring education in the middle school grades.* Richmond, VA: Author.

Vogel, D. (1995). Should the development of a healthy lifestyle be the primary purpose of physical education? *Journal of Physical Education, Recreation, and Dance, 66*(8), 6.

Vygotsky, L. (1978). *Mind in society: The development of higher mental processes.* Cambridge, MA: Harvard University Press.

Walberg, H. J. (1988). Synthesis of research on time and learning. *Educational Leadership, 45*(6), 76–85.

Walker, K. (1991). All students are at-risk. *NASSP Bulletin, 75*(539), 112.

Walsh, K., & Shay, M. (1993). In support of interdisciplinary teaming: The climate factor. *Middle School Journal, 24*(4), 56–60.

Warren, L. L., & Muth, K. D. (1995). Common planning time in middle grade schools and its impact on students and teachers. *Research in Middle Level Education, 18*(3), 41–58.

Watson, D., & Crowley, P. (1988). How can we implement a whole language approach? In C. Weaver (Ed.), *Reading process and practice* (pp. 232–279). Portsmouth, NH: Heinemann.

Weber, A., & Ingvarsson, M. (1996). Growing from grass roots: Writing-across-the-curriculum. *Middle School Journal, 28* (1), 37–41.

Weir, C. (1998). Using embedded questions to jump-start metacognition in middle school remedial readers. *Journal of Adolescent and Adult Literacy, 41,* 458–467.

Welsh, S. (1994). Students and TV . . . Anything but a passive role. *Middle School Journal, 25*(5), 52–53.

Westheimer, J., & Kahne, J. (1993). Building school communities: An experienced-based model. *Phi Delta Kappan, 75*(4), 324–328.

Williams, C. (1997). Families + schools = learning. *Schools in the Middle, 7*(1), 39–41.

Williams, D. L., & Chavkin, N. F. (1989). Essential elements of strong parent involvement programs. *Educational Leadership, 47* (2), 18–20.

Wilson, C. (1998). The real meaning of middle school advisory programs. *Contemporary Education, 69*(2), 100–102.

Windschitl, M., & Irby, J. (1999). Tapping the resources of the World Wide Web for inquiry in middle schools. *Middle School Journal, 30*(3), 40–46.

Winn, M. (1983, May 8). The loss of childhood. *New York Times Magazine,* 18–23+.

Wolfe, D. T., & Manning, M. L. (1997). Taking charge of school reform: English teachers as leaders. *English Journal, 86,* 36–38.

Women's Educational Equity Act. (1997). http: www.edc.org/Women's equity.

Wood, K. D., & Jones, J. P. (1996). Integrating the language arts: from the classroom to the community. *Middle School Journal, 28*(2), 49–53.

Wood, K. D., & Jones, J. P. (1997). When affect informs instruction. *Childhood Education, 73,* 292–296.

Woody, R. H. (1998). Music in the education of young adolescents. *Middle School Journal, 29*(5), 41–47.

Wraga, W. G. (1997). Interdisciplinary team teaching: Sampling the literature. In T. S. Dickinson & T. O. Erb (Eds.), *We gain more than we give: Teaming in the middle school* (pp. 325– 344). Columbus, OH: National Middle School Association.

Yao, E. L. (1985). Adjustment needs of Asian-American children. *Elementary School Guidance and Counseling, 19,* 223–227.

Zorfass, J., & Copel, H. (1995). The I-search: Guiding students toward relevant research. *Educational Leadership, 53*(1), 48–51.

Zorfass, J., & Copel, H. (1998). *Helping young adolescents become active researchers: How to promote inquiry in the middle school.* Alexandria, Va.: Association for Supervision and Curriculum Development.

Author Index

Subject Index

Note: Page entries in *italics* refer to figures.